TREASON ON TRIAL

CONFLICTING WORLDS

New Dimensions in the American Civil War

T. Michael Parrish, Series Editor

TREASON ON TRIAL

THE UNITED STATES v. JEFFERSON DAVIS

ROBERT
ICENHAUER-RAMIREZ

LOUISIANA STATE UNIVERSITY PRESS
BATON ROUGE

Published with the assistance of the V. Ray Cardozier Fund

Published by Louisiana State University Press

Manufactured in the United States of America
First printing

Designer: Michelle A. Neustrom
Typeface: Sentinel
Printer and binder: Sheridan Books, Inc.

Library of Congress Cataloging-in-Publication Data
Names: Icenhauer-Ramirez, Robert, 1955–
Title: Treason on trial : the United States v. Jefferson Davis / Robert Icenhauer-Ramirez.
Description: Baton Rouge : Louisiana State University Press, 2019. | Series: Conflicting worlds: new dimensions in the american civil war | Includes bibliographical references and index.
Identifiers: LCCN 2018046608 | ISBN 978-0-8071-7080-9 (cloth : alk. paper) | ISBN 978-0-8071-7141-7 (pdf) | ISBN 978-0-8071-7142-4 (epub)
Subjects: LCSH: Davis, Jefferson, 1808–1889—Trials, litigation, etc. | Trials (Treason)—United States. | Secession—United States—History. | United States—History—Civil War, 1861–1865.
Classification: LCC KF223.D3855 I34 2019 | DDC 345.73/0231—dc23
LC record available at https://lccn.loc.gov/2018046608

The paper in this book meets the guidelines for permanence and durability of the Committee on Production Guidelines for Book Longevity of the Council on Library Resources. ♾

For
Jennifer Barrett Poppe

CONTENTS

PREFACE

THE TREASON PROSECUTION against Confederate president Jefferson Davis in the aftermath of the American Civil War ended abruptly and without a conviction. In the closing days of the war, Davis was tracked, imprisoned, and indicted for treason. He faced the prospect of being hanged for his role in levying war against the United States—a conflict that resulted in the deaths of over 700,000 people and the widespread devastation of the South. Although the United States government pursued the charges for over four years, the case never went to trial.

Historians have largely ignored why the trial never occurred. Most historical surveys interpret the political reasons by analyzing them in the broadest national contours. This global assessment never attempts to discern how the lives and experiences of the individuals responsible for prosecuting or defending Davis, and the people who had a direct interest in the case, influenced the handling of the treason prosecution. While national politics had a role in the direction of the case, it was the actions and decisions of lesser-known men and women that ultimately bear responsibility for the failure to try Davis for treason. This book examines those actions and the reasons why the prosecution was ultimately dismissed.

The beginning of the story is straightforward. By May 1865, Jefferson Davis was implicated in the assassination of Abraham Lincoln and considered an arch-traitor to the country that had educated him and in which he had risen to political prominence. Many northerners also held him responsible for the abuse of Union prisoners of war at Andersonville. At that time, both northerners and southerners believed that he might be hanged for these crimes. In the ensuing four years, his case was set for trial many times. But the trial was repeatedly postponed. Ultimately, in 1869, the federal government simply dismissed the case against him.

Historians of Reconstruction have generally not attributed much significance to the failed Davis prosecution. An early standard work on Reconstruction, *Reconstruction and the Constitution,* by John W. Burgess, a political scientist from Columbia University, does not mention Jefferson Davis or the treason indictment.[1] In part 2 of *The Confederacy and Reconstruction, The Sequel of Appomattox,* by Walter Lynwood Fleming, the Davis trial received no mention. All that Fleming had to say on the subject was that the Radicals "wished to uproot a civilization, while [Andrew Johnson] wished to punish individuals."[2]

To the extent historians have touched upon Davis's indictment, most summarized the outcome without analysis. In *Reconstruction Political and Economic, 1865–1877,* for example, William Dunning found that "though many prominent Confederates were kept in strict confinement, and were treated in some cases with much more rigor and harshness than was necessary, the policy of bringing them to trial and punishment gradually was abandoned. That Mr. Johnson willingly gave up this policy in the case of Jefferson Davis is more than doubtful." According to Dunning, the "political leaders [of the South] were being made to feel the bad, and expect the worst, consequences of failure in civil war."[3] Claude G. Bowers, in *The Tragic Era: The Revolution after Lincoln,* discusses the Davis prosecution only in terms of how Andrew Johnson "appears to have inspired confidence in women" and uses his meeting with Mrs. Clement Clay and their discussion regarding Davis being tried before a military commission to emphasize that point.[4] Similarly, the trial of Davis was considered to be "one of Johnson's chief problems, because of its reactions in the South as well as in the North," according to George Fort Milton in *The Age of Hate: Andrew Johnson and the Radicals.*[5] Milton offers a significant discussion of the Davis prosecution but one that is entirely from the viewpoint of the political leadership of the nation. His analysis of the Davis trial ends with the release of the former Confederate president on bail in 1867. E. Merton Coulter, in his study *The South during Reconstruction 1865–1877,* gave Davis's imprisonment and criminal prosecution two paragraphs, ultimately writing that "his release was brought about by the strangest of the many strange uses to which the Fourteenth Amendment has been put."[6] As this book will show, Davis was not released because of a strange use of the Fourteenth Amendment. Even the eminent historian Eric Foner, in his landmark book *Reconstruction: America's Unfinished Revolution, 1863–1877,* relegated the postwar prosecutions to near insignificance. Foner mentioned Johnson's "amazing leniency," writing that "Jefferson Davis spent two years in federal prison but was never put on trial and lived to his eighty-second year." As for Henry Wirz, Foner wrote that "only Henry Wirz, commandant of Andersonville prison camp, paid the ultimate penalty for treason."[7] While technically correct, Wirz did not pay the ultimate price for treason. He was hanged for war crimes. The military commission found Wirz guilty of conspiring with Davis and others "who were engaged in armed rebellion against the United States" of "traitorously and in violation of the laws of war, to impair and injure the health and to destroy the lives" of federal prisoners.[8] He was also found guilty of murder. Subsequently, he was hanged for the war crimes at Andersonville. The treason prosecutions undertaken by the federal government after the war have been minimized into complete inconsequentiality.

Christopher Phillips, in his article entitled "Lincoln's Grasp of War: Hard War and the Politics of Neutrality and Slavery in the Western Border States, 1861–1862," found evidence that supports the argument that during the war northerners, through Union military personnel, had a "collective belief in the coercive authority of a democratically elected government to discipline and punish disloyal citizens alongside enemy combatants."[9] This view was held before the sovereignty of the Union had been reestablished after four years of bloody civil war. But by spring 1865, the southern states had been beaten into submission. With this complete victory, the federal government found itself in a position to dramatically demonstrate for posterity that the obligation of loyalty that a citizen had to the country could not be abrogated without consequence. The trial of Davis would bring that concept into sharp focus. His conviction and punishment might ensure that no other generation of Americans would have to undergo the horrors of a bloody civil war. Yet he was not tried. How was it, then, that the political face of the Confederacy escaped a hangman's noose?

This book will examine the questions that bear directly on the controversy surrounding the decision not to put Jefferson Davis to trial for treason. Douglas Southall Freeman wrote in 1908 that "published material on the [Jefferson] Davis trial is not abundant."[10] A century later, Cynthia Nicoletti wrote that work on the Davis case "has been quite minimal."[11] Her book, *Secession on Trial: The Treason Prosecution of Jefferson Davis,* stands as the first study to attempt to explain the reasons for the failure of the Davis prosecution. As is evident from its title, Nicoletti views the prosecution through the lens of the issue of secession, arguing that "in the months following the war's conclusion, the U.S. government sought to mitigate the war's disruption of the regular legal process by selecting a test case that would provide a final determination of secession's constitutionality and the war's legitimacy."[12] That is a bold proposition, but the historical evidence is unconvincing.

Roy Nichols correctly perceived that the issue of secession evolved as the Davis prosecution unfolded. He wrote that the government "conceived the idea of punishing [Davis] for treason, a purpose which gradually transformed itself into a project for trying him in order that the highest courts might officially and finally declare secession to be treason."[13] Nichols correctly stated that the issue of secession played a role in the Davis prosecution as the case advanced; however, I disagree that the prosecution ever became an effort to declare secession unconstitutional except insofar as that finding would permit a jury to convict Davis of treason. Certainly, most historians and legal scholars agree that whether secession was a right maintained by a state or its citizens after the adoption of the Constitution was a question that had not been clearly answered at the time of the Civil War. The Constitution did not plainly set out the legality of this momentous question. It was, of course, the ambiguity of the American Constitution that gave it the chance to be ratified. And the Constitution was vague on many issues that plagued the young nation in the first half of the nineteenth century. Indeed, George B. Forgie has written that the "constitutional law on the subject of slavery was so murky that a search for precedents would yield whatever one sought."[14] The same may be said about the subject of secession. Still, the historical record does not support a conclusion that the Johnson administration chose to indict Davis for treason for the purpose of litigating the legality of secession.

This book examines Jefferson Davis's prosecution from the perspectives of the individuals involved and their actions. Davis was prosecuted for treason because President Andrew Johnson and key members of his cabinet believed the former Confederate leader was guilty of that crime. Initially, they held him complicit in Lincoln's murder. Moreover, Johnson had campaigned on the promise to hang Confederate leaders and undoubtedly believed that this was the proper policy to pursue. There is no evidence that the government actively sought to litigate in a courtroom the results of the war. It made no sense to do so. It made less sense that Johnson and his attorney general would seek to do so in a Richmond courtroom. Instead, secession became an issue in the Davis prosecution after the decision was made to seek a treason indictment against the former Confederate president. The question of the legality of secession and the role it would play in the Davis prosecution was first raised by Davis's defense counsel. It took no one on the government team by surprise. Davis's lawyers reasoned that if secession was legal, he had not committed treason because he owed no duty of loyalty to the United States after Mississippi seceded. The issue of secession did not appear to loom large in the view of government lawyers until they used it as one basis to convince Johnson to permit the dismissal of the case. The evidence supports a conclusion that the government lawyers were not so much concerned by the potential power of the secession argument, of which they had been aware for four years, as they were convinced that the trial was pointless and used the argument as motivation for Johnson to concur in their request to dismiss the prosecution. The United States government sought to punish Davis for treason, not to litigate an issue that could only cause problems for the victors of the Civil War.[15]

The politics of Reconstruction were divided very neatly by Lincoln's murder. As H. W. Brands has written, "Had Lincoln lived, the war's end would have forced him to answer questions he had avoided amid the fighting."[16] One of those questions revolved around what ought to be done with the Confederate leadership, both military and political. Lincoln never expressed the sentiments that Andrew Johnson made manifest about the issue. Lincoln was far too politically astute to place himself in a political corner by asserting that "treason should be made odious," as Andrew Johnson had publicly proclaimed. Lincoln was trying to win a war. Making statements like that, if they had any effect on the conduct of the war, would likely extend the fighting by the rebels. No leader would willingly surrender to a government that he knew would hang him for his participation in the war. And even if Lincoln believed that such pronouncements would not extend the fighting, he would not have wanted to muddy the postwar waters by inhibiting his ability to make decisions about rebel leadership at a time when the issue was truly ripe. And at the root of the question was whether Lincoln believed that these men should be hanged.

Furthermore, Davis was not the only Confederate indicted for treason. Months before Jefferson Davis was indicted, over a dozen Confederate leaders were indicted for treason by U.S. attorney Lucius Chandler, the very man who would subsequently indict Davis. Those charged included Robert E. Lee. The indictment of Lee and other military leaders threatened to overturn the parole policy articulated at Appomattox. As historian William Blair put it, "Grant paroled Lee and other officers partly to show to the remaining forces in the field that the government intended no harsh treatment of those who accepted the surrender and tried to live peacefully under the law of the United States."[17] There is little doubt that the policy advanced the Union cause. According to Charles Roland, "Advising fellow southerners to lay aside old animosities and rear their children to be Americans, Lee became a potent force in the efforts to erase the sectional animosities that had caused the Civil War and had been immensely inflamed by it."[18]

The colossal prestige wielded by Grant after the war proved assurance enough that Lee would not be brought to trial. He was never arrested or jailed on the charge. The language of the parole proved enough of a legal hurdle against prosecution that the case was never brought to bar. When it appeared to Grant that the agreement reached during Lee's surrender might be breached by the Union government, Grant wrote the War Department. "In my opinion," he said, "the officers and men paroled at Appomattox C. H. and since upon the same terms as given to Lee, can not be tried for treason so long as they observe the terms of their parole."[19] The decision not to prosecute Lee involved facts and motivations much easier to explain than did the failure to bring Jefferson Davis to trial. Lee escaped trial because of the parole given him by Gen. Ulysses S. Grant at Appomattox. The entire Confederate military leadership found the same protection in the terms of their surrender. Not so, however, for Davis. He went right to the brink of trial several times. Andrew Johnson believed that Davis should be tried for treason. Johnson's will never wavered that Davis should be punished, but he was guided by the advice of attorneys and deferred to their expertise.

Other motivations and factors that contributed to the decision not to try the rebel leaders will also be examined. A treason trial of Jefferson Davis would have far-reaching political and legal implications for the actors involved and the efforts to reunite the nation. The evidence indicates that Abraham Lincoln preferred that rebel political leadership escape the United States mainland to safety abroad, which would obviate the need for a decision on trying them. His successor, Andrew Johnson, once the outspoken advocate of putting the Confederate leaders on trial for treason, advocated their indictment but did not bring them to bar. His political struggle contributed to this outcome but was not the primary reason for the failure. Instead, the lawyers involved in the prosecution played a bigger role than has commonly been acknowledged. This book will investigate the evidence of the decision surrounding the choice to charge the Confederate leader with treason. It will attempt to explain how Davis escaped trial after levying a war against the United States that was so costly in lives and possessions.

The Davis indictment has a fascinating backstory. John Underwood, the district judge presiding over the case, was a Radical Republican who had been badly treated by the residents of northern Virginia before the war and whose ability to be evenhanded was suspect. The U.S. attorney for the Eastern District of Virginia, Lucius Chandler, struggled as a trial lawyer and had political aspirations beyond that of being a U.S. attorney that may have influenced his actions in the case. The high-profile lawyer brought on to assist in the prosecution, William Evarts, and the equally highly regarded lead Davis defense attorney, Charles O'Conor, had engaged in legal battles against one another for years before this case. The chief justice of the U.S. Supreme Court, Salmon Chase, acted in the case with the full recognition that his role would affect his political future, often using "legal technicalities to block the progress of the trial."[20] Into this mix are added the formidable personalities of Jefferson Davis and his wife, Varina.

No matter what the basis was for the failure of Andrew Johnson's government to bring Davis to trial, the dismissal of the case had a profound effect on the narrative offered by the South after the war. A defiant postwar South rewrote the story of the American Civil War. The myth of the Lost Cause was born. Robert E. Lee became the "Marble Man." Jefferson Davis published defenses of his actions up to the time of his death in 1890. The right of secession was defended. That rebel leaders had committed treason was vehemently denied. Consequently, the Davis prosecution played a significant role in the history of the United States in the aftermath of the war. An understanding of that failed prosecution is essential to an understanding of the decades following the war. This book will examine why Jefferson Davis was not brought to trial for treason after he led the Confederacy in the bloodiest war in American history. It is a story worth telling.

ACKNOWLEDGMENTS

MY PATH FROM lawyer to historian was made much easier by the support of the faculty of the University of Texas at Austin. George Forgie, a friend and brilliant historian of the Civil War, spent many hours talking to me about my work and freely sharing his vast knowledge of this period in American history. The remarkable imagination of H. W. Brands, and his willingness to help other scholars, made him the person most responsible for me writing about the Jefferson Davis prosecution. Jacqueline Jones, Wm. Roger Louis, Erika M. Bsumek, Alan Tully, and Robert Olwell each supported my aspirations. Marilyn Lehman, graduate program administrator, also deserves special mention.

Michael Parrish, of Baylor University, patiently guided me through the process of getting this work published. I am indebted to him for his work.

Sandra Spicher assisted me immensely with adapting the work from a dissertation to a book. Her hard work and expertise was invaluable and much appreciated. Several people read parts or all of the manuscript and offered helpful suggestions. My daughter, Elizabeth, a historian herself, read the entire manuscript. Rick Poppe also read the entire manuscript. Writing a book about a criminal prosecution may be complicated by an author's own past defending clients in criminal cases. Valuable perspective was gained during discussions about this book with Linda Icenhauer-Ramirez, a distinguished criminal defense attorney and wonderful friend.

My children, Michael Icenhauer, Katie Icenhauer-Ramirez, and Elizabeth Icenhauer-Ramirez, and their spouses, Whitney Priddy Icenhauer, Lt. Deanna Lichter, and Lt. Adam Mendoza, have been constant supporters of my work. I am grateful to them for their steadfastness and the grandchildren that they have given our family—Harrison Robert, Kianna Grace, and Palmer Reese. Alex Damianov is always a bright spot in my life. My brother, Gocha Allen Ramirez, who likely has never understood my reading yet another book on Abraham Lincoln, has been a great source of encouragement for me. Other family members have cheered on this project. Rick Poppe and Jana Edwards are foremost, with Jana offering insights that can only come from an author. Kathy Tedrick and John Tedrick are two of the many others. Vincent Damianov supported my aspirations of a doctorate in history. Ron Meyerson, who has been as close as a brother to me nearly since I began my practice of law, is always a stalwart friend. I truly appreciate them all.

My parents were probably surprised by my interest in the American Civil War, given that I grew up in Hebbronville, Texas, a small ranching community in South Texas. My father, Zaragoza Ramirez, nurtured in me a love of reading that led to my interest in American history and my lifelong fascination with the Civil War era. My mother, Ruth Anne Icenhauer Ramirez, instilled in me a confidence and work ethic that I value as a part of my character.

Finally, I cannot fail to mention the one person most responsible for whatever success I have had over the last fifteen years—my wife—Jennifer Barrett Poppe. Jennifer has listened to my thoughts on American history. She has read and edited my writings. She has encouraged my work and heartened me during the tough times that we all face. All of this she did while working long hours as a lawyer. Jennifer has never been too busy to share in my work. Her beautiful smile and generous heart evoke a love and gratitude in me that is too deep for words. I can only aspire to be to her what she is to me.

TREASON ON TRIAL

1

THE FATE OF THE REBEL LEADERS

I do not know the method of drawing up an indictment against a whole people.

—Edmund Burke

JEFFERSON DAVIS AWOKE on May 10, 1865, to the sound of gunfire. Davis and his wife, Varina, and a small group of Confederates had spent days trying to evade lawless marauders and the Union army. The president of the Confederate States of America was desperately attempting to flee the country. His flight had begun in Richmond, Virginia, when the Army of Northern Virginia, commanded by Robert E. Lee, had begun to collapse. Now in Georgia, his destination was the coast of Florida, where he hoped to gain passage to a foreign safe haven. He was a most wanted man, not only for his role as head of the rebellion but because he was suspected of being involved in the brutal assassination of Abraham Lincoln. Davis had intended to separate from his wife the night before so that he could travel alone, and faster, on horseback. But hearing that his camp was going to be stormed by a roving band of men looking for the wagons full of Confederate gold that he was rumored to be traveling with and fearful for the safety of Varina, he decided to stay until morning to help ward off any attack. Now his worst fears were realized.

Luckily for him, he had slept fully clothed, his horse saddled and his pistols in their holsters. An African American man, described by Davis as "my coachman, a free colored man, who faithfully clung to our fortunes," alerted Davis to approaching gunfire.[1] Davis emerged from his tent wondering if the group was going to be attacked by a lawless band. Instead, he immediately recognized that the horsemen belonged to the Union cavalry beginning to deploy around the camp. Desperate not to be caught, Davis stepped back into the tent and told his wife that the intruders were indeed cavalry.

Varina insisted that her husband flee. Davis hesitated, losing several critical seconds, doubtless torn between leaving his wife to fend for herself and trying to decide how he could possibly escape capture. His horse and firearms were down the road over which the Union cavalry had advanced. He knew that he could not reach them to escape. His only route was in the opposite direction. Later claiming that the tent was still dark, he put on his wife's raglan, an item of clothing that he described as "a water-proof, light overcoat, without sleeves," thinking that it was his own similar item. Then, he wrote, "as I started, my wife thoughtfully threw over my head and shoulders a shawl."[2] This act would haunt the rebel president for the rest of his life, as his detractors would claim that he attempted to escape while dressed in a woman's clothing. After putting the shawl on her husband, Varina then told a female servant to take a bucket and walk with Davis so that it would appear that they were only walking to the creek for water.

He had gone only a few steps when a Union horseman ordered him and the servant to stop. The two changed directions, only to encounter a second mounted soldier, who told them he would shoot if they did not stop. Davis wheeled and threw the shawl from his shoulders. Quickly, he advanced on the trooper, who took aim at the slender man approaching him. At such close range, Davis supposed that the man would not have the ability to aim and fire and would likely miss. Intending to grab the man's foot from beneath the stirrup and throw him from the horse, he stepped in the direction of the cavalryman. This was his last chance to commandeer a horse and race from the camp. But Varina, seeing the threat to her husband, ran between him and the horseman and threw her arms around him to protect him from being shot. Imploring the man not to fire, she ended whatever possibility her husband had of maintaining his freedom. Jefferson Davis was under arrest.[3]

Davis was a nationally known politician before the Civil War. He had risen to prominence in the federal government. Educated at the United States Military Academy at West Point, he served as an army officer. In the two decades before the Civil War, he held office as a U.S. representative and, later, senator from Mississippi and served as secretary of war. Davis was in the Senate in 1861, when Mississippi seceded. He resigned his seat and followed his home state in leaving the Union. His prewar career resembled, though perhaps was more successful than, those of most leaders of the Confederacy. After the war, Jefferson Davis explained his view of a citizen's national allegiance: "His relation to the Union arose from the membership of the State of which he was a citizen, and ceased whenever his State withdrew from it."[4] From the onset of war in 1861, many in the federal government, believing that the rebels were traitors, wanted to prosecute the leaders of the rebellion for treason if the North prevailed in the war. But while the war was fought, deciding what to do with southern leaders after the war was secondary to preserving the Union. This was true for Abraham Lincoln, and no policy had been advanced on what to do with Davis or other Confederate leaders if the war was won.

The North Divided: Politics and Appointments

Only seven months before Davis was captured, in the midst of the war, the North conducted an unprecedented act during warfare in a republican form of government—it held a presidential election. The election of 1864 provided northerners a referendum on Abraham Lincoln's management of the war. The passionate arguments advanced by both parties reflected the deeply emotional principles that underpinned their differences. The war was not yet won, and it was not clear that it would be won. The Democrats denounced what they perceived to be Lincoln's war aims. Lincoln supporters found Democrats to be all but unfaithful to their country for their proposed views on reconciliation with the South on southern terms after so much bloodshed. To many in the North, Jefferson Davis, the president of the Confederacy, stood as the symbol of secession, human bondage, and treason. The Congressional Union Committee, a pro-Republican organization, accused the Democratic Convention of 1864 of uttering no word of "disapproval of Jefferson Davis" during its convention in Chicago, thereby drawing a link between the treasonous Davis and the almost treasonous Democratic Party Copperheads. "The blood and crimes, the hardships and deprivations, the infringements on personal liberty which we all endure, were not, during the entire setting of the Convention, once charged to the rebellion or its leaders," the committee wrote.[5] According to the pamphlet, speakers at the Democratic Convention made audacious statements that underscored the white-hot temper of the times. The Democratic Party leader, S. S. Cox, exclaimed from the podium that a judge had been arrested in Missouri because "he happened to say that Jefferson Davis was no greater enemy to the Constitution than Lincoln. He [the speaker] would say it boldly; let them arrest him. [Cheers and cries, 'They dare not.']"[6] On election eve, there remained deep divisions in the North on the issue of whether to continue to fight the war or make peace with the South.

It is not surprising, then, that the more remote question of whether Davis and other rebel leaders had committed treason was one the North failed to answer with one voice. Even after Lincoln's reelection, the North had not decided what Davis's fate would be if the Union won the war. Many Democrats refused to acknowledge that he was a traitor, even after years of intense warfare, underscoring the difficulty that might face a prosecutor in attempting to convict Davis of treason. Some Peace Democrats based their position on that intoned by an icon of American politics, Daniel Webster. Indeed, Webster had given expression to his uniquely American doctrine in June 1825 in an address dedicating work on the Bunker Hill Monument: "The Battle of Bunker Hill was attended with the most important effects beyond its immediate results as a military engagement. It created at once a state of open, public war. There could now be no longer a question of proceeding against individuals, as guilty of treason or rebellion."[7] If a revolt that had raised a regular army and engaged in pitched battle against the government to which the revolting soldiers had formerly owed allegiance removed the potential accusation of treason from the soldiers at Bunker Hill, then surely, many Peace Democrats reasoned, the Army of Northern Virginia's having fought at Antietam, Gettysburg, and the Wilderness would shield the southern leadership from prosecution under Webster's announced doctrine, despite the army's surrender at Appomattox. Doubtless, had the British won the Revolutionary War, London would not have recognized this doctrine. Most in the North were unpersuaded as well.

But as the presidential election of 1864 approached, Davis's postwar treatment was not the voters' main concern. Instead, they would determine whether the conduct of the war would be continued under Lincoln or take a dramatic change under George B. McClellan. Democrats' defense of Davis might make for good campaign fodder for Republicans, but how he would be treated if the North prevailed was subsumed in the vastly more important question of who would prosecute the war. Still, the campaign rhetoric of 1864 revealed fissures in American opinion toward the Confederate president. During the hot summer of 1864, the Union war effort seemed to have stagnated, and many in the North began to question whether the war could be won. Lincoln's reelection appeared to be in jeopardy. His fortunes reversed dramatically when Maj. Gen. William Tecumseh Sherman's armies routed the Confederate forces under Lt. Gen. John Bell Hood outside Atlanta and seized the crucial railway hub in that city on September 2, 1864. This military victory made Lincoln's reelection certain, and the end of the war appeared to be in sight.

Lincoln's reelection offered assurance that he would decide whether Davis would stand trial after the war. But Congress also would play a role, and Lincoln's decisions would be closely scrutinized by the Radical Republicans in both houses, who often found Lincoln hesitant to adopt their punitive measures. Many prominent leaders in the radical wing of the party had sought to have Lincoln replaced on the ballot. Only after it became clear that he would win the nomination did they throw their support behind him. Leaders such as Thaddeus Stevens, Ben Wade, and Zachariah Chandler in the Senate would not stand by idly if Lincoln failed to act as they wanted. Likewise, Radical Republicans such as James Ashley in the House would expect to have a say in these decisions too. The road ahead was going to be rocky.

On election day, it appeared that the prosecution of Davis, if it occurred, would be undertaken by the capable Edward Bates, Lincoln's attorney general. Bates was an advocate of strong executive leadership. He had steadied the new president when Lincoln hesitated to order the reluctant George B. McClellan to move against the Confederate army in December 1861 and January 1862. "Being 'Commander in Chief' by law, [you] must command," Bates told Lincoln.[8] In late November 1864, just after the election, Bates submitted his resignation. Gideon Welles happened to be at the Executive Mansion while Bates waited outside the president's office. Not knowing the reason for Bates's meeting with Lincoln, Welles recorded how anxious the attorney general appeared.[9] Bates's decision did not surprise Lincoln; Bates had told him months earlier that he intended to resign as soon as Lincoln was reelected.[10] The attorney general was certain that the time was right for him to leave the administration. He had competently discharged the duties of his office and now longed for retirement. The end of the war appeared to be in sight, and the nation had the experienced executive needed to guide it through Reconstruction. It seemed like a good time to leave.[11] But it would deprive Lincoln of a strong, proven attorney general.

Lincoln accepted Bates's resignation. By 1864, the office of the attorney general had evolved into an important cabinet position, even though the creation of the Justice Department was still six years away. The position had not been crafted by independent legislation but was created by the first Congress on September 24, 1789, in the same act that set up the federal judicial system. Section 35, the very last of that law, included three sentences that brought the office into existence. The qualifications for the position were only generally stated: a "person, learned in the law." Similarly, the duties were outlined broadly: "to prosecute and conduct all suits in the Supreme Court in which the United States shall be concerned, and to give his advice and opinion upon questions of law when required of any of the departments, touching any matters that may concern their departments."[12]

Initially, the attorney general was not given any control over how the local federal district attorneys should handle lower court litigation. Since it was his job to represent the interests of the United States before the Supreme Court, this lack of authority led to considerable frustration for the men who held the post in the early part of the nineteenth century. It took more than thirty years for the attorney general to be assigned a clerk, office space to be furnished by the government, and a stipend to be provided for office supplies. In 1853, the salary of the attorney general was adjusted to match that of other cabinet officials, and in 1861, Congress finally gave the attorney general the power to control federal district attorneys and marshals in all the districts. Bates, then, was the first attorney general to have the responsibility of directing the work of locally appointed federal district attorneys. While those attorneys might prosecute any rebel indicted for treason, it would be under the direction of the attorney general, who would bear ultimate responsibility for the conduct of the case.[13]

Bates had made his opinion of treason cases known to his prosecutors: "Treason is only the highest crime known to our law. But the law of treason, and the duties of the officers in regard to it, are as plainly laid down in the Constitution and the Statutes, as in regard to any other crime." His strategy, however, was to encourage prosecutors to be very careful in selecting persons to prosecute for treason. "Better let twenty of the guilty go free of public accusation—than to be defeated in a single case," he counseled.[14] His advice was not always heeded. In the area of Virginia that became West Virginia, the federal district attorney had over seven hundred cases of treason pending in his district. Frustrated with the grand juries that enthusiastically handed down indictments in these cases, the attorney declined to call any further grand juries into session. So, while Bates's monitoring of the activities of his federal district attorneys and treason charges was not unusual during the Civil War, it did not necessarily translate into his policy's being adhered to by local prosecutors or grand juries.

The president had clearly given some thought to who would be Bates's successor because he did not hesitate to approach Joseph Holt, the judge advocate general, and offer him the post. The choice would have surprised few people. The members of Lincoln's cabinet reflected considerations beyond their qualification for the job. Even before the suggestion was made, Welles wrote in his diary that he thought the post had to go to a man from a border state and that Holt was likely to be Lincoln's nominee.[15] Welles viewed the appointment from the kind of political and geographic perspectives that characterized Lincoln's course in 1860. But with Lincoln elected to a second term and with Sherman's capture of Atlanta and the South's approaching defeat, Lincoln was less likely to be bound by those geographic considerations that had so clearly marked his choices for his first cabinet.

Joseph Holt, who hailed from Kentucky, was a good choice for more than political reasons. An accomplished, highly regarded lawyer from a slave state, he had a brilliant legal mind and was staunchly loyal to the Union.[16] But according to John Nicolay and John Hay, Lincoln's secretaries, Holt balked at the offer because he believed "that the length of time which had elapsed since he had retired from active service at the bar had rendered him unfit for the preparation and presentation of cases in an adequate manner before the Supreme Court."[17] Holt asked for a few days to consider Lincoln's offer. On November 30, 1864, he wrote to Lincoln to decline the position. It is difficult to know Holt's reasons for doing so. People oftentimes offer less-than-candid reasons for declining positions that they did not want in the first place. This may have been the case with Holt. It was no secret that he had faced immense pressure from his family to join the southern cause immediately before the outbreak of the war and that his tenacious defense of the Union strained his bonds with his closest family members. He knew that if he assumed the job of attorney general, his office would issue opinions, over his signature, on the legality of the thorny issues surrounding Reconstruction. On top of that, the prosecution of southern leaders for treason, if those trials took place, would be directed by the attorney general. Many people thought that the attorney general himself should prosecute the rebel leaders. There is no direct evidence that such considerations played a role in Holt's refusal of the office, but his stated reasons for doing so simply do not ring true.

Holt's decision was not seen as a major news story by the nation's editors. The people of the North were reading exciting accounts of the Battle of Franklin and Maj. Gen. George Thomas's defeat of his Confederate adversary, John Bell Hood. The announcement of Holt's decision was buried on page four of the *New York Times,* which found the news so insignificant that it placed it two pages after the "List of Letters Unclaimed in the New York Post Office" and just below a sentence advising readers that the Army of the Potomac had "no movements in progress."[18] Holt's rejection of the job did have unforeseen consequences. It meant that his dynamic, forceful personality would not be at the helm of the post charged with the prosecution of Confederate leaders. It is difficult to overestimate the difference that a leader like Holt might have made to the prosecution of Davis.

If Holt truly thought that his legal skills were inadequate for the job, then his recommendation of a replacement to Lincoln makes little sense because that man had even less legal experience than Holt. Shortly after his interview with the president, Holt suggested his and Lincoln's mutual friend James Speed for the job: "Referring to our conversation of yesterday, I beg to say that the opinion there expressed in regard to Mr. S. remains unchanged. I can recall no public man in the State, of *uncompromising loyalty,* who unites in the same degree, the qualifications of professional attainments, fervent devotion to the union, & to the principles of your administration & spotless points of personal character. To these, he adds—what I should deem indispensable—a warm & hearty friendship for yourself, personally & officially."[19]

Holt's letter to Lincoln allows readers to infer that when the two men discussed Speed, the matter of geography must have arisen, for Holt refers to Speed as foremost "in the State" of Kentucky in certain characteristics. But Holt gives little hint of believing that legal accomplishments should be the primary reason for offering Speed the job of top federal prosecutor. He emphasizes Speed's "uncompromising loyalty," his "fervent devotion to the union," and his "hearty friendship" with Lincoln as among his greatest qualifications. He fails to mention a single accomplishment by Speed in the legal profession. Almost in passing, he notes Speed's "qualifications of professional attainments."

Speed, a Kentucky lawyer, was woefully unprepared to be attorney general. But his legal acumen appears not to have been a motivating factor in the appointment. In fact, it makes sense that Lincoln did not view the office as one that necessarily required a strong legal background in the issues facing the administration. An excellent attorney himself, Lincoln understood better than anyone the legal issues that would confront him in his second term. Also, there were other excellent lawyers in his cabinet. Edwin Stanton, the secretary of war, had briefly served James Buchanan as attorney general. Secretary of State William Seward was a brilliant lawyer. It can be persuasively argued that Lincoln did not need another accomplished lawyer in his circle of advisors. Moreover, once Speed was confirmed, Lincoln closely supervised him. As Speed later recalled, "[President Andrew Johnson] interfered with my appointments very much less than Mr. Lincoln had done during his lifetime."[20] Lincoln's close monitoring of Speed extended to other issues as well and would likely have ensured that Speed's tenure as attorney general took the path directed by the president.

Lincoln appointed Speed because he was a friend whose advice Lincoln could depend on to be given honestly and with the good of the country in mind. Speed's brother Joshua had been Lincoln's closest friend as a young man. When the country had divided on the explosively divisive question of slavery, Lincoln's personal ties with Joshua were strained, but they were never broken. Once he became president, Lincoln depended on the Speed brothers to advise him on keeping their native Kentucky in the Union, a necessary goal to Lincoln in the first two years of the war. In late July 1862, just as Lincoln had shown the first draft of the Emancipation Proclamation to his cabinet, he trusted the brothers enough to discuss it with them during their visit to Washington, D.C. Both men were shocked at the proposal and cautioned the president about the negative reception they were certain it would receive in the crucial border state.[21] Most revealing in Lincoln's confiding in them this intention was the confidence that he showed that they would give him their best advice and keep the information to themselves.

Lincoln must have known, when he offered the post to Speed, that Speed would not advance a personal or political agenda that deviated from the president's. During Lincoln's second term, Speed would not need to concern himself with the formulation of legal policy. Instead, he would be relied on to offer Lincoln sound, honest advice that the president knew to be untainted by political ambition—exactly what Lincoln needed from an attorney general. If Lincoln had lived, Speed's appointment might have proven to be a good choice. There is no doubt that Lincoln would have personally decided whether to prosecute rebel leaders after the end of the war. Any trials would have taken place with close scrutiny, advice, and supervision from a great trial lawyer—Lincoln himself. But in hindsight and in light of Lincoln's tragic murder, Speed was a poor choice for attorney general with regard to being prepared to head the prosecution of southern leaders. While events that shaped history were still months in the future, Lincoln was anxious to get Speed on board.

On December 1, 1864, Lincoln sent Speed a two-sentence telegram: "I appoint you to be Attorney General. Please come on at once. A. Lincoln."[22] Speed was thrilled. He admitted to a family member in a letter four days later that "the call was sudden and unexpected."[23] Unlike Holt, he did not appear to have seriously considered himself inadequate for the post. He responded at once to the president's call and traveled to Washington. On December 5, he met with Lincoln to discuss the offer. Immensely pleased with the courtesy shown to him by the president, Speed heartily accepted, with the caveat that he would not begin work until his nomination had been confirmed by the Senate. In anticipation of fulfilling the duty "to prosecute and conduct all suits in the Supreme Court in which the United States shall be concerned," Speed applied for membership in the Supreme Court bar. Two days later, according to the *Trenton (N.J.) Daily State Gazette,* Speed was admitted to practice before the U.S. Supreme Court.[24]

Speed's nomination faced no opposition in Congress. Within a week of Lincoln's offer, Speed's name was referred to the Judiciary Committee. The *New York Times* reported that "the committee are understood to be nearly unanimous in his behalf."[25] Indeed, he was quickly at his post.

Speed approached the job with determination. At fifty-two, he was a fit, compact, balding man. He wore glasses and sported a full beard and mustache. He was described by the *New-Hampshire Sentinel* as looking "like a man of ability, great force, sharp opinion and large capacity for hard work."[26] His reputation for physical courage had been cemented in the early days of the secession crisis when he had walked through a room crowded with secessionists, pulled down the rebel flags adorning the meeting room, and unfurled two American flags in their place. He then demanded the right to be heard on the issue and delivered a very strongly worded, pro-Union speech that elevated his reputation throughout the North. That he was a staunch Union man could not be doubted. The war's end, however, would bring questions of deep constitutional and legal consequence to Speed's desk, along with the thorny question of how—practically and politically—to address the problems. Among the most significant matters was whether to try southern leaders for treason and, if so, how to accomplish that task. Unfortunately, he was unprepared to be at the helm of the Office of the Attorney General, especially without supervision by someone like Lincoln.

Upon assuming office, Speed was lauded by the nation's press for his accomplishments. According to the *New Orleans Tribune:* "That exquisite judgment of men which has distinguished Mr. Lincoln's selection of his constitutional advisers is again exhibited in the appointment of James Speed, Esq., of Louisville, Ky., to the Attorney Generalship of the United States, vacated by the retirement of Hon. Edward Bates of Missouri. Mr. Speed brings to his high office studious and laborious habits, a perspicuous and analytical mind and a professional integrity which no breath of slander has ever impeached and which is made more illustrious by an unspotted private character."[27] Lavish praise notwithstanding, it would take much more than earnestness and a strong work ethic to succeed as attorney general. Speed soon realized that he was facing a mountain of work and that fulfilling his duties would be challenging indeed. Six days after accepting the job, Speed wrote, "I find that the labor of my office will be great; with a watchful eye over my health and habits, I think that I will get through them."[28]

Within five months of Speed's assuming office, a whirlwind of events changed the course of the Civil War. It began with the crumbling of the Confederate lines protecting Petersburg, Virginia. Forced to abandon the defensive trenches, the Army of Northern Virginia marched away from Richmond in an effort to link up with Joseph Johnston's army farther south. Jefferson Davis evacuated Richmond just ahead of the army. The Union army pressed the Army of Northern Virginia relentlessly, recognizing that its destruction would signal the end of the war. Union forces trapped the Confederates at Appomattox, Virginia; Lee, his army utterly exhausted, surrendered to Ulysses S. Grant.

Lee's Surrender and the Significance of Grant's Terms

When Lee and Grant met at Appomattox, Virginia, in April 1865 for Lee to surrender his army, Lee's command was on the verge of dissolution. Once the envy of the entire continent, the army was weak from hunger, surrounded, and at the mercy of the Army of the Potomac and its general. The two men discussed the terms of surrender on April 9. Grant was decidedly magnanimous to the Confederate soldiers, especially since they were utterly unable to continue the fight against the vastly superior Union forces. But the surrender agreement represented much more than simply the laying down of arms by a defeated army; it became a critical document in Lee's later fight against the charge of treason.

Grant had twice previously accepted the surrender of large Confederate forces. On February 16, 1862, he had famously demanded the unconditional surrender of Fort Donelson, in Tennessee, despite Confederate general Simon Buckner's request to discuss terms. The nearly fifteen thousand Confederate troops capitulated to the demand, although Grant then proved more generous than his demand of "unconditional surrender" might have suggested. There was no formal surrender ceremony, and southern officers were permitted to keep their sidearms and personal baggage. On July 4, 1863, Grant accepted the surrender of Vicksburg, Mississippi, after a six-week siege. Initially, on July 3, Grant had indicated that he would accept only an unconditional surrender of the thirty thousand men led by Lt. Gen. John C. Pemberton. But recognizing the difficulties involved in an assault on the city and the bloodshed that would result, Grant had a change of heart after meeting with his corps and division commanders. He wrote Pemberton that the Confederates would be paroled to their homes, instead of being sent to prison camps, if they surrendered rather than forced an attack by the Union army. Additionally, officers would be permitted to keep their sidearms, personal belongings, and one horse each. The Union commander further agreed to distribute rations to the surrendered troops. When Pemberton received this offer, he quickly accepted. As one historian put it, "At both Fort Donelson and Vicksburg, Grant combined devastating military victories with sensible and even sensitive surrender policies, pointing toward reunion of the two warring countries."[29]

Grant had a clear idea of the surrender terms for Lee by the time he sat down to write them out, even though he did not go to the meeting with a prepared text. Rejecting ceremony, Grant laid down simple, generous terms. Again, soldiers were given their parole. The arms and artillery he ordered to be parked and stacked. As for the leaders of the Army of Northern Virginia, Grant ordered simply that the officers were "to give their individual paroles not to take up arms against the Government of the United States." After providing for the property of the southern army, Grant wrote that "each officer and man will be allowed to return to his home, not to be disturbed by U.S. authority so long as they observe their paroles and the laws in force where they may reside."[30]

While at Appomattox Court House, Lee and his staff signed a parole letter on April 8, 1865. The terms of the letter included a promise not to serve in the army of any enemy: "We, the undersigned prisoners of war belonging to the Army of Northern Virginia, having been this day surrendered by General Robert E. Lee, C.S. Army, commanding said army, to Lieut. Gen. U. S. Grant, commanding the Armies of the United States, do hereby give our solemn parole of honor that we will not hereafter serve in the armies of the Confederate States, or in any military capacity whatever, against the United States of America, or render aid to the enemies of the latter, until properly exchanged, in such manner as shall be mutually approved by the respective authorities."[31] Strengthening the argument that this parole letter carried the sanction of law was the endorsement made by George H. Sharpe, assistant provost marshal general. He wrote immediately beneath the parole that "the within named officers will not be disturbed by the United States authorities so long as they observe their parole and the laws in force where they may reside."[32] The affirmation by Sharpe did not include any legal limitations in stating that these men, including the commanding general of the Army of Northern Virginia, were not to be disturbed by federal authorities so long as they did not thereafter take up arms against the United States or prospectively violate the laws in effect where they chose to reside.

Grant's terms to Lee were a product of his evolving view of the war and its aftermath as well as of his conversations with Lincoln. The terms appear to have been brilliantly thought through. Whether they were only what Grant knew was in his head, the conditions of Lee's parole at Appomattox later formed the basis of Lee's defense against the charge of treason. He would argue, if necessary, that a charge of treason against him was legally barred by the terms of his parole. Given Sherman and Grant's talks with the president, Lincoln's fingerprints may as well be on the surrender papers. An attorney as talented as Lincoln could not have failed to notice that Lee's parole probably barred any prosecution of him. It is reasonable to assume that Grant's terms were in full accordance with Lincoln's wishes. If so, then Lincoln's vision of the postwar United States centered on reconciliation with, rather than retribution against, the southern leadership.

Grant and Lincoln spent many days together at City Point, Virginia, preceding the collapse of Lee's army in late March and early April 1865. Their relationship was clearly a close one. On March 20, Grant wrote the president, asking: "Can you not visit City Point for a day or two? I would like very much to see you, and I think the rest would do you good."[33] Lincoln responded enthusiastically to the invitation.[34] It makes sense that they would have continued to discuss what to do with the rebels as the end approached. While at City Point, Lincoln and Grant would have certainly spoken of the disposition to be made of Lee's troops after the war. On April 6, Lincoln was still at City Point and writing to Grant in the field. He spoke of the administration's policy, "which you remember," regarding the confiscation of rebel property: "Confiscation shall be remitted to the people of any State which will now, promptly and in good faith, withdraw its troops and other support from resistance to the Government." In the same letter, Lincoln told Grant, "I have thought best to notify you so that if you should see signs you may understand them."[35]

Given the close collaboration between the two leaders on a number of political matters concerning surrender by the rebels, the evidence strongly supports the idea that the president and Grant discussed terms to be offered to Lee if he surrendered. The written evidence also strongly supports the conclusion that Lincoln was well aware of the generous terms that Grant would present to Lee. The bar to prosecution that Grant included at Appomattox had every indication of bearing Lincoln's stamp of approval. Lee's capitulation was met with unrestrained joy in the North. No group was more relieved than the Union soldiers recovering from their wounds in field hospitals in Virginia. David B. Lyman, in charge of the Fifth Corps hospital at City Point, wrote to his friend, Massachusetts attorney Richard Henry Dana Jr., that "we have had nearly two thousand patients each day and not enough agents to do our work as it should be done." Lyman recounted that "President Lincoln visited the hospital yesterday and shook hands with every patient." As the war drew to a close, the bond between the simple soldiers and the American president could not be stronger. When word of Lee's surrender arrived, the convalescing men received it "with the wildest joy. Many burst into tears and cried like children. The rejoicing seemed to have no bounds. The past victories have been received with a quiet satisfaction; this with the most unbounded emotion."[36] The terrible wounds experienced by the men and the nation seemed to be healing.

John Minor Botts, a Virginia politician, former congressman, and staunch Unionist (jailed by the Confederates during the war), described the subdued mood in the South after Appomattox: "At the time of the surrender of General Lee's army and the restoration of peace I think there was, not only a general, but an almost universal acquiescence and congratulation among the people that the war had terminated, and a large majority of them were at least contented, if not gratified, that it had terminated by a restoration of the state to the Union. At that time the leaders, too, seemed to have been entirely subdued. They had become satisfied that Mr. Lincoln was a noble, kind-hearted, generous man, from whom they had little to fear."[37] But an assassin's bullet changed that forecast.

2

ANDREW JOHNSON ASSUMES THE PRESIDENCY

I inquired of Dr. H[all], as I entered, the true condition of the President. He replied the President was dead to all intents, although he might live three hours or perhaps longer.

—Gideon Welles

BY MAY 1865, the United States of America had in custody the man who, more than any other, personified the Confederate States of America. The intense effort to capture him had paid off. But his imprisonment opened many more questions that now needed to be addressed. It was a legal and political quagmire that was to fascinate the nation for the next four years. Yet the wishes of the man who had been elected to decide such questions had never been made explicit.

Perhaps the most compelling evidence of Lincoln's thoughts regarding the postwar treatment of Davis was offered by Maj. Gen. William Tecumseh Sherman in his *Memoirs.* On March 28, 1865, Sherman, Adm. David Porter, and Lt. Gen. Ulysses S. Grant met with President Lincoln aboard the *River Queen,* a steamer lying at wharf at City Point, Virginia. Sherman asked what should be done with political leaders like Davis. Should they be allowed to escape?[1]

Lincoln said that he was not able to speak frankly on the subject but hinted, according to Sherman, that Davis should "'escape the country,' only it would not do for him to say so openly." "As usual," Sherman continued, "he illustrated his meaning by a story: 'A man had taken the total-abstinence pledge. When visiting a friend, he was invited to take a drink, but declined, on the score of his pledge; when his friend suggested lemonade, which was accepted. In preparing the lemonade, the friend pointed to the brandy-bottle, and said the lemonade would be more palatable if he were to pour in a little brandy; when his guest said, if he could do so "unbeknown" to him, he would not object.' From which illustration I inferred that Mr. Lincoln wanted Davis to escape, 'unbeknown' to him."[2]

Sherman was not alone in his view of Lincoln's intentions. Lincoln's new attorney general, James Speed, stated that immediately after the collapse of the rebellion, "clemency, and not persecution, was, I think, the policy of the government."[3] General Grant, too, echoed Sherman's belief, writing: "Mr. Lincoln, I believe, wanted Mr. Davis to escape, because he did not wish to deal with the matter of his punishment. He knew there would be people clamoring for the punishment of the ex-Confederate president, for high treason. He thought blood enough had already been spilled to atone for our wickedness as a nation."[4]

Lincoln left historians precious little evidence of what he would have ordered done with the leaders of the rebellion. His first inaugural address struggled to define the nature of the rebellion, but it was his position that "acts of violence, within any State or States, against the authority of the United States, are insurrectionary or revolutionary, according to the circumstances."[5] The word *revolutionary* was substituted for *treasonable* in the speech, but it was still clear that Lincoln did not view the actions of southern leaders as constituting civil war. Acknowledging that the nation was engaged in a civil war would have had legal implications that Lincoln was not then willing to confront. He believed that the vast majority of southerners were loyal to the Union. That opinion, in addition to the practical issues that would be raised if the struggle were acknowledged to be a civil war, such as the possibility of international recognition of the Confederacy, shaped his view. As the war progressed, the Lincoln administration's treatment of the rebellion evolved into a legal policy that has been labeled "a strange inconsistency."[6]

As the scope of the war broadened, practicalities made such an inconsistency both understandable and inescapable. While Lincoln strove to keep the conflict defined as a rebellion, the widespread fighting and the organized government of the Confederacy made clear that the conflict was, in fact, a full-scale war. The Union needed to blockade southern ports. Rival armies needed to exchange prisoners. The line between rebellion and war became blurred by the actions that the North took in trying to subdue the South.

Lincoln believed that southern leaders were responsible for the war. But Lincoln never claimed that the North exclusively occupied the moral high ground. To Lincoln, "good did not correspond to North, nor evil to South."[7] In September 1862, he told a group of Chicago Christians who presented him with a memorial in favor of national emancipation: "I admit that slavery is the root of the rebellion, or at least its sine qua non. The ambition of politicians may have instigated them to act, but they would have been impotent without slavery as their instrument."[8] But it was the politicians who led the South out of the Union, and Lincoln's view that these southern leaders had committed treason was clear. His published letter of June 1863 to Erastus Corning and others is often quoted for the memorable question "Must I shoot a simple-minded soldier boy who deserts, while I must not touch a hair of a wiley agitator who induces him to desert?"[9] More important to this discussion, in that letter, he also discussed his view of treason and men like Lee. Lincoln was responding to Corning's resolution condemning Lincoln's suspension of the writ of habeas corpus. At issue was the recent arrest of Clement Vallandigham for violating an order issued by Gen. Ambrose Burnside in Ohio against the expression of disloyal opinions. Corning's resolution asserted that Lincoln had overstepped his constitutional authority by suspending habeas corpus in areas not actively in rebellion and that arrests should not be made except upon evidence of a crime having been committed.

Lincoln responded that "the man who stands by and says nothing, when the peril of his government is discussed, can not be misunderstood. If not hindered, he is sure to help the enemy. Much more if he talks ambiguously—talks for his country with 'buts' and 'ifs' and 'ands.' Of how little value the constitutional provision I have quoted will be rendered, if arrests shall never be made until defined crimes shall have been committed, may be illustrated by a few notable examples." Having written in generalities, he next named specific people in Confederate service: "Gen. John C. Breckenridge [*sic*], Gen. Robert E. Lee, Gen. Joseph E. Johnston, Gen. John B. Magruder, Gen. William B. Preston, Gen. Simon B. Buckner, and Comodore [*sic*] [Franklin] Buchanan, now occupying the very highest places in the rebel war service, were all within the power of the government since the rebellion began, and were nearly as well known to be traitors then as now. Unquestionably if we had seized and held them, the insurgent cause would be much weaker. But no one of them had then committed any crime defined in the law. Every one of them if arrested would have been discharged on Habeas Corpus, were the writ allowed to operate."[10] Historians of the war have backed Lincoln's view. According to Gary W. Gallagher: "Without Lee and that famous field command, the Confederate experiment in rebellion almost certainly would have ended much sooner."[11]

Lincoln's letter to Corning offers historians a glimpse of his opinion on treason trials. Most important, he saw the difficulty of securing convictions for treason. "A jury," he said, "too frequently have at least one member more ready to hang the panel than to hang the traitor."[12] His thought proved remarkably similar to that of the Davis prosecutors five years later. Lincoln believed that Robert E. Lee and Jefferson Davis had committed treason, but he was a good enough lawyer to know that securing convictions would be difficult.

Jay Winik has written about the "remarkable compassion and charity toward the Confederates that was to be the backbone of [Lincoln's] postwar policy."[13] He is not alone in this assessment. Many of Lincoln's contemporaries believed that his benevolence would be extended even to the rebel leadership. Given Lincoln's extensive experience as a trial lawyer and the opinion he expressed to Corning, it stands to reason that his reluctance to try men like Davis and Lee for treason after the war might stem from his view of the difficulty of securing convictions, in conjunction with his interest in reconciling the two sections of the country.

The president was also a practical politician. During the Union army debacle at Fredericksburg, Virginia, in mid-December 1862, in which Burnside's repeated frontal assaults against Lee's fortified positions on Marye's Heights made suspect the military capabilities of Union military leaders, Lincoln responded to a letter from Fernando Wood, a Democratic congressman from New York. In it, he addressed the possibility of the Confederacy's sending representatives to the next Congress to discuss peace. Wood had indicated that according to his information, the only request that would be made by the Confederacy before sending the mission was that "a full and general amnesty should permit them to do so." Lincoln began his response by indicating that he thought Wood's information would "prove to be groundless." But he artfully dodged the question regarding amnesty except to note that if the seceded states wanted to return to their proper place within the Union, "in such case, the war would cease on the part of the United States, and that, if within a reasonable time, 'a full and general amnesty' were necessary to such end, it would not be withheld."[14] Consequently, it is undoubtedly correct that President Lincoln was open to granting a "full and general amnesty" years before the war's end.

On other occasions, Lincoln gave assurances that he was not vindictive. Writing privately on July 26, 1862, to Reverdy Johnson, a Democratic senator from Maryland, he stated, "I am a patient man—always willing to forgive on the Christian terms of repentance; and also to give ample *time* for repentance." But forgiveness did not indicate weakness. Responding to Johnson's complaint that pro-Union sentiment was being snuffed out in areas of the South occupied by Union forces because of rough treatment of the civilian population, Lincoln graphically stated his case: "You are ready to say I apply to *friends* what is due only to *enemies.* I distrust the *wisdom* if not the *sincerity* of friends, who would hold my hands while my enemies stab me."[15]

Consequently, the president was perfectly willing for the military to arrest and incarcerate civilians, even members of the judiciary, who worked against the Union war effort. Judge Richard B. Carmichael of Talbot County, Maryland, charged a grand jury that it had the duty to indict persons, including several officers of a Delaware regiment, who had been responsible for arresting secessionists. Gen. John A. Dix sent a deputy provost marshal and four policemen to Easton, Maryland, to arrest the offending judge while he was presiding in court, "in order that the proceeding might be more marked." The marshal and two police officers ascended the bench and informed Judge Carmichael that they had an order, by authority of the United States, to take him into custody. The judge angrily denied that the government had the authority to arrest him and reportedly attacked one of the police officers. During the struggle, the judge ("unfortunately," according to the report) received a superficial wound to the head. The officers restrained him and led him from the courtroom under arrest. When Maryland politicians appealed to Lincoln to release Carmichael, the president gave them his thoughts on the matter.

"I have been considering the appeal made by yourself, and Senator Pearce in behalf of Judge Carmichael," Lincoln wrote. "His charge to the Grand-Jury, was left with me by the Senator, and, on reading it, I must confess I was not very favorably impressed towards the Judge. The object of the charge, I understand, was to procure prosecutions, and punishment of some men for arresting or doing violence to some secessionists—that is, the Judge was trying to help a little, by giving the protection of law to those who were endeavoring to overthrow the Supreme law—trying if he could to find a safe place for certain men to stand on the constitution, whilst they should stab it in another place. But possibly I am mistaken."[16]

Ultimately, the president agreed to release the judge if he took the oath of allegiance. Lincoln did not hesitate to use military justice against civilians during the Civil War. It would not have been unreasonable, based on the wartime evidence, for him to have sought military justice for the Confederate leadership. But the question remains, what did he intend to do with the rebel leadership after the war?

Much of the rest of the nation was not ready to reconcile with the men who had led the nation through such a bloody trial. Only days after the surrender of the Army of Northern Virginia, there were rumors that Lee intended to travel to New York City, amid suggestions that he be treated with dignity and respect. One anonymous letter to the editor of the *Hartford (Conn.) Daily Courant* addressed reconciliation with Confederates: "We have not been pouring out millions of treasure and oceans of blood, parents have not submitted to become childless, wives to become widows, and children to become orphans, and the whole nation to be draped in sorrow, for the poor privilege of honoring a traitor."[17] The writer reminded readers that the stern realities of war compelled an army's execution of deserters; how then, he asked, could honors be bestowed on Lee, who had deserted the flag "after he has been *educated by the nation to skill in its defense*"? The letter then makes clear Lee's treason: "More than that, who fires upon the flag that has given him the position and honor that he once enjoyed and shoots down in thousands those who, not base and traitorous like himself, rather die than desert. Such is Gen. Robert E. Lee." The writer closed with what must have been the hopes of many in the North: let the "government seize him, try him and execute him as a traitor." This was the sentiment of many before Lincoln's assassination; calls for clemency rather than persecution were likely to be shouted down by those who believed punishment was in order. And the howls for rebel blood became deafening after his murder.

The Assassination of Lincoln

The murder of Abraham Lincoln by John Wilkes Booth on April 14, 1865, sent a shock wave through the North. Washington, D.C., was transformed, literally overnight, from a jubilant capital to one draped in mourning. Reportedly, groups of men gathered at hotels and street corners, angered by the assassination and eager to find rebel sympathizers to punish for the crime. Mob violence against people with southern leanings became a real threat. Stranded in the District of Columbia because of the ban against anyone leaving the city, southerners wisely stayed off the streets. Whether through fear of reprisal or genuine sorrow, many of them joined in the public display of mourning; the houses of prominent rebels displayed crape and funeral decorations. Persons seen being transported under guard were threatened in the streets by angry crowds.[18]

African Americans, whose lives they felt had been so intimately tied up with Lincoln's, reacted with horror. "No common mortal had died," wrote Elizabeth Keckley, a woman who after spending decades as a slave had found employment in Lincoln's White House. "The Moses of my people had fallen in the hour of his triumph."[19] A member of the famed Fifty-Fourth Massachusetts wrote that the assassination was "too overwhelming, too lamentable, too distressing."[20]

The terrible split in the Republican Party was evident in private comments made by Radicals who saw Lincoln's death, and the accession of Andrew Johnson, as a boon to their plans for Reconstruction. George Julian, an Indiana congressman and leading House member of the Committee on the Conduct of the War, captured their sentiments in his journal: "Hostility towards Lincoln's policy of conciliation and contempt for his weakness were undisguised. The universal feeling among radical men here is that his death is a god-send."[21] A lesser-known Radical, Francis Lieber, who codified the principles of war, wrote without regret to Charles Sumner that "Lincoln could not die a more glorious death."[22] Only days after the murder, Lieber publicly lamented the assassination while trying to leverage it into a harsher Reconstruction policy against the South. As shocking as those words sound to Americans today, politics in the mid-nineteenth century had plunged to appalling depths. A more common reaction was captured by Richard Henry Dana Jr. in a letter to his son. "It is the most frightful tragedy in history," he said simply. He attributed it to a conspiracy "formed by some malignant copperheads."[23]

Blame quickly settled on the "leading men" of the South. The men who had led the lower states out of the Union were an understandably easy target of northern anger. Davis, as Confederate president, was especially so. People from all walks of life held the opinion. A "woman in Vermont wanted Jefferson Davis hanged from the same gallows as John Brown."[24] A thirteen-year-old girl in Richmond, Virginia, "never dreamed of the Yankees getting to Richmond sure enough, but the wretches are here"; she wrote in the same letter, "I am so sorry Lincoln was killed I don't know what in the world to do, because I believe the whole South will be punished for it."[25] In the ensuing weeks, calls for vengeance would fade in intensity, but the belief that somehow Davis was responsible would be slower to change.

Many in Lincoln's cabinet waited up all night at the president's bedside. The secretary of the navy, Gideon Welles, described "listening to the heavy groans, and witnessing the wasting life of the good and great man who was expiring before" them. Feeling faint, Welles rose at about six in the morning and "took a short walk in the open air." He noted: "It was a dark and gloomy morning, and rain set in before I returned to the house, some fifteen minutes. Large groups of people were gathered every few rods—all anxious and solicitous. Some one stepped forward as I passed, to enquire into the condition of the President, and to ask if there was no hope." Welles reveals that he answered the person very frankly: "Intense grief exhibited itself on every countenance when I replied—that the President could survive but a short time. The colored people especially—and there were at this time more of them perhaps than of whites—were painfully affected."[26]

When he returned to the parlor, he found Attorney General James Speed and Secretary of War Edwin Stanton taking evidence concerning the shooting. When Lincoln died, shortly after seven that morning, the cabinet, except Treasury Secretary Hugh McCulloch and Secretary of State William Seward, met and signed a letter written by Speed to Vice President Andrew Johnson, informing him that the president was dead and that the "government devolved upon him."[27] Welles rode home with Speed on the attorney general's trip to deliver the letter. As they rode, they agreed to have a cabinet meeting that day at noon at the Treasury Department.

As later events showed, it was the men who had been in Lincoln's cabinet—one of whom, William Seward, was savagely stabbed on the night of the murder by a coconspirator in Lincoln's assassination; others, among them Edwin Stanton and Gideon Welles, sat at Lincoln's bedside as he died—who formed the core of those most intent on trying Jefferson Davis for treason, even after the momentum for the trial was lost. The emotions generated by watching a man die who had been an admired leader during the struggles of the war years did not quickly fade. Whether or not they consciously attributed Lincoln's death to Davis, they believed that he had plunged the nation into war and led the South in an unjust conflict. The monstrous nature of Booth's act stayed with Stanton, Seward, and Welles. The combination of the long war and the senseless murder of Lincoln after the close of the fighting appeared to harden these men's resolve to punish southern leaders. They continued to believe, long after others had given up resolve, that someone should pay for the damage incurred by the Union. But with Booth dead, who should pay? The answer was clear: Jefferson Davis, the traitor.

Andrew Johnson Becomes President

When Welles arrived at the Treasury Building for the first cabinet meeting after Lincoln's death, Andrew Johnson had already been sworn in as president by Chief Justice Salmon Chase. Speed told Welles that Johnson had "expressed a desire that the affairs of the government should proceed without interruption." The new president told the members of the cabinet that he wanted to conduct business consistent with Lincoln's policies and that "in all essentials it would, he said, be the same as that of the late President."[28] It is unclear whether Johnson was acknowledging uncertainty about his own path of governance or whether he believed it his duty to advance the Lincoln agenda now that the president was dead. A third possibility is that he was merely reassuring the cabinet that he did not want Lincoln's death to disrupt the government any more than it must. Each of these scenarios raises a question. Did Johnson know what Lincoln's policies were or how to discern them? If he did, could he sign on to their continuance? All indications were, in regard to the rebel leadership, that Lincoln preferred reconciliation to punishment. This was in direct contradiction to the position espoused by Johnson, who had, during the war, explicitly stated that the rebel leaders should be tried for treason. In the short time that he had been vice president, Johnson had expressed this opinion to Charles Dana and, on the very day that Lincoln was shot, had visited the president at the White House to urge him to not be lenient on the rebels.[29] One thing is certain: Johnson had not had time to reconsider his position.

There were those in the South who recognized that Johnson's postwar plans might differ significantly from Lincoln's. The staunch Unionist and Virginia politician John Minor Botts testified before the Joint Committee of Fifteen on Reconstruction about southerners' initial responses to a Johnson presidency. "They remembered Mr. Johnson's declarations in the Senate of the United States before the war, his own treatment during the war by the secession party, and his declarations after he came to Washington as the Vice-

President of the United States, in one or more speeches, but especially in a speech in which he declared that treason was a crime which must be punished," he reported. "They felt exceedingly apprehensive for the security of their property, as well as for the security of their lives."[30] Their apprehension was well founded, especially after it was discovered that the assassins had also targeted Vice President Johnson. He was only spared being murdered when George Atzerodt, a coconspirator of John Wilkes Booth, lost his nerve upon finding Johnson drinking at a Washington, D.C., hotel on the night of Lincoln's death.

Even the unflappable Grant, another target of Booth's plan, could not immediately dismiss the possibility that Lincoln's assassination was but part of a wider conspiracy. He ordered measures taken to address that threat. On the day after the shooting, Grant telegraphed an order to Maj. Gen. Edward Ord in Richmond, directing him to "arrest J. A. Campbell, Mayor Mayo, and the members of the old council of Richmond, who have not yet taken the oath of allegiance and put them in Libby Prison." Grant's entire view of Confederates appears to have undergone a transformation by virtue of Booth's bloody act. "Extreme rigor," he wrote, "will have to be observed whilst assassination remains the order of the day with the rebels."[31] Ord responded very quickly to Grant's telegram, warning him of the implications of his order. "Lee and staff are in town among the paroled prisoners," he reminded Grant. Then he offered his unsolicited view: "Should I arrest them under the circumstances I think the rebellion here would be reopened. I will risk my life that the present paroles will be kept, and if you allow me to do so trust the people here who, I believe, are ignorant of the assassination, done, I think, by some insane Brutus with but few accomplices."[32]

Ord's belief that the conspiracy was not widespread and did not involve Lee or other officers made sense to Grant. Only four hours later, Grant seemed to have recovered somewhat from the shock. "On reflection," he telegraphed Ord, "I will withdraw my dispatch of this date directing the arrest of Campbell, Mayo, and others so far as it may be regarded as an order, and leave it in the light of a suggestion, to be executed only so far as you may judge the good of the service demands."[33] He wrote a revealing but reassuring letter to his wife, Julia, the next day about the crisis: "All seems very quiet here. There is but little doubt but that the plot contemplated the distruction [*sic*] of more than the President and Sec[retary] of State. I think now however it has expended itself and there is but little to fear."[34] Grant was not one to panic, but as H. W. Brands has written, "he appreciated that the death [of Lincoln] killed the chance of an easy reconstruction" and might have sparked northern vengeance against the rebels.[35]

On Sunday, the cabinet met with the new president at the Treasury Department for the second time. Stanton arrived late with a bundle of papers that, he suggested, carried forward Lincoln's intentions. With Seward indisposed because of the serious injuries he had suffered on the night of Lincoln's assassination and with Salmon Chase out of the cabinet, the secretary of war seemed poised and anxious to fill the power vacuum. The future treatment of the Confederate leadership was discussed and recorded for the first time in the Johnson administration. Welles caught the mood in his diary: "President Johnson is not disposed to treat treason lightly, and the chief Rebels he would punish with exemplary severity."[36] Welles did not say whether any cabinet member voiced a belief that Lincoln would not have sought retribution. Speed certainly believed that "clemency, and not persecution, was, I think, the policy of the government," but there was no sign that the Johnson administration would advance that policy.[37] Stanton, writing from Lincoln's deathbed at one thirty in the morning of April 15, 1865, to Maj. Gen. Dix in New York, stated: "At a Cabinet meeting yesterday, at which General Grant was present, the subject of the state of the country and the prospects of speedy peace was discussed. The President was very cheerful and hopeful; spoke very kindly of General Lee and others of the Confederacy, and the establishment of government in Virginia."[38] Every indication was that Lincoln would have treated the rebel leadership with much less harshness than what Johnson advocated. Clemency marked Johnson's policy toward almost everyone who supported the rebellion but did not extend to the Confederate leaders. Whether he realized it or not, Johnson had already begun to shift Lincoln's postwar policy.

The shift proved to be dramatic and understandable. Perhaps the assassination of a president made the reversal of policy inevitable. Could any new president sustain an approach to southern leadership that did not involve some measure of retribution after the murder of his predecessor by a known southern sympathizer? Even if it were possible, could someone of Johnson's predisposition, who for years had advocated the punishment of rebel leaders, believe that softening his stance was the correct course of action? Lincoln's death disrupted the government's transition from wartime to peace. When

Lincoln drew his last breath, he took with him his presidential policy toward the South and the reintegration of the South into the Union. Initially, his successor and his cabinet members were relegated to attempting to surmise what his policy might have been. Then, as time passed, the struggle for ascendency on federal policy toward the South tore the cabinet apart, as Stanton broke with President Johnson and endorsed the Radical Republicans' Reconstruction plans.

Meanwhile, Washington was awash in rumor, fear, and sorrow. The streets were filled with people overwhelmed by grief, and no one knew how far the conspiracy to destroy the federal government extended. Members of the government, concerned for their safety, attempted to manage bureaucratic affairs of state in this tense crisis. Seagoing vessels, trains, and other potential means of escape were ordered searched for possible conspirators. Stanton wired Winfield Hancock about his proposed meeting with the Confederate colonel John Mosby: "In holding an interview with Mosby it may be needless to caution an old soldier like you to guard against surprise or danger to yourself," but "the recent murders show such astounding wickedness that too much precaution cannot be taken."[39]

Maj. Gen. Henry W. Halleck issued an order to the officer commanding Union forces in Washington: "Should either of the murderers or assassins of last night be caught put them in double irons and convey them, under a strong escort, to the commander of the navy-yard, who has orders to receive them and to confine them on a monitor to be anchored in the stream."[40] Shortly thereafter, Halleck prohibited passengers from leaving Washington or Alexandria aboard seagoing vessels. The federal government meant to find the Lincoln conspirators even if it meant shutting down the District of Columbia until they were located.

Many Confederate military leaders also reacted swiftly to the president's death. Lt. Gen. Richard S. Ewell, of the Confederate States of America, wrote Grant on April 16, 1865, to voice his repugnance at the crime: "Of all the misfortunes which could befall the Southern people, or any Southern man, by far the greatest, in my judgment, would be the prevalence of the idea that they could entertain any other than feelings of unqualified abhorrence and indignation for the assassination of the President of the United States."[41] He was not alone in his feelings. Brig. Gen. J. R. Jones stated: "I trust in God that no Southern man, when all is brought to light, will be found to be in any way accessory to the hellish crime, but on the contrary, that all will feel the utter abhorrence of the act, which is merited by all men."[42] Maj. John W. M. Appleton, a Union officer stationed at Fort Warren in Boston Harbor, oversaw Confederate prisoners housed there. He reported their revulsion at the crime: "The general officers confined at this post as prisoners of war have, from the moment of the reception of the news, expressed their regret for the loss of President Lincoln, and their utmost horror of the act and detestation of his murderers."[43] In Elmira, New York, Confederate prisoners held meetings and passed resolutions expressing their condemnation of the assassination.[44]

From a position of safety across the Atlantic, the erstwhile Confederate envoy to France and Britain James M. Mason published a letter that angrily refuted any charge that rebel leaders had played a role in Lincoln's death. "It is the crudest conception, too," he wrote, "that the murder of Abraham Lincoln was planned and executed for the purpose of 'aiding the rebel cause.'" Mason's letter may have voiced what many Confederates thought but were too afraid to say. Who, he questioned, gained from the president's death? "I can well understand that [the claim of southern involvement] may have material influence in aiding the cause of that overpowering party in the United States, of which Mr. Stanton is the type, and Andrew Johnson, who succeeds as President, with Butler of that notorious prefix, are the exponents and leaders—a party in whose path the late President and his Secretary [Seward] were acknowledged obstacles in their projected schemes of plunder and rapine to follow their domination over the Southern States."[45] It was just as well for Mason's continued longevity that he wrote this from across the ocean.

Not surprisingly, Confederates in the United States were unwilling to go as far as Mason. But newspaper editors across the South recognized what the assassin's bullet meant. The *Charleston (S.C.) Courier* reported that the murder "was a calamity unlooked for, and will stamp with still deeper infamy the leaders and abettors of the accursed rebellion."[46] The *Augusta (Ga.) Chronicle* told its readers that while the murder "has aroused a tempest of indignation throughout the North, . . . the more sober journalists are disposed to regard it as the act of a half crazy fanatic; while none, we believe, have been so reckless as to charge the Confederate authorities with complicity in his designs."[47] This proved to be wishful thinking at its best.

Grant's View of Reconciliation after Lincoln's Assassination

Grant's belief that Lincoln sought reconciliation with the South, and his efforts to advance this policy, continued after Lincoln's death. On April 17, 1865, Major General Ord addressed Grant from Richmond, where he found several thousand convalescing rebel soldiers at Libby Prison. The question was whether to parole the prisoners under the same terms given Lee's army. Ord informed Grant that he "was trying to make the military government acceptable by kindness where the interests of the Government allowed it."[48] The same day, General Order No. 27 announced that "all officers and soldiers of the Army of Northern Virginia who were not present at the surrender of that army by General Robert E. Lee, at Appomattox Court-House, on the 9th of April, 1865, are hereby informed that the terms of capitulation are extended to them."[49]

The interpretation of the surrender terms granted to Lee began almost immediately. On May 6, 1865, an army chief of staff wrote that Grant had decided "that under the terms of the capitulation all soldiers surrendered by General Lee, or under the terms granted by General Grant, *have a right* to return to their homes at Alexandria, or elsewhere in Virginia, and to remain there as long as they respect their paroles and the laws in force where they reside."[50] In another letter written the same day, the chief of staff indicated that this quasi amnesty extended seemingly to all paroled rebel soldiers: "Good faith demands that the privilege be secured to the men [to remain at home in West Virginia], and under General Grant's decision the general cannot permit these paroled men to be driven from their homes by the citizens, in the absence of any specific charges showing that it is dangerous for the community for them to remain."[51] Such was the power of Grant in the aftermath of the war that he felt comfortable stating, unequivocally, what rights might be derived from the terms of Lee's surrender. His prestige was immense, and his interpretation was not challenged insofar as the terms of surrender influenced the rights of former Confederate soldiers. Either Grant believed that he should not attempt to influence the treatment of Confederate political leaders or felt that he did not have the authority to do so. In any case, Jefferson Davis was not afforded the protection that Confederate military men found in Grant.

Disparate treatment of civilian and military personnel had existed during the war. Residence in a loyal state did not protect people from arrest. It was not unusual for those suspected of harboring rebel sympathies to find themselves under arrest. From the war's beginning, military commanders in loyal states maintained control of the civilian populations by arresting civilians suspected of disloyalty. As early as September 1861, Gen. John C. Fremont began the practice of trying civilians before military tribunals. As Jonathan W. White has noted, when Lincoln suspended the writ of habeas corpus, other constitutional protections, including the right to be tried criminally in a civil court rather than before a military tribunal, fell by the wayside. Indeed, civilians were routinely tried in military courts for actions as minor as verbally abusing Union soldiers.[52] On August 8, 1862, Edwin Stanton authorized United States marshals and other law enforcement officials "to arrest and imprison any person or persons who may be engaged, by act, speech, or writing, in discouraging volunteer enlistments, or in any way giving aid and comfort to the enemy, or in any other disloyal practice against the United States."[53] This order received presidential confirmation shortly thereafter. In the Proclamation Suspending the Writ of Habeas Corpus, signed on September 24, 1862, Lincoln subjected to arrest those individuals who had committed specific acts but also those who were "guilty of any disloyal practice," a vague phrase giving military commanders vast authority to arrest virtually anyone known to be a southern sympathizer. A key provision of the proclamation allowed commanders to substitute a court-martial or trial by military commission for a civilian court. It has been estimated that over four thousand civilians faced court-martial or were tried before military commissions during the war.[54] Indeed, the *Official Records* include over fifteen hundred pages in a section titled "Treatment of Suspected and Disloyal Persons North and South." Many prisoners were alleged to have engaged in "treasonable language" or "general disloyalty."[55] No one, North or South, would have been surprised if the leaders of the rebellion had been handed over to military tribunals for trial.

Prosecution of those who had conspired against the Union government did not suddenly end with Lee's surrender. On May 9, 1865, the secretary of war directed that members of the secret society known as the Order of American Knights, or the Order of the Sons of Liberty, be hanged. These men, Lambdin P. Milligan and seven others, had been tried by a military commission in Indianapolis in October 1864. They were charged with conspiring against the United States government, affording aid and comfort to rebels, inciting insurrection, engaging in disloyal practices, and committing acts in violation of the laws of war.[56] Milligan was a citizen of Indiana who was not in the military or naval service, yet he was tried before a military commission rather than a civil court in Indiana. In mid-1864, when the fate of the nation hung in the balance, this action may have been understandable. But Confederate leaders must have been worried when the federal government upheld the verdict rendered by a military commission after the war had ended. By their composition, military commissions posed a threat of serious punishment for those tried before them. Union officers sitting on the commissions, who had suffered the privations of war and seen the terrible toll that it took on their lives and the lives of those in their units, would be much less likely than civilian jurors to sympathize with the accused. The punishment of civilians by military commissions in the northern state did not bode well for the treatment of southern leaders.[57]

The terms of Lee's surrender gave southerners reason to believe that Confederate leaders might be treated under extraordinarily generous terms. But John Wilkes Booth and the conspiracy that he headed had murdered the most powerful Republican leader in the North, one whose conciliatory spirit might have blocked the effort to punish southern leaders for treason. Union leaders feared that Booth's plot might have germinated in Richmond, with the knowledge of Jefferson Davis. From that vantage point, the flight of Davis and members of his cabinet after Lincoln's murder took on a sinister tone to northerners. Davis had left Richmond before the assassination in an attempt to gather the Confederate forces and continue the war. But his continued flight through the South after Lincoln's death contributed to the belief among northerners that he had been involved in the assassination plot. In the charged atmosphere after April 14, 1865, the cool reflection necessary for making a decision about whether to try Confederates for treason was lost. Capturing Davis became the paramount goal. The question of what to do with him became secondary to placing him in Union custody. What was certain was that the one man who had both the will and the power to ensure that Davis would not be put to death for warring against the Union—President Lincoln—had been murdered.

3

THE STRANGE "FLIGHT" OF JEFFERSON DAVIS

Jeff. Davis has more lives than a cat and we must not trust him.

—William Tecumseh Sherman

DAVIS LEFT RICHMOND before Lincoln's murder, believing that the Confederacy still lived. His conduct did not change after word of Booth's crime reached him. Perhaps he feared being caught and put on trial for treason, but if he harbored this fear, it was not evidenced by his words. In his copy of *The Prison Life of Jefferson Davis,* published in the summer of 1866 and acquired by Davis while he was still incarcerated, he underlined the word *flight* in the sentence that read, "Mr. Davis then spoke of the circumstances attending his flight from Richmond." In the margin, he annotated the word with a simple question mark.[1] To the contrary, his actions and speech exhibited an inflexible mind-set that the Confederate States of America was still a viable nation. Lincoln considered this a reflection of "senseless obstinacy" on the part of Davis that could not be representative of the sentiments of the southern people.[2] Varina Davis still believed in the viability of the Confederate state and encouraged this false confidence in her husband. "You are the country's only hope," she wrote. "Why not cut loose from your escort? Go swiftly and alone, except for two or three," she advised.[3] But the month progressed, and soldiers deserted to return to their homes; the armies surrendered, and the Confederacy died. Davis was reduced to trying to escape the United States mainland. These shifting concerns occupied his mind as he moved south with his cavalry escort. There is little evidence to suggest that how he fit into Lincoln's political plans for the future motivated his movements. In spite of this, the Lincoln administration's blueprint for the nation after the war was a critical consideration regarding Davis if he was overtaken.

Implicit in Lincoln's comment that he would not mind if Jefferson Davis escaped capture is Lincoln's perception that having the Confederate president in custody would bring a host of problems that could be avoided if Davis simply eluded federal authorities and fled the country. By nature, Lincoln was not a bloodthirsty man. His statement might have reflected his feeling that enough sacrifice had been made in the war. But it betrayed Lincoln's belief that Davis would become a distraction to reunion of the North and South. Once in federal custody, Davis might delay, if not block, a smooth reconciliation of the two sections of the country. Debates over whether Confederate leadership should be indicted for treason would certainly lose steam if the head of the rebel government, because of his absence from the country, was not susceptible to trial. And actually putting Davis to trial for treason would divide the nation even further while exposing the federal government to the negative consequences of an acquittal. Lincoln's perception was insightful.

Jefferson Davis had his own ideas about what would be good policy for the North after the war. In *The Rise and Fall of the Confederate Government,* Davis wrote that after the war's end, "nothing remained to be done but for the sovereigns, the people of each State, to assert their authority and restore order. If the principle of the sovereignty of the people, the cornerstone of all our institutions, had survived and was still in force, it was necessary only that the people of each State should re-consider their ordinances of secession, and again recognize the Constitution of the United States as the supreme law of the land. This simple process would have placed the Union on its original basis, and have restored that which had ceased to exist, the Union by consent."[4] Sixteen years after Lee's surrender, his suggestion was that all simply should have been forgotten and forgiven. His solution ostensibly would have permitted the same men who had led the South out of the Union to lead their states back into the national government. This was a result that many in the North found wholly unacceptable. But there were men, both North and South, who would attempt to make it a reality.

However, in April 1865, reconciliation with his former nation was the furthest thing from the mind of Jefferson Davis. With the disintegration of the Confederacy, many rebel leaders were working to escape to foreign countries. If the Confederate States of America died, Davis hoped to join them in exile. But he had not given up hope that the war could still be won. Davis moved away from advancing Union troops, but his acceptance of the inevitability of the Confederacy's dying took time. Others recognized what was yet unclear to Davis.

When he left Richmond on Sunday, April 2, 1865, Davis held the delusion that he could rally the South. The chaos surrounding him did not dim his view. He traveled by train accompanied by several members of his cabinet: Secretary of State Judah Benjamin, Secretary of the Treasury George Trenholm, and Secretary of the Navy Stephen Mallory. Together they carried with them much of the gold and silver that remained in the nearly bankrupt treasury. Losing the national capital would not mean the end of the bloody struggle if Lee could unite his army with that of Joseph Johnston. Davis's retinue reached Danville, Virginia, to await Lee. While there, Johnston wrote to find Lee's location. Such was the state of the Confederacy. Days later, a young lieutenant arrived from Lee's headquarters to tell Davis of the disaster that had occurred at Sayler's Creek, Virginia, on April 6, 1865. The Confederate army had been split by Union cavalry under Maj. Gen. Phil Sheridan. Over seven thousand southern soldiers had surrendered, while the rest of Lee's army was diverted away from Danville. The young officer made clear that Lee's army would not be able to withstand the pressure of the Union forces.

Upon leaving Richmond, Davis immediately ordered a withdrawal into North Carolina. He put his close aide Burton Harrison, recently returned from escorting Varina and the children out of Richmond, in charge of arranging for a train. Again, officers of the government, luggage, and important papers were hastily loaded. The scene at the railway station was frenzied. Orders were given to guards not to allow any person or item to be placed on the train unless authorized by Harrison. As he was supervising the evacuation, two Confederate officers rode up on horses spattered with mud. Harrison saw that one of the men rode a fresh, spirited horse. Finding that the officer was not the owner but had been charged by the owner with getting the horse to the owner's son, Harrison offered to assume responsibility for it. The officer declined to give the horse to Harrison and rode away. He returned shortly, after finding that he could not board the train without an order from Harrison. The officer told Harrison that if Harrison "would furnish such an order, he would accept my proposition about the horse. The arrangement was made immediately, and the colonel became a passenger on the train."[5] In another instance, Harrison recounted a general "besieging me for permits to enter the train . . . with several daughters and one or more of his staff officers."[6]

Confederate refugees trying to get out of Danville crowded the station. To their disappointment, the train was reserved for Davis and his staff and others authorized by Harrison. Many at the station would be left behind. One Confederate War Department official complained in his diary that "the President and Cabinet made hasty preparations to leave Danville that night for Greensboro, North Carolina, and did so without giving any orders to the bureau offices, which caused great confusion."[7] The panic was growing.

Once loaded, the train made it to Greensboro, where Davis spent the next four days. The reception that he received there was noticeably cold. Harrison reconciled this by noting that the area had not been a hotbed for secession in 1861 and that the people there had never been strong supporters of the Confederacy. Much to Harrison's dismay, however, many of the staff officers were relegated to sleeping in the uncomfortable railway cars. Davis was not invited into the home of any local citizen. He escaped sleeping in the train only because a member of Davis's staff had earlier sent his own family from Richmond to Greensboro and allowed Davis to stay at their home.

The presence of Confederate officials in the state did not deter the North Carolina governor, Zebulon B. Vance, from corresponding with Sherman to surrender the state. Vance's immediate concern were the Union columns bearing down toward the capital, Raleigh. Vance asked for safe passage to Sherman's headquarters and for a personal interview with the general for the purpose of ending the war in North Carolina. Davis got wind of Vance's intentions and ordered the arrest of anyone attempting to meet with Sherman. Despite this order, the Union army was not to be slowed, and Sherman met with the leading citizens of the city in the governor's mansion on April 13. Noticeably absent was Governor Vance, who had fled Raleigh, fearing arrest. But Sherman was not interested in acquiring territory. The surrender or destruction of Johnston's army was still foremost in his mind. "I think I can force Johnston to disperse his army or accept battle in a few days," he wrote to his cavalry commander, "and will proceed as fast as I can get troops into position."[8]

Two days earlier, Davis had dispatched a message to General Johnston, headquartered near Raleigh, about seventy-five miles east of Greensboro, instructing Johnston to travel to Greensboro to confer. Johnston took the first train, at midnight, and arrived at about eight the morning of April 12. He and Gen. P.G.T. Beauregard waited for an hour or two within sight of Davis's quarters before being summoned to meet. Judah Benjamin, Stephen Mallory, and John Reagan were with Davis when Johnston and Beauregard arrived.

The generals were under the mistaken impression that they were "to be questioned concerning the military resources of our department, in connection with the question of continuing or terminating the war." To their dismay, "the President's object seemed to be to give, not obtain information,"[9] and they were asked for no news about the state of their forces or their opinions regarding the continuation of the war. Instead, they were astonished to hear Davis claim that he would have a large army in the field in two or three weeks. The conference ended with the two generals stunned by the unrealistic view held by the civilian leadership of their government.

Johnston and Beauregard knew that the Confederate armies were defeated. But until John C. Breckinridge arrived that afternoon, they did not know how they would convince Davis of that fact. Once he arrived and met with the two generals, Breckinridge promised Johnston that he would give Johnston the opportunity to talk candidly with Davis. Not long after this, Stephen Mallory came to Johnston and commiserated with the general about Davis's failure to accept reality. Mallory urged him to tell Davis that the war needed to end and demurred when Johnston suggested that Mallory should tell him. This must have given Johnston a taste of the character of the men now surrounding Davis.

Breckinridge did get another meeting between the generals and Davis. Again, this summit began with Davis making observations about the condition of the Confederacy. The military situation was dire, he acknowledged. He then made statements that must have sounded utterly senseless to the officers in the room. Davis offered that "our late disasters are terrible; but I do not think we should regard them as fatal. I think we can whip the enemy yet, if our people will turn out." General Johnston's bronzed face betrayed his barely suppressed anger that Davis did not recognize the actual condition of the Confederacy, but Johnston stewed in silence until the president asked him for his opinion. Joe Johnston was about five feet eight inches tall and weighed about 150 pounds, but he held himself with an undeniable *air militaire*. He stood completely erect and, while genial and good-humored generally, was also known as an intellectual power of great military stature. When he spoke on this day, he did so very candidly and forcefully.

Mallory later wrote that Johnston spoke in a "terse, concise, demonstrative way, as if seeking to condense thoughts that were crowding for utterance." Johnson told the president and the war council, "Our people are tired of the war, feel themselves whipped, and will not fight." Nothing could be more clearly stated. Mallory wrote that the words from Johnston were almost spitefully spoken. That was understandable. Johnston had been in the field with his men, watching them suffer and die at the hands of a much stronger Union army. He wanted the misery to end. "Since Lee's surrender they regard the war as at an end," he said. "I shall expect to retain no man beyond the by-road or cow-path that leads to his home. My small force is melting away like snow before the sun."[10] Confederate soldiers, loyal so long, were voting to end the war with their feet. Johnston had done his duty to his men; he had told the Confederate leadership the truth.

Davis listened quietly while folding and refolding a piece of paper. He did not look at Johnston but stared intently at the paper in his hands. In a low voice, he asked General Beauregard for his thoughts, doubtlessly hoping for a more optimistic view. The general responded, "I concur in all General Johnston has said." A quick survey of the cabinet members present found that they also agreed with Johnston. This ended all hope of continuing to fight. Davis and Johnston were not on friendly footing, but the president needed to find out what Johnston proposed. Davis asked if terms could be gotten from Sherman. Johnston suggested that terms better than those given to Lee at Appomattox could be obtained.

Even with the Confederate president and the remnants of his cabinet in Greensboro, along with two of the top remaining military commanders, soldiers in that city deserted in droves. Brig. Gen. Alfred Iverson reported "the desertion of numbers of the troops from the lines around the town, the Virginia troops generally leaving. I am pained to say that the disposition of the command is not good, there being much demoralization. Large numbers of stragglers are constantly arriving. Arrangements have been made to collect these men, but the difficulty is to keep them from deserting."[11]

Davis and his men knew that the options available were very limited. But they continued to seek a better end to the war than simple surrender. Writing nearly a week after the war council that "the enemy is still unconscious of the full extent of our weakness," Postmaster General John H. Reagan stressed to Davis that he should seek terms that would allow the states to reintegrate smoothly into the Union. His proposed terms included the withdrawal of Union forces from the seceding states while the states called conventions to reestablish their place in the Union and the payment of the Confederacy's war debt in common with the debt of the United States. Reagan said that the justification for these terms could be found in the fact that "we did not seek this war, but only sought peaceful separation to secure our people and States from the effects of unconstitutional encroachments by the other states."[12] If Reagan still held that absurd opinion a week after Johnston had made clear that the Confederacy was finished, his position must certainly have bolstered Davis's belief that a negotiated settlement favoring the Confederacy might still be possible. It appears that only the military men grasped that the Confederacy was dead. Davis and the civilians around him remained in utter denial. The Confederate president adjourned the meeting having given Johnston specific directions on what terms to attempt to negotiate with Sherman.

General Johnston left Greensboro at 3:30 a.m. on April 14 and immediately resumed command of his forces, which had retreated to the outskirts of Greensboro. General Beauregard left town on the morning of the fifteenth. Johnston undertook the mission agreed upon by Davis and his cabinet to end hostilities with terms better than those given to Lee. While outwardly maintaining his bearing, Davis privately wrote to Varina on April 14. He seemed to finally understand the obvious: "I will come to you if I can. Every thing is dark—you should prepare for the worst by dividing your baggage so as to move in wagons." He urged her to go to Abbeville, South Carolina, to meet him if she could, confessing to her, "I have lingered on the road and labored to little purpose."[13]

Johnston wasted no time in contacting Sherman. Citing the recent loss of Virginia, he asked Sherman "whether, in order to stop the further effusion of blood and devastation of property, you are willing to make a temporary suspension of active operations, . . . the object being to permit the civil authorities to enter into the needful arrangements to terminate the existing war."[14] Sherman would have none of it. He replied immediately that the foundation of an agreement would be "the same terms and conditions as were made by Generals Grant and Lee at Appomattox."[15]

Sherman continued sending detailed orders to his subordinates. To Maj. Gen. Judson Kilpatrick, his cavalry commander, he confided, "I will not suspend hostilities till Johnston's army is captured or scattered." Sherman knew the South was near defeat but expressed caution: "The people here manifest more signs of subjugation than I have yet seen, but Jeff. Davis has more lives than a cat and we must not trust him."[16]

On April 16, Johnston had telegraphed John Breckinridge, urging him to come immediately to Johnston's headquarters near Greensboro. Since Sherman refused to suspend fighting while civil authorities negotiated a surrender, Johnston needed to personally conduct any negotiations. He sought the advice of Breckinridge on how to best accomplish that task. He sent a second and then a third telegram the next day emphasizing the need to confer with the Confederate secretary of war before April 18. Davis waited nervously in Charlotte and sent his own message asking whether Breckinridge had arrived. As the Confederacy teetered, its leaders had difficulty even communicating with each other. Breckinridge did finally arrive, to the relief of everyone. Johnston, heavily pressed by Sherman's army, could now begin talks.

Meanwhile, Major General Kilpatrick believed that Johnston was using the exchange of dispatches simply to stall while his forces slipped away. Kilpatrick reported to Sherman that "Johnston's whole army is still marching on." Sherman's cavalry commander warned his commanding officer, "If Johnston can escape I believe he will do so."[17] Sherman did not agree, but his response made it clear that he was not a man to be trifled with. "I have faith in General Johnston's personal sincerity," he wrote, but he added ominously that "if he gains on us by this time lost we will make up at the expense of North Carolina."[18]

Sherman's faith was vindicated when Confederate lieutenant general Wade Hampton sent a dispatch that very day proposing a meeting of the two senior commanders at 10:00 a.m. on April 17. Kilpatrick was ordered to prepare for Sherman's arrival by having about twenty officers, a cavalry escort, and horses ready to travel to the site of the proposed meeting, which would take place about equidistant between the lines of the two armies. Sherman and his staff would travel by locomotive to Durham, bringing with them their saddles.

It was now raining in torrents, and Sherman took the time to inform his superiors of what was transpiring in North Carolina. He wrote to Secretary of War Stanton and Gen. Ulysses S. Grant about Johnston's proposal to pause the fighting. Knowing that the war was nearly over, he told them, "If any cavalry have started toward me caution them that they must be prepared to find our work done." Completely unaware of what had happened at Ford's Theater, he must have felt it was a grand moment to share. Sherman assured Grant and Stanton that he would extend only the terms given at Appomattox "and be careful not to complicate any points of civil policy."[19]

The next morning was likely one that Sherman awoke to with much joy. But any feeling of exultation was short-lived. As he was boarding the train, a telegraph operator whose office sat above the train depot ran downstairs to breathlessly tell Sherman of an urgent message that he was receiving at that very moment. He implored Sherman to wait for the full message to be transmitted. The general delayed the train for half an hour while the telegram came in. It contained dreadful news from Edwin Stanton: Lincoln had been assassinated.

According to Stanton, the assassin had exclaimed, "Sic semper tyrannis!" in revenge for Virginia. Stanton continued. "I find evidence that an assassin is also on your track."[20] A second message came from Henry Halleck, the chief of staff of the Union army, which provided more detail about Sherman's would-be assassin. Reportedly, the man was the same person who had assaulted and nearly killed William Seward and Seward's son, Frederick. The man was a Texan by birth, about five feet nine inches in height and of a slender build. A very detailed description of his clothing and facial hair was provided. Halleck said that the assassin was traveling with another man.

Sherman needed time to think through the implications of this horrific act. It came at a critical moment. Was Johnston to be trusted? Was Sherman walking into a trap? He asked the telegraph operator if the man had told anyone else. When he was assured that he had not, Sherman told him that he was not to reveal, by word or manner, that the North had suffered a serious blow. He should keep it to himself until Sherman returned that afternoon. The man agreed. Then Sherman boarded the train. The shocking news transformed the mood as he rode the rail to Durham. It must have been a terrible time. Sherman's staff was aware that the war was nearly over, and their mood must have been joyful. Their leader could not have joined in their elation.

Once in Durham, all the men mounted their horses and rode toward the meeting behind a rider carrying a white flag. After about five miles, the flag bearer met another riding toward him. Sherman discovered, upon riding up, that Joe Johnston and Wade Hampton, a lieutenant general leading Johnston's cavalry, were close behind the truce bearer, riding side by side. The three men shook hands and introduced their staffs. The courtesy extended on this occasion masked some deep emotions. Hampton disliked Sherman intensely, and Sherman reciprocated the feeling.

Less than two months earlier, the Union commander now mounted before him had written to Hampton complaining of Union foragers being murdered after capture and their bodies being left behind with placards saying "Death to all Foragers." This had happened to seven Union soldiers near Chesterville, South Carolina, and another twenty near a town called Fosterville in Tennessee. Sherman wrote a blistering letter to Hampton. Foraging was "a war right as old as history," Sherman wrote, and then reminded Hampton that Sherman held about a thousand Confederate prisoners. While not blaming the Confederate cavalry commander directly, he told him that "he would suggest that you give notice to the People at large, that every life taken by them simply results in the death of one of your confederates." Sherman could not stop at that. Consistent with his personality, he continued: "Personally, I regret the bitter feelings engendered by this war: but they were to be expected, and I simply allege that those who struck the first blow, and made war inevitable, ought not in fairness to reproach us for the natural consequence."[21] Sherman was, as always, unfiltered in his words; Hampton must have believed them to be very sharp.

Sherman asked if there was somewhere private to speak. Johnston said that he had passed a farmhouse a short distance back, and the entire group rode in that direction. Despite having served in the United States Army together prior to the war, Sherman and Johnston had never met. They reached a small frame house that belonged to a Mr. and Mrs. Bennett, who were home. The couple must have been astonished to have Sherman and Johnston ask for the use of their modest home, but they left the house and waited as the men met inside.

The meeting could not have started worse for Johnston. Sherman showed him the telegram announcing Lincoln's murder. Johnston was visibly shaken. When he spoke, he denounced the assassination as a disgraceful act. Then he told Sherman that he hoped that Sherman did not believe that the Confederate government was behind the murder. Sherman answered tersely that he did not believe that Johnston or Lee would ever countenance such an act but that he could not be sure about Jefferson Davis or men like him. Sherman later recalled their conversation: "We talked about the effect of this act on the country at large and on the armies, and he realized that it made my situation extremely delicate. I explained to him that I had not yet revealed the news to my own personal staff or to the army, and that I dreaded the effect when known in Raleigh. Mr. Lincoln was peculiarly endeared to the soldiers, and

I feared some foolish woman or man in Raleigh might say something or do something that would madden our men, and that a fate worse than that of Columbia would befall the place."[22]

When the talk turned to the surrender of Johnston's army, the rebel officer admitted that any further fighting would be little more than murder. But he inquired whether Sherman might not take the broader surrender of all the Confederate armies. The Union general questioned his counterpart's authority to surrender more than his own army. Johnston assured Sherman that he could get authorization from Jefferson Davis to accomplish this. With this larger question now before them, the men parted to meet the next day.

To the Confederacy's apparent good fortune, Johnston faced a foe willing to engage in negotiation. Unbeknownst to Sherman, Johnston already had the authority he was supposedly seeking during the break. Sherman, perhaps under the impression that Lincoln's position on reconciliation was still the Union posture and under the added misfortune of not being connected by telegraph to Washington, D.C., was about to make some critical errors. That night, however, he wrote to Grant about the meeting. He called the talk "a full and frank interchange of opinions. [Johnston] evidently seeks to make terms for Jeff. Davis and his cabinet."[23] Sherman was not naive, but he was ill informed of the changes that were occurring in the Union capital. The delay, he thought, would work to the Union advantage, even if terms could not be arrived at, since roads were drying and becoming more passable each day. The only concern that he revealed was the possibility that Johnston's army would splinter and fill the South with robbers and murderers. In the meantime, Sherman returned to Raleigh and published the news of Lincoln's assassination to the Union army.

The notice contained equal parts anger, admonitions to the men, and forewarning to the South. "It seems that our enemy, despairing of meeting us in open, manly warfare, begins to resort to the assassin's tools," Sherman said. "Your general does not wish you to infer that this is universal, for he knows that the great mass of the Confederate Army would scorn to sanction such acts, but he believes that it is the legitimate consequence of rebellion against rightful authority. We have met every phase which this war has assumed, and must now be prepared for it in its last and worst shape, that of assassins and guerillas; but woe unto the people who seek to expend their wild passions in such a manner, for there is but one dread result."[24] Sherman waited nervously, hoping that no incident would engulf Raleigh in flames. None did.

Later that evening and the next morning, Sherman spoke to his ranking officers about Johnston's proposal. John M. Schofield, Henry W. Slocum, O. O. Howard, John A. Logan, and Frank P. Blair each urged him to come to terms that would end the entire war. They even spoke of whether Sherman should permit Jefferson Davis to safely leave the country, with one of his subordinates going so far as to propose that Davis be provided with a federal ship for his passage.

At about 2:00 p.m. on April 18, 1865, the two antagonists met again at the Bennett farmhouse. Johnston told Sherman that he had acquired the authority to surrender all Confederate forces but considered this move such a major concession that Sherman ought to guarantee the political rights of the officers and men in return for their capitulation. Sherman told him that Lincoln's amnesty proclamation of December 8, 1863, was still in effect and accomplished that purpose, certainly when combined with the terms enunciated at Appomattox. Johnston said that his officers and men were unconvinced.

At this point, Johnston told Sherman that John Breckinridge was waiting nearby and asked Sherman to allow him to join the discussions. Sherman objected because he believed that the discussion should be restricted to military men, not Confederate civil authorities. Johnston pointed out that Breckinridge was not only the Confederate secretary of state but also a major general in the Confederate army. He suggested that Breckinridge be permitted to participate as a general, not as a cabinet member of the Confederate government. Although this was a weak distinction, Sherman agreed.

Breckinridge appeared, and shortly thereafter, a messenger arrived with a parcel of papers from Confederate postmaster general Reagan. Sherman looked the papers over and saw six terms sought by the Confederacy written in Reagan's hand. The fifth paragraph from Reagan protected Jefferson Davis and everyone else who had a hand in waging war against the Union. It granted to all people "freedom from future prosecution or penalties for their participation in the present war."[25] Sherman rejected Reagan's proposal as too long and wordy.

Instead, Sherman sat down at a table and took a pen in hand. He quickly drafted a document that he believed encompassed the conversation he had had with Lincoln at City Point. Not being privy to a subsequent message that Lincoln had sent to Grant, which restricted Grant to dealing with Lee only to accept the surrender of his army, Sherman thought that he was working within the framework set out by Lincoln for a settlement of the war. When he finished writing, he allowed Johnston and Breckinridge to see the terms and told them that he was willing to submit these to Washington, D.C., for approval. Both rebel leaders agreed. As copies were prepared for signature, the Confederate and Union officers and their staffs mingled in the yard. Everyone must have been relieved that the war was over.

Sherman told Breckinridge that he should leave the country immediately. He explained that the people of the North were largely hostile to the politicians of the South. And Breckinridge, as a former vice president of the United States, was especially loathsome. Breckinridge intimated that he would quickly leave. Sherman recalled, "I may have also advised him that Mr. Davis too should get abroad as soon as possible."[26] Davis was eager to hear directly from Breckinridge about the meeting and sent him a very short message: "Join me at Charlotte, N.C."[27]

A firestorm of criticism would erupt because of these proposed terms. It must be said, in Sherman's defense, that the face of the document acknowledged that he lacked the authority to bind the federal government to the terms but merely pledged to submit the proposal for approval. Sherman sent the document to Grant in Washington, D.C., by the most expeditious means possible. Unfortunately, this was not via telegraph but by steamer. Grant received it from a special messenger on April 21, 1865. He immediately recognized that the proposed terms went well beyond what was politically possible in the charged atmosphere of the capital. In fact, they went well beyond the instructions that Grant had from Lincoln before Lee's surrender, which gave Grant only the authority to accept the surrender and nothing else. Grant informed Secretary of War Stanton of the dispatch. Grant's tone reflected his concern. The dispatches "are of such importance," he wrote, "that I think immediate action should be taken on them and that it should be done by the President in council with his whole cabinet. I would respectfully suggest whether the President should not be notified and all his cabinet, and the meeting take place to-night."[28]

The proposed terms between Sherman and Johnston were untenable. While the document Sherman composed provided for the surrender of Confederate forces, it also intruded on the executive and congressional prerogatives by binding the Union to a reunion of the nation on terms very favorable to the South. Under the terms of the surrender, there would be a general amnesty, and the rights—including property rights—of citizens of the former

Confederacy would be restored and protected. Sherman wrote that Johnston and Breckinridge "admitted that slavery was dead,"[29] but this must have been of little consolation to the men in Washington reading that southerners' rights to property would be guaranteed. Perhaps most egregious was the proposal that preserved the state governments then in control of Confederate states once the officers and legislators of the states took an oath of allegiance to the United States. This agreement would mean that the leaders of the rebellion would remain in their leadership roles in state government and likely send the same men to Washington as senators and representatives. Jefferson Davis could return as a senator from Mississippi. There was no provision for the freedmen either.

Stanton could not contain his outrage. He immediately disapproved Sherman's submission and directed that Sherman "resume hostilities at the earliest moment."[30] The cabinet assembled at eight o'clock that night. Grant and Preston King were also there. King had been credited as being "largely instrumental in procuring the nomination of Andrew Johnson for the Vice-Presidency," and the new president leaned on him for advice. "Remarkable for obesity," King stood only five feet six inches but weighed over 250 pounds.[31] The meeting was short and limited to the question of the propriety of Sherman's proposed terms for the end of the war.

Stanton and James Speed, the new attorney general, condemned Sherman's proposal. Speed's denunciation of the proposed terms was tempered with a profession of his personal friendship for Sherman. Stanton's censure was devoid of anything of that nature, which made his words about Sherman sting a bit more to the other men in the room. Whether he truly believed what he said or had an ulterior motive for questioning Sherman's patriotism cannot be known, but he had been at Sherman's headquarters in mid-January 1865 and knew, firsthand, how vigorously Sherman had pressed the fighting. He voiced four specific objections against Sherman and the proposal, counting each off on his fingers as he spoke. Gideon Welles confided to his diary that "some of [Stanton's] argument was apt and well, some of it not in good taste nor precisely pertinent."[32]

Sherman's close friend Grant refused to join in any censure of the general, although he agreed that the terms could not be approved. He knew his subordinate well enough not to impugn the man's integrity or his patriotism. The proposal was simply a bad one that needed to be rejected. The cabinet recognized this as well, and Grant was instructed to immediately inform Sherman of the decision. He was also instructed to order Sherman to resume military operations against the Confederate forces at once. Stanton warned the cabinet to keep Sherman's proposal secret. The next day, Grant left Washington to deliver the instructions to Sherman in person. He knew the general to be prickly and prideful and wanted to make certain that the rejection of the proposal was not seen by Sherman as a personal or professional rebuke.

That day, Secretary of the Navy Welles was visited by the Radical Republican Charles Sumner, asking about Sherman's proposal. He had just come from Stanton's office, so it was clear to the naval secretary that Stanton was not abiding by his own order for secrecy. Stanton was known to engage in intrigue, striving to advance his own agenda. This instance was but another example. By Sunday morning, the entire story was in the newspapers. In addition to the news of the proposed terms of surrender, the papers carried an incendiary dispatch from Stanton to Maj. Gen. John A. Dix in New York. It stated, "The orders of General Sherman to General Stoneman to withdraw from Salisbury and join him will probably open the way for [Jefferson] Davis to escape to Mexico or Europe with his plunder, which is reported to be very large, including not only the plunder of the Richmond banks, but previous accumulations."[33]

The paper speculated that the Confederate leaders had previous knowledge of the conspiracy to murder Lincoln and his key cabinet members and thought that his assassination would lead to terms better than those received by Lee during the late president's life. Welles knew better. Sherman's "error, if it be one, had its origin, I apprehend, with President Lincoln, who was for prompt and easy terms with the Rebels."[34] The cabinet was well aware that Lincoln had met with Grant and Sherman at City Point near the end of the war and had talked to them about the prospect of the war ending. This did not keep James Speed from becoming frantic with fear that Sherman intended to put himself at the head of the army and take over the government. Attorney General Speed feared that Sherman might arrest Grant when Grant arrived at Raleigh. Welles and Postmaster General William Dennison Jr. tried to assure Speed that Sherman would not betray his trust, but the attorney general was worried that Sherman had fallen under the sway of Breckinridge. In the wake of the assassination and the very easy terms in Sherman's dispatch, anything seemed possible. In hindsight, Welles admitted that the cabinet had become influenced by the avowals of Stanton and Joseph Holt that they possessed proof positive that Jefferson Davis and others had conspired to kill Lincoln.

Ominously, the *New York Herald* also trumpeted that Jefferson Davis had escaped during the armistice and that Grant had gone to Carolina to direct the operations against Johnston. Unknown to federal officials in Washington, Davis was not yet trying to escape. He continued to wait in Charlotte for word on the negotiations. On the day that the *Herald* announced that he had escaped, Davis wrote to Varina and told her of the secret meetings between Johnston and Sherman and their agreement to suspend the fighting under agreed-upon terms. Davis told her that the terms "are secret and may be rejected by the Yankee govt.—to us they are hard enough, though freed from wanton humiliation and expressly recognizing the state governments, and the rights of person and property as secured by the Constitutions of the United States and the several states."[35]

During the suspension of hostilities, the Confederacy was further breaking down. Governor Vance wrote to Johnston that southern troops under his command had taken property belonging to North Carolina and threatened to sack more property. Vance told Johnston that Sherman had offered to protect public property from looting and implied that he would ask for that protection if Johnston could not control his troops. The collapse affected Davis too. There was no train that could operate south from Greensboro, so the president and his remaining cabinet had to travel by horseback and wagon. Just before leaving, Judah Benjamin, who was very overweight, emphatically stated that he would not mount a horse except as a last resort. This left Burton Harrison scrambling to find an ambulance that could be used to transport the large man. Recent rains slowed travel almost to a halt. Wagons and horses pulling them sank into the soft mud and had to be pulled out. Davis's group faced capture even before leaving Greensboro. They crossed one bridge just before Union cavalry arrived and burned it. After an exhausting day, they stopped at the home of a hospitable Confederate sympathizer. For the first time in a week, the men were able to have a good meal and a nice place to sleep. They did not stay long at the house.

After leaving Greensboro, Davis spent a night each at Jamestown, Lexington, Salisbury, and Concord, before reaching Charlotte. Breckinridge, meanwhile, was having difficulty finding a locomotive to take him to Davis. The train that he thought would transport him to Charlotte had been seized, he believed, by stragglers from the Confederate army also trying to reach Charlotte. Breckinridge wrote to Davis on April 20, asking that the commandeered train be met and the ringleaders be dealt with severely. Davis responded that a train, this time under armed guard, would be sent to Breckinridge. The next day, fleeing soldiers again intercepted the train meant for the Confederate secretary of war. This time, the engine and tender escaped to finally reach the stranded man. When Breckinridge complained to Johnston about the great confusion caused by southern stragglers, including the burning of important railway bridges, Johnston replied that the government should use the treasure being transported to pay the men who were now deserting the army. Tensions were at their highest levels.

Waiting for news and running from capture must have created an oppressive atmosphere for the rebel president, but it did not keep him from working furiously to keep the Confederacy alive. He tried to direct military events when he reached Charlotte, North Carolina. Telegraphing Howell Cobb in Macon, Georgia, on April 21, Davis implored him to defend Macon with the "absentees, including very many who belonged to captured companies of the Army of Northern Virginia" who, Davis thought, might want to continue the fight.[36] The Confederate president was taking leave of reality. Lee's men were done with warfare. At Lee's urging, they were making their way home but not with any inclination to sacrifice their lives for the Confederacy. In the midst of this maddening panic, Davis asked his cabinet members for a memorandum giving their advice on the prospect of southern independence.

On April 19, 1865, Varina wrote her husband. All news was delayed in reaching her, and she was still unaware of Lee's surrender but was worried. "The fearful news I hear fills me with horror," she said. "I do not believe all, yet enough is thrust upon my unwilling credence to weigh me to the heart. Where are you—how are you—What ought I to do with these helpless little unconscious charges of mine are questions that I keep asking myself always." By the time she added a postscript, on April 24, she confessed that "the dreadful news, with its dreadful confirmation has rendered us very wretched." Reports of Appomattox had arrived.

Other men shared an unrealistic hope of success. Gen. Wade Hampton, who was with Johnston during the meeting with Sherman, wrote to Davis, admitting that "the military situation is very gloomy" but arguing that it was "by no means desperate, and endurance and determination will produce a change." He claimed that there were forty to fifty thousand men willing to join the Confederate standard "if they are allowed to enter the cavalry service." He made no mention of where horses were to be found for these recruits. He clung to the hope of intervention by a European power but warned Davis, "If we disband we give up at once and forever all hope of foreign intervention." The future was bleak if the Confederacy surrendered. He foresaw a war between the United States and England and France in which "we of the South, under a more rigorous conscription than has yet been obtained here, shall be forced to fight by the side of our own negroes and under Yankee officers." He added that "no sacrifice would be too great to escape this train of horrors."[37] Hampton envisioned leading these men west into Texas and, if need be, into Mexico to continue the fight.

The Confederate armies were dwindling. Johnston's army had once numbered seventy thousand men and now could muster only twenty thousand, according to Judah Benjamin. Even that number was "daily diminishing by desertion and casualties."[38] On April 22, John Reagan wrote to Davis of Johnston's force, "from demoralization and despondency, melting away rapidly by the troops abandoning the army and returning to their homes singly and in numbers large and small."[39] In the chaos, not everyone was deserting. Orders that came over the signature of Jefferson Davis still carried the weight of a commander in chief. Brig. Gen. Thomas Munford, in command of a Confederate cavalry brigade that was disbanding, commanded his men to continue fighting, after having received a communication from Davis "ordering us again to the field in defense of our liberties." Reliant upon the news that General Johnston still had an army in the field capable of upholding the Confederate banner, Munford urged his men to assemble once again and resume the war. The futility of his call was evident by the order asking the men to "renew our vows, and swear again by our broken altars to be free or die."[40]

Davis believed that Johnston's army "holding its position with determination to fight on, and manifest ability to maintain the struggle, will attract all the scattered soldiers and daily and rapidly gather strength."[41] On April 19, Davis made a very short speech in Charlotte, North Carolina, in which he told a crowd that if they would "only show by your determination and fortitude that you are willing to suffer yet longer, . . . we may still hope for success."[42] This was a fantasy.

According to Davis's host in Charlotte, Lewis Bates, Davis had bowed and was about to turn from the talk when he was handed the telegram announcing Lincoln's assassination. Bates testified that Davis read the telegram aloud to the crowd and then said, "If it were to be done, it were better it were well done."[43] Davis vigorously denied ever making the statement, and at least one person was present who said that he had not uttered the words. There were many in the North willing to believe both that Davis had said these cold words and that their utterance revealed a conspirator's involvement in the murder of the late president.

Davis expressed no regret at Lincoln's death when he wrote Gen. Braxton Bragg the next day. "It is difficult to judge the effect thus to be produced [by Lincoln's murder]," he wrote analytically. "His successor is a worse man, but has less influence." Davis was, by now, informed of Johnston's entering into a "temporary suspension of hostilities" with Sherman, yet he told Bragg that he was "not without hope that recent disaster might awake the dormant energy and develop the patriotism which sustained us in the first year of the war."[44]

Stephen Mallory saw Davis shortly after the news of the assassination had reached them. He told the Confederate leader that he feared "that the South would be accused of instigating his death." He said that Davis replied sadly: "I certainly have no special regard for Mr. Lincoln; but there are a great many men of whose end I would much rather have heard than his. I fear it will be disastrous to our people, and I regret it deeply."[45] Mallory's oft-quoted recollection of what Jefferson Davis said to him was published in 1901 but still needs to be evaluated along with other evidence of what Davis expressed. It could easily be seen as being made in defense of the honor of Davis and the Confederacy, since Davis was still considered by many, even in 1901, to have been involved in the Lincoln conspiracy, but it may be an accurate reflection of the sentiments of the Confederate president.

The question of whether Davis was complicit in the assassination of Abraham Lincoln was a hotly contested one at the end of the war. One of Davis's preeminent biographers, William C. Davis, has written that there is no ground to suspect that Davis had "foreknowledge of or involvement in the murder." Yet a reader is left with an uneasy feeling about this assessment when considering the historian's next words: "At this point Davis probably did not even suspect that Lincoln's death at the hand of John Wilkes Booth might have a distant connection to those kidnapping plots that Davis almost certainly knew of, if he did not condone them." The reasoning of the historian is that by March 1865, Confederate agents were beyond "the reach or control" of the rebel president and that "by April Booth and his friends, originally participants in the kidnapping scheme, were beyond the control of Davis' agents. In the evolution from kidnapping to killing, Booth acted alone. Jefferson Davis would have recoiled from assassination."[46]

There are several logical flaws in this argument if Jefferson Davis did actually know of and condone a scheme to kidnap Lincoln. Kidnapping the president was a very serious crime, attended with many unforeseeable risks. It placed Lincoln in danger of serious injury or death. John Wilkes Booth and his coconspirators may have been outside the control of the Confederacy, but their decision to murder instead of kidnap does not necessarily vindicate the Confederate president. If Jefferson Davis condoned the kidnapping plot, he should have realized that the men undertaking the plot, once cut loose from their moorings after Lee's surrender, might consider it better to eliminate the target rather than kidnap him. Unless explicit prohibition of such a tack had been made, condoning a kidnapping plot did not exculpate Davis in the assassination simply because another crime—murder—was committed in its stead.

It was not only people from the North who thought that Davis was involved in Lincoln's murder; there were some in the South, in April 1865, who believed it too. When Davis, Burton Harrison, and others on his staff attended a Sunday church service in Charlotte, the minister spoke adamantly about the wickedness of Lincoln's murder. Sitting in the pews, Davis was struck with the belief that he was the object of the reproach. "I think the preacher directed his remarks at me," he told the staff with a smile as they left the church, "and he really seems to fancy I had something to do with the assassination."[47] If his perception was correct about being the preacher's mark, it was odd that he found it amusing in the least.

In a letter to Varina dated April 23, 1865, Davis informed her that he was sending Burton Harrison to help her and the children escape. He admitted that the plans they had made in Richmond before she left were hopeless. His only suggestion was that during the suspension of hostilities between Sherman's and Johnston's armies, she might take the children to Mobile and sail to a foreign nation or cross the Mississippi and travel to Texas. "For myself," he said, "it may be that our Enemy will prefer to banish me."[48] His uncertainty about what to do was evident from the letter, as he wrote of going to Mexico and deciding where to live after getting there. He remained in Charlotte hoping for a negotiated settlement. It was not until April 24 that he first heard of the proposed agreement. He quickly penned a note to Johnston, approving its terms but having no idea that the entire process had been abjectly rejected by the federal government. Davis learned of this only later that night. Davis immediately wrote to Burton Harrison to give him the news, while Breckinridge sent Johnston the unrealistic advice to continue the war. Refusing to prolong the fighting that would bring senseless slaughter, Johnston surrendered his army on April 26, 1865, to Sherman.

Davis was suffering the shock of having lost everything, but the reality of his situation was becoming apparent to him. Staying in Charlotte after Johnston's surrender was not an option. He had been told, no doubt, by John Breckinridge that Sherman had suggested that they both flee the country. This advice was given while the Union commander was under the impression that his proposed terms would be agreed to in Washington. Now that they had been rejected, Davis knew that his life was at risk. He left Charlotte in haste. Within several days, Joe Johnston was writing other former Confederate officers that "it is not doubted here that we are abandoned by the Government."[49] Indeed, they had been.

4

THE CAPTURE OF JEFFERSON DAVIS

I never cease to regret that Jeff. Davis was
not shot at the time of his capture.
—Charles Sumner

JEFFERSON DAVIS was on the run. The stakes were raised by two acts of Andrew Johnson: On May 1, Johnson issued an order that the Lincoln conspirators would be "lawfully triable before a Military Commission."[1] Then, on May 2, the new president proclaimed that the Bureau of Military Justice had evidence linking Davis and others to the conspiracy that resulted in the murder of Lincoln. A reward of $100,000 was offered for the arrest of Davis.[2]

Davis made a critical mistake when news reached him of this accusation—he continued his flight. At least one man saw the implication of continuing to evade the pursuit by federal officials. Clement C. Clay Jr. had been a close, trusted friend of Davis prior to the war. Davis had considered nominating Clay to be secretary of war, refraining only because of Clay's fragile health. When the Confederate Congress gave Davis five million dollars as a secret service fund in February 1864, Davis appointed Clay as a commissioner to go to Canada on behalf of the Confederate government. He took with him one million dollars, a vast sum at that time, to utilize at his discretion. Charged as they were with operating from Canada with only vague verbal directions coming from Davis, Clay worked to further the interests of the Confederacy with little else to guide him. Union officials suspected that he had organized the plot to kill the president. Clay was in La Grange, Georgia, when he heard of the accusation. He was trying to elude Union forces. In an exhibition of southern honor, Clay wrote to the Union general James Harrison Wilson, commanding the troops searching for the Confederate leadership: "I have just seen a proclamation by the President of the United States offering a reward of $100,000 for my arrest on a charge of having, with others therein named, incited and concocted the murder of the late President. Conscious of my innocence, unwilling even to seem to fly from justice, and confident of my entire vindication from so foul an imputation upon a full, fair, and impartial trial, which I expect to receive, I shall go as soon as practicable to Macon to deliver myself up to your custody. I am, respectfully, C. C. Clay, Jr."[3] Clay, unlike Davis, understood the grave criminal allegation under which he was cast. Clay's sense of honor impelled him to stop his flight and turn himself in to Union authorities and underscored the realistic view he had of the accusations against him. Two days after sending this telegram, Clay gave himself up. If flight could be construed as an indication of a person's guilt, Clay wanted nothing of it. Jefferson Davis would have been better served had he done the same.

Davis received the bad news that Sherman's proposal had been rejected on April 24, while still in Charlotte. The rejection came with the added notice that hostilities would resume at noon on April 26. This gave General Johnston adequate time to surrender but not enough hours to do much else. Anxiety racked the rebel president about both the state of the Confederacy and his personal life. He had earlier sent his trusted aide Burton Harrison south to find Varina and his family. Although he hoped that Harrison would find Varina in Abbeville, he was uncertain if she was there. Harrison traveled to Chester, South Carolina, a town about fifty miles south of Charlotte by train. Although he moved on rail, he took his horse with him in case locomotives became unavailable. He and Davis had agreed to rendezvous in Chester if matters became worse. Davis hurriedly sent a message to Harrison there, hoping he would receive it. It was only one sentence long, written partially in cipher, which told him of the resumption of hostilities. The two must have spoken of this contingency; the information was simply stated, as if that would be enough for the recipient to know how to react.

Davis then wrote Gen. Braxton Bragg, in Chester, that he expected to join Bragg in a few days. Davis and his group met with Bragg and his men close to Cokesbury, South Carolina, on May 1, 1865. They traveled south together, accompanied by cavalry and men who had been separated from their units. When they reached Washington, Georgia, on May 5, Bragg left Davis and headed toward his home in Mobile, Alabama, only to be captured on May 9.[4] The chaotic state of the Confederacy made it difficult to ascertain the truth. In the Deep South, rumor had it that Davis was headed toward Texas. One Confederate officer wrote his father that if Davis made it to Louisiana, he would "make a last effort to sustain himself, but his efforts will all be in vain."[5] Wade Hampton, meanwhile, who had accompanied Johnston to his meeting with Sherman, now tried to withdraw from the terms of the surrender by claiming that he was away from Johnston's army, moving toward South Carolina under orders from John Breckinridge, at the time of Johnston's surrender. In truth, he hated the notion of reunion with the North and hoped to continue the fight. His letter to Johnston stating "I do not regard myself as embraced in the capitulation" was more than simply a courteous note to his erstwhile commander.[6] If he was a part of the surrendering army and chose to ignore the terms of laying down his arms, he risked losing the protection given him by Sherman's terms. He was, in other words, subject to being shot upon capture for violating his parole. While willing to continue the fight, he was not anxious to lose his one chance to surrender and receive a parole from the Union army.

While Hampton was trying to wriggle out of the terms given by Sherman to the military, others were trying to get included within them. Samuel Cooper, the inspector general, with whom Davis had left the records of the Confederate War Department, wrote to Johnston claiming that he was unable to travel to Greensboro but pleading for him and his assistant to be included in the terms. He had been physically unable to travel when Davis left Charlotte and felt stranded. He worried, as many soldiers did, that an individual surrendering would not be immediately paroled.

Hampton was being pulled in two different directions. Certain of Hampton's zeal, Davis instructed him to leave his command, select a small group of men, and ride to join the president. Hampton's escort would prove invaluable to Davis if it could be arranged. The problem was that Joseph Johnston considered Hampton part of his command that had been surrendered. At 1:00 p.m. on April 27, Johnston received a telegram informing him that "General Hampton has left here with Butler's division," a cavalry unit. Johnston was outraged. One of Johnston's staff officers relayed an order to Hampton: "General Johnston directs that you cause this division to return immediately to the position near Hillsborough, in which it has been serving under his orders."[7]

In his response to Johnston, Hampton revealed the truth behind his actions. "I went to consult with the President," he wrote that night, "the armistice having been annulled. After full conference with him, a plan was agreed on to enable him to leave the country. He charged me with the execution of this plan, and he is now moving in accordance with it." Hampton admitted to having put himself "in a position of great delicacy" by having returned for the cavalrymen he intended to use to help Davis: "I must either leave him to his fate, without an effort to avert it, or subject myself to possible censure by not accepting the terms of the convention you have made. If I do not accompany him I shall never cease to reproach myself, and if I go with him I may go under the ban of outlawry. I choose the latter, because I believe it to be my duty to do so. But I leave my command to abide the terms, as I shall not ask a man to go with me. Should any join me, they will be stragglers like myself and, like myself, willing to sacrifice everything for the cause and for our Government."[8]

Hampton rode to Charlotte, hoping to overtake the Confederate president. He reached that city only to find that Davis had left for Yorkville, South Carolina. Hampton was nearing exhaustion but, after only a few hours rest, mounted a fresh horse at sunset and rode through the night. To his chagrin, he reached Yorkville on the morning of May 1, 1865, after Davis had departed for Abbeville. Worn-out, Hampton, who happened to live in Yorkville, went home.

The collapse of the South took a physical toll on all of the Confederates, but Hampton's wife was not prepared for the man she greeted. She immediately sent a message to Maj. Gen. Joseph Wheeler, a subordinate of her husband, asking for him to come to their home the next morning. When Wheeler arrived, he admitted that he "was shocked at the broken appearance of my fellow-officer. He was harassed in mind, and worn in body."[9] Wheeler convinced Hampton to remain at home while Wheeler attempted to find the rebel chieftain. Hampton insisted that Wheeler tell Davis that he would serve the president in any manner in which he was capable of serving to the last.

Wheeler started south toward Washington, Georgia, with a large body of Confederate soldiers. Federal cavalry roamed the countryside, and Wheeler soon became convinced that he could not advance safely without splitting his command. He did so, sending small detachments out in search of Davis. Wheeler likely thought back to his meeting with Davis in Charlotte on April 27, when the cavalryman was struck by how detached from reality the president appeared. Davis had "preserved the semblance of power and routine of government" that allowed him to operate as if the Confederacy was merely retreating, not collapsing. Wheeler remembered being dumbstruck that "a young cadet underwent a regular form of examination for promotion to the office of lieutenant" when the entire army was disintegrating. According to Wheeler, Davis "did not yet realize the completeness of our undoing."[10]

Though he was only a day or so behind Davis, Wheeler found it impossible to ascertain the precise location of the man. Couriers carrying messages were intercepted, making it even harder for southern cavalry to communicate. Federal cavalry seemed to be everywhere, and the local citizenry talked to the Union horsemen fairly openly. As a result, neither Davis nor Wheeler were anxious to make their presence known to the citizenry. Local citizens told Wheeler that the federal troops were actively working to collect the reward for Davis's capture. The intelligence that locals offered was correct. Many southerners would have been happy to collect the reward too. The Union army worked tirelessly to cut off Davis's possible routes of escape and capture him. Orders went out to those involved in the search to "make every endeavor to capture or kill Jeff. Davis, the rebel ex-President."[11] Suggestions were offered that federal military officers "use every persuasion to induce the disgusted secesh to join in hunting him."[12]

Varina Davis on the Run

Meanwhile, Burton Harrison had found Varina Davis in Abbeville, South Carolina, staying in the beautiful home of Armistead and Martha Burt. Martha Burt was a niece of John C. Calhoun. The Burt and Davis families were old friends, and she was warmly welcomed. The Davis children traveling with Varina enjoyed the respite, but it was brief. Varina was terrified of being captured by the Yankees. She believed that her husband wanted her to escape to a foreign country, and she insisted on heading for the Atlantic coastline to secure passage. Burton Harrison and the Burt family argued that the best course of action was to wait, but Varina was not convinced.

According to an account written by Harrison years after the war, the first lady of the Confederacy expressed an "unwillingness to subject them [her host family] to the danger of having their house burned for sheltering her.... Colonel Burt magnanimously replied that there was no better use to which his house could be put than to have it burned for giving shelter to the wife and family of his friend."[13] Harrison's recollection differed from the account offered by Varina on May 1, 1865. In a letter to her husband, she stated, "I left Abbeville against my convictions but agreeably to Mr. Burts and Mr. Harrisons opinion."[14] The discussion in the household must have been wrenching.

After Harrison found a suitable wagon and a troop of young Confederate officers willing to act as an escort, she and her family left Abbeville. Ostensibly, their hope was to reach Florida, gain passage on an Atlantic-bound ship, and escape the American mainland. If successful, they would hope for similar fortune for her husband. Then they could begin their life anew in a foreign country. Varina was intensely loyal to him. The feeling was mutual. No one who knew her would doubt that she wanted to be reunited with Jefferson and share the danger, and perhaps the fate, of her beloved husband, rather than trying to escape without him. Her wish would come true soon enough, as their parties would cross paths one May night in Georgia. From that point onward, Jefferson and Varina Davis would face his perils together, despite the separations that the coming months would bring.

The Johnson Administration's Attitude toward Confederates

Even by late April 1865, no clear policy had been articulated by the federal government regarding what would be done with the civilian leadership of the Confederacy. The past treatment of individual rebel leaders was haphazard and offered little guidance to Jefferson Davis to consider. For instance, Henry S. Foote, a member of the Confederate Congress, traveled to Washington, D.C., ostensibly to negotiate a peace treaty on behalf of the South. He had no authority to try to end the conflict, and James A. Seddon, the Confederate secretary of war, ordered that he be arrested. The Confederates did not catch him.[15] Once within northern lines, Foote was taken prisoner by Union officials and paroled. He traveled to New York City, where he lodged until the end of the war, completely unsupervised. On May 1, Foote wrote to President Johnson from his residence, requesting a modification of the parole given him by the Union. He asked for permission to travel to the Pacific Coast via Ohio, where he wanted to visit an old friend. The new president's view of the former Confederate congressman was dimmer than that of his deceased predecessor. Johnson referred the request to Edwin Stanton "with the suggestion that unless Mr. Foote goes beyond the limits of the United States proceedings be had with a view to his indictment for treason."[16] Stanton telegraphed that Foote had forty-eight hours to leave the United States. Foote left the country within the specified time frame.[17] Clearly, some prizes were bigger than others. But the question remained: if Foote could be charged with treason, why had he been allowed to remain in the North for months? And why, when Johnson became aware of the presence of a man whom he considered to be a traitor, was Foote not arrested, instead of being told to leave the country?

Meanwhile, southern state leaders found out that their state's comity vis-à-vis the federal government was to be redefined, again, quite arbitrarily. Once defeated, they would not simply rejoin the Union. Georgia governor Joseph E. Brown attempted to call the Georgia state legislature into session to address "the complete collapse in the currency and the great destitution of provisions among the poor."[18] He was told by military authorities that he must first seek authorization from Washington, D.C.

His letter to Andrew Johnson was met with a response drafted by Stanton. The response to Governor Brown that the secretary of war suggested contained no sympathy for the plight of the State of Georgia. The proposed draft addressed Brown's telegram, point by point: "The collapse in the currency and the great destitution of provision among the poor of the State of Georgia mentioned in his telegram have been caused by the treason, insurrection, and rebellion against the authority, Constitution, and laws of the United States, incited and carried on for the last four years by Mr. Brown and his confederate rebels and traitors, who are responsible for all the want and destitution now existing in that State." Stanton proposed that "what Mr. Brown calls the result which the misfortunes of war have imposed upon the people of Georgia and all the misery, loss, and woe they have suffered are chargeable upon Mr. Brown and his confederate rebels, who usurped the authority of the State and, assuming to act as its Governor and Legislature, waged treasonable war against the United States, and by means of that usurped authority protracted the war to the last extremity, until compelled by superior force to lay down their arms and accept the result which the fortunes of war have imposed upon the people of Georgia as the just penalty of the crimes of treason and rebellion." Johnson's response should end, in Stanton's view, with the admonition "that the restoration of peace and order cannot be intrusted to rebels and traitors who destroyed the peace and trampled down the order that had existed more than half a century and made Georgia a great and prosperous State."[19] A warrant was issued for Brown's arrest.

R.M.T. Hunter, a Confederate senator, was arrested by order of Gen. Ulysses S. Grant on May 11, 1865, as was Judge John Campbell, the former U.S. Supreme Court justice and one of the Confederate emissaries at the Hampton Roads Conference shortly before the end of the war. Hunter immediately wrote "to know if I could obtain the amnesty upon the conditions mentioned in the amnesty proclamation."[20] According to Maj. Gen. Henry Halleck, Campbell, "very destitute and much broken down," surrendered himself "to such punishment as the Government may see fit to impose."[21] Halleck's sympathy for Campbell proved to be of no avail. Stanton responded to Halleck that Judge Campbell had "labored as far as he dared to keep the rebellion alive. This impression is very strong in the North."[22]

Part of the problem was that fantastic rumors spread, frightening people in the North and leading Union authorities to investigate the truthfulness of wild claims. Joseph Holt sought proof that Libby Prison had been mined with explosives to kill all the prisoners prior to their release.[23] Emotions ran high in the North as terrified citizens believed unsubstantiated rumors. Lincoln's assassination made it appear that the South was capable of any atrocity. It was under these conditions that southern leaders were being pursued and apprehended.

The net cast by northern political leadership was wide. Not only was Capt. Henry Wirz, the commander of Andersonville prison, ordered arrested, but so was Col. George C. Gibbs, who claimed to have nothing to do with maltreatment of any Union soldier held at the prison. In a postscript denying that he had ever had the power to influence events at the prison, Gibbs offered evidence that damned Jefferson Davis and his cabinet. Gibbs related that "Wirz commands by order of the Secretary of War."[24] Since the secretary of war was in Jefferson Davis's cabinet and had been appointed by Davis, Wirz derived his authority directly from Richmond. As the horrid conditions at Andersonville were uncovered, Davis would find himself implicated in the atrocities found at the camp. Day by day, Union public opinion crystallized that the Confederate president was involved in crimes as despicable as could be imagined, each act finding its genesis in his treason. But Davis's sole interest was in eluding federal forces.

As Davis fled through Georgia, he found it more and more difficult to move undetected with his cavalry escort. By May 7, federal officials were able to report that they were so close on his heels that Davis had, in an effort to elude them, disbanded his escort. Three of the regiments that had served as his protection surrendered themselves to Union officials in northern Georgia.[25] Telegraphic inquiries into the whereabouts of Davis now rushed over the wires several times a day. Bvt. Maj. Gen. James Harrison Wilson, part of William Tecumseh Sherman's command and the officer whose troops were bearing down on Davis, pressed his subordinates to keep him informed of their progress. Wilson urged his men to "watch every train closely; he might try that way."[26] The pressure from Washington to capture the Confederate was intense, and Union officials pushed the officers in the field relentlessly.

Stanton's micromanagement began to grate on the nerves of the high-strung Sherman, who had been harshly criticized for the proposed terms of Joseph Johnston's surrender. Sherman feared the censure that would doubtless be heaped upon him if Davis escaped. Stanton was writing directly to Wilson, bypassing Sherman in the chain of command. This was more than the prickly general was willing to bear. At midnight on May 8, Sherman telegraphed Ulysses S. Grant, updating him on Davis's flight and Wilson's pursuit. Sherman told Grant that Davis "cannot escape save in disguise." He posed the question to Grant: "Does the Secretary of War's newspaper order take Wilson from my command or shall I continue to order him? If I have proven incompetent to manage my own command let me know it."[27]

Without Lincoln's steady hand, the Union high command showed signs of unraveling. The annoyance that Sherman felt toward Stanton's hand in the pursuit was well-founded. Stanton routinely telegraphed Wilson directly to issue orders, such as the one for Governor Brown's arrest and the seizure of his papers, that should have gone through Sherman. As might be expected, Wilson responded directly back to the secretary of war.[28] Stanton, to the annoyance of many, filled the power vacuum at the top of the executive branch of the nation's government whenever he could. He used every ounce of energy to drive his subordinates in an effort to abort Davis's escape.

Even Wilson began to sense a straining of his relationship with Sherman caused by Stanton's intervention. Wilson dutifully wrote to Sherman, who was hundreds of miles away, to tell him that Wilson's three divisions had marched over 220 miles in six days and that while Davis was a fugitive, the rebel president had been forced to drop the treasure that he had been carrying while Wilson's men were "looking for him in all directions."[29] If the two men found their military relationship now slightly awkward, Wilson did his best to maintain his place in the chain of command. On May 8, Wilson ordered the publication and distribution of the presidential proclamation offering rewards for Davis's capture as handbills and broadsides to encourage civilians to assist in locating Davis.[30]

As the dragnet tightened, the fear that he might escape mounted. Wilson confessed, "My scouts have not yet been able to get upon a substantial trail since Davis left Washington [Georgia]."[31] A rumor circulated that the Confederate president had reached a rebel ship and sailed away from Florida, perhaps for Cuba.[32] Officials in Washington, D.C., agonized over the prospect of him slipping through their fingers. In fact, federal soldiers were rapidly bearing down on his party. While the searchers perceived their quest as looking for a needle in a haystack, Davis was not willing to break away from his wife and family and race away on horseback across fields and meadows. He was bound to a party that required wagons, which relegated him to roadways and wagon trails that were easily crossed by Union cavalry.

Joseph Wheeler's cavalry was nearby as well, but he had no better luck making contact with Davis. His efforts to avoid Union forces governed his movements while tracking Davis. Just outside of Atlanta, his efforts ended when federal soldiers captured his force. Wheeler made one last bid to remain free—he pointed out to the Union officer in charge that there was an agreement between Sherman and Johnston that provided for the parole of Confederate prisoners and boldly asked to be included pursuant to that measure. Wheeler later recounted that "the officer, in some doubt, replied that he did not feel justified in setting us free."[33] Wheeler's war was over. He was taken prisoner just miles away from the Confederate president, whose escape he had hoped to secure.

The dragnet found its man when Jefferson Davis stepped out of his tent in the early morning hours of May 10, 1865, just over a month after Lee's surrender. Members of the Fourth Michigan Cavalry surprised and arrested Davis at Irwinville, Georgia. They overtook him and his party, along with five wagons and three ambulances.[34] Armed and capable of resisting his arrest, Davis chose not to fight. Worn-out by the years of warfare and exhausted by the unfamiliar role of fugitive, when confronted by an armed Union cavalryman, he simply surrendered. Jefferson Davis, Varina, and the rest of their party were now in Union custody. The North would rejoice in their downfall.

To Davis and his family, the federal government's colossal efforts to capture him were completely unwarranted. A Union officer present at his capture reported that "he expressed great indignation at the energy with which he was pursued, saying that he had believed our Government more magnanimous than to hunt down women and children."[35] The vigorous nature of the search for Davis should have indicated to him that the perception of him in the North was not what he understood it to be. He later admitted to being perplexed at why the Union forces would pursue him so aggressively. It should also have revealed to him a glimpse of the long and dangerous road on which he was now to travel. In his exhaustion and embarrassment, it does not seem to have occurred to him that the pursuit was more than simply an attempt to capture him for his role as president of the Confederacy. Instead, he was thought to be a notorious traitor, assassin, and war criminal.

The Union cavalryman leading the hunt for Davis was a unique product of the American civil war—a boy general. James Harrison Wilson, known as "Harry" to his friends, was an 1860 graduate of West Point who rose from the rank of second lieutenant to brevet major general. The assignment to find the Confederate president fell to him, in part, because his cavalry was already in the Deep South. His horsemen had entered Alabama in March 1865. While in the state, they defeated the outmanned Confederate legend Nathan Bedford Forrest, destroyed the arsenal at Selma, took over seven thousand soldiers prisoner, and captured three hundred cannon, all while organizing a brigade of three thousand African American soldiers.

Riding into Georgia, the Union cavalry took Columbus on April 16, 1865, and accepted the surrender of Macon on April 20. Brimming with confidence, Wilson confided, "My health is splendid and I have the best cavalry and the best cavalry officers in America." Wilson admitted, "The zeal and activity displayed by my entire force have been heightened by the general belief that the murder of Mr. Lincoln was concocted by Davis and his confederates."[36] Wilson was working in his makeshift headquarters in Macon, Georgia, when the electrifying news arrived that Davis was in Union custody.

The captured Davis and his party reached Macon at two in the afternoon of May 13. The streets of the city were crowded with southerners in a sullen mood. The reception he received was icy. His popularity was at a low, and the people of this town reflected the entry found in Mary Chestnut's diary for May 21, 1865. Chestnut was a close friend of the Davis family and kept a sober journal throughout the war. At the end, she was disheartened by the view that her compatriots had of Davis: "Harriet is radiant. She had heard that Jeff Davis has been captured."[37] Davis was the face of defeat to the South and the face of treason to the North. Wilson, who was awaiting his arrival, was surprised that no man from Macon appeared at his headquarters to ask about the Confederate president.

Wilson tried to accommodate everyone in the party as well as he could. He assigned Davis and the others the finest rooms in the hotel and permitted them to rest while he directed his staff to prepare the best dinner that the local resources would allow. After dinner, Davis was invited to Wilson's room, where they talked at length. The Confederate president was likely taken aback by the youthful man sitting before him. Wilson was three decades younger than Davis and a major general at age twenty-seven. Wilson tried to put Davis at ease by turning the conversation to West Point, where they both had been educated. As they spoke, Wilson sized up the man. Forty-seven years later, Wilson wrote that Davis was "bronzed and somewhat careworn, but hardy and vigorous, and during the conversation behaved with perfect self-possession and dignity."[38] Later that night, however, he wrote his friend Adam Badeau and described Davis differently. In his letter, he wrote that "Davis seemed quite cheerful and talkative, but in his whole demeanor showed no dignity or great fortitude. He remarked with a smile that he thought the U.S. would find graver charges against him than the murder of Lincoln, and seemed to regret that Mr. L. had been killed."[39]

The conversation turned to the generals, both Union and Confederate, and Davis expressed his opinion freely of these men. Lee, he told Wilson, was "one of the boldest generals of whom he had any knowledge, never needed urging. This was in comparison with Johnston in regard to whom his silence was marked."[40] As to northern military leadership, Davis "expressed surprise at Grant's skill and persistency, admiration for Sherman's brilliancy, and respect for Thomas's solid qualities. He did not hesitate to say that he had expected more from McClellan, Buell, and Fitz-John Porter than they had performed."[41] At some point, Davis brought in his son Jeff to meet Wilson. When the topic turned to politicians, Davis expressed his regret that Lincoln had been assassinated and, like many others in the South, feared that Andrew Johnson would prove to be vindictive and unforgiving toward the southern people. As the talk wound down, he expressed his satisfaction with his treatment at the hands of the men who had captured him and asked Wilson to convey that message to the officer in charge, Lt. Col. Benjamin D. Pritchard of the Fourth Michigan Cavalry.

Then the conversation turned to the immediate future. Wilson said that Davis would be transported that afternoon by way of Atlanta and Augusta to Savannah, where he would go by sea to a destination as yet unknown to Wilson. The secretary of war would decide the location and inform the officers in charge of the prisoners. Davis was not surprised. Later that night, Wilson wrote: "The thought struck me once or twice that Jefferson Davis was a mad man. The indifference with which he seemed to regard the affairs of our day savored of insanity. He was polite and gracious in his intercourse with me and almost affectionate in taking leave of me."[42] The high-strung Davis was doubtlessly mentally exhausted and struggling to maintain his equilibrium.

Wilson noted that the southern leader asked for no favors but also stated that his wife "insinuates once in a while that the 'President' is not treated with becoming dignity." Varina complained to Colonel Pritchard that whenever Davis went out, the guards accompanied him with cocked triggers. She was apparently offended by the colonel's reply that the guns were not cocked but only half-cocked and that the "men had orders to shoot *Mr. Davis* if he made any attempt to escape and would certainly execute the order."[43] Varina Davis was offended, no doubt, by the allusion to the Confederate president as "Mr. Davis," but she was beginning her role as caretaker of the image and memory of Jefferson Davis. Her quest to make him a martyr of the Lost Cause could find no better platform than that of portraying him as a man patiently suffering abuse at the hands of his captors.

Wilson wisely recognized that there was no need to delay Davis's departure. By five in the afternoon, the Confederates in custody were put on a heavily guarded train bound for Augusta via Atlanta. General Wilson gave the honor of conveying the prisoners to Colonel Pritchard. The prisoners' train was preceded and followed by others, eight hundred men between the two escorts. Aboard the middle train, which actually carried the Confederate president, Colonel Pritchard rode with twenty handpicked soldiers. The young Union general would take no risk of losing his prisoners. Given the woeful condition of the southern states, the unpopularity of Davis, and the desire of most paroled soldiers to get home, there was little chance of an attempted rescue. Still, it was not a danger that Wilson would hazard, thus the strong show of force.

Davis and his family were placed in a car separate from the others as they waited on the tracks. He and Varina were, no doubt, glad when his old friend Clement C. Clay and his wife, Virginia, stepped into the car. Davis stood and embraced Virginia Clay warmly, saying, "This is a sad meeting, Jennie."[44] The two sat together as they rode through the night to Atlanta. Arriving at daybreak, everyone was immediately transferred to a waiting train to Augusta. The ride was very uncomfortable, and Virginia Clay remembered that only the children slept. There was little chance that the passengers could be comfortable in a car that had no bedding. Moreover, the understandably palpable stress and fear in the closed car ensured that there was no ease for its passengers. No one was allowed off the train, and meals were brought on board to be eaten en route to the sea. The long day ended when the train reached Augusta at sunset.

What happened at Augusta serves as a reminder that the war was fought by people who saw themselves in their erstwhile enemies. Virginia Clay spoke to Colonel Pritchard and asked permission for her and her husband to visit the home of a close family friend in Augusta on her promise that they would return at the appointed time at the boat for passage to Savannah. She later said that "Pritchard gave a somewhat reluctant consent and we drove rapidly away."[45] His hesitancy may have been grounded in the fact that Clement Clay was a suspected conspirator in Lincoln's murder, but the officer nevertheless permitted the couple to depart from his custody. After a brief visit with their friends, the couple rejected the idea of their hosts that they should try to escape. At the appointed time, their carriage appeared at the Union boat docked on the riverbank, and they returned themselves to custody. It is nearly inconceivable that this would have happened in a war that was truly being waged by two different peoples.

Pritchard had his hands full now that everyone was on the riverboat *Standish*. Alexander Stephens, the former vice president of the Confederacy and a man on very cool terms with Jefferson Davis, expressed a desire to have no contact with Davis. The Union officer agreed to attempt to accommodate the request. Stephens had famously argued against secession, but when Georgia passed articles of secession, he followed the state out of the Union. Nevertheless, his personal courage in speaking out against disunion endeared him to many northerners. When the Confederacy fell, he did not attempt to flee but awaited arrest at his home. These facts likely played a part in his somewhat deferential treatment by Colonel Pritchard.

Neither Varina Davis nor Virginia Clay believed that they were treated with enough deference. Varina; her four children; her sister, Maggie Howell; two women described as "waiting-maids," one African American and one white; as well as several other "servants" were there to assist her.[46] Both women believed that they were treated disrespectfully by the Union soldiers. Yankees clearly did not value chivalry as their southern counterparts did. Their attitude, as well as their circumstances, assured them a miserable voyage. Jefferson Davis was in intense pain from his chronically inflamed eye, and the two women were further distressed by the lack of concern exhibited by Union officers to his discomfort. Varina, her sister, and Virginia Clay took turns nursing Davis by bathing his temples in an effort to ease his pain.

The men were more reconciled to their fate. Along with Davis and the Clays, the boat transported Maj. Gen. Joseph Wheeler, who had searched in vain for his rebel chieftain, and his staff; John Reagan, the Confederate postmaster general; Stephen Mallory, the Confederate naval secretary; and Davis's aides Burton Harrison and Preston Johnston—the son of Gen. Albert Sidney Johnston, who was killed at Shiloh. The most reliable sources evidence no misbehavior by the men being transported north.

Years after the war, Wheeler wrote of an escape plan that was discussed by some of the men on board, but there is little likelihood that a serious undertaking was made. Clay had turned himself in to disprove the allegation that he was involved in Lincoln's murder. Stephens had awaited arrest at his home. Davis was not physically or emotionally capable of assisting in an escape attempt. Furthermore, the *Standish* was shadowed by other watercraft, and there was a more than adequate armed force on board that likely would have made such an attempt foolhardy. But given the importance of courage and manhood in southern culture, it is not surprising that postwar memories reflected a boldness that did not exist at the time of the transport.

Savannah came into sight shortly after midnight on May 16. Pritchard reported to Gen. Henry Birge at four o'clock in the morning. Birge immediately ordered the steamer *Emilie* alongside the *Standish,* transferred the prisoners, and began steaming toward Hilton Head, South Carolina. Orders were telegraphed to Hilton Head to make the steamer *Clyde* ready to take the prisoners to Washington, D.C. There would be no opportunity for a rescue party to light upon a docked riverboat and free the Confederate officials. The transfer to the seagoing *Clyde* was smoothly done, and the three-day journey to Fortress Monroe was under way. The *Clyde* was a brig-rigged steamer that was large and comfortable, compared to the smaller transports used to get them to the sea.

The anxiety of Union officials concerning Davis's transport on the steamer *Clyde* to his destination at Fort Monroe reveal how federal officials considered this to be a trip fraught with danger. Secretary of War Stanton, who had been closely involved in most of the decisions regarding the detention of Confederate leaders, orchestrated virtually every detail of Davis's movement from Georgia and his incarceration at Fort Monroe. It was also revealed in his undeniable obsession with the rebel commander in chief's imprisonment. Stanton admonished Lt. Col. Benjamin Pritchard "to take every precaution to secure your prisoner and prevent rescue or escape. For that purpose he must be treated as any other criminal. Call on the naval commander at Savannah for convoy if you need it, and upon all military commanders for force. Report your arrival from point to point."[47]

Pritchard did not need to be admonished about his charges. The *Clyde* was a three-decker steamboat filled with men from the Fourth Michigan Cavalry and did not sail alone. The steamer was followed by the *Tuscarora,* with its guns trained on the *Clyde* day and night. It would have been utter foolishness for anyone to attempt to escape. The only fear that Union officers on board expressed was the possibility of a Confederate warship attempting to intercept the *Clyde.* As they steamed out into the Atlantic, the chance of this occurring kept the crew alert.

Davis was depressed and restless during the voyage. He was uncertain about his destination, and members of the party believed that he would ultimately be executed. Others in the party were treated better than he. Stephens and Clay were on parole while on the *Clyde* and were able to have their run of the ship. Stephens requested and was granted the right to correspond with his brother. Despite his reluctance to meet Davis, Stephens did encounter him on deck early in the trip. It was the first time that they had seen each other since they had parted the night after Stephens returned to Richmond from the Hampton Roads Conference months earlier. The two men did not talk for long. While melancholy and lonely, Stephens engaged in long conversations with Clay, Reagan, and Wheeler. He also wrote in his diary that "Colonel Pritchard introduced to me Captain Hudson, of his regiment, and a Mr. Stribling (?), who was a correspondent of the New York *Herald.* We talked a good deal on the state of the country, etc. The entire day was clear, mild and beautiful."[48] They were given complete freedom of movement aboard the steamer.

The contrast between the reported treatment of the Confederates by the prisoners is stark. The women wrote of their meals being "served at a table reserved for prisoners" and took "note of culinary deficiencies."[49] Joseph Wheeler recalled that "we prisoners were sent down to breakfast first, before the soldiers, who were grumbling and hungry," and that the southerners returned "in great good humor, for the meal had been an excellent one."[50]

Alexander Stephens described the ship: "This was the *Clyde,* a new boat, a propeller of about 500 tons; there were several good berths in the cabin below, and quite a number of state rooms on deck above. The ladies and most of the gentlemen selected state rooms. I preferred a berth below, and chose my place there, which I found on the voyage was a most excellent choice."[51] Virginia Clay expressed outrage at a sentinel in place outside her stateroom door, with musket and fixed bayonet. After admonishing him, he replied that he was there to guard her against being bothered by anyone on the ship. This softened her toward him but revealed her inclination to taking offense to otherwise understandable actions by Yankee soldiers. Stephens noted in his diary that the officers "were all courteous and agreeable."[52] The harsh treatment claimed by Varina Davis and Virginia Clay was likely exaggerated, given Colonel Pritchard had allowed them to pick out which stateroom to occupy.

Husbands were not isolated from wives, nor were Davis and Varina separated from their children during the voyage. Neither were the prisoners subjected to demeaning searches or confiscation of property. In fact, Virginia Clay had in her possession a pistol that was not discovered until after Jefferson Davis left the steamer at Fort Monroe. John Reagan carried a small knife with him and about two thousand dollars in gold until he reached Fort Warren, where he was allowed to keep his knife but not the gold. Moreover, complaints were listened to. At Fort Warren, Reagan grumbled about his fare and was told that he "could order my meals by the sergeant from the post quartermaster, who furnished meals to the [Union] officers."[53] But it is still understandable that men and women from the highest stations in their culture would find the entire process of being transported to unknown destinations and uncertain fates very objectionable and demeaning.

By May 20, the *Clyde* anchored off Fort Monroe in northern Virginia. The weeklong journey was nearing an end, but Davis still was not certain that he would be confined at Fort Monroe. The prisoners spent the next couple of days waiting on board to be told the decision regarding where they would be kept. Pritchard spoke to Stephens and told him that he expected orders very soon. Still, the day was dreadfully dull. Rumors spread that Gen. Henry Halleck was on shore and would come aboard to speak to Davis, but hours passed with no hint of his fate. Stephens, always well treated, was told to be ready to move the next day. He would be transferred to Fort Warren in Boston. Davis's sense of helplessness was magnified when a tugboat came alongside the *Clyde* and took William Preston Johnston, Francis Lubbock, and Joseph Wheeler and his men from the boat for eventual transfer to Fort Delaware.

That night, Stephens and Clay saw the New York newspapers and read about the trial of the Lincoln assassins. Of course, Davis and Clay were accused of the crime as well. Clay told the former Confederate vice president that he was fully confident that nothing could be brought forward to implicate him in the murder. Clay told Stephens about his reaction when he first heard the news and how he deplored Lincoln's death. Stephens was moved by the man's steadfast denial of any knowledge of the conspiracy, but whether that would prove enough to keep him from hanging for it was something neither man could possibly know. The long talk that they had might have proven therapeutic for Davis if he had he been close enough to Stephens to confide in him. Instead, when Stephens bade farewell to the other passengers as he left the *Clyde* on the twenty-first, he was surprised by the emotion Davis showed to him. Davis, choking on tears, said nothing but "goodbye" and squeezed the hand of his estranged vice president. He then watched Stephens descend a rope ladder to be taken to prison.

Jefferson Davis was often described in postwar writings as being perfectly tranquil while being transported to prison. His demeanor "taught a lesson of heroism that should not be forgotten," wrote one author some three decades afterward.[54] Joseph Wheeler wrote that Davis, in discussing the prospect of being executed, "showed not the slightest trepidation, but reviewed the situation as calmly as if he had no personal interest in it."[55] These depictions are in sharp contrast to the descriptions of the man given at the time. Throughout his life, Davis tried to suppress his emotions. Men like George Washington and Robert E. Lee, who were capable of masking their emotions except in very rare instances, were much admired. Davis, however, was not one of these men. He hid his emotions as best he could, but they were revealed in other ways. Severe neuralgia, insomnia, depression, and other ailments plagued him throughout his life. These symptoms appeared very clearly while he was being transported on the *Clyde,* where he largely kept to himself. When physically reduced by severe headaches, he attempted to escape the pain by having wet towels applied to his head by his wife and Virginia Clay. Postwar descriptions were intent on portraying Davis heroically but, in doing so, removed the very traits that made him human.

5

THE REBEL'S FATE DEBATED

My early prophecy in 1862 will be fulfilled,
and nobody hanged for treason.

—Charles Sumner

ON MAY 19, 1865, a Union lieutenant wrote from Charlotte, North Carolina, "I have possession of . . . all the rebel War Department documents together with their captured flags."[1] Secretary of War Edwin Stanton, who kept close watch over the telegrams coming from the field, did not care about recovering captured flags, but he expected to find a treasure trove of documentary evidence linking Davis and others to the Lincoln murder in the files of the Confederate War Department. He pressed Henry Halleck about getting them to Washington, D.C.: "It is very important to have the rebel War Department papers here immediately for use on the present trial."[2] Then, in characteristic haste, he bypassed Halleck and wrote directly to John Schofield, ordering him to get the files to Washington as soon as possible. The records consisted of two train car loads of documents. He ordered that they be sent to one of his trusted assistants, Charles A. Dana.

Stanton's enmity toward Jefferson Davis was clear from the tone of his dispatches. "Jeff Davis was caught in the woods trying to escape in his wife's clothes," he wrote Halleck on May 14.[3] Halleck suggested that "if Jeff. Davis was captured in his wife's clothes I respectfully suggest that he be sent north in the same habiliments."[4] The readiness to humiliate Davis permeated the North. Shortly thereafter, Stanton wrote to Gen. Quincy A. Gilmore, revealing the decision to incarcerate Davis at Fort Monroe on Chesapeake Bay at the southern tip of the Virginia peninsula. But try as he might, events were moving too fast for Stanton to fully command from Washington. "It is said that Davis' wife and family accompany him," wrote the secretary of war. "You will not allow them to come North, but will require them to remain where they are, within your command, until further orders."[5] He ordered that updates be telegraphed to him concerning the progress of transporting Davis and the others. "These prisoners," he warned, "are to be dealt with as criminals and enemies of the Government of the most dangerous character."[6]

The Confederacy had, from the beginning of the rebellion, sanctioned many acts that the leaders of the federal government considered criminal. In the second year of the war, Henry Halleck had commissioned a study by Francis Lieber, a noted legal scholar, on the question of guerrilla warfare. The South claimed that men, dressing as civilians, might attack northern troops and destroy property within the customs of war. Union authorities considered them marauders who were liable to summary punishment. Rebel officials threatened retaliation against Union prisoners of war if this occurred. Halleck commissioned Lieber to consider this issue and render an opinion on whether men like these should be afforded the treatment and safeguards of belligerents.

Lieber responded within days. Halleck, in turn, had the opinion published in a small pamphlet entitled *Lieber on Guerrilla Parties, Considered with Reference to the Law and Usages of War.* It was disseminated to serve as a rationale by the Union in grappling with the large numbers of men from the South, attached to no military body, who preyed on Union soldiers and property. Lieber wrote that "the armed prowler, the so-called bushwhacker, is a simple assassin, and will thus always be considered by soldier and citizen; and we have likewise seen that the armed bands that rise in a district fairly occupied by military force, or in the rear of an army, are universally considered, if captured, brigands, and not prisoners of war. They unite the fourfold character of the spy, the brigand, the assassin, and the rebel, and cannot—indeed, it must be supposed, will not—expect to be treated as a fair enemy of the regular war. They know what a hazardous career they enter upon when the take up arms."[7] Yet Davis had threatened retaliation against regular Union troops being held as prisoners of war if northern military commanders dealt with guerrillas as irregulars. Men wearing blue considered the deaths of their comrades in arms by these guerrillas as simple murder. If Davis countenanced this act as within the rules of a civilized society, then it was a short stop to authorizing the murder of an American president.

Lieber presciently ended his opinion by averring that "so much is certain, that no army, no society, engaged in war, any more than a society at peace, can allow unpunished assassination, robbery, and devastation, without the deepest injury to itself and disastrous consequences, which might change the very issue of the war."[8] Many in the northern states believed that at the moment of Union victory, Jefferson Davis had undertaken to change the course of the war by ordering Lincoln's murder. Edwin Stanton was determined not to allow such a traitorous act to go unpunished.

Stanton telegraphed Halleck ordering him to bombproof Fort Monroe in preparation for Davis's confinement. He stated that Davis would remain there "until tried, which will be immediately after his arrival. His trial and punishment, if there be any, shall be in Virginia."[9] Halleck instantly set to work preparing ten to twelve escape-proof casements.[10] Officials in Washington continued to closely supervise the prisoners. Stanton filled the power vacuum in the nation's capital and displayed an obsessive interest in the fallen Confederate leadership. His hand was visible in virtually every detail. It was over Stanton's signature that orders went out detailing where each Confederate leader was to be housed. He also decided that Varina Davis had lost her freedom to travel. Davis's wife and children were ordered away from Norfolk, Virginia. The one concession was that Varina was allowed to decide where in the South she wanted to proceed. Absolutely no one was allowed to visit with Davis or communicate with him in writing.[11]

Stanton did not want to leave Washington, but he wanted a set of eyes on the ground to report back to him about the preparations being made at Fort Monroe to imprison Davis. He sent Charles A. Dana, a trusted assistant in the War Department, to Virginia. Just three days earlier, a young brevet major general, Nelson A. Miles, had been reassigned from the Army of the Potomac to become the man in charge of the fort. The officers at the base were admonished to guard against "surprise, attack, or any effort at rescue or escape."[12] Despite Union military successes, the threat of a rebel effort to free Davis was considered to be very serious.

Dana knew the type of detail that would satisfy his boss. His initial telegram to Stanton began with a reassurance that Davis and Clement C. Clay had been jailed with guards both within and outside the cells. He went so far as to report that the locks had been fastened. Then he began the narrative of Davis's removal from the *Clyde*. Miles took a tugboat out to the prisoner's ship, bringing a heavy guard from the garrison. Davis tried to maintain his composure when he was taken from Varina and his children, but it was clear that he was deeply affected. He assured his wife that she would see him that very evening.

She intended to continue on to Washington, D.C., to begin lobbying on her husband's behalf.

After only a few minutes, the general started back to the wharf with his prisoners. A cavalry squad preceded Miles and Davis toward the fort. Miles, Dana reported, walked next to Davis, holding him by the right arm. Behind them were six armed soldiers. Next came Col. Benjamin Pritchard with Clay. Behind them marched the men whom Miles had taken with him as a guard aboard the tugboat. "The arrangements were excellent and successful, and not a single curious spectator was anywhere in sight," according to Dana.[13]

Stanton's view of Davis was reinforced by Dana's description of him: "Davis bore himself with a haughty attitude. His face was somewhat flushed, but his features were composed and his step firm." The prisoner was dressed in gray, topped by a thin, dark overcoat. His head was covered with a slouch hat. "His hair and beard are not so gray as has been represented, and he seems very much less worn and broken by anxiety and labor" than War Department officials had been led to believe.[14] In a private letter, Dana was more forthcoming about his feelings about Davis, writing, "Davis marched with as haughty and defiant an air as Lucifer, Son of the Morning, bore after he was expelled from heaven."[15] At some point in the transfer, Davis asked to speak to Henry W. Halleck. His request was denied. Instead, he was placed in his cell. Davis was to have no contact with family or friends.

The cell that he was imprisoned in was a converted casement with a single, heavily barred window. Inside it, a guard would share the small space with the prisoner. The door would eventually be grated, but in the rush to convert the room to its purpose, bars were fastened outside the door. Two other sentries stood outside the cell. An officer was constantly on duty in the outer room. The key to the cell was kept exclusively by the officer in charge of the guards. Outside the rooms, a strong line of sentries cut off any access to the casements where Davis was held. Then, if that was not enough, a second line of sentries guarded from the parapet, while a third line was posted across the moats. The security was "as complete as could be desired."[16]

The only furniture was a hospital bed with an iron bedstead, a table and chair, and a movable stool closet. Linen was issued to him as if he were a soldier, and he was given a soldier's ration as food. It would be prepared by a guard. A lamp was to be kept burning in each room at all times. Halleck ordered that the officer on duty walk to the cell and see the prisoner every fifteen minutes. Davis, a deeply religious man, was permitted to have a Bible to read. The guards were not allowed to talk to Davis. No one was allowed to communicate with him verbally or in writing. Questions by Davis would be referred up to the officers in charge.

Dana next touched on a subject that would become highly controversial. He told Stanton, "I have not given orders to have them placed in irons, as General Halleck seemed opposed to it, but General Miles is instructed to have fetters ready if he thinks them necessary."[17] The directive to Miles, sent "by order of the Secretary of War," stated that "Miles is hereby authorized and directed to place manacles and fetters upon the hands and feet of Jefferson Davis and Clement C. Clay whenever he may think it advisable in order to render their imprisonment more secure."[18] The day after receiving this directive, Miles ordered Davis's feet shackled. The men who entered Davis's cell found him unwilling to allow this humiliation. He "violently resisted" the effort but to no avail.[19] The leg irons were put on him. It was an unnecessary and cruel act.

If Davis had ever believed that he would be treated with gentility upon his capture, he was certainly relieved of that notion by the time he had spent forty-eight hours at Fort Monroe. Anxious to make contact with any of his former friends, he asked Miles to be allowed to see Secretary of State William H. Seward or the elder Francis Blair. Miles passed the request on to Stanton, along with letters from Varina Davis to the same two men. His treatment in custody began to generate newsprint. The *Daily National Intelligencer* in Washington reported that "among the many rumors flying about to-day in regard to the confinement of Jeff Davis, has been one to the effect that yesterday afternoon he was manacled."[20] The *New York Herald* editorialized that "there is a sensation story published in one of the Philadelphia papers that Jeff. Davis has been put in irons; that he resisted terribly when the manacles were put on; that he first raved and then wept, and wanted the guards to shoot him. There is probably not a word of truth in the statement. If true, the act is certainly without the sanction of the President, and will not be tolerated by him. There is no need of any such mode of securing the rebel chief. All accounts show that he cannot escape from the casement which has been prepared for his confinement. No good and strong government does an unnecessary act. This, if true, base as Jeff. Davis is, would come under this head. It is, therefore, fair to believe that the whole story was made up to sell, regardless of all other considerations."[21] Unfortunately for Stanton, the rumor was true.

The secretary of war reacted in a most deceitful manner. Stung by the negative press, Stanton wired Miles a two-sentence telegram: "Please report whether irons have been placed on Jefferson Davis. If they have been, when was it done, and for what reason, and remove them."[22] Within hours, a disbelieving Miles responded that "anklets" were placed on Davis only because the door to the cell was made of light wood and had no lock, contradicting the report that Charles Dana had given Stanton about the high level of security for Davis. "I directed anklets to be put upon his ankles, which would not interfere with his walking, but would prevent his running, should he endeavor to escape," Miles wrote to the war secretary. "In the meantime I have changed the wooden doors for grated ones with locks and the anklets have been removed."[23] Stanton treated Davis with a heavy hand but was unwilling to accept criticism for it.

Attracting less notice by the newspapers was another order issued by Stanton through Halleck. It was more brash even than the communication authorizing shackles. On May 28, Halleck telegraphed Miles that Davis, "having been confined in Fort Monroe by order of the Secretary of War, . . . will be removed from that place only on orders from the same source, communicated in the same way. No writs or orders of any civil courts will be recognized or obeyed."[24] Stanton did not intend to cede power over Davis without a fight. While Davis was unaware of this order, there was little in his treatment that would raise a doubt about him being tried. The only remaining questions were the criminal charge and the forum that he would face.

The jurisdiction of military commissions extended deep into the lives of ordinary citizens during the Civil War. Prosecutions were conducted against individuals for charges stemming from violations of the laws of war, for manufacturing arms for the enemy, and for cutting telegraph wires between military posts, allegations that derived directly from the conduct of the war. But the types of cases heard by military commissions also involved ordinary crimes. The jurisdiction of a military commission was determined by whether the geographic area was under a military government and the status of martial law in the area. If an area was under military government or martial law but the civilian courts continued to operate freely, then there could be a concurrent jurisdiction over ordinary crimes.[25] Davis, imprisoned in Virginia, fell within the jurisdiction of a military commission on any charge that could have been brought against him. Officials in Washington were faced with making serious choices about how to treat Davis.

Many people sought to assure the new president that his inclination to punish treason was correct. Former Lincoln vice president Hannibal Hamlin wrote, "Whatever timid or time serving men may say we the people believe treason is a crime to be punished, and that is the only *security* for the future."[26] Johnson showed no hint of moderating his long-held opinions. Speaking to a delegation from Pennsylvania, he said, "I, too, think the time has arrived when the people of this nation should understand that treason is a crime." He did distinguish between the roles people took in the rebellion. In his view, there were "some who have been engaged in this rebellion, who, while, technically speaking, are guilty of treason, yet are morally not." To these men, he would offer reconciliation. But, the president told the delegation, "to those who have deceived—to the conscious, influential traitor, who attempted to destroy the life of a nation, I would say 'On you be inflicted the severest penalties of your crime.'"[27]

President Johnson initially involved himself extensively in the decision-making process involving the former Confederate president. In May 1865, he and his close friend, Preston King of New York, met with Judge John C. Underwood, the federal district judge for the Eastern District of Virginia, in Washington, D.C., to discuss the Davis prosecution. With Congress not in session until December, Johnson held the reins of action. The president and King told Underwood that it was their opinion that the more prominent and guilty leaders of the Confederacy had committed treason and should be indicted and punished for their conduct. Salmon P. Chase, chief justice of the U.S. Supreme Court, was not present for the interview but wrote a "Statement of the Case" years later that included details that he indicated were taken from a "memorandum furnished by Judge Underwood." According to Chase's rendition, Underwood had taken the position during the war, perhaps influenced by his "education in the principles of the Society of Friends and his former hostility to capital punishment," that the great conflict had outgrown the character of a rebellion and assumed the dimensions of a civil war. It stood to reason, then, that "sound policy and humanity demanded that the technical treason of its beginning should be ignored, and that it should be treated only as a civil war, and those engaged in it only as enemies."[28] Caught up in the events of the day, the judge agreed to present a newly formed grand jury with a charge, proposed by Johnson and King, to obtain treason indictments against Confederate leaders.

That Underwood met with Andrew Johnson and Preston King is undoubtedly correct. However, Chase's account, written years later, is possibly slanted by his seeking to justify his own legal position and bolster his political aspirations. Chase made it appear that Underwood held the legal opinion during the war that Chase took after the war—that leading a rebellion might be treasonous but that engaging in a civil war was not. Whether the substance of Chase's account is accurate or not, the one important fact that can be established is that President Johnson had decided that Davis and others should be prosecuted for treason after the war and took the unusual step of meeting with a federal judge to encourage formally charging the leading rebels.

Upon Underwood's return to Norfolk, he met with the members of the grand jury and charged them with bringing to justice men who had waged war against the United States. The charge began with the statement "You will be compelled by your regard for country, freedom and humanity to present for trial the authors and conductors of the most gigantic, bloody and unprovoked crimes that ever cursed our world." He admonished the jurors to consider indicting not only those who caused battlefield deaths but also those who caused "the greater agonies and tortures of starvation in Libby Prison, on Belle Island, at Salisbury and Andersonville."[29] Belle Island and Libby Prison were Confederate prisons housing Union soldiers in Richmond, Virginia, within the jurisdictional boundaries of the Eastern District of Virginia. Not so with Salisbury prison camp in North Carolina and the infamous Andersonville prison in Georgia. If the grand jury found that the executive leadership of the Confederacy had caused the war crimes committed at these distant prisoner of war camps, President Johnson wanted them to be prosecuted for it.

The charge was rife with explosive language. The jurors were "to review the conduct and motives of men whose lust of power and greed of gain are without a parallel; whose thirst for notoriety, strangely desired and courted, and finally acquired the public gaze, only to sink them to disgrace and infamy." In a single paragraph, Underwood defined treason for the jury, reminding them that the guilty may be civilians who would be no less guilty than those who raised arms against the Union. The judge acknowledged that "universal prosecution would be unreasonable and impossible" for the hundreds of thousands who "are technically guilty of treason" but left it for the grand jurors "to decide who and how many of the most prominent and guilty, are to answer to the violated laws of the Country."[30] Judge Underwood, already hatred by southerners, would find himself demeaned by the press in the North and South alike for this jury charge.

The *Petersburg (Va.) News* informed readers that "the first official function of a public character which he [Underwood] discharged on the return of peace, is to launch against a citizen of this State, the latchets of whose shoes he is unworthy to loose, a proclamation which, for violence, blasphemy and unfounded aspersion of a brave and chivalrous people, beggars imagery and defies comparison. No sooner had this charge been issued than its object was unfolded in the summoning of a cloud of witnesses before the grand jury, in order to base on their evidence an indictment against General Lee."[31]

The fact that "General Grant could afford, not only to pardon General Lee, but to exhaust the etiquette of conventional respect in all his intercourse with him" was pointedly remarked upon by the southern press.[32] Grant's conduct toward the rebels had not deterred Underwood. Similarly, the *Philadelphia Inquirer* urged that the grand jury inquiry begun by Underwood be shut down. The newspaper did not challenge his loyalty or impugn his integrity but noted that treason trials would lead to many unforeseen difficulties. Its editors argued that "the Government of the United States should be allowed, as the guardians of the whole people, to manage this whole question in its own way."[33] The public perception was that the grand jury proceeding initiated by Underwood was overreaching. The *Inquirer* implored the president and his advisors to determine who might be an offender worthy of prosecution, not a grand jury from Norfolk, Virginia.

Complicating the messy legal questions swirling after the war, Underwood wrote that "to an inquiry which has been made by an officer of the Court, whether the terms of parole agreed upon by Gen. Lee were any protection to those taking the parole, the answer is, that was a mere military arrangement, and can have no influence upon civil rights or the status of the persons interested."[34] This contradicted the understanding held by members of the military forces, both southern and Union, that was reached during the last days of the war. The written terms of parole of nearly every Confederate officer and soldier who surrendered to a Union force stated that "each officer and man will be allowed to return to his home, not to be disturbed by U.S. authority so long as they observe their paroles and the laws in force where they may reside,"[35] or contained language very similar to that. As previously noted, Lt. Gen. Ulysses S. Grant had staked the immense prestige of his position on the understanding "that under the terms of the capitulation all soldiers surrendered by General Lee, or under the terms granted by General Grant, have a right to return to their homes at Alexandria, or elsewhere in Virginia, and to remain there as long as they respect their paroles and the laws in force where they reside."[36]

The charge, standing alone, was a remarkable document. It gave members of the grand jury no guidance on who, if anyone, should be tried for treason or war crimes. Judge Underwood's jury charge also struck down the magnanimous terms of the Union army at Appomattox and elsewhere that seemed to move so well toward the reconciliation of the two warring sections of the country. By the judge's interpretation, Grant's guarantee to Confederate soldiers and officers was not legally binding on the question of treason. If Underwood was correct, every military officer who had surrendered with the understanding that there would be no legal recriminations could be subjected to prosecution for treason. No other branch of the federal government had made that claim, making the reading appear unreasonable. Adding to the perception that Underwood was the wrong man to try treason trials because of bias were the newspaper accounts that indicated that he "is sincerely desirous that the Wilson, Sumner and Wade policy may be adopted, as the only sure means of saving the South from civil anarchy and ruin."[37] Being linked to the Radical Republicans by the press could only cause concern for his ability to impartially administer justice.

Chief Justice Chase gave an opinion that may have explained the quick work of the grand jury. He wrote that "concerning acts which have reached such a measure of notoriety that they can not lawfully be gainsaid, judicial investigation or trial is impossible. It is obvious that every material fact in the action of Jefferson Davis against the government was of this public nature."[38] In much that vein, a grand jury might have gone into deliberations without extensive testimony to establish who the major leaders of the South were. Perhaps this common knowledge influenced the decision to permit the grand jury to operate independently. Even if this was the reasoning behind the lack of direction provided by the prosecution, it gave the appearance that the government's prosecution of the rebel leaders was haphazard.

The criminal indictments, filed on June 4, 1865, in Norfolk, Virginia, charged rebel military leaders—including Robert E. Lee, Jubal Early, Richard Ewell, Wade Hampton, Benjamin Huger, Fitzhugh Lee, James Longstreet, and William Mahone—with treason. Also indicted were James A. Seddon, Henry Wise, John Breckinridge, and George W. Alexander, the commandant of the notorious Castle Thunder prison in Richmond. A review of the list of men indicted makes the process appear haphazard at best. In all, the grand jury returned indictments against eighteen rebel leaders. Most prominent of the men, of course, was the commander of the Army of Northern Virginia, Robert E. Lee, who had just two months earlier been paroled at Appomattox. It did not take long for the Johnson administration to realize that the indictments had opened up a highly charged controversy about the propriety of bringing charges against these men. Missing from the list of individuals indicted was the prominent Confederate against whom Andrew Johnson actually wished to proceed—Jefferson Davis.

After the grand jury returned, Judge Underwood traveled to meet with Attorney General James Speed in June 1865 to talk to him about the indictments that had just been handed down against the high-ranking Confederate leaders.[39] It fell to the judge to offer an explanation of why Davis had not been indicted. There is no record of how he explained that fact. The reaction of the Johnson administration revealed how the lack of direction from the executive branch could seriously embarrass the new president. On June 20, 1866, Speed wrote to Lucius Chandler about the newly indicted cases. "I learn that many of the rebel officers and soldiers that were paroled by capitulation have been indicted," he said. "I am instructed by the President to direct you not to have warrants of arrest taken out against them, or any of them, until further orders."[40] The meeting between Andrew Johnson, Preston King, and Judge Underwood directing Underwood to secure indictments against Confederate leaders had resulted in the indictment of men paroled by the terms of their surrender and embarrassed the administration. It should have come as no surprise. Because the government provided no direction as to who should be indicted and the federal prosecutor, Chandler, was not involved, the grand jury could be excused for returning indictments against the prominent military leaders of the Confederacy instead of the politicians who had led the South out of the Union. The first run at prosecuting Davis was inauspicious.

If the prosecution of rebel leaders was haphazard and disorganized, Andrew Johnson was also alienating Radical Republican congressional leaders by his efforts to rapidly bring the rebellious states back into the Union. Pennsylvania congressman Thaddeus Stevens wrote at the end of May 1865, "I see our worthy president fancies himself a sovereign power."[41] Within six weeks, his anger boiled over in a letter to the president himself. "I am sure you will pardon me for speaking to you with a candor to which men of high places are seldom accustomed. Among all the leading Union men of the North with whom I have had intercourse I do not find one who approves of your policy," he said to Johnson. Pleading with him to wait until Congress was back in session before making important decisions, he asked, "Can you not hold your hand and wait the action of Congress and in the mean time govern them by military rulers?"[42] Radical Republicans found Johnson's actions intolerable but could not meet until their recess was over without the president calling them into special session. They seethed as they watched and waited.

The Unpopularity of Davis in the South

In the months after the war, Davis had another intangible problem with which he had to deal—he was not well liked even in the South when he began his imprisonment. It was under his watch that the South had been devastated by the Union armies. As James McPherson noted, Davis "led a cause that went down to disastrous defeat and left the South in poverty for generations."[43] One correspondent wrote: "I have seen many persons from the South lately and they all agree in saying that the world has never seen a more subjugated or conquered people. Everyone is utterly and I fear irretrievably ruined. My own relations and friends were actually on the verge of starvation." He found southerners to be of one opinion: "They all blame Davis as the cause of their defeat."[44] Gen. James H. Wilson also addressed the attitude of southerners he encountered: "From the contempt they feel toward Davis government, the disgrace of its termination, as well as its tyranny while in force, they feel a sentiment of relief at the restoration of national authority."[45] The *New York Tribune* editor, Horace Greeley, agreed, comparing southern treatment of Davis to an "idolater, who adores his god after a victory, but flogs him when smarting under defeat."[46] If the prosecution acted quickly and decisively in bringing Davis to trial, the unpopular Davis might have lacked support even in the South. All that was necessary was a clear direction from the government in what was to be done with the former president.

Arriving at Fort Monroe, Davis was reduced to waiting to learn what might become of him. Would he be tried and executed? Would his fate be left in the hands of a military commission, or would a civil court try him? Might he escape trial altogether? None of these questions had been answered in May 1865, but there is ample evidence that federal officials were discussing the options. Stanton's inveterate hatred of the southerners who had led the rebellion and his attempt to manage every aspect of Davis's treatment and prosecution did not mean that he effectively controlled everyone who might have a hand in prosecuting the rebel chief. Despite Stanton's May 14 telegram that Davis would be tried in Virginia, the federal attorney for the District of Columbia had, apparently, not been made aware of that decision.

On May 26, 1865, the first indictments were handed down against Davis and John C. Breckinridge for treason. The *Washington Evening Star* reported that "the overt act was the raid in July last within the District of Columbia, and the jurisdiction of this court, killing citizens and destroying property, Breckinridge being present and Davis constructively so." A warrant was requested for Breckinridge. The district attorney, E. C. Carrington, indicated to the court that he would request that Davis be brought to the District of Columbia for trial. The reporter advised that "the announcement produced no excitement in the court room, the indictment having been expected for some time."[47] If the prosecution of rebel leaders was unsystematic and disorganized, there was no better proof of it than this.

News of the charge spread quickly. Greeley printed the indictment in its entirety on the front page of the *New York Tribune* on May 29. The New Jersey *Camden Democrat* ran a more detailed story on exactly what the indictments alleged. Davis was accused of having been in league with a large number of insurgents as their commander in chief and attacking Fort Stevens in the District of Columbia on July 12, 1864, killing and wounding U.S. troops, "contrary to the duty of his said allegiance and fidelity to the United States."[48] The newspaper informed its readers that the court was expected to bring Davis to be formally arraigned in court within a few days. The indictment was secured less than three weeks after he was apprehended in Georgia. The federal prosecutor charged Davis with treason and sought a conviction based upon Davis's "constructive presence" in the District of Columbia during the 1864 Confederate attack. Constructive presence was, of course, a legal doctrine, permitting the finding by a jury that Davis was present in the District of Columbia despite the fact that he was not physically present at the time of the attack. He could be found to be constructively present by virtue of him being the commander in chief of Confederate forces and having ordered the strike. The indictment carried some risk in that Article III, Section 2, of the United States Constitution states that "the trial of all crimes . . . shall be held in the state where the said crimes shall have been committed."[49] Members of Johnson's cabinet were uncertain whether the doctrine could be applied in treason cases. Had Carrington even considered whether constructive presence was permitted in treason cases?

Anticipated or not, the indictment was considered problematic for some in the administration. In late May, Stanton met with Joseph Holt in Holt's office. Holt was in the middle of the prosecution of Mary Surratt and the other Lincoln conspirators. Their conversation was brief but touched upon the question involving the treason indictments of Davis and Breckinridge just announced in the criminal courts of the District of Columbia. Could the two men be legally tried in the District of Columbia, they wondered? Stanton left the meeting without having expressed a definitive conclusion. Over the next week, however, it weighed on his mind, and he finally addressed the question in a lengthy letter to Holt.

Ten days after their meeting, in a letter dated June 7, 1865, Stanton wrote to Holt to express his now considered opinion as to the proper venue of a treason trial for Breckinridge and Davis. The original indictments of Breckinridge and Davis have since been lost to history, but contemporary newspapers published the pertinent portions of the charging instruments. Stanton's discussion is relevant to explaining the subsequent measures taken by the government in the prosecution of Davis in Virginia. It was the attack on Washington, D.C., by Gen. Jubal A. Early and fifteen thousand troops, including John C. Breckinridge, in mid-July 1864 that led to the criminal charge. The Confederate force came within five miles of the White House and put a scare into the entire city that it might fall to the southern forces. The rebels drove their lines so near that they could see the Capitol dome from their positions. It was this treasonous act that formed the foundation of the indictment in Washington. Stanton conceded that a trial of Breckinridge in the District of Columbia was proper because Breckinridge was actually present in the district when the overt act charged was committed. Stanton opined, "I do not understand that there is any controversy but the Court has rightful jurisdiction over him, *if they catch him.*"[50]

Jurisdiction over Davis, however, was a much thornier question. Stanton was troubled that if jurisdiction existed, it was to be had only on the basis of the constructive presence of Davis in the district during the time that the overt acts of treason were committed. But he was also concerned about the appearance of fairness in the process of trying Davis. "The trial of Jefferson Davis for treason will be a marked event in the Judicial history of the country," he told Holt. "It is of vast importance that it should be conducted in such a manner as to meet the approval of the American Bar." Stanton clearly wanted to sustain the government's effort to prosecute Davis in the District of Columbia. However, he expressed his doubts on several points to Holt. He had reviewed the decision by Chief Justice John Marshall in the Aaron Burr treason trial and concluded that it was Marshall's holding that a person could not be convicted of treason unless the person was personally present within the jurisdiction of the court in which the overt act was committed. Moreover, Stanton had spoken to J. J. Coombs, a man he described as "probably the best lawyer in the District" and an author of a work on the Burr treason trial who had grave doubts about the jurisdiction of a District of Columbia court over Davis. Ultimately, Stanton claimed that it was the U.S. Constitution that required that treason be tried in the district where the crime was committed. He came to that conclusion by reading the text of the Constitution itself and recognizing that there was little room for interpretation, especially in light of Marshall's opinion in the Burr trial. This conclusion—that Davis should be tried in Virginia, a state that had seceded from the Union—might have given pause or even deterred a less determined man from advocating the trial of Davis for treason. Stanton was undeterred. The secretary of war argued that "a jury might be found in Virginia, and the trial had at Alexandria, Norfolk or Richmond. And why not in Wheeling! He committed treason enough to hang a legion of men before the State of West Virginia was organized."[51]

Stanton was also concerned that Davis not be tried by a mere district judge. Instead, he argued that the former Confederate president should be tried before the chief justice of the Supreme Court. Evidently, he believed that the prestige of the office of the chief justice should be lent to the proceedings. But Salmon P. Chase, a highly ambitious politician known by Stanton to be an inveterate schemer and aspirant to the presidency, would be the man overseeing the trial. Did Stanton really trust Chase to oversee a trial so important to the federal government without his rulings being colored by his ambition? If he harbored this concern—and he likely did—he did not address it in his letter to Holt.

The secretary of war was silent in his letter about what to do with the U.S. attorney in Washington if the case against Davis proceeded to trial there. The controversy swirling around that officer certainly would have caused Stanton and Holt concern. The federal prosecutor, E. C. Carrington, a Virginian by birth, had been the subject of a congressional investigation into his loyalty during the Thirty-Seventh Congress of 1861–62. The legislature had investigated dozens of federal employees from virtually every federal department in an effort to detect any hint of disloyalty among the nation's government workers. It was a massive undertaking, with occasionally unfair results. Carrington's name was on the list of "those against whom the evidence of disloyalty was deemed conclusive." Carrington was reputed to have admitted that he was appointed district attorney by virtue of having raised a company of men for the District of Columbia. However, when the company was ordered into Virginia, Carrington refused to go. According to witnesses from his company, Captain Carrington told the men in his company that "we were under no obligations to go—that we had only taken an oath to fight in the District." His colonel testified that Carrington told him that he would not go into Virginia to fight but would defend the District of Columbia if it was attacked by the Confederates. Witnesses against him claimed that his reluctance to accompany his unit into Virginia stemmed from the fact that his mother was a resident of Virginia and his two brothers served in the rebel army. The committee found that Carrington's loyalty was doubtful and that he could "not be depended upon either to repress rebellion or to defend the Constitution and laws, which he has, as district attorney, taken a solemn oath to support."[52] Despite the findings, he retained his appointed post.

Stanton did not address Carrington's loyalty in his letter to Holt. As a result, no conclusion can be drawn that the findings of the House Committee pertaining to the alleged disloyalty of the district attorney played a part in Stanton's reluctance to try Davis in the District of Columbia. There is no direct evidence that Stanton was aware of the claims made by the committee. Still, there were several military officers within the War Department who had serious allegations of disloyalty made against them in the same House report that investigated Carrington. Stanton had succeeded Simon Cameron as secretary of war only a few days before the report was printed. He certainly would have reviewed the report as to his own department. The secretary of war was also well known for his concern for the security of officials in Washington. Carrington would have been the chief law enforcement official in charge of prosecuting those who posed a threat to officials within the district.

It is very likely that he would have seen the findings made against the U.S. district attorney for the District of Columbia while studying the report. It is possible that Stanton dismissed the legislative finding because of evidence of Carrington's loyalty. It is also conceivable that the allegation played a part in his belief that the treason trial of Davis was better left to be prosecuted by someone in another jurisdiction. In May 1865, Stanton was, perhaps, the most powerful member of Johnson's cabinet. If he did not cede the decision, however, the president would decide if and where Davis would be tried.

An indictment was pending in Washington, D.C., against Davis for treason and other crimes. Davis, however, had yet to even be arraigned on the charges. Instead, the attorney general had presumably made the decision that the proper venue was Virginia and so declined to prosecute the pending charges in Washington. Meanwhile, Chase was said to not be contemplating holding court in Virginia for an indefinite period of time. Stanton's exasperation was understandable to anyone hoping for a speedy trial of the Confederate leader.

As Davis languished at Fort Monroe, the trial of the Lincoln conspirators came to a close. The trial had lasted for nearly a month. The conspirators, Mary Surratt and eight others,[53] were alleged in charge 1 to have aided—with Jefferson Davis and others, including Beverly Tucker and Clement C. Clay—in the murder of President Lincoln and the plot to kill Secretary of State William H. Seward and Vice President Andrew Johnson.[54] On June 29, the military commission rendered its findings against the conspirators, recommending the death penalty for Surratt and three others. Johnson approved the findings and sentences on July 5. On July 7, the four executions were carried out when the condemned were simultaneously hanged.

The hanging of the Lincoln conspirators did not end the Lincoln murder investigation. Joseph Holt continued to take sworn affidavits from men who falsely claimed to be witnesses who could link the former Confederate president to the Lincoln assassination. As late as November 1865, Charles A. Dunham, known by the alias of Sandford Conover, produced two witnesses for Holt who claimed "that they along with Surratt joined Davis in plotting Lincoln's death." After the witnesses gave their sworn statements, Holt took at least one of them to the White House to read their statements to Johnson and Seward. While the two men later recanted their declarations, when brought before a congressional committee, and Dunham was convicted of perjury, men like Holt and Stanton harbored grave reservations that Davis was innocent in Lincoln's slaying. They would pursue leads in the investigation while Davis was held in Fort Monroe.[55] Conover's testimony "stained the government's case and eventually raised a serious question of whether Holt had been gulled by Conover's perjury or complicit in it."[56] Under either circumstance, the rapid trial by military commission of the conspirators revealed the lengths to which the federal government would go to secure convictions of individuals whom they considered guilty of serious offenses.

Davis must have wondered what was in store for his future. Even after the end of the war, military commissions operated to quickly dispose of cases like that of the Lincoln conspirators. Union officers composed the members of military commissions, making the body less impartial than a civilian jury. It was presided over by a high-ranking officer, rather than a civilian judge, making the evidentiary rulings less likely to follow the rules of evidence. No decision had been made that would have eased the mind of the Confederate leader. What would he be charged with? Who would he be tried before? Would he receive a fair trial? These were all questions that understandably raised his anxiety and made life difficult for the high-profile prisoner of Fort Monroe. The struggle to answer the questions would occupy the energy of Davis's advocates and opponents in the coming months.

In the days following Lincoln's murder, Radical Republicans met with Johnson and found his views on punishing rebel leaders harshly as sweeping as their own. In a meeting in April 1865 with Senator Benjamin Wade, the radical senator from Ohio, Johnson was advised by Wade to hang a dozen or so rebels. The president disagreed with the suggestion and stated that he thought the executions should be more numerous. What the Radicals did not realize was that the new president was not an open-minded man. While his views on treason and the need to punish southern leaders aligned neatly with their own, they would find in the coming years that Johnson was a conservative man on race and the status of the states in relation to being brought back into the Union. Instead of being their godsend, Johnson would come to be hated by the Radicals. Their attention would be turned from punishing Jefferson Davis to destroying Andrew Johnson. That shift, in turn, would divert Johnson's attention from trying Davis for treason.[57]

6

THE NATION'S BEST LAWYERS TAKE SIDES

Open the case, and when you are doing it, talk to the jury as though your client's fate depends on every word you utter.

—Abraham Lincoln

A New York Lawyer Volunteers His Services to Davis

Within days of the capture of Jefferson Davis, prominent lawyers began vying to work on his defense. The case was so publicized, and the issues involved in the trial of the former Confederate president so novel, that it would come as no surprise that many lawyers were interested in defending him. Given the great decisions that needed to be made by the government and that might be influenced by a good defense attorney, the advocates realized that it would be advantageous to get on the case as early as possible. But Davis had a particular man in mind for the job. He had told his wife, Varina, while sailing north under arrest, that if they should be separated during the voyage, she should request that Charles O'Conor represent him.[1] O'Conor, a preeminent New York defense lawyer, was considered to be "an advocate almost without peer in his day," according to *Harper's Monthly Magazine*.[2] What was striking about O'Conor was "his full embrace of slavery as a positive good" before the war.[3] Varina Davis was not able to contact the lawyer before she found that he had volunteered to represent her husband.[4] She must have been greatly relieved that O'Conor would be so interested in the case. This also signaled to the federal government that the accused rebel would be given the highest-quality defense.

O'Conor was sixty-one years old in 1865 and had reached the pinnacle of his profession in New York City. His prominence came despite his early years of poverty and lack of formal education. His grandfather had left Ireland with his extended family, hoping to avoid persecution after being involved in the Irish Rebellion of 1798. O'Conor was born six years later into this destitute family of Irish immigrants.[5] The school that he attended for about two months as a child constituted the only formal education he would ever receive. When he was eleven years old, his mother died. His father, perhaps unsuccessfully grappling with raising a son alone, apprenticed young Charles to a man who manufactured tar pitch, turpentine, and lampblack. The adolescent received no pay but was given his board. When he left this occupation at age thirteen, his father placed him with an acquaintance who held a rude and unprofitable law practice.[6] Bright and extremely ambitious, O'Conor earned membership to the New York bar in 1824 at the age of twenty and began a career that spanned nearly sixty years.[7] He changed the spelling of his name, dropping a letter *n* after a trip to Ireland convinced him that the original spelling contained only one.[8]

Known more for his prodigious work ethic rather than the brilliance of his arguments, O'Conor attributed his success at the bar to one word: *study*.[9] His preparation for cases was legendary; he once remarked, "I have not left a stone unturned under which there crept a living thing."[10] In a time when formal pleadings in lawsuits might make or break the success of a case, O'Conor considered every pleading filed by his adversary as potentially flawed. In many ways, he was not a likable man. His younger but great professional adversary, William M. Evarts, claimed that O'Conor was "endowed by nature with these prodigious gifts of intellect, of insight, of discussion, of manifestation, of oratory, and with the added power of industry, that if it was not born in him, was burnt into him by ten years of poverty and struggle at our Bar, had everything in his favor to make a great lawyer."[11] But he carried with him a resentment that his being Irish and Catholic had needlessly placed obstacles in his path to success. Whether his youthful poverty and ethnic and religious background played any role in his developing a confrontational and oftentimes unsocial personality is a matter of speculation. That he had this personality is undeniable. He "left in the minds of many the impression that he was a harsh, severe and unamiable man," a fellow lawyer said of him at his death.[12] This truth was so obvious that even those eulogizing him at a memorial in his honor could not fail to mention it.

Every adversary respected his abilities. Through sheer hard work, O'Conor very quickly attained prominence in the New York bar. A contemporary of his, Charles A. Peabody, also an attorney, found O'Conor to be supremely confident in his ability to present cases: "His courage, his fearlessness in attacking obstacles, was remarkable; nothing daunted or discouraged him. I do not think he knew such a feeling as fear or distrust of his case. He always felt himself equal to the attainment of justice."[13] His courtroom style included "a cutting irony and a power of sarcasm that was, at times, withering. His manner was formal and his ordinary speech defiant."[14] Accounts of his demeanor before juries leave no doubt that he was a pugnacious fighter who enjoyed the confrontation that is inevitable in the trial of any case. In the best tradition of the law, O'Conor was acknowledged to keep the secrets of his clients. This reserve in preparing and presenting his cases was turned into a weapon at trial. He understood juries and determined that "the great lawyer is not the one who knows the most law, but who understands what the point involved is."[15] But personally, he could not avoid the isolation brought on by his antisocial behavior. Samuel J. Tilden, the future Democratic candidate for president, knew O'Conor well and said of him, "Mr. O'Conor is a man of extensive and accurate legal learning, of an acuteness of reason somewhat excessive even for the higher uses of his profession—of great mental activity—indefatigable, vehement and sarcastic in controversy—remarked at the bar as able rather than wise, and remarkable for a want of tact."[16] He was seen as honest and able but lacking the ability to be diplomatic or compromise on issues.[17]

Politically, he was well connected in the Democratic Party in New York and held many of the conservative views of that party. His youthful poverty and the challenges that he faced by being Irish and Catholic did not make him sympathetic to the plight of African Americans, neither free nor those held in bondage. During the 1850s, he not only undertook representation of southern causes in New York, but he also asserted the southern position in his personal and political life. His view of slavery coincided with the most extreme southern view of the institution. As the sectional crisis deepened, O'Conor advocated the southern cause in New York City, answering the cries of abolitionists with a strident speech given at the Union Meeting at the Academy of Music entitled "Negro Slavery Not Unjust," which he subsequently had printed and distributed in pamphlet form.[18] Many in the New York bar regretted the "powerful aid he has given the cause of slavery by his superior talents."[19] After the war came, he openly "condemned the prosecution of the war by the North," giving him views that placed him squarely in the Copperhead circle during the conflict.[20]

His efforts on behalf of the southern cause lost him many friends. When Columbia Law School considered honoring O'Conor with an LLD degree, largely in hope that he would donate his considerable law library to the college, George Templeton Strong, a New York lawyer and trustee of Columbia College, confided to his diary that many "seem unwilling that the College confer any academic honor on any man who has been using his great talent and learning to weaken the national cause and to uphold the cause of secession and of slave-breeding, all through these years of war. I think Columbia College cannot confer academic honor on so maleficent a Copperhead as O'Conor, not even for the bribe of a cart-load of law books. I will not vote for it, anyhow."[21] No matter how good a figure he cut in the courtroom, his politics made him anathema to many in the United States.

He did, however, make a formidable opponent in any case in which he appeared. He viewed litigation as a physical ordeal as well as a cerebral one. Shortly after volunteering to represent Davis, he wrote to Franklin Pierce, the former United States president, "In order to put myself in good physical trim, a very important point in the preparation for an intellectual combat as well as for a prize fight, I design going to Saratoga Springs tomorrow."[22] O'Conor was a tough, intimidating trial lawyer and believed that keeping physically fit added to his ability to endure long, stressful trials. If the federal government vigorously prosecuted the rebel leadership, O'Conor would need every ounce of energy that could be mustered.

In his letter to Pierce, he explained his reason for volunteering to represent the former Confederate president as well as the events that had transpired since he made his offer: "When the newspaper reports indicated the near approach of a trial and as yet no one had volunteered to defend, I thought fit to intervene for the purpose of saving our (northern) country from the reproach of unanimity. On my request the War Department permitted an open note containing my tender to be delivered to Mr. Davis. But his reply was perused by the Attorney General and pronounced an improper communication. It was consequently returned to him for correction. He has made no further attempt to correspond with me and my application for a personal interview with him is deemed inadmissible at present."[23]

Franklin Pierce was a "beloved old friend" of Jefferson Davis as well as a correspondent with O'Conor.[24] Pierce saw the fight as more than simply a question of whether Davis had committed treason or some other crime. Writing to Jeremiah Black, he urged the lawyer to assist O'Conor in the defense. "I hope you will assist Mr. O'Conor in his defence of Davis," he wrote, "if not in Court by conference for it is not Mr. Davis alone but civil and constitutional liberty is on trial."[25] But primarily, Pierce sought help for a dear friend on trial for his life.

From the very beginning, O'Conor recognized that a collaborative effort was needed for the defense. He admitted that "it is entirely impossible to divine what course may be adopted by the ruling powers. The signs of their interest are very various and it may task 'one poor-head' to determine some questions that must be regarded as within the compass of possibility. I would like to call a counsel board together for consultation upon them."[26] O'Conor asked that Pierce help him put together a group of people to talk about Davis's case. O'Conor's willingness to work jointly with other lawyers did not mean that he conceded the lead to any other attorney. He reserved the authority to decide on the correct strategy to take in the case completely for himself.

Across the Atlantic, in England, Confederate representatives came forward to help Davis and the others charged by the United States government. James Mason wrote to O'Conor from London in June, expressing gratitude that O'Conor had volunteered to handle Davis's defense and to place five hundred pounds sterling at his disposal for the fees and investigative costs of mounting a defense for Davis. Mason wanted no corners cut in the case. "I am aware," he wrote, "that to conduct the defense properly, expenses must be incurred besides the fees of counsel, in preliminary preparations as regards obtaining rebutting or other evidence."[27] Mason also wanted a network of former Confederates to be located with the aim of helping Davis defer the expense of trial. To that end, he suggested that O'Conor talk to Davis about locating the Confederate agent to Canada, Jacob Thompson, for help.

The five hundred pounds yielded O'Conor about thirty-five hundred dollars, and the defense lawyer received notice that a credit of ten thousand pounds would be placed at his disposal from which he could draw for the Davis defense. O'Conor used the money judiciously. By June 1867, O'Conor reported to Davis that he had cashed, and presumably paid himself, about seven thousand dollars from that source. He also reported that the ten thousand–pound line of credit had been withdrawn and replaced by five bills for five hundred pounds each, of which O'Conor had cashed one.

R. H. Gillett, another very capable New York attorney, was hired by friends of Davis to assist O'Conor in the defense of the indictment returned in May 1866.[28] He was described as "one of the most prominent lawyers and politicians north of Albany" by the *New York Herald* and was said by the same paper to rank "high as a criminal lawyer."[29] Supporters of the former Confederate president were moving quickly to assemble a very high-quality defense team. The prosecution, however, was moving much more slowly.

Assembling the Prosecution Team

At the cabinet meeting of August 22, 1865, James Speed reported to the president that he was waiting to hear back from private counsel whom he hoped to employ in the Davis prosecution. He had contacted William M. Evarts, the lawyer from New York who was well acquainted with Charles O'Conor, to work on the case. Speed also contacted a former Massachusetts attorney general and governor, John H. Clifford, through a third party to gauge his interest in working on the case. Clifford agreed to meet Evarts at the luxurious Astor House hotel in New York City to talk about the case. Evarts was an accomplished professional who, four years earlier, had been mentioned as a possible candidate to replace Seward in the Senate. A New Englander by birth, Evarts had amassed a large fortune as an attorney and had been an early Republican supporter of Lincoln. Speed had indicated to the lawyers that he would be taking the role of lead prosecutor in the case, with them being in a supporting position. In a case of this importance, Speed believed "that, as the highest law officer of the government, I should prosecute in person."[30]

The president was apparently taken by surprise by the selection of these two men, who were not known to members of the cabinet as strong trial lawyers. Gideon Welles, the naval secretary, thought that Speed had made the offers based on the recommendations of Stanton and Seward, whom he perceived to be the only members of the cabinet not surprised by Speed's presentation. It was the view of Welles that Benjamin Butler, whom he believed to be an outstanding trial lawyer, should have been brought on for the trial as well, not only for his trial skills but also because "he belongs to a school which at this time and in such a trial should have a voice."[31]

Davis had quickly retained Charles O'Conor as his lead counsel, while the United States attorney general was still trying to assemble a prosecution team for the treason trial. The delay seemingly did not affect the government's case vis-à-vis the defense, since O'Conor had not yet even had a visit with his client; however, Davis had been in custody for three months, and there was no sense of urgency apparent in the government's actions. Any prosecutor intent upon trying a case like Davis's would be cognizant that a delay would work against the government's interest, since the passage of time would inevitably draw attention to more pressing national problems and allow northern hostility toward the southern leader, now at a high fever, to wane.

Nevertheless, in August 1865, Evarts received a telegram from Speed asking that he come to Washington. During that visit, Evarts, Speed, and President Johnson discussed bringing Evarts on to assist in the prosecution. The meeting must not have been as clear as it should have been, since Evarts left with the impression that he had been retained to prosecute not only Davis but also any other rebel leaders who might be indicted for treason.[32] Historians have portrayed Andrew Johnson as a man unsure of what he was to do with Davis after the war. William J. Cooper Jr., author of *Jefferson Davis, American,* advanced this position.[33] This is not entirely fair. President Johnson wanted Davis brought to trial. Any delay was not due to Johnson's lack of clarity on that question. He did what he believed he could to accomplish that end. On August 22, Johnson told the assembled cabinet that he had tried to speak to Chief Justice Salmon P. Chase about the time and place of the trial but that Chase had declined to discuss the subject with the president. James Speed admitted that President Johnson was "anxious for a speedy and prompt trial of Jefferson Davis."[34] Johnson, however, deferred to his advisors in their field of expertise. Speed, as attorney general, and his successors after he left office, recognized that the responsibility devolved upon them to prosecute Davis. The president made clear his wishes and did not intrude upon their prerogative as to time and place. He also backed his attorney general on the choices he made for his trial team. If the failure to bring Davis to trial for treason ultimately must fall on the president's shoulders, his shortcoming lay in his not ordering that the trial begin by a date certain.

William Maxwell Evarts

In the early stages of the prosecution, the government made excellent choices in drawing together the trial team. The man chosen by Speed to assist in the prosecution, William M. Evarts, was characterized by another New York attorney as a "great lawyer and brilliant advocate."[35] The contrast between Evarts and O'Conor was dramatic. A man of medium stature and slim build, Evarts was descended both from Roger Sherman, a signer of the Declaration of Independence, and an otherwise prominent family in Boston. A second-generation lawyer, his education was first-rate: he had graduated from Yale in 1837 and Harvard Law School. One of his classmates at Harvard was Richard Henry Dana Jr., a man who would later join the Davis prosecution team. Dana characterized Evarts as one of Harvard Law School's "leading men" in terms of his ability to offer a "complete, systematic, precise and elegantly spoken law argument." He noted that "if he does not become distinguished, he will disappoint more persons than any other young man whom I have ever met with."[36] Thereafter, Evarts moved his practice of law to New York City.

As Evarts himself later recalled, he "came to this city from the law school in 1839, and had the great advantage of being received into the office of the eminent and excellent lawyer who then stood at the head of professional employments in this city."[37] He was smooth where O'Conor was rough; he maintained the self-assurance born into a man confident in his place in society, whereas O'Conor grasped and clung to success with a fear that only great labor could save him from falling back into poverty and disgrace. Yet Evarts believed that it was O'Conor's background that gave him advantage as an attorney, being "that the discipline of poverty and of necessity is the one best assurance for the making of a great lawyer and the gaining of the great fame and the great enjoyments accompanying success at the Bar."[38] Undoubtedly, O'Conor would have found this sentiment of a brilliant lawyer, born into wealth and society and imbued with high intellect and a first-rate education, amusing.

Like many lawyers, Evarts became involved in politics. He began as a Whig, initially in the Millard Fillmore wing of the party, before he moved to back the more progressive Whig leader, William Seward, then the governor of New York. The friendship between him and Seward would last until Seward's death. It was an association that greatly benefited the younger Evarts. Subsequently, he was appointed assistant U.S. attorney by Fillmore's appointee, doubtless reaping the advantage of his skills and his contacts. After the passage of the Fugitive Slave Act in 1850, he joined Fernando Wood, the conservative New York Democrat, and others in speaking in support of the act. This caused him no small problem with his claim to being an antislavery man, but as it was explained years later by another New York attorney, "Evarts, like Webster, was inimical to slavery but Union was to him more than the antislavery cause and hence he sought to allay sectional irritation by urging obedience to an abhorrent law."[39]

As a prosecutor in the United States Attorney's Office for the Southern District of New York, Evarts made a name for himself when he tried a high-profile case known as the *Cleopatra* expedition to Cuba. The trial involved the prosecution of individuals who had undertaken an odyssey to Cuba in an effort to extend southern slavery to an island already a part of the slave culture. The Neutrality Act of 1818 prohibited vessels from being outfitted for war against countries with which the United States was at peace, making the Cuban adventure illegal. In April 1851, Evarts became aware that sailors and men were being recruited in New York City and about to leave for the southern coast. The young lawyer had the leaders arrested and the ship detained while the case was prepared for trial. Nearly a year later, the case went to trial. Evarts lost the case but gained public attention through the prosecution.

His reputation in the antislavery community was recovered only after he undertook the *Lemmon* case by defending a New York statute that pronounced free every slave brought into New York voluntarily or by consent of the slave's master. Jonathan Lemmon and his family, citizens of Virginia, were traveling from Virginia to Texas with eight slaves when they stopped in New York merely to transfer ships to Texas in November 1852. During the stop, a writ of habeas corpus was issued for the eight slaves, alleging that they were being unlawfully restrained in their liberty because by virtue of their having stepped foot in New York, they were free. A New York state court upheld the statute. The controversy created by this writ was immense and provocative to both sections of the country. Merchants of New York who were dependent upon southern trade immediately raised five thousand dollars to compensate Lemmon for the value of his slaves. Abolitionists led by Lewis Tappan raised hundreds of dollars to finance the relocation of the newly freed slaves to Canada.[40]

Pro-southern newspapers derided activist judges: "Instead of administering the law as they find it, they usurp the authority of the Legislature, and make law according to their notions of what it ought to be."[41] This opinion, of course, ignored the fact that the New York legislature had passed the very statute under which the slaves had been freed. Jonathan Lemmon returned to Virginia with the money given him by merchants and abandoned both his intended move to Texas and his pursuit of his legal claim to the slaves. In February 1857, when no one appeared at the appellate court on his behalf, the case was dismissed.[42]

The Commonwealth of Virginia did not give up so easily. The day after the dismissal, lawyers appeared on behalf of Virginia, and the case was reinstated on the docket. The attorney general of Virginia began the prosecution of the appeal in the case and hired local counsel to represent the state. The case had generated much notoriety in the South, and many were outraged by the court decision. Howell Cobb, the governor of Georgia, claimed to regard the 1852 decision as a "just cause of war."[43] The Commonwealth took the case to the New York Supreme Court, an intermediate appellate court, which heard the case in December 1857. By this time, the *Dred Scott* decision had been handed down by the U.S. Supreme Court, dealing a blow to the antislavery movement. Southerners hoped that federal courts would next extend their right to take slaves wherever they chose. Proslavery advocates did not have confidence that a New York appellate court would make that ruling.

The man hired by the Commonwealth of Virginia to fight the writ was none other than Charles O'Conor, whose well-known southern sympathies would ensure that his legal positions would not be compromised by his personal views. Chester Arthur, the future president, was the attorney for the State of New York, but William Evarts was hired to assist and argued the case before the appellate court. As they had in other cases, Evarts and O'Conor locked horns in October 1857. O'Conor urged the court to honor the property rights of the slaveholders while they were in New York. Evarts responded that the New York statutes "operate as a universal proscription and prohibition of the condition of slavery within the state."[44] By the time the case reached the New York Court of Appeals for argument, in January 1860, the nation was reeling from the shock of John Brown's raid on Harpers Ferry just months earlier. The arguments became high drama for the nation.

O'Conor's arguments before the court of appeals were astonishingly broader than the narrow legal position that he could have taken, that slaves were property entitled to be transported through a free state, as would any other property. The courtroom was jolted by his words. "The cruelties of vicious slaveowners and the horrors of the slave trade are topics quite irrelevant," he told the judges.[45] He argued, in part, that "Negroes, alone and unaided by the guardianship of another race, cannot sustain a civilized social state" and "that, alone and unaided, he never can sustain a civilized social organization is proven to all reasonable minds by the fact that one single member of his race has never attained proficiency in any art or science requiring the employment of high intellectual capacity,"[46] an assertion completely outside the narrow legal question before the court. When confronted with the point that Great Britain freed slaves immediately upon them stepping foot on British soil, O'Conor responded in a biting and somewhat misleading way that the law did not apply to white men held as slaves so that "the air of England had not its true enfranchising purity till drawn through the nostrils of a negro."[47] Mocking the legal position advanced by lawyers from the State of New York, O'Conor attempted to insert the issue of social equality into the case: "The moment an African-negro comes within the State of New York, he is elevated to the rank of a freeman; almost elevated to political equality—entirely so, indeed, if he have but a little speck of real property. He is elevated to political equality with the most favored of the Anglo-Saxon race; and but for a vulgar, but inveterate prejudice, he would also be elevated to social equality."[48] O'Conor attempted to bait the judges into viewing the case from the perspective of race. Whether this was a posture that he prepared in advance and intended to take or whether he shifted his approach as the lengthy arguments advanced is not known. What is known is that he recognized that members of the audience, perhaps even the judges, would find his taunting assertions offensive but undertook to advance them nonetheless.[49]

Evarts limited his argument before the judges to the law pertaining to the case much more than did Charles O'Conor, perhaps because O'Conor was playing to a sectional audience but also likely because Evarts's training and experience guided him in the direction of a narrow, legal approach. The statutory law of New York prohibited slavery within the boundaries of the state. "It remains only to be considered," Evarts contended, "whether, under the principles of the law of nations, as governing the intercourse of friendly States, and as adopted and incorporated into the administration of our municipal law, comity requires the recognition and support of the relation of slave owner and slave between strangers passing through our territory, notwithstanding the absolute policy and comprehensive legislation which prohibit that relation and render the civil condition of slavery impossible in our own society." He drew an interesting analogy for the court by arguing that the relationship between a master and slave, similar to "incestuous marriage or polygamy, lawful in the foreign domicile, cannot be held as a lawful continuing relation here."[50] Even assuming for the sake of argument that the movement of property could be governed in a manner alleged by O'Conor, Evarts responded that "by the law of Nations, men are not the subject of property."[51] A large audience listened to Evarts's argument in evident support for the propositions he advanced.[52]

Evarts prevailed in the highly publicized and closely watched case. But the reputation of both lawyers was elevated in the political circles in which they moved. On the one side was O'Conor, fighting for the interests of the peculiar institution. On the other side was Evarts, seamlessly advancing the rights of man. The vehement arguments advanced by O'Conor endeared him to the slaveholding South and would not be forgotten after the war, when Davis was in need of a preeminent trial attorney who truly believed in the cause of the South. Nor would the efforts of Evarts be forgotten when a brilliant Republican lawyer was needed to assist in the prosecution of alleged traitors after the war.

By the time of the Republican convention of 1860, Evarts was "a leading Wall Street lawyer and one of the most eloquent supporters of the Sage of Auburn," his fellow New Yorker William Henry Seward said, according to historian Michael Burlingame.[53] Evarts had won such a name for himself in the law and in politics and his reputation for persuasive speaking was so well-known, that he was chosen to nominate Seward for president at the Republican convention in Chicago. During the war, Seward twice asked Evarts to sail to Great Britain to represent the interests of the United States. On the first occasion, it fell to Evarts to attempt to convince the British government to enforce its neutrality laws and prohibit the launching of gunboats intended for the Confederacy. On the second trip, in 1864, Evarts engaged the British on the progress of the war and the duties of neutrals, which he also commenced in a cross-channel visit to France.[54] The missions that Evarts undertook to Europe during the war made his name conspicuous as a lawyer in the United States. It is not surprising, then, that when Speed sought assistance in the prosecution of Davis that Evarts, with backing by William H. Seward, would be brought on for that role.

By August 29, Speed told the cabinet that Evarts, Clifford, and an attorney from Kentucky, Lovell Rousseau, had agreed to associate themselves with him for Davis's trial. Benjamin Butler was suggested as a cocounsel on the case. Speed did not dismiss the possibility of bringing him on board, but the prospect of Butler proving to be an "unpleasant associate" became a topic of conversation. No one doubted his ability as a trial attorney, but it was thought that his personality might prove to be alienating to other counsel. Speed was open to Butler but thought it prudent to consult the other members of the prosecution team.[55] Butler would never be brought on as counsel for the government. His exclusion, given how deeply despised he was in the South and how polarizing he was even in the North, was a sensible decision by Speed.

Lucius H. Chandler

The federal district attorney for the Eastern District of Virginia was Lucius H. Chandler. Richmond, Virginia, was within the district, which made Chandler's court the potential venue for prosecutions of rebels. Jefferson Davis had directed the conduct of the Civil War from Richmond. If Davis was to be indicted and tried for treason in Virginia, Chandler would likely prove to be the U.S. attorney in whose district the case would be tried. There is no evidence that Chandler sought this distinction or that he relished the opportunity to play a part in the trial, though many attorneys seeking to enhance their reputations might have savored the prospect.

A transplanted Yankee, Chandler had graduated from Colby University in Waterville, Maine, at age nineteen.[56] He married Susan, a young woman from Virginia, and they had at least five children over a nine-year span, all of whom were born in either Maine or Massachusetts. Eventually, the family moved to Virginia, where Chandler found himself at the start of the war.[57] The life of a person from the North living in a southern state immediately before the outbreak of the war was not easy. The scant evidence that can be found about Chandler would lead to the conclusion that he was a genial man who wanted to be liked by his neighbors, not an individual who sought out confrontation. Neither characteristic would be helpful in his role in the Jefferson Davis trial.

Chandler had not supported the Republican ticket in 1860. Instead, he had thrown his support behind John Bell and Edward Everett of the Constitutional Union Party in the presidential election. Chandler had joined William M. Evarts as a speaker in New York for the election of the Union ticket.[58] After Lincoln's election and the secession of the South, he joined thousands in the Norfolk area of Virginia as a Union man during the war. Norfolk was a major naval base for the federal government; as soon as Gideon Welles was appointed secretary of the navy, he began to replace much of the leadership of the base. Chandler, as a Union Party man, traveled to Washington, D.C., in an attempt to convince Welles to retain many of his friends.[59] Despite meeting with mixed success, he was clearly trying to use his political influence to advance the interests of his friends and himself in northern Virginia.

Like many lawyers, Chandler had an interest in politics that had led him to run for the United States House of Representatives on more than one occasion. He won a seat in the House from the second district in Virginia in the election of May 1863, garnering 778 votes out of 779 cast, but faced resistance in taking his seat. To his chagrin, his election was not immediately recognized as legitimate; his bid to be seated was referred to the Committee of Elections, and an investigation was had into the vote. Nearly a year after his electoral victory, the committee made findings that kept Chandler from occupying the office. In short, the committee found that the second district comprised eleven counties, but votes were only cast in Norfolk County, while "all the other counties composing this district, except that of Norfolk, were either under the entire control and occupation of the rebels, or so nearly so that no man could go to the polls in safety, if any had been opened for the reception of the votes."[60] The congressional conclusion was "that in no proper sense can the vote in one county be treated as the choice of the other ten counties, prevented by the strong arm of the rebellion from expressing any wish at the ballot-box," and Chandler was denied a spot in the Thirty-Eighth Congress.[61] Until he took on the Davis prosecution, Chandler, who was characterized as a brilliant orator, was perhaps best known for his speech in the failed defense of his seat, which was described by the *Richmond Whig* as "a magnificent argument."[62] Despite this, Chandler was not able to sway enough votes to be seated.

Chandler failed in his bid to become a federal congressman while he held the post of consul for the United States at Matanzas, a municipality and province in Cuba.[63] It was an office that he had held since being nominated in 1861 and confirmed in February 1862.[64] There is no evidence that he ever served as consul in Cuba. Fortune smiled upon him, however, and Chandler's name was soon before the Senate for confirmation as Lincoln's nominee for the post of U.S. attorney for the Eastern District of Virginia. This office would assume oversized importance in comparison to other federal attorneys in the postwar period. The prosecution of Davis and other rebel leaders under indictment in Virginia for treason was a responsibility of immense moment. Nominated on June 18, 1864, Chandler was referred favorably by the Senate Committee on the Judiciary only nine days later and confirmed three days after that.[65]

At age fifty-two, Chandler began work as the United States attorney for the Eastern District of Virginia under very unusual circumstances. As a result of the rebellion, the number of attorneys who were licensed to practice in the court in Richmond, even in November 1865, was reduced to Chandler and one other attorney. Every other attorney was disqualified by virtue of an inability to take the "iron-clad" oath, the loyalty oath required by the federal government for prospective members of the bar. When the constitutionality of the oath was argued before the federal court, the lawyer arguing that it was unconstitutional was a recently elected Virginia state senator who was not even licensed to practice in federal court.[66] Chandler, by virtue of being the U.S. attorney for the Virginia district encompassing Richmond, had the Davis treason prosecution land on his desk.

Many lawyers, recognizing that prosecuting the president of the Confederacy would make their reputation as an attorney, would have aggressively pursued the professional opportunity. Not so with Chandler, who immediately balked. Chandler "felt all along, that it was quite important that I should know what the views of the administration were in reference to the trial of Mr. Davis."[67] Chandler went to Washington to speak to President Johnson on two or three occasions to determine whether Johnson thought the case should be tried. According to Chandler, each conversation ended with Chandler not getting a very clear answer to that question. Instead, he felt that Johnson merely referred him to the attorney general on the important matter.

President Johnson had received correspondence about Chandler that proved to be correct. John Underwood, the district judge for the Eastern District of Virginia, wrote to Johnson on July 10, 1865, about Chandler. Underwood penned the missive to "state one apprehension and my reason for it." The judge had learned that Attorney General Speed had asked Chandler about a special application for pardon that had been made by a recently disloyal citizen. Speed's reliance on Chandler's opinion troubled Underwood, who said, "Mr. Chandler is a very clever gentleman and my friend, but being remarkably social in his disposition and long an aspirant for a seat in Congress, the rich rebels have urged him to come out for Congress and have induced him to do so in opposition to a candidate nominated by a convention of union men promising him their hearty support which of course is equivalent to his election."[68] Underwood's concern was that Chandler would become beholden to the rebels for political support, which could sway the prosecutor's view in favor of lenient, and perhaps unwarranted, pardons. Although Underwood's hesitation about Chandler did not involve the Davis prosecution, the judge's fear must have extended to the handling of the case if he thought that Chandler's gratitude and political ambition would lead the attorney to make poor judgments on pardons.

The United States attorney was not completely comfortable proceeding with the case, and the hesitancy that Chandler displayed in his approach to the case would cause problems from the beginning. While it is impossible to ascertain the precise reason for his hesitancy, there are several possibilities that stand out. First, the prosecution would be unpopular with the former Confederates among whom he lived. It is difficult for some lawyers to proceed with a case that negatively affects their personal lives. The Davis prosecution certainly fell into this category. Since he had run for Congress, Chandler must have recognized that his political aspirations would be compromised, if not entirely destroyed, by the trial. Yet however strong these reasons might have been in assessing the foundation for his tentative start, the historical record points to a lack of professional confidence and competence on Chandler's part. Fear of failure causes many lawyers to recoil from handling major cases. Chandler appears to fall into that category of advocate. Finally, heading an office that was so small meant that every decision devolved upon his shoulders. It was a difficult post to occupy and one whose challenges Lucius Chandler would not rise to meet.

Trial Teams for the Case of the Century

Two of the nation's most prominent lawyers were now engaged in the Davis treason trial. With Evarts and O'Conor once again squaring off against each other, both the conservative and radical elements of the political spectrum were well represented. It was expected to be a highly publicized trial with significant constitutional implications to be played out before a deeply interested public. The parties appeared to be very motivated to try the case, relying on advocates who would leave no evidentiary stone unturned. The reputations of both lawyers also guaranteed that they would make compelling presentations of their differing perspectives of how the constitutional questions involved in a treason trial after the war.

There were decisions that remained unresolved. Attorney General Speed announced that he intended to lead the prosecution against Jefferson Davis personally. His resolve to do so had several effects on the case. First, Evarts and Chandler would not play the leading role in the treason trial—Speed would. Evarts was the most accomplished lawyer of the three, so the decision would cast him in a supporting role, when it might have been better for him to act as the lead attorney. This assessment must be weighed, however, against the argument that Speed was a man from a slave state, courageous enough to have withstood a call to disunion. Speed's advocacy in a southern state, calling for Jefferson Davis to hang for treason, may have compensated for a more polished New York attorney, believed in the South to be an abolitionist, calling for the same result. Second, Chandler would easily be able to put off essential work on the case because Speed was the lead attorney. The defense had neither the capacity nor the inclination to force the case to trial. Underwood would look to the government for word on when the case was ready to try and would show himself very respectful of the preparation that he knew was essential to the trial of this major crime. It proved to be up to the prosecution to prepare and bring the Jefferson Davis case to trial. Unless James Speed made very clear the tasks each man was to accomplish and then made certain that the work was done, the case could simply languish for lack of prosecutorial leadership. But that, perhaps, was only clear in hindsight.

7

TWO JUDGES FOR ONE TRIAL

Chase has mental power and resources, but he is politically ambitious and restless . . . he will be likely to use [the Supreme Court justice position] for political advancement.

—Gideon Welles

THE JEFFERSON DAVIS prosecution had a very unique quality: there were two judges. The genesis of this strange feature was likely the Aaron Burr treason prosecution. Chief Justice John Marshall, sitting alongside federal judge Cyrus Griffin, presided over the trial of the former vice president. At the beginning of the nineteenth century, Supreme Court justices also acted as trial court judges.

In 1807, at the time of Burr's treason trial, each member of the Supreme Court rode a circuit that included a specific geographical part of the United States. Burr was indicted in Richmond, Virginia, which happened to be Marshall's circuit. That made Marshall the member of the Supreme Court who, along with Griffin, presided over Burr's circuit court criminal trial. From a practical standpoint, the potential difficulty of trying a case before two judges is in the rulings of the court. If the judges disagree on a point of law, there is no third judge acting as a tiebreaker. According to Dumas Malone, biographer of Thomas Jefferson, the trouble was resolved in the Burr case because Cyrus Griffin "played a negligible part in the proceedings."[1] This would not be true in 1865. The district judge in the Jefferson Davis case would play the larger part in the courtroom, while the chief justice of the Supreme Court assumed a greater role in the politics of the case.

Both judges were guided by American law on treason, which had been honed by John Marshall. In the Burr conspiracy trial, Marshall had considered the long history of treason rulings from Britain in juxtaposition with the American constitutional provisions on treason and set the legal precedent on many aspects of a treason trial. "Marshall was forced to clarify the constitutional meaning of treason" and determined that, under the Constitution, "treason consisted solely in actually 'levying war' against one's country or aiding and abetting the enemies of the country in time of war."[2] No one would argue in 1865 that Davis and the Confederacy had not levied war against the federal government. But there was another legal precedent set in the Burr prosecution that would cause many in the Union to question whether a treason prosecution against Davis was winnable. What if Davis had to be tried in Virginia?

Critically for the Jefferson Davis prosecution, Chief Justice Marshall expounded upon the question of constructive presence in 1807. This legal issue became a major hurdle for the federal prosecution in 1865. Jefferson Davis, as commander in chief of the Confederate army, had authorized the Army of Northern Virginia to advance into Maryland and Pennsylvania during the war. Confederate naval raids were also not uncommon up and down the New England seaboard. Was Davis, because he had authorized these military and naval incursions, constructively present under the constitutional law of treason? Marshall addressed that question from the bench in Burr's trial in 1807 and made it difficult for a federal prosecutor to argue that point in the affirmative. Marshall had decided that "the place in which a crime was committed is essential to an indictment, were it only to shew the jurisdiction of the court. It is also essential for the purpose of enabling the prisoner to make his defence. That at common law an indictment would have been defective, which did not mention the place in which the crime was committed, can scarcely be doubted. . . . This necessity is rendered the stronger by the constitutional provision that the offender 'shall be tried in the state and district wherein the crime shall have been committed.'"[3] If the federal government chose to put Jefferson Davis on trial for treason somewhere other than in Virginia, where he resided during the war, the indictment might be dismissed because it was brought in a jurisdiction not authorized by the Constitution. But could a conviction be gained in the former capital of the Confederacy?

Federal District Judge John C. Underwood

If Edwin Stanton and James Speed had their way, Judge John C. Underwood, the federal district judge for Virginia, would try Jefferson Davis. Judge Underwood had come to the bench in Virginia in a most roundabout manner. Born in central New York in 1809, Underwood graduated from Hamilton College, in Clinton, New York, before moving south to work as a tutor for the children of Edward B. Jackson, a slave owner in western Virginia. Underwood continued his education by studying law. In 1839, he married one of his former pupils, Maria Jackson, who happened to be a cousin of Thomas J. Jackson, the eccentric professor who became the renowned "Stonewall" Jackson. The marriage into one of Virginia's first families was a good one for Underwood. By the 1850s, he had become a well-respected planter and farmer in Clarke County, Virginia, one of the very northernmost counties in the state. But the marriage was good for more than simply economic reasons. Underwood was a stouthearted, independent man who, despite living and working in a slave state, was antislavery. His wife, Maria, shared his views just as deeply and courageously.

Not surprisingly, Underwood's political and social leanings caused him considerable trouble in Virginia. His decision to attend the Republican convention in Philadelphia and support John C. Fremont for president in 1856 caused a rupture with his neighbors in Virginia that eventually drove him from his home. He was one of only a handful of men from the South at the Republican convention and served on the resolutions committee. While in Philadelphia, Underwood made a speech "enunciating the doctrines held by Washington and Jefferson on slavery."[4] He not only quoted Jefferson's statement that "he trembled for his country when he reflected that God is just" but also spoke of spending time at the table of James Madison and hearing the elderly man expound upon the evils of slavery.[5] Then he embarked on a speaking tour of the North in support of Fremont, often assailing the negative consequences of slavery on the free white population of the South.[6] His efforts were widely reported in the nation's press and did not go unnoticed by his neighbors. They were not well received.

On July 26, 1856, many of the prominent citizens of Clarke County, Virginia, met at the courthouse to take action against Underwood. A committee on resolutions was appointed with sixteen members who resolved that Underwood had committed "an atrocious fraud" by attending the Republican convention as a Virginia delegate when no citizen of Clarke County had ever authorized him to attend the convention in that capacity. The resolution accused Underwood of having made statements there that would have earned him a "felon's reward," if true, and of conspiring against the South. Finding that Underwood stood "guilty of moral treason, at least, if not legal treason, against the Commonwealth of Virginia" for his speech at the convention, they sought to punish him in absentia. The men unanimously resolved, "We have no respect for the sickly, morbid sentiment, which holds slavery to be a 'moral evil.'" The committee then agreed not to tolerate Underwood's presence in their community any longer, declaring "that if he dare return to reside, we will take steps to eject him—peaceably if we can, forcibly if we must."[7] Since Underwood's whereabouts were unknown, the men indicated that they would have their resolutions printed in northern papers for him to be given notice of his eviction. By early December 1856, a letter from Turner Ashby addressed to Underwood was printed in papers throughout the North, offering him personal protection only if he returned to Virginia to settle up his business with an eye to leaving the state forever. Ashby closed with a thinly veiled threat: "Should you persist in renewing your citizenship among us, we shall withdraw our protection and leave you to suffer whatever may follow at the hands of the community."[8] The ill treatment by his neighbors angered many people in the North.

The *Portland Advertiser* in Maine wrote that Underwood, "laboring under the fearful hallucination that this is a free country, attended the People's Convention in Philadelphia; for which offence he has been ordered to leave the State."[9] While the nation watched the unfolding drama, Underwood's neighbors were trying to force him out of Virginia for his advocacy of free labor and antislavery sentiments. The citizens of Clarke County appeared to be oblivious to the hubris that their actions exhibited to readers across the northern section of the nation.

The outrage over his treatment spilled over into Congress. Philemon Bliss, a Republican congressman from Ohio, addressed Underwood's treatment from the floor of the House on January 15, 1857. As the debate intensified over the extension of slavery into the territories, Underwood became a symbol of the intolerance of the slave South toward those within the borders of slave states who disagreed with slavery. Bliss spoke about Underwood's plight, reminding his colleagues that citizens who still held dear the liberty fought for by the founding fathers would speak up against slavery, "but slavery forbids it." Having the courage to express an antislavery sentiment places a person in the position of being "guilty of disloyalty to the slave interest." He continued his defense of Underwood and the attempts made by the transplanted New Yorker to bring free labor to Virginia:

> The poor around him found a friend, and one who sought to aid them in that career, that gives character to the free-State laborer; and instead of being surrounded with gangs of ragged and shirking slaves, the deficiency of whose thriftless labor must be supplied by the sale of their young men and women; he gave employment to the dependent free white, and was thus enabling them to overcome their doom. Thus enlisted in the elevation of labor, he was of course a Republican, and vindicated his principles by his action. This man, thus noble and true, not even suspected of violating any law, just or unjust, merely for the security of slave domination, is driven from his property and home, and thus are crushed his experiment of free speech, and his attempt to elevate free labor. Virginia, not he, feels the blow; for the name of John C. Underwood will be honored.[10]

Underwood, not understanding the seriousness of the threats against him, attempted to return to his home in February 1857. As he exited a railway car at Markham Station near his home, he was met by Turner Ashby, Dr. Thomas H. Fisher, and a crowd. Underwood's wife later wrote that Ashby "rushed out like a madman" at her husband, exclaiming, "Tar and feathers—let's give him a coat of tar." Dr. Fisher took issue with Maria Underwood's rendition of the facts. He wrote that "upon seeing Mr. Underwood, he [Ashby] was much excited, and in reply to a remonstrance from me, said to me in an audible voice, but not to the crowd, 'don't you think we ought to give him a coat of tar.'"[11] The distinction that Dr. Fisher drew was one without a difference. That Ashby did not direct the audible statement toward the crowd would be of no significance when the wife of the man that he suggests should be tarred and feathered is within earshot. Whether Ashby attempted to incite the crowd against Underwood or not, it was clear that his return to Virginia would be troubled. Despite his protestations that he continued to be "a citizen of Virginia, and a temporary sojourner" in New York, Underwood quickly determined that his "life, to say the least, would be exceedingly insecure" if he remained, and he soon sold much of his property and moved away from northern Virginia.[12]

Underwood's expulsion from Virginia did not end his efforts to change the lives of his former neighbors. From his new home in New York City, he was elected secretary of the American Homestead and Emigration Company, an organization that raised over $200,000 in less than half an hour after its books were opened.[13] The company was formed to encourage the emigration of free men into Virginia. The board of directors hoped to infuse free-soil men into the border states of the South by making wholesale purchases of large tracts of cheap land and selling that land to actual settlers for small farms. The *New York Herald,* announcing the formation of the company, attributed the homestead movement as "but one of the accidents consequent upon the passage of the Kansas-Nebraska bill."[14] The southern press viewed the company as a serious threat to the region. The *Daily Advocate* in Baton Rouge, Louisiana, warned that "immediately our land will be filled with vagabonds and paupers of every description" and urged the people of Virginia to "hasten to repel the invasions of Abolitionism before it is too late."[15]

Underwood read papers and gave lectures to antislavery audiences in an effort to educate the northern public, traveling from New York to Portland, Maine.[16] He also became involved gathering subscriptions, for no wages, in eastern states for the publication of a tract called "Helper's Impending Crisis of the South."[17] When he appeared before the Compensated Emancipation Society and spoke against the compensated emancipation of slaves as immoral, instead arguing that the estimated billion dollars be spent to educate poor whites, the southern press published an account of his appearance and noted that "the meeting is regarded as unfavorable to the plan of compensated emancipation."[18] His activities were closely monitored by an anxious citizenry in his home state.

After the Virginia border was electrified by the John Brown raid, Underwood became the subject of intense scrutiny. Governor Henry Wise was telegraphed a rumor of an armed invasion by 250 men near Berry Ferry, Virginia, near Underwood's former home. Wise immediately dispatched a military force of 40 men and two cannons to repel the invasion. Armed citizens and the Clarke Guards joined the force and conducted a search of Clarke County and the homes of individuals thought to be antislavery. According to the *Berryville (Va.) Conservator,* the militia "searched several houses—among them the unoccupied tenement of the notorious John C. Underwood—but found nothing worthy of consideration."[19] It was apparently lucky for Underwood that no one was home, as the paper reported that "upon application for entrance into the house of a known Abolitionist, the wife of the man living there (her husband being absent) seized an ax and defied their entrance. They finally wrested the weapon from her grasp, but not without first giving her a bayonet wound on the arm."[20] As tensions rose, men like Underwood faced deadly threats to their lives and property in Virginia. Underwood was deeply despised by the white secessionists in Virginia.

When Virginia seceded from the Union on April 17, 1861, Underwood remained in the North, working for the federal government. He worked as an auditor in the Treasury Department under Salmon Chase and was involved in establishing the Tax Commissioner's Board for the sale of the estates of rebels for nonpayment of direct taxes.[21] He continued his work as a social progressive, serving on the board of directors of the Institute for the Education of Colored Youth in the District of Columbia, which had been established by Congress in 1863.[22] It was then that he was considered for appointment to the bench of the District Court of the Eastern District of Virginia, comprising the area east of the Blue Ridge Mountains and the area of northern Virginia now occupied by Union military forces.[23] Nominated by Lincoln and confirmed by the Senate, there was at least one ambitious politician ready to take credit for Underwood's selection. The *New York Herald* commented that he was appointed "at the instance of Secretary Chase."[24] But it was Attorney General Edward Bates who sent Underwood, on March 28, 1863, a commission appointing him judge of the District Court of the United States for the Eastern District of Virginia.[25]

It was announced that the court would be organized on June 1, 1863, at Norfolk, Virginia. Underwood, the well-known antislavery man, was going to be the federal judge in the Old Dominion. The northern press relished the appointment, characterizing it as Underwood being called "to administer justice among traitors who but a few years ago drove him from the state on account of his anti-slavery convictions."[26]

A Radical Judge in Northern Virginia

Underwood's tenure as judge began in controversial fashion. In November 1863, he approved the forfeiture of real and personal property of fifteen rebels, including three men who had previously served in the United States Navy but joined the Confederate navy after the beginning of the war. The ruling was based upon his interpretation of paragraph two of Article III, Section 3, of the Constitution, which provides that "the Congress shall have the power to declare the punishment of treason, but no attainder of treason shall work corruption of blood, or forfeiture except during the life of the person attainted."[27] His reading of the constitutional provision found that the word *except* meant "unless." Under that analysis, if a person was found to be treasonous and was still alive, his property was subject to confiscation. The southern press expressed no surprise that this decision could be made by "a notorious Abolitionist," while the *New York Herald* presumed that "the subject, in some shape or other, will be brought before the Supreme Court of the United States, at its approaching term, for a final decision; and, as upon its interpretation of that one word, 'except,' will depend the inheritance or confiscation of thousands of millions of Southern property, the decision will be a matter of supreme importance."[28] Judge Underwood's controversial ruling jeopardized the property of every living rebel officer who had ever served in the U.S. military forces.

Southerners found Underwood's judgments appalling. One former Confederate official examined the document and expressed outrage that the Constitution was being tread upon and "*violated* wholesale." Rumors of Underwood being corrupt began to swirl; for example, he was "said to have made large purchases of lands under his own decrees at prices not exceeding a year's rent."[29]

Confiscation became a powerful tool in Underwood's court, and he proved to be aggressive in cases involving rebels. In one instance, an attorney appeared to seek the reversal of a decree of confiscation against Dr. Orlando Fairfax of Alexandria, Virginia. Underwood "informed the attorney, from the bench, that he would allow no appearance for any 'rebel' or 'traitor'; that this was the rule of his court as before that publicly announced, and that he had in every case ordered the appearance of counsel for, and the answer of 'rebels,' to be stricken from the files."[30] In fact, the record shows that Fairfax faced the same reception in three different cases in Underwood's court, with the same result. In his short tenure as a federal judge, Underwood proved himself ready to administer harsh justice against rebels in Virginia. While his rulings were decried in the South, he was admired in certain Radical Republican circles in the North.

Radical Republicans looked to Underwood's experience in Virginia in trying to determine how to address Reconstruction. One of the concerns was the fear of a resurgence of the Democratic Party after the war's end. The judge counseled the Joint Committee on Reconstruction against allowing the Democratic Party to become the dominant party. Underwood believed that if the

Copperheads of the North joined with the former rebel party in the South, this could occur. And if it did, the Democratic Party would sponsor and pass a national "acknowledgment of the Confederate debt, and compensation for their negroes."[31] The result would be that antebellum wealth would be restored to the very people who had brought the rebellion and whose finances had been ruined by the war. The wealthy elite would be restored to power.

From the perspective of many Virginians, Underwood's testimony to Congress exposed an agenda on his part to impoverish the prosperous families of the South. Yet Underwood was the judge hearing confiscation cases in their state. He was perceived by those appearing before him as a vengeful tyrant bent on advocating a hostile position rather than the voice of an impartial tribunal. By the war's end, Judge Underwood was not a magistrate before whom any rebel leader charged with treason would want to find himself.

Had these individuals known the complete story, they would not have felt any better. Before any indictments were ever handed down, Underwood had met with President Johnson and discussed the question of whether there should be prosecutions "of those who had been engaged in the rebellion, and he [Johnson] expressed himself very decidedly on the subject in favor of prosecution."[32] Underwood made no secret of his views—he agreed.

Chief Justice Salmon P. Chase

The chief justice of the U.S. Supreme Court, Salmon P. Chase, had occupied that seat for less than six months when Jefferson Davis was captured in Georgia. He succeeded Roger Taney, the author of the *Dred Scott* decision, who had died on October 12, 1864, at the age of eighty-seven. Chase brought a dramatically different point of view to the bench than that of his predecessor. Born in 1808 in New Hampshire, when Chase was nine, he was sent to Ohio, after the death of his father, and was raised by an uncle. The education that he received was first-class. He graduated from Dartmouth College in the 1820s and studied law while working as a teacher. Once admitted to the bar, Chase returned to Ohio, where he gained a reputation as a staunch abolitionist, taking up the cases of runaway slaves as part of his practice. His antislavery credentials were unassailable.

Chase became active in Ohio politics and became a leading voice in the slavery question plaguing the nation. He served in the U.S. Senate from

1849 through 1855 and returned to Ohio to serve as governor from 1855 through 1860. An early member of the Republican Party and one of its brightest lights, Chase threw his hat into the 1860 presidential primary race. The nomination appeared to be between William H. Seward and Chase until the Chicago convention failed to nominate either man and, instead, turned to a dark horse candidate by the name of Abraham Lincoln.

Losing the nomination, especially to the Illinois lawyer, was a bitter blow to Chase, who considered himself much better qualified than Lincoln to serve as president. But he agreed to take a prominent position in the Lincoln cabinet, and the Treasury Department became his. It was a good fit for Chase. He ran the department energetically and with great innovation. The government was heavily in debt when the war began. To compound the problem, Congress was not in session, so the new Treasury secretary was relegated to putting together bank loans to pay for the war. Lincoln also relied on him to organize a small group of men to contract for weapons and supplies, a job that ordinarily would have been accomplished by the secretary of war. Later, a banking bill that Chase authored passed and filled government coffers. The leadership that he displayed allowed the war to be financed and prosecuted efficiently. Without the money to pay for the immense cost of the effort, the war could not have been won.

But Chase never recovered from his loss to Lincoln and his belief that he served a lesser man than himself. Instead of putting his ego aside, Chase schemed and plotted to enhance his own reputation at Lincoln's expense. The president was a shrewd man and knew of Chase's attempts to undermine his authority but kept Chase in the cabinet precisely because of his value to the war effort. By June 1864, though, Chase's efforts to undermine Lincoln became too much for the president to overlook. When Chase offered his resignation (as he had three times before), Lincoln surprised him by accepting it. "Your resignation of the office of Secretary of the Treasury is accepted," wrote the president. "Of all I have said in commendation of your ability and fidelity, I have nothing to unsay; and yet you and I have reached a point of mutual embarrassment in our official relation which it seems can not be overcome, or longer sustained, consistently with the public service."[33] Chase was dumbstruck. A friend of Chase, Lucius Chittenden, confided to the president that the loss of the Treasury secretary would be catastrophic for the nation. Lincoln disagreed and pointedly told the man that Chase "thinks he has become indispensable to the country."[34] Lincoln knew better and was unwilling to budge from his decision to accept the resignation.

When Chief Justice Taney died in October of that year, Lincoln turned back to his old Treasury secretary. It was not for a lack of interest in the vacant Supreme Court seat. Just within his own cabinet, Montgomery Blair, Edwin Stanton, and Edward Bates each had a strong interest in being appointed. But Lincoln chose Chase despite the bitter intrigue that his former cabinet officer had engaged in against him. It was Chase's intellect, his clear ability, and his commitment to the principles of the Republican Party that drew Lincoln to the conclusion that Chase was the right man for the job. So, on December 15, within the crowded Supreme Court, Salmon P. Chase was sworn in as only the sixth chief justice of the court. The sole doubt that Lincoln was known to express about the appointment was whether Chase would be able to put aside his unbridled ambition to become president and not engage in the political intrigue to which Chase had too often succumbed. If Chase failed to set aside his presidential aspirations, Lincoln feared that Chase's work as chief justice might be compromised. Lincoln was a perceptive judge of character.

Rather than retiring from the political arena, Chase continued to privately attempt to influence the terms under which the South would be reconstructed. He wrote to Gen. William T. Sherman on January 2, 1865, asking the Union commander to "avoid any appearance of harshness and severity" toward African Americans, after Sherman had filed a report that classed the freedmen with cattle needing to be ridded from Sherman's camp. Chase reminded the senior officer that "the Attorney General, in a well considered opinion, has asserted the citizenship of those who are free. And it seems to me not doubtful that, in the political reorganization of the states in insurrection, political, as well as natural, rights, must be conceded to a portion at least of the colored population. For myself, indeed, I freely say that I see no reason why all citizens may not vote subject only to such restrictions as are applicable to all irrespective of color."[35] While the point of his letter to Sherman was laudable, Chase would step further out into politics the more time went on.

The new chief justice was aware of the perception of impropriety that might follow his opining on these critical topics. Writing to Francis Lieber, the respected legal scholar who had written opinions regarding the conduct of the war, Chase confided that "upon matters which cannot possibly present a question for adjudication by the Courts, I feel as free to express my opinion as ever."[36] With that caveat, Chase then proceeded to discuss several issues. He wrote of universal suffrage and the ability of the Union to impose terms upon the defeated southern states. "It is clear," he told Lieber, "that, involved as the National Government is, in a civil war with the Rebel States, it can, and must, make peace upon some terms; & these terms must be agreed upon between the National Government and that body of citizens in each Rebel State, whom that Government is willing to recognize as competent to act for the State."[37] It is disingenuous to believe that Chase did not recognize at this stage of the war that suffrage and the terms under which the states would be readmitted to the Union might come before his court for adjudication. Less than a month after being sworn in, Chase was back in politics, although entering through the back door.

By the middle of April, he was writing directly to Lincoln about the readmittance of Virginia and cautioning the president against yielding to "pressure for the recognition of the rebel organization on condition of profession of loyalty."[38] The very next day, he wrote another lengthy letter to Lincoln, discussing the terms under which amnesty might be offered to the rebels, the participation of African Americans in Reconstruction, the restoration to the Union of the seceded states, universal suffrage, and the conditions under which Louisiana should be readmitted to the Union. Chase's letter to Lincoln was not just private, personal advice on political questions. On the same day that he wrote Lincoln, Chase also wrote Massachusetts senator Charles Sumner, a Radical Republican, enclosing a copy of the letter that had been sent to Lincoln. He wanted Sumner to know where he stood on these issues and that he had sent his views to the president.

On April 14, Chase sent Stanley Matthews, a superior court judge in Cincinnati, Ohio, a letter. "Now comes the question of reconstruction," he wrote. "I was anxious that it should be provided for in advance eighteen months ago; and my plan was a very simple one. I proposed that the loyal citizens should be enrolled." He acknowledged that his plan had not been adopted: "And now the President has given a sort of sanction, & a pretty strong one too, to the meeting of the rebel Legislature, with a view to its putting itself right by a simple declaration of submission & acquiescence in Emancipation. This greatly alarms those of us who want the hydra of rebellion killed not scotched; & there are signs of trouble."[39]

Perhaps a man like Chase may be forgiven for not scrupulously abiding by a duty to not address questions that might come before his court for decision when he had been, like Chase, involved in the political process for so many years prior to becoming chief justice. Maybe his passion for causes that we now concede were the right path to advocate make us judge his actions less harshly. Had he been taking positions less admirable, however, he would indeed be judged severely. The consequence of his unwillingness to withdraw from politics would later have effects, for better or worse, on the treason trial of Jefferson Davis.

Fig. 1. "Jeff's Race for the Last Ditch"—northern press depiction of Davis's capture, May 10, 1865. F. N. Carter, G. D. Russell & Co., Boston, 1865. From the author's collection.

Fig. 2. "Jeff's Last Shift"—Davis's capture as depicted in the northern press. *New York Daily News,* May 15, 1865.

Fig. 3. Southern press photograph of "Jefferson Davis—In the Riding Dress He Wore When Captured." Source unknown [1869]. American Civil War Museum.

Fig. 4. Davis in his Fort Monroe prison cell. Alfred Waud, 1865.
Library of Congress.

Fig. 5. Northern satire of Jefferson Davis in his Fort Monroe prison cell.
Gibson & Co., Cincinnati, 1865. Library of Congress.

Fig. 6. Charles O'Conor, Jefferson Davis's defense attorney. Brady's National Photographic Portrait Galleries, between 1855 and 1865. Library of Congress.

Fig. 7. James Speed, Lincoln's last attorney general. Brady's National Photographic Portrait Galleries, between 1860 and 1865. Library of Congress.

Fig. 8. William M. Evarts, prominent New York City lawyer hired to assist with the prosecution. Brady's National Photographic Portrait Galleries, between 1865 and 1880. Library of Congress.

Fig. 9. John C. Underwood, U.S. district judge presiding over the Davis prosecution. Brady's National Photographic Portrait Galleries, between 1865 and 1880. Library of Congress.

Fig. 10. Salmon P. Chase, chief justice of the U.S. Supreme Court, presided over the Davis prosecution. Brady's National Photographic Portrait Galleries, between 1861 and 1865. Library of Congress.

Fig. 11. The interracial grand jury that indicted Jefferson Davis. Source unknown [1868]. American Civil War Museum.

Fig. 12. Jefferson Davis being led into the courtroom for his habeas corpus hearing. *Frank Leslie's Illustrated Newspaper,* June 1, 1867.

Fig. 13. Horace Greeley meets Jefferson Davis at Richmond. *Harper's Weekly,* June 1, 1867. From the author's collection.

Fig. 15. Trial of Jefferson Davis, *Harper's Weekly,* June 1867. From the author's collection.

Fig. 14. Horace Greeley, editor of the *New York Tribune,* who posted part of Jefferson Davis's bond. Photographer unknown [between 1860 and 1865]. National Archives.

Fig. 16. Robert Ould, former Confederate commissioner of prisoner exchange, then defense counsel for Davis. Francis Trevelyan Miller and Robert Sampson Lanier, *The Photographic History of the Civil War,* 10 vols. (New York: Review of Reviews Co., 1911), 7:101.

Fig. 17. Davis released on bail. *Harper's Weekly,* June 1, 1867.

Confederate Veteran.

Published Monthly in the Interest of Confederate Veterans and Kindred Topics.

Price 5 Cents. Yearly 50 Cents. Vol. I. Nashville, Tenn., May, 1893. No. 5. S. A. Cunningham, Editor and Manager.

JEFFERSON DAVIS. (TAKEN SOON AFTER HIS RELEASE FROM PRISON.)

FOSTER & WEBB, PRINTERS, NASHVILLE, TENN.

Fig. 18. Jefferson Davis, taken soon after his release from prison.
Confederate Veteran (Nashville), May 1893.

Fig. 19. Henry Stanbery, attorney general under Andrew Johnson. Brady's National Photographic Portrait Galleries, between 1860 and 1865. National Archives.

Fig. 21. Richard Henry Dana Jr., a prominent attorney brought on to assist with the prosecution. Asa Eaton, ca. 1868. National Portrait Gallery.

Fig. 20. Jefferson Davis's interracial petit jury. David Anderson, ca. May 1867. American Civil War Museum.

Fig. 22. Jefferson and Varina Davis in Montreal after the war. William Notman, 1869. American Civil War Museum.

8

THE HENRY WIRZ TRIAL FOR CRIMES AT ANDERSONVILLE

> Their sufferings, and what is called the inhumanity of their treatment, were in great measure an unavoidable necessity.
>
> —Alexander H. Stephens

FROM HIS CELL in Fort Monroe, Jefferson Davis was not permitted to have any direct correspondence with anyone. Any type of letter or message to Davis had to be sent first to the War Department for review by officers there. Not everything was allowed to be forwarded to Davis. He was considered terribly dangerous to the federal government. Charles O'Conor, his newly retained lawyer, did not even know exactly where to find his client. Consequently, in his first letter to the former Confederate president, on June 2, 1865, he stated in the transmittal letter to Gen. Edward D. Townsend, an assistant adjutant general in Washington, D.C., that "the statements in the public prints render it doubtful where the gentleman to whom it is addressed may be confined at this moment, and consequently I am constrained to request that you will overlook the omission of an address and nevertheless cause the note to be delivered."[1]

Enclosed with the transmittal letter was the introductory letter O'Conor had written to Davis. It was carefully worded and not completely truthful. O'Conor was leery of the prying eyes and doubtful motives of federal officials and was careful not to reveal how he had been retained. He feared, no doubt, adverse consequences for the people who had hired him. Consequently, he revealed little in his letter. "Dear Sir," he wrote falsely,

> Gentlemen who have no personal acquaintance with yourself, and who never had any connection by birth, residence, or otherwise with any of the Southern States, have requested me to volunteer as counsel for the defense in case you should be arraigned upon an indictment which has been announced in the newspapers. No less in conformity with my own sense of

> propriety than in compliance with their wishes I beg leave to tender my services accordingly. I will be happy to attend at any time and place that you may indicate in order to confer with yourself or others in relation to the defense. The Department of War having given its assent to the transmission of this open letter through the proper military authorities I infer that if my professional aid be accepted you will have full permission to confer with me in writing and orally at personal interviews, as you may judge to be necessary or desirable.[2]

There were several untruthful statements made by O'Conor, which he must have known would not be believed by War Department officials reading his letter. He claimed that he had been contacted by men who were not from the South, who had no connection to the southern cause, and who did not know Jefferson Davis personally, nevertheless asking him to volunteer to represent the former Confederate president. No one would have believed that transparent lie. But O'Conor did not care about being thought a liar. His handling of this initial letter reveals his sophistication in high-profile cases.

O'Conor released his request to the New York press. He knew that Andrew Johnson and Edwin Stanton would face a storm of criticism if the administration did not allow Davis access to an attorney. After all, the Sixth Amendment to the Constitution guaranteed the assistance of counsel for every person accused of a crime. If Davis was not accorded his right to an attorney, public opinion would quickly coalesce around the idea that the treason trial was a sham. O'Conor's offer to represent Davis spread quickly and worked to the lawyer's advantage. "Even those most bitter against the imprisoned rebel, express gratification that he is to be defended by a lawyer of Mr. O'Conor's unsurpassed learning and ability. They say that preservation of the forms of administering justice are not less important than the punishment of the guilty," the *New York World* opined in an article that was reprinted around the country.[3]

As O'Conor waited for a reply to his letter, he wasted no time in bringing attention to the Jefferson Davis cause. On June 8, he was announced as the person who would preside over a meeting at the Cooper Institute to discuss reconstruction and reunion. It was known that the meeting would be against the prosecution of former Confederates for treason. That night, the Cooper Institute was filled with an audience described by the *New York Herald* as "warm sympathizers with the rebels,"[4] but O'Conor did not appear. No reason was given for his absence. Still, it was the first hint that a strange mix of former political foes might help shape the dialogue about Davis's prosecution. Present were Horace Greeley, the abolitionist editor of the *New York Tribune;* Gerrit Smith, a man who had helped finance John Brown's foray into Harpers Ferry; and Henry Ward Beecher, the abolitionist Congregationalist clergyman. The meeting was not well received by much of the nation's press. "It will be seen by a glance," the *Herald* told its readers, "at the names of the signers to this call that Barnum's Happy Family does not afford a more striking illustration of the possibility of reversing the laws regulating the animal's kingdom than the association of such discordant spirits as these individuals were four years ago."[5]

Gerrit Smith was the main speaker, and his oration lasted over two hours. He warned that while the South had plunged the nation into war and was guilty of the great crime of the age, the North, if it persisted in trying to punish the South for treason, would be in danger of committing the mean crime of the age. Calling for an end to bloodshed, except for those guilty of murdering Lincoln or starving or murdering prisoners, Smith urged that Confederates not be put to trial for their lives for the crime of treason. After Smith finished his long speech, Greeley was called upon by the crowd to remark on the issues. According to newspaper accounts, he did not touch on the issue of treason but did say that anyone who had been paroled—even Lee, whom he saw as the worst of traitors—should not be prosecuted. So soon after the end of the war, these influential abolitionists now showed themselves to be unlikely allies of Jefferson Davis and his lawyer, Charles O'Conor, who had espoused such hateful positions before the war about African Americans held in bondage.

Davis Accepts O'Conor's Offer

Courage displayed on a battlefield does not necessarily translate into boldness in all areas of life. Nelson A. Miles, the general in charge of keeping Jefferson Davis in custody at Fort Monroe, would receive the Medal of Honor for the courage he displayed at Chancellorsville in 1863. A Massachusetts youth of twenty at the beginning of the war, Miles volunteered for the Union army and began a meteoric rise from lieutenant to major general in the short span of the war. Wounded four times in battle, Miles saw action at Antietam, Chancellorsville, the Wilderness, Spotsylvania Court House, and the Appomattox Campaign. But a person's initiative often reflects the character of the commander in charge. Miles was ultimately reporting to Edwin Stanton, a micromanaging boss not to be crossed.

Miles, no doubt, also remembered shackling Davis with what he correctly thought to be Stanton's explicit permission, only to find no support from the War Department when that issue became a national controversy. Once bitten, twice shy. Miles received O'Conor's correspondence to Jefferson Davis as well as the transmittal letter from General Townsend stating, "By direction of the Secretary of War I enclose herewith an open letter from Ch. O'Conor, Esq., of New York, dated June 2, 1865, to be delivered to Jefferson Davis. Please report its receipt."[6] Miles replied as requested but asked a question: "Shall I furnish Jeff. Davis writing materials to answer Mr. O'Conor's letter, received this a.m.?"[7] Apparently, Townsend felt unauthorized to go out on this limb, too, because his response revealed that he had spoken to Stanton to get the question answered. He wrote back saying, "The Secretary of War says you may furnish writing materials to Mr. Davis sufficient for the specific purpose of accepting or declining Mr. O'Conor's offer."[8]

Only two days later, the authority that Miles may have thought he had was further circumscribed after Miles allowed a chaplain to visit Davis. Townsend informed Miles that people seeking to meet Davis were restricted to persons who possessed signed, written permission from Stanton or his adjutant. The restrictions on Davis were so tight that the War Department returned the letter that he wrote to O'Conor accepting the lawyer's offer of representation because of a sentence that the department found objectionable. Davis removed the offending sentence, explained to O'Conor what the now omitted sentence referenced, and re-sent the letter. He made it clear that he was not allowed to stray from a response to the offer from O'Conor, writing: "To-day permission has been granted to me to make a specific reply to your offer. Formally, then, I accept your tender of services as my counsel and offer my grateful acknowledgements for your kindness."[9]

Davis admitted that he was in the dark: "Since my arrival here all knowledge of passing events has been so rigorously excluded that I am quite ignorant as to any proceedings instituted against me, as well as the character of the evidence on which they could have been founded, and consequently cannot judge what kind of testimony will be required for my vindication." There was only one way to remedy that concern. O'Conor must visit him. "Though reluctant to tax you with the labor of coming here," Davis wrote O'Conor, "I must, for the considerations indicated, request you to obtain the requisite authority to visit me for the purpose of a full conference."[10] There was a long road ahead for Davis, but he knew that the first step was meeting and discussing the case with his lawyer.

In spite of having accepted O'Conor as his lawyer, nearly two months after his arrest, Davis sat in Fort Monroe, effectively denied the assistance of counsel because the attorney general for the federal government deemed it inexpedient for him to meet with an attorney. There is no apparent legal justification for the denial. Whether Davis was to be tried before a military tribunal or a civilian jury, there was no reason why he should have been denied counsel. The clumsy handling of his incarceration would gradually shift the public's perception of him and make him a hero to southerners while softening the attitudes of the northern public.

In early September, Charles O'Conor still struggled to learn any facts that might assist in Davis's defense. He had earlier written James M. Mason, the former Confederate envoy to England, who from Great Britain had raised money for Davis's defense, that he expected Davis to be tried before a military tribunal. His view gradually changed, although he still had no final word on the question. He now believed, from information that he thought "seems quite trustworthy," that the individuals "most likely to control action are opposed to any punishment. Their wish is to get rid of the matter; they are quite resolutely determined against using the 'military commission.'" O'Conor did not believe, at this time, that Johnson was entirely in charge of the government's policy. In the same letter, he betrayed a hope that Davis might avoid trial altogether but suggested that if he had to face a jury, it would be a "regular trial for treason in a judicial court." As would any good defense attorney, he considered what groups of people might prove influential to his client's benefit. He shared his surprising revelation that "the abolitionists are averse to any further infliction upon the persons of 'traitors.'" In his judgment, Andrew Johnson might prove an unlikely ally with abolitionists on this point, despite the animosity and lack of confidence between Johnson and the abolitionists. O'Conor thought that those seeking the punishment of Davis consisted of people, like Edwin Stanton and Joseph Holt, who had been involved in the Lincoln conspiracy trials—what O'Conor termed the "Surratt tragedy."[11]

Delays in the expeditious handling of criminal cases after the war were unusual. The Davis prosecution was the exception. Four months after the end of the war, a military commission began proceedings against Capt. Henry Wirz, the Swiss-born commander of the notorious Andersonville prisoner of war camp. Since Davis was not tried for the atrocities committed against Union prisoners, historians writing about the trial of Henry Wirz often fail to see a connection between it and the Davis treason case. The attorneys defending Davis were well aware of the cases' dangerous parallel, though, and worried very much about it, as did Davis himself. In August 1865, as Davis sat in Fort Monroe, isolated from his family and friends and denied access to counsel, the Wirz trial portended badly for him. The federal government had moved quickly to bring Wirz to trial. Despite evidence that originated in Georgia and witnesses who were scattered after the war, an indictment had been handed down in Washington, D.C., only weeks after Davis's capture. The federal government's prosecution appeared to be well organized and intent upon punishing the rebels.

Two issues significant to Davis, Lee, and other Confederate leaders took a troubling turn for the rebels. First, Wirz was tried before a military commission, not a civilian court and jury. Second, of consequence especially to Davis, the trial was being held in Washington, D.C., not in Georgia, where the crime was alleged to have been committed. The questions of venue and forum were critical to the Davis trial. If Wirz could be tried before a military tribunal, there seemed to be little reason why the commander in chief of the Confederate armies could not be tried in the same manner. However, if Davis could be tried before a civilian court and jury, he certainly would prefer to be tried in the South, rather than in the North. Just as critically, the prospect existed that Davis would be charged with the crimes committed at Andersonville. If that occurred, then the defense faced the prospect of an immediate trial for Davis. In late summer 1865, these questions were still unanswered. That Wirz faced trial in Washington before a military tribunal must have caused Davis much anxiety about his own future, as he became accustomed to his prison cell at Fort Monroe. The facts that led to the Andersonville prosecution had some ugly facts for any accused person to address.

* * *

The Crime of Andersonville

The maltreatment of Union prisoners of war generally, and the abuses found in Andersonville, Belle Isle, and Libby prisons in particular, had long horrified the population of the North. Published accounts of the appalling treatment of Union soldiers were common. After the war, it was estimated that one Massachusetts soldier died at Andersonville prison for every five Massachusetts soldiers who died in battle.[12] During the war, Congress had appointed a committee to investigate the growing evidence and rampant rumors that Union soldiers were being subject to shocking abuse. Simultaneously, another organization was involved that might be able to shed some light on the camp. The United States Sanitary Commission, a humanitarian and philanthropic organization that relieved "our men in rebel prisons whenever it is permitted to do so,"[13] regularly issued reports on Confederate prison camps during the war that informed the northern public about the horrible conditions of many southern prisoner of war camps. Families lived in fear that their captured sons, fathers, or husbands would end up in a place like Andersonville. Established on February 24, 1864, the Andersonville prison camp rapidly became known in both the North and the South as a hellhole.[14]

Samuel White, representing himself as "an old man" who "could do nothing," wrote President Lincoln on behalf of his son, a husband and father of two, from Rushford, New York. His letter reflected the fears and uncertainties of thousands of others in the North:

> One of my boys, who is a prisoner of war in the hands of the enemy, and who was last heard of from on Belle Isle, is now supposed to be in Andersonville, Ga., if living, suffering for want of food and clothing. . . . Winter is approaching, and my son and 30,000 more brave soldiers must perish unless the Government should relieve them by bringing about an exchange. . . . Humanity prompts me to lay the case before you, hoping that if an honorable negotiation for an exchange of prisoners cannot be made with the infernal rebels, I would suggest that a sufficient force be immediately detailed, and Kilpatrick or some other brave officer sent to liberate from captivity the brave soldiers now confined in the State of Georgia. . . . The rebel prisoners at Elmira in this State live better than many poor people. They have wholesome food and enough of it, and are well provided for

> in sickness. The contrast is great between these prisoners and ours. Mr. President, what can be done and what will you do to liberate them from this cruel bondage?[15]

White obviously knew that Gen. Judson Kilpatrick, a Union cavalry commander, was part of Sherman's force fighting deep in the Confederacy. The calls for action were not ignored but did not result in the implementation of any effective measures.

The United States Christian Commission, a philanthropic agency, sought to reach the Union men held by the Confederacy and alleviate their suffering. Their efforts were in good measure fruitless, but they were intent upon trying. George H. Stuart, chairman of the commission, wrote Secretary Stanton on October 31, 1864, asking if the North would agree to an exchange of delegates with the South to allow both sides to visit their own held in the opposing camp's prisons. The request was forwarded to Grant for his thoughts. Grant responded, "I see no impropriety in granting permission to the commission to send a certain number of good Christian men to make the attempt within proposed, and if successful I know of no special reason why proper Christian agents from the South should not [be] permitted to visit and administer to rebel prisoners in our hands."[16] Southerners were not quite so open to the idea of inspections of these facilities by northern groups.

The North's attempts to initiate inspections of the prison camps failed. Soon the United States Sanitary Commission began an independent investigation. In 1864, it published its findings in the *Narrative of Privations and Sufferings of United States Officers and Soldiers while Prisoners of War in the Hands of the Rebel Authorities.* The pamphlet was 283 pages in length and contained photographs of emaciated Union soldiers, testimony from witnesses to the murder and abuse of prisoners, and medical reports from the commission's staff.[17] Significantly, Libby Prison and Belle Isle were in Richmond, Virginia, capital of the Confederacy and residence of Davis. The Confederate president might plausibly plead ignorance when it came to the conditions at Andersonville because it was located in Georgia, but he could not do that for Libby Prison or Belle Isle unless he had willfully turned a blind eye to it.

Libby Prison was generally understood by the North to be a prisoner of war camp designed for officers of the Union army, although it also was used to house other soldiers. In badly overcrowded conditions, the men found themselves robbed of their clothing and blankets upon arrival at the prison. They were then housed in an area that was poorly ventilated and ill heated in the winter. Camp rules prohibited prisoners from going within three feet of windows, and those who ventured too close were shot without warning. The food provided to these men, according to the investigation, was putrid and spoiled, often filled with worms and maggots. But the reports of exposure and starvation lent themselves to apologists who claimed that southern soldiers suffered from the same problems. The North could not be certain at this stage of the war whether the abuse was planned and systematic or simply the result of a Confederacy in which soldiers, civilians, and prisoners of war suffered alike. The evidence offered by the Sanitary Commission of murder gave muscular expression to those who believed the cruelty was intentional. Testimony by former prisoners of brutal and unrestrained guards pepper the publication, but evidence of this nature was not confined to this report. Men who came home from these prison camps published their own accounts of their treatment. Northern civilians became familiar with the term *dead-line,* a point "beyond which no one was allowed to pass, without being immediately shot by some of the sentries in the boxes."[18]

The conclusion of the Sanitary Commission report was that abuse of Union soldiers was so pervasive that it could only be attributed to a policy sanctioned by the very top of the Confederate leadership. "No supposition of negligence, or thoughtlessness, or indifference, or accident, or inefficiency, or destitution, or necessity, can account for all this," it maintained. "So many and such positive forms of abuse and wrong cannot come from negative causes. The conclusion is unavoidable, therefore, that 'these privations and sufferings' have been 'designedly inflicted by the military and other authority of the rebel government,' and cannot have been 'due to causes which such authorities could not control.'"[19]

Rumors about the treatment of prisoners at Andersonville terrified northern families. In August 1864, Gen. William Tecumseh Sherman wrote his wife, Ellen, from his headquarters near Atlanta, saying: "I have already lost [Gen. George] Stoneman and near 2,000 Cavalry in attempting to rescue the Prisoners at Macon. I get one hundred letters a day almost asking me to effect the exchange or release of these Prisoners." He candidly confessed to her that "it is not in my power."[20] Although Sherman had witnessed carnage throughout the past four years, the knowledge that Union soldiers might be starving just miles from his headquarters led him to take a chance he would not have normally taken in an attempt to relieve these soldiers. Two days later, Sherman wrote to Thomas Ewing of Lancaster, Ohio. He admitted: "I have made no professional mistakes but one, in consenting that Stoneman should make the premature attempt to reach our prisoners of war at Macon & Anderson & release them. Stone begged for it & I consented, my judgment being warped by our Feelings for 20,000 poor men penned up like cattle."[21] Stoneman was captured by the Confederates in the ill-fated attempt.

It would have been difficult for the leaders of the rebellion in Richmond to deny knowledge of the horrible abuses, as the conditions at Andersonville were well documented within the Confederate government. Within five months of its establishment, Andersonville prison officials reported deaths of 4,585 Union soldiers. In March 1864, there were 7,500 prisoners housed at Andersonville. By April, there were 10,000. The population grew to 15,000 men in May; 22,291 in June; and by July, there were 29,030 Yankee prisoners of war housed in the Confederate military prison. In July alone, there were 1,817 deaths. In a report dated August 2, 1864, the chief surgeon of the post, Isaiah H. White, reported that the hospital accommodations were insufficient, medical supplies deficient, and "during the entire month of July the commissary has been without funds." White reported that scurvy was rampant within the densely crowded prison and that "the lack of barrack accommodation exposes the men to the heat of the sun during the day and to the dews at night, and is a prolific source of disease." Despite these conditions, White attributed the "chief cause of mortality" to be the "mental depression produced by long imprisonment." White also noted the "deposit of fecal matter over almost the entire surface of this bottom land," which he attributed to the lack of facilities. Ultimately, he blamed the prisoners themselves, citing "the filthy habits of the men."[22] Two days later, White reported to his commanding officer, Gen. John H. Winder, that "the prisoners are without barracks or tents, 30,000 men being densely crowded together, sheltered only by blankets and low hovels densely and irregularly arranged."[23] General Winder, writing the same day to an assistant adjutant general, Lt. Col. D. T. Chandler, complained that the prison, which was initially meant for 6,000 men and was later expanded to accommodate 10,000, now had over 32,000 Union soldiers.

The next day, Chandler submitted a report to Col. R. H. Chilton, an assistant adjutant and inspector general in the Confederate capital. Chandler's lengthy report constitutes some of the most damning evidence against the Confederate leadership. He described an area of 540 by 260 yards that shaped the boundaries of the prison. A "dead-line" of 20 feet from the perimeter and about 3.25 acres of marshes near the center of the prison reduced the usable area for the thirty-two thousand men to 23.5 acres. A small stream that ran through the enclosure furnished the only water available to the men, but Chandler reported that the guards' camp, the bakery, and the cookhouse, which utilized the stream before it entered the prison, "render the water nearly unfit for use before it reaches the prisoners."[24] The area used as toilets was found to be "in a shocking condition and cannot fail to breed pestilence." Chandler also noted that "the sanitary condition of the prisoners is as wretched as can be." He wrote that "no shelter whatever, nor materials for constructing any, has been provided by the prison authorities, and the ground being entirely bare of trees, none is within reach of the prisoners." The men were left to utilize a blanket as best they could for shelter. "Of other shelter there is and has been none," Chandler said. There was no medical access within the stockade. At the daily sick call, Chandler witnessed crowds so great that only the strongest could push their way to the front, while the weakest and those in most need of treatment could not.[25]

During his inspection, Chandler witnessed twenty deceased men carried from the stockade. The dead were carted out daily with no effort to ascertain their cause of death. Most, he reported, had never been seen by medical staff. Chandler wrote that the hands of the dead were mutilated with an ax to remove any rings they wore. As to the living, there were no barracks or tents, and "no soap or clothing has ever been issued." Despite the claim that the lack of food was unavoidable, Chandler stated, "After inquiry I am confident that by slight exertions green corn and other antiscorbutics [to counteract scurvy] could readily be obtained." He found that most of the medical staff accepted their positions "to avoid serving in the ranks" and were "generally very inefficient; and not residing at the post, only visiting it once a day at 'sick-call.' They bestow but little attention to those under their care."[26]

On October 31, 1864, the surgeon in charge at Andersonville, R. R. Stevenson, wrote to General Winder that, during the month of October, there had been 1,595 deaths at the prison camp. Remarkably, Stevenson stated that "there has been a marked improvement in the health of the prisoners" during October. Winder forwarded the report to the adjutant and inspector general.[27]

These reports made their way up the chain of command. J. A. Campbell, an assistant secretary of war, sent the report to the Confederate secretary of war with the notation that "these reports show a condition of things at Andersonville which calls very loudly for the interposition of the Department in order that a change may be made."[28] The appalling conditions at Andersonville were clearly known to Jefferson Davis's wartime cabinet.

Federal Prosecutors Attempt to Link Davis and Lee to Andersonville

Col. N. P. Chipman, judge advocate of the military court, prosecuted the Andersonville case at the behest of both Secretary Stanton and Joseph Holt, the judge advocate general of the United States and the prosecutor of the Lincoln assassins. Chipman's investigation of the deaths of over thirteen thousand Union soldiers at Andersonville convinced him that "the heads of the rebel government were largely responsible for the awful suffering" there. He wrote that it was not until he had spent "months in searching out proofs, and arranging the facts, that this suspicion deepened into conviction."[29] Many southerners saw Henry Wirz, the commandant of Andersonville prison, as a victim of Yankee vengeance. One correspondent referred to him as "poor Capt. Wirz" and wrote that "he appears to have no friends, and a Confederate without money or friends has but a slim chance for justice or acquittal in a Federal Court."[30]

Former Confederates perceived a more sinister reason for Wirz's prosecution to commence prior to the Davis trial and to be held before a military commission. C. J. McRae wrote to Davis's attorney that the tribunal and timing of the Wirz trial "induces the belief that Capt. Wirz has been selected as the subordinate officer to be convicted and capitally punished in order to establish a precedent for a like conviction and punishment of more eminent persons."[31] McRae hardly evidenced any concern about Wirz personally. Instead, he confided in Charles O'Conor that "it is deemed of the utmost importance that Capt. Wirz's case hereto be properly managed, and I take the liberty of writing to request that you will add to the pains already conferred on us to see that Capt. Wirz has able counsel and that *his case* is so managed as not to damage those of persons that may be hereafter tried."[32] To that end, McRae authorized O'Conor to use a portion of the money sent to him for Davis's defense to help Wirz in his trial. O'Conor was cautioned to not reply directly to James Mason but to go through the channels that had been established for their correspondence. Clearly, they believed that their mail might be compromised if the American government officials became aware of the identities of the correspondents. They also perceived a link between the Wirz trial and a potential capital charge against Jefferson Davis.

By the beginning of August 1865, the Wirz prosecutor was certain that Davis, Robert E. Lee, and many other top rebel leaders bore responsibility for the atrocities at Andersonville. Unlike the conclusions of the Sanitary Commission, Chipman would need to present evidence that supported the allegation that the responsibility for the abuse emanated from the top of the Confederate government. The widespread pervasiveness of deplorable conditions, while perhaps raising an inference of knowledge, would not suffice to prove guilt in a military tribunal.

With the indictment in hand and the belief that he had proof to support his allegations, Chipman read aloud the document charging Robert E. Lee and other Confederate leaders as coconspirators with Henry Wirz for the deaths of thirteen thousand Union soldiers at Andersonville. The first charge alleged a conspiracy between Wirz, Lee, James A. Seddon (the Confederate secretary of war), and others to "injure the health and destroy the lives, by subjecting to torture and great suffering, . . . large numbers of federal prisoners, soldiers in the military service of the United States of America."[33] After Wirz was arraigned, the commission recessed until the following day, when Colonel Chipman intended to begin presenting evidence. The electrifying allegation that Robert E. Lee was linked to the horrors of Andersonville was telegraphed around the country and provided front-page news. Evidently, Chipman thought that he had the concurrence of Stanton and Holt in charging the Confederate leadership. He did not.

The next day, as the commission reassembled, Colonel Chipman received an order from the War Department dissolving the military court and ordering him to report immediately. The reason behind this stunning order only became clear when he arrived at the War Department and found an "unusually disturbed" Edwin Stanton, angry at Chipman's indictment of the rebel leadership in the Wirz case. Although Chipman had had extensive conversations with Joseph Holt, Stanton was apparently unaware of Chipman's intentions to include the Confederate leadership among the parties charged in the Andersonville case. Stanton ordered Chipman to reindict Wirz and drop the charges against Jefferson Davis, Robert E. Lee, James A. Seddon, and other leading rebels. While Joseph Holt was intimately aware of the nature of the evidence that Chipman had garnered against the Confederate leadership, Chipman believed that Stanton was not. Chipman was downcast at the prospect of not having this evidence come to light at trial. Now, relegated to trying only Wirz, a man he found to be "of comparatively small consequence," Chipman believed that the government had lost a chance to bring to light his belief that the war crimes led directly to the desk of Jefferson Davis.[34]

Once involved, Stanton decided to personally intervene and approve any new indictment filed by Colonel Chipman in the Wirz case. Chipman brought the same language to the new pleading, omitting the names that he had been required to delete, adding names of individuals of less note, and inserting the words *and others unknown* to the conspiracy count. The hurried changes allowed the trial to begin August 23, 1865. Stanton must have been satisfied to have stopped the military trial before it started and to have once more placed the prosecution of Davis in the hands of those he thought most appropriate. But Stanton was unaware that his decision to require the dismissal of the rebel leadership from the Andersonville trial may have been the last opportunity to try Jefferson Davis and Robert E. Lee for their actions during the Civil War. Of course, Colonel Chipman's indictment did not contain allegations of treason against the two men. Still, Chipman had put together a case that he was confident would expose Confederate leadership to judgment. But he had even more than that. Chipman had a military commission ready to try the case. He had evidence assembled that he believed supported his allegations. And he had the willingness to try the case to judgment. At no other time would the United States government again have a court, a prosecution team, and evidence ready at the same time to try Jefferson Davis. So far as Lee went, there would never be a serious attempt to prosecute him—and there likely should not have been.

The military tribunal was held in the basement of the Capitol building in the Court of Claims. Fresh from his stint as a member of the nine-man commission that had tried and condemned the Lincoln conspirators, Maj. Gen. Lew Wallace headed the commission. Henry Wirz was a slight man of about five feet eight inches in height and only about 135 pounds. The accused had a very thin face with a full beard. He wore a black coat, vest, and brown pants.

He was, in the words of the *Boston Daily Advertiser,* "scorned, loathed, despised, hated of all men and women" as his trial began.[35] There is little wonder why the North hated Wirz, despite his being a mere representative of the prison camp officials. Many men held at the camp recounted the same horrors. One veteran, Charles Tibbles, testified that when tracked down by hounds and threatened with death by rebel guards, he and other escapees told the rebels "to shoot; that we would rather die anyhow than go to Andersonville."[36] Wirz sat with his legs crossed as the charges and specifications were read in court. The *Daily Advertiser* "wondered that there was no outraged soldier to take the law into his own hands, and shoot the miserable creature as he walked with his guard or sat on the luxuriously cushioned lounge between his counsel."[37]

The tribunal found Wirz guilty as charged. The "Findings and Sentence" of the court implicated others, including the former Confederate president. The sentencing court found that "Wirz, did combine, confederate, and conspire with them, the said Jefferson Davis, James A. Seddon, Howell Cobb, John H. Winder, Richard B. Winder, [and others] who were then engaged in armed rebellion against the United States, maliciously, traitorously, and in violation of the laws of war, to impair and injure the health and to destroy the lives, by subjecting to torture and great suffering, by confining in unhealthy and unwholesome quarters, by exposing to the inclemency of winter and to the dews and burning suns of summer, by compelling the use of impure water, and by furnishing insufficient and unwholesome food, of large numbers of federal prisoners."[38] To no one's surprise, Wirz was sentenced to be hanged. But of course, the significance to Davis and his lawyers was that Davis was linked by a military tribunal's finding that the leader of the Confederacy had conspired to commit the crimes at Andersonville.

Speculation abounded in Washington that Johnson would commute Wirz's death sentence.[39] That rumor was quickly quashed when, in the first week of November, Johnson approved the sentence of Henry Wirz and ordered that his execution be carried out on November 10, 1865.[40] Wirz's counsel, Louis Schade, immediately requested and was granted an interview with President Johnson. During that meeting, he intimated to Johnson that he should commute the sentence of Wirz by claiming that the physical health of the man was so fragile that he would perish of natural causes within six months. Apparently because of the presence of others at the meeting, Schade thought that it was better that he not press Johnson for a direct answer to the request. Johnson told the lawyer that he would consider the matter.[41] The president let the sentence stand.

Two days before his scheduled hanging, Henry Wirz granted an interview to the *New York Herald.* The prisoner's quarters were found to be closely guarded, day and night. His right arm, which he said had been hurt by a shell in the Battle of Fair Oaks, was in a sling. His sore arm did not appear to hamper his willingness to talk about himself. He claimed to be a tailor's son from Switzerland. At the time of his trial, Wirz was forty-one years old. He had immigrated to the United States in 1849, and his work took him from New York to Connecticut and eventually to Kentucky, where he married. Prior to the war, he had overseen a plantation in Natchez, Mississippi.

Wirz joined the rebel army in August 1861 as a private. His first duty was as a guard at a military prison in Richmond. Early in the war, he was noticed by General Winder and given assignments that were better carried out by an officer. He claimed to have been made assistant adjutant general to Joseph Johnston and was wounded by a shell at Fair Oaks. When he recovered, he was eventually ordered to Libby Prison in Richmond in early 1863. "I did not like the way in which prisoners were treated, as they did not have enough to eat," he said. He asked for a transfer but was denied. In March 1864, Wirz was ordered by General Winder to Andersonville to relieve W. S. Winder, General Winder's son. Shortly before the war ended, Wirz claimed to have been ordered to Richmond, where he remained until the surrender of the Confederacy.[42]

Wirz seemed reconciled to his execution. "As far as I am concerned," he told the *New York Herald,* "I have no hope of reprieve. These things which were done (meaning Andersonville) somebody must suffer for. I have never denied that the prisoners were mistreated; but it was not my fault. If I am the last one that is to suffer death for the Southern confederacy I am satisfied. I do not fear death." The newspaper correspondent described Wirz as "composed throughout" the interview and said that his statements were made in a "remarkably direct manner." The "command of thirty-five thousand men," which is how he described the position of Andersonville prison commandant, had "to be strict, but when I am accused of conspiring with Jefferson Davis and others it is all a lie," he said.[43] Rebel sympathizers would seize on these words by the condemned man as evidence of Davis's innocence on the charge of violating the laws of war. However, Wirz did not clear Davis of these charges when he gave this statement. Whether Davis had conspired with Wirz to commit these crimes, the president of the Confederacy was personally aware of the privations and did nothing to alleviate the suffering of these Union men. Davis implicitly approved the treatment of the prisoners of war. Despite his view that the sufferings of Union soldiers at Andersonville was "an unavoidable necessity," Alexander H. Stephens, the vice president of the Confederacy, made a simple yet damning statement about Davis's failure to act, writing, "When I was satisfied of the inability of the Confederate Government to provide for its prisoners as humanity required, I wished them all (or at least all in such places as Andersonville) to be released and sent home on parole."[44] The solution to the suffering of Union prisoners was easy to determine and governed only by the dictates of the requirements of humanity. But Jefferson Davis did not act "as humanity required" toward these suffering Union men. Later in life, Colonel Chipman lamented the lost opportunity to link Davis to the crimes that resulted in Wirz being hanged on November 10, 1865. At the time, the chance did not appear to have been missed.

Davis himself saw the danger of being prosecuted for Andersonville. On Christmas Day 1865, Nelson Miles visited Davis to report on his health. He found Davis to be in good health, and "as the newspaper reports were so favorable he assumed more the airs of a prince than a prisoner." But one observation that Miles made indicated that Davis harbored concerns about the maltreatment of prisoners of war at the Georgia camp. "I noticed in his cell," Nelson recounted, "the reports of the evidence in the case of Wirz, which he had carefully preserved."[45]

With the trials of the Lincoln conspirators and Captain Wirz now over, the remaining criminal accusations were against the men indicted in Norfolk, including Robert E. Lee and other military leaders. Since Lee had never even been arrested on a warrant pursuant to the indictment issued against him, it seemed very unlikely that the government would proceed against him. The other military men under indictment took comfort that the parole granted them at the time of surrender would protect them from prosecution. Several others were uncharged but incarcerated and awaited a fate unknown. These men included Jefferson Davis and individuals who held lesser civilian posts in the Confederate government. Gradually, the federal government lost the desire to prosecute. John H. Reagan, for instance, the former Confederate postmaster general and close confidant of Davis, was released from imprisonment in mid-October 1865 and was able to eventually return to his home in Texas.[46] As the likelihood of prosecution diminished for others, Davis remained behind bars. He was the one rebel still targeted by the federal government for trial as a traitor.

9

PUSHING THE DAVIS CASE TO TRIAL IN 1865

I consider [trial by jury] as the only anchor ever yet imagined by man, by which a government can be held to the principles of its constitution.

—Thomas Jefferson

Jefferson Davis was unaware of the Johnson administration's plans for getting him to trial. All that he knew in 1865 was that he was being held in military custody without charges and without bail. Sitting in his cell, a modified casement at Fort Monroe, Davis was relegated to waiting for some action to be taken against him by the federal government. In hindsight, the delay in bringing the treason charge to bar allowed time for the public perception of Davis to change. Over the coming months, the shift in public opinion would work to Davis's benefit.

It is safe to say that the majority of white southerners came to believe that Davis was being mistreated by his Union captors. Andrew Johnson was aware of the charge and took action to determine whether the accusation was true. Early in his incarceration, as we have seen, Davis was held in irons. This news stirred the sympathy of people both South and North. Even Union general Benjamin Butler, known to southerners as "Beast," wrote that he regretted Davis's being placed in irons. But Butler also moderated his position slightly while implicitly placing the blame for the decision to shackle Davis on the correct man: "I do not know how far I should have been stirred in the direction of putting Davis in chains had I stood beside the death bed of Mr. Lincoln as did Stanton."[1]

President Johnson wanted trustworthy information on the subject of Davis's treatment. To find out, he asked his Treasury secretary, Hugh McCulloch, to travel to Fort Monroe to see for himself. Johnson's request of McCulloch for a report on Davis did not mean that Johnson's feelings about the Confederate were softening. Davis "was the head devil among the traitors, and he ought to be hung; but he should have a fair trial, and not be brutally treated while a prisoner," Johnson told McCulloch.[2]

Traveling in an unofficial capacity, McCulloch arrived at the fortress and found Davis walking upon the ramparts with two Union soldiers as escorts. Davis approached McCulloch in apparent good health. They spent a couple of hours conversing in Davis's cell. The quarters were sparsely furnished: a cot, a pine table, and two cane-bottomed chairs accounted for the furniture, but Davis remarked that the furnishings were "such as a prisoner charged with high treason ought not to complain." McCulloch reported to Johnson that Davis "had not the appearance of one who was suffering in health by imprisonment."[3]

The backstairs efforts to force the military to accommodate Davis more comfortably reached the highest executives of the federal government. In the summer of 1865, Varina Davis undertook a writing campaign that requested favors from her friends to enlist their aid in inducing federal authorities to grant her requests for travel and access to her husband. "Enclosed please find a letter to Mr. Seward—read it and if it will not damage my hopes of leaving here, send it to him," she wrote to Francis P. Blair in July 1865.[4] At other times, Varina Davis wrote directly to federal officers, as she did to Maj. Gen. James B. Steedman, the postwar commander of the Department of Georgia, asking, "May I appeal to you to use the very great influence which I hear you possess to obtain permission for me to go to the North." She was not above employing flattery: "So soldierly a man as I hear you are can readily appreciate the helpless and afflicted state of a woman," she stated to Steedman. Her letters were also filled with sentiments that appealed to southern sympathies: "I long since offered to take any parole if permitted [to] go so near Mr. Davis as to hear daily of his health. I have entreated to share his imprisonment, and if not permitted to be in his prison, to be permitted to send a few words of all the many I would like to say to him."[5]

Francis P. Blair, the elder patriarch of a conservative, pro-Union family of Maryland, had long been a man to whose advice presidents listened. Born during the Washington administration, Blair's involvement in politics spanned many decades, and his influence as editor of the *Globe* during Andrew Jackson's presidency made him a part of Jackson's "Kitchen Cabinet." Before the war, the Blair family held slaves, but Blair became convinced that slavery should not be extended beyond its present borders and freed his slaves during the war. In 1860, his support eventually went to Abraham Lincoln during the presidential nomination process, and his son Montgomery became postmaster general in Lincoln's cabinet. Lincoln spent time at the Blair House, which was very near the White House, seeking advice and taking the temperature of Democrats from the elderly leader of the family. Despite Blair's support for Lincoln, he remained a conservative voice in Washington, D.C. The friends of Jefferson Davis recognized the elderly patriarch as a valuable ally in their attempts to persuade President Johnson not to prosecute Davis.

"Old Man" Blair used his access to Andrew Johnson to try to sway the president by forwarding notes from Varina Davis that she had written to Blair detailing her tribulations. "I trouble you," Blair wrote to Johnson, "because you ought to know the condition of the unhappy, innocent ones who are at your mercy." In the space of a single page, Blair managed to include Varina's familiar refrains—those of maltreatment and bitter feelings toward the captors of her husband and her desire to be able to leave Savannah, Georgia. Undoubtedly, Johnson was not impressed. However, he also conveyed that "in her letter she asked that her husband may have a 'fair trial before a jury,'"[6] laying bare the fear of everyone in Davis's camp that the former Confederate president would be tried before a military tribunal. With the recently ended military trial of the Lincoln conspirators and the soon-to-begin trial of Henry Wirz, the possibility loomed large that Davis would face the same fate. Joseph Holt was still investigating whether Davis was implicated in the assassination and seeking to determine if "yet, more conclusive testimony bearing upon the complicity of the rebel leaders named in the murder of the President existed."[7] There is no evidence that Varina Davis was coached by Charles O'Conor to try to influence Johnson on the question of whether Davis would face a civil or military court, but the disadvantage of appearing before a military tribunal was clear enough for a woman of her sophistication and intelligence to have seen on her own.

The lead counsel for Davis was directing other efforts to influence what he could not directly control. Through his associate George Shea, O'Conor worked to dispel the idea that Davis had been involved in the atrocities at Andersonville. Shea wrote to Horace Greeley at the *New York Tribune:* "I received from Mr. O'Conor, and want you to read, a letter, which . . . ought to be published. It is an exoneration of Davis from any participation by act or word in the abuse of our prisoners and a most interesting and valuable historical testimony *coming from the highest and best informed source.* I am glad to possess this, as it relieves Davis' case from that odious feature. And I notice with pleasure that the charges and specifications preferred against *Wirz* (printed in this morning Tribune) does not state the name of Davis as among the persons with whom Wirz is therein said to have conspired. After I see you, it may be deemed advisable to publish the letter and have an editorial on the subject."[8]

Shea thought that it was imperative that Davis not be perceived as responsible for the horrors of Andersonville, remarking to Greeley that "if the contrary cannot be made to appear, the case [defending Davis] is hopeless."[9] It becomes abundantly clear that the Davis defense team worked tirelessly to influence both political leaders and the general public. On August 25, 1865, Greeley published an editorial in the *New York Tribune* that reflects the defense lawyers' effectiveness: "We can probably say nothing affecting the management of Military Trials that will not be attributed to spite against the present Secretary of War; and yet we cannot suppress our feeling that the false start in the Wirz trial was a bungle, and not a fair business transaction. There either was or was not evidence attainable which justified the indictment of James A. Seddon (late Confederate Secretary of War,) Gen. Robert E. Lee and L. D. Northrop, as conspirators to murder our soldiers when in prison at Andersonville. If there was such evidence, the trial should have proceeded as it began; if there was not, it was unfair and unjust to arraign these persons, and send the blasting indictment all over the world. We don't believe in striking foul blows, especially at those who are down."[10]

The indirect efforts to influence having borne little fruit, Varina Davis wrote personally to President Johnson in August 1865. Still not permitted to leave her home in Georgia, she wrote: "I see by a recent paper, my husband has been permitted to correspond with Mr. Gillet, who is said to be one of the counsel employed for his defense. I am led to hope that I will now be permitted at last to send open letters through the proper channels. My anxiety about his health is intense and I am separated from all my children because I had a faint hope that in diminishing my family so much you might perhaps consent to let me go to Mr. Davis. I would bear any privations, imprisonment, or restrictions, take and keep any parole, to be with him, even if only for an hour each day. His health is always frail, and I have been used to ministering to him at such times as he has been suffering, and consider it the chief privilege of my life. Before you refuse me, pray remember how very long I have been separated from him."[11] Enclosed in the letter to Johnson, Varina placed a letter to her husband that she hoped would be forwarded to him.[12]

Varina Davis chafed at being subjected to restrictions on her travel and being confined to Georgia. But likely without her realizing it, the bitterness and haughtiness that her letters displayed hampered her efforts to have the restrictions removed. Visitors who met with President Johnson in October 1865 asked whether these restrictions might be lifted so that she could travel into South Carolina to see her friends. Johnson told the people imploring him on her behalf that he "had received letters from Mrs. Davis, but they were not very commendable. The tone of one of them, however, was considerably improved, but the others were not of the character becoming one asking leniency."[13] Johnson went on to discuss his general beliefs about southern attitudes, tying Varina's attitude to the South as a whole. He reportedly stated that "the character of an individual may characterize a nation which is nothing but an aggregate of individuals, and when a proper spirit is manifested, all can act harmoniously. The man who goes to the stake is almost dignified by his bearing. It lifts him above humiliation. In these cases, gentlemen, we will do the best we can. While there was sympathy there was a public judgment which must be met. I assure you, gentlemen, no disposition exists for persecution or a thirst for blood."[14] The president was unmoved by the haughty letters from Varina Davis. In his view, northern public opinion demanded some sign of repentance by the former Confederate elite; Johnson shared this expectation. In the eyes of many northerners, it was southern hubris that began the war. Without a proper submission to the federal government, these elites should not expect to be helped by the president.

Blair also tried to assist the Davis defense team gain access to their client. Two months into his imprisonment, Davis had still not met with his lawyers. Regular visits between O'Conor and Davis would have helped build the relationship necessary for O'Conor to gain the trust of his client and to provide effective legal representation. Their meetings could have garnered factual information that might have proven critical to Davis's defense, but the meetings would have also established a level of assurance to Davis that O'Conor was working diligently on the case. Davis had no such reassurances in the first months of his plight, despite the efforts of many to gain him face-to-face visits with his attorney. He was relegated to sending letters to O'Conor through the War Department and receiving correspondence from his lawyer through the same channel, ensuring that no confidential information, so necessary to prepare his defense, could be transmitted.

If Davis could not directly assist in his defense, his former associates continued to display a marked sense of loyalty to him and often tried to help in his case. John H. Reagan, the former Confederate postmaster general, was released from Fort Warren in Massachusetts and immediately traveled to New York City. In his *Memoirs,* he stated that "while in New York I called to see Charles O'Connor, the great lawyer, who had been engaged to defend President Davis, in order to confer with him about that defense."[15] As a former cabinet member, Reagan could have offered his knowledge of what was known and discussed by Davis about Andersonville and the treatment of prisoners during cabinet meetings. He also would have been able to assure O'Conor that, to Reagan's knowledge, the former rebel president was not involved in the conspiracy to assassinate Lincoln. O'Conor must have been very pleased to meet with Reagan.

Other influential southerners felt compelled to try to help Davis. Richard Taylor, son of the late President Zachary Taylor and a high-ranking general in the Confederate army, immediately decided to go to Washington to speak to Andrew Johnson about releasing Davis when he heard that the former president was going to be charged with treason. Short of cash, Taylor raised money from his friends in New Orleans and booked travel on a steamer to New York City in mid-July 1865. Once there, he met with Samuel Barlow, a prominent Democratic attorney, looking for advice and funds to secure Davis's release. From there, Taylor traveled to Washington and stayed at the Willard Hotel. Stanton, Taylor learned, had issued an order prohibiting former Confederates from entering the capital, after a rumor circulated that another assassination plot existed. A third party contacted Johnson, who issued Taylor a pass permitting him to stay in Washington. Johnson also invited Taylor to the White House.[16]

Taylor was "ushered in to the President—a saturnine man, who made no return to my bow, but, after looking at me, asked me to take a seat." While Johnson had a disdain for men of Taylor's southern aristocratic background, he shared their concern about the Radicals in Congress. Johnson and Taylor talked about the condition of the South, and Taylor came away with the impression that, despite Johnson's early talk of hanging traitors, the president "had now somewhat abated his wolfish desire for vengeance." Still, Taylor was loath to bring up the purpose of his trip and asked for another meeting with Johnson to discuss "a matter of much interest to lay before him."[17]

The ease with which Taylor made his way through the capital, dining with William Seward and meeting with other members of the cabinet, is worthy of remark. There appears to have been little fallout from the role that he played in trying to sever the nation in two. When he presented his case to Johnson, the president pondered Taylor's request to visit Davis but did not make a decision. Instead, he asked Taylor to return for a third meeting at the White House. As Taylor waited on the day to arrive, he found the capital filled with "volunteer generals" whose "women sat at meat or walked the highways, resplendent in jewels, spoil of Southern matrons." His description of Washington immediately after the war sounded much like Sodom, with "courtesans swarmed everywhere, about the inns, around the Capitol, in the antechambers of the 'White House,' and were brokers for the transaction of all business," except, presumably, his. "Of a tolerant disposition and with a wide experience of earthly wickedness," he noted, "I did not feel called upon to cry aloud against these enormities, remembering the fate of Faithful; but I had some doubts concerning divine justice; for why were the 'cities of the Plain' overthrown and this place suffered to exist?"[18]

Several more meetings with Johnson got Taylor no closer to getting permission to visit Davis. Finally, Johnson told Davis that if Taylor could convince, among others, Thaddeus Stevens and Charles Sumner to recommend that Taylor be allowed to visit Davis, he would issue the order. Stevens received Taylor politely but told him, "Johnson was a fool to have captured Davis, whom it would have been wiser to assist in escaping." He remarked that "had the leading traitors been promptly strung up, well; but the time for that had passed," and he predicted that "nothing would be done with" Davis. Stevens ended the conversation by saying that "it was silly to refuse me permission to visit Jefferson Davis, but he would not say so publicly, as he had no desire to relieve Johnson of responsibility."[19]

Nevertheless, Johnson eventually gave Taylor permission to go to Fort Monroe. Taylor met Davis with a silent handshake and remembered the former Confederate president remarking, "This is kind, but no more than I expected of you." Taylor described him as "pallid, worn, gray, bent, feeble, suffering from inflammation of the eyes," but making no complaint. Taylor told him of the men he had met with in Washington, including Grant, and that he was confident that Varina would soon be allowed to stay at Fort Monroe with him. The two men spoke of the condition of the South. The thin-skinned Davis asked Taylor about rumors that had reached him, even in prison, that he was being blamed for the Confederate defeat. Taylor could not deny this but tried to assure Davis that the attacks on his character were being made by people trying to curry favor with the federal government. Taylor also told Davis that his imprisonment "served to endear him to all," a remark that Davis found consoling. The two men spent the day talking.[20] Indeed, Davis would soon become a symbol of northern oppression even as he was joined by his family at the fort.

The Davis defense team was working hard to address a number of issues in the case, but the time slipped by, despite their efforts. Shea had already met with Chief Justice Salmon P. Chase about the case. Recall that Chase had earlier declined to discuss the Davis trial with President Johnson because of the impropriety of such a discussion. The chief justice did not have the same hesitancy in discussing the case with Davis's lawyers. He told Shea that he considered "the late armed strife between the States as an open and public war, and that no charge of treason attaches to anyone engaged in it on the part of the Southern States."[21] This dovetailed completely with Daniel Webster's 1825 view of treason, and it did not escape Shea's notice that Chase was telegraphing him a potential defense to the treason charge. Chase then began a remarkable conversation about his own political ambitions that would be borne out only three years later. Shea remembered the chief justice saying: "I have always been somewhat Democratic in my opinions; and now that slavery is at end, there is no reason why I should not be more so. You may yet see some old abolitionist candidate of that party for Presidency."[22] Doubtless, Chase intended to curry favor with Davis's attorneys, who were, by and large, Democratic Party stalwarts. Ever ambitious, his political aspirations would color his handling of the Davis case throughout the proceedings, for better or worse.[23]

President Johnson addressed the plight of southerners who engaged in rebellion and their claim to have simply followed the dictates of their state in his message to the House and Senate dated December 4, 1865. "The States," he said, "cannot commit treason, nor screen the individual citizens who may have committed treason, any more than they can make valid treaties or engage in the lawful commerce with any foreign power." He announced that the Virginia circuit court, which would have had jurisdiction over the Davis treason trial, would not meet during the autumn or winter term for that trial. Johnson called on Congress to provide for an early resumption of the civil judiciary in Virginia, citing the need to expedite the treason trials. His words conveyed his steadfast belief that "it is manifest that treason, most flagrant in its character, has been committed. Persons who are charged with its commission should have fair and impartial trials in the highest civil tribunals of the country, in order that the Constitution and the laws may be fully vindicated; the truth clearly established and affirmed that treason is a crime and that traitors should be punished and the offense made infamous." However, he added a final element to his refrain that might have troubled his listeners. Astonishingly, he called for these trials as vehicles "that the question may be judicially settled, finally and forever, that no State of its own will has the right to renounce its place in the Union."[24] Lincoln would never have made this mistake or put the question of the legality of secession back into the public arena for debate—the issue of the legality of secession having been conclusively determined on the field of battle. Johnson's statement, which was poorly thought out, played into the hands of southern Lost Cause apologists.

Johnson voiced a variation of that position weeks before his congressional address. On October 13, 1865, several South Carolinians met with Johnson to present him with a petition from their state convention seeking the pardon or parole of Davis and several other prominent men. After the initial introductions, the president asked the petitioners to sit and engaged them in a conversation that revealed some of his thoughts about the power to pardon and the crime of treason. Johnson reportedly told the southerners that pardons must be deliberately considered. Too often, he heard the rationale that one person should be pardoned because another who was just as bad had already been pardoned. This reasoning did not appeal to him. Justice must be done, but the government must also show "a proper degree of humanity," he reportedly said. But, he said, "if treason has been committed there ought to be some test to determine the power of the Government to punish the crime." He did not stop at that sentiment. A trial of persons charged with treason served more than simply as a vehicle to potentially punish the offender. In Johnson's view: "Looking at the Government as we do, and the laws violated in an attempt at the overthrow of the nation, there should be a vindication of the Government and the Constitution, even if the pardoning power were exercised thereafter. If treason has been committed, it ought to be determined by the highest tribunal and the fact declared, even if clemency should come afterwards. There was no malice or prejudice in which to carry out that duty."[25]

While Johnson persisted throughout the autumn of 1865 in his desire to punish southern leaders for treasonous acts, a rift between the president and many of the Radical Republicans began to grow. The disagreement centered over the terms under which the states would be reunited. The difference would eventually widen into a deeper political problem for the president than that of whether Jefferson Davis faced trial on the charge of treason. It was once common to read that Andrew Johnson simply did not go far enough to satisfy the Radical Republicans. This is incorrect. Johnson and the Radical Republicans viewed Reconstruction in fundamentally different ways. Johnson was open about his position. In late October 1865, he spoke to Alexander McClure and stated emphatically that he intended for the South to reenter the Union "with all its manhood—I don't want it to come eviscerated of its manhood!" By this, "Johnson meant the dignity and pride that would allow Southerners to lead their communities, that would give a man command over his household and black people."[26] Absent slavery, Johnson would return the South to the Union with the same white-dominated society after punishing a small, select group of men for leading their states out of the Union. Radical Republicans sought to give the freedmen an equal political footing in the South.

Early on, though, Johnson was not seen as having a completely different vision for the region. Instead, he was thought to have disagreed with some of the tactics that were advocated by the Radicals. In September 1865, for instance, Pennsylvania congressman Thaddeus Stevens advocated in a speech that "we especially insist that the property of the chief rebels should be seized and appropriated to the payment of the National Debt, caused by the unjust and wicked war which they instigated."[27] Johnson did not regard this measure as necessary and did not seek to punish the rebel leaders in this manner for the war. If his position had been well analyzed, it would have hinted at his belief that the antebellum wealthy, white leadership of the South should continue to dominate politics and society even after Reconstruction.

The Question of a Speedy Trial for Davis

A little over seven months after Davis was captured in Georgia, the United States Senate passed a resolution calling on President Johnson to explain the charges that Davis faced and why he had not been brought to trial. Congress had gone into session in December 1865. On December 13, the two houses appointed a joint committee to examine the condition of the states that had previously formed the Confederacy. The members of the legislative branch clearly intended to assert a right to lead the reconstructive process over the seceded states. The Senate resolution inquiring as to the reasons why Davis had not yet been brought to trial was consistent with the view that Congress had oversight responsibilities on the broadest range of postwar concerns. Indeed, the *Report of the Joint Committee on Reconstruction* found that Johnson "as President of the United States, had no power, except to execute the laws of the land as Chief Magistrate. These laws gave him no authority over the subject of reorganization."[28] The fissures in late 1865 would eventually lead to a break between the legislative and executive branches of government in 1868. The legislative assertion of oversight responsibilities in the Davis treason prosecution was only one minor point of contention early on the road to Andrew Johnson's impeachment.

It fell to Edwin Stanton and James Speed to provide the answer to the Senate's inquiry. Rather than integrating the information into a single response, Johnson forwarded the individual responses of both Stanton and Speed to the Senate. The letters were eventually released to newspapers for publication. Their correspondence was worthy enough, in the opinion of many editors, to publish in full. Stanton's letter subtly revealed a frustration with the lack of prosecution. He stated that Davis "has not been arraigned upon any indictment or formal charge of crime, but has been indicted for the crime of high treason by the grand jury of the District of Columbia." Davis was "also charged with the crime of inciting the assassination of Abraham Lincoln, and with the murder of Union prisoners of war, by starvation and other barbarous and cruel treatment toward them." Stanton went on to say that Johnson "was advised by a law officer of the government that the most proper place for such trial was in the State of Virginia." The secretary of war did not reveal the identity of the "law officer" who had told the president that Virginia was the "most proper place" for Davis's trial, nor did he attempt to explain why, if that were true, the trial could not be held in another jurisdiction. Revealing that Davis was apparently under indictment in the wrong jurisdiction, Stanton then wrote of a second serious problem with the potential prosecution of the rebel leader. Virginia was within the judicial circuit assigned to Chief

Justice Salmon Chase, "who declines, for an indefinite period, to hold any court there."[29] Any reader would immediately infer that after seven months in custody, Davis was not close to being tried. Stanton clearly was frustrated with the lack of movement in the case.

Speed's response was not a model for legal reasoning. Instead, his letter offered only legal conclusions that he did not even attempt to explain. He wrote the president that "the Senate respectfully requests to be informed upon what charges and for what reasons Jefferson Davis is still held in confinement, and why he has not been put upon his trial." Speed began his analysis by stating the conclusion that Davis was properly in military custody, since he was taken during the war and was being held as a prisoner of war, without any legal support for that claim. Then he stated that "trials for high treason cannot be had before a military tribunal. The civil courts have alone jurisdiction of that crime." If this was true, then the next question to be answered involved the proper venue or location of the trial to be held. That was answered by Article III, Section 2, of the Constitution, where "it is plainly written that they must be held in the State and district 'wherein the crime shall have been committed.'" Speed found the argument that Davis could be tried anywhere that the rebel forces reached during the war, under the doctrine of constructive presence, to be "of doubtful constitutionality." In his opinion, Davis could not be tried in any state or district in which he had not actually been present during the war.[30]

Speed next turned to the potential prosecution of rebel military leaders: "Some prominent rebels were personally present at the invasions of Maryland and Pennsylvania; but all or nearly all of them received military paroles upon the surrender of the rebel armies. Whilst I think that those paroles are not ultimate protection for prosecutions for high treason, I have thought that it would be a violation of the paroles to prosecute those persons for crimes before political power of the Government has proclaimed that the rebellion has been suppressed." It was his opinion that Davis would have to be tried in one of the states that had seceded from the Union, since Davis had not traveled outside of the Confederacy during the war. While on firm constitutional footing, it placed the venue of any treason trial in very hostile terrain. What, then, was the answer to the senatorial inquiry?[31]

No trial had been held because the civil courts had not yet resumed full authority over the states in which a prisoner would be tried. Speed asserted that "though active hostilities and flagrant war have not for some time existed between the United States and the insurgents, peaceful relations between the Government and the people in the States and districts in rebellion have not yet been fully restored. None of the justices of the Supreme Court have held circuit courts in those States and districts since actual hostilities ceased. When the courts are open and the laws can be peacefully administered and enforced in those States whose people rebelled against the Government—when thus peace shall have come, in fact and in law, the persons now held in military custody as prisoners of war, and who may not have been tried and convicted for offenses against the laws of war, should be transferred into the custody of the civil authorities of the proper districts to be tried for such high crimes and misdemeanors as may be alleged against them."[32]

The loyal Union man who hailed from Kentucky then offered his opinion as to the wisdom of trying Davis and the others. "I think that it is the plain duty of the President to cause criminal prosecutions to be instituted before the proper tribunals and at the proper times against some of those who were mainly instrumental in inaugurating and most conspicuous in conducting the late hostilities. I should regard it as a direful calamity if many whom the sword has spared the law should spare also; but I would deem it a more direful calamity still if the Executive, in performing his constitutional duty of bringing those persons before the bar of justice to answer for their crimes, should violate the plain meaning of the Constitution, or infringe in the least particular the living spirit of that instrument."[33]

The letter indicated that several hurdles must be overcome before Davis could be tried. These obstacles to the trial rested entirely upon conclusions that the attorney general made without offering facts in support of them. Speed also failed to offer an explanation or timetable for resolving the issues inquired about. If that was not enough, Speed muddied the legal waters that Lincoln and his cabinet had taken great pains to avoid stepping into. For instance, Speed wrote of a continued "state of war" and of Davis being a "prisoner of war." If Davis was, indeed, a prisoner of war, then the legal position that Salmon Chase reportedly expressed to one of Davis's lawyers, George Shea—that in a civil war treason could not have occurred—was made stronger. Speed appears to have taken no pains to avoid controversy by writing a clear, well-reasoned letter addressing the narrow question of why Davis had not been tried.

Speed's written opinion did not quiet the fears that Davis would not be tried or clearly state the steps that needed to be taken before the case could be tried. His use of terms of great significance—*prisoner of war* and *war*—were much too loose. In trying to justify why a trial had not begun, Speed wrote that "though active hostilities have ceased, a state of war still exists over the territory lately in rebellion." He made this assertion despite Virginia having surrendered in April and holding statewide elections in early June 1865. These elections were not for Confederate offices but were held in an effort to set the stage for elections to the federal Congress. Newspaper accounts about the polling related "quiet and orderly conduct at the voting places."[34] Virginians were called to the polls again from the middle of July through early August 1865.[35] Elections could not have been held if a state of war existed. The attorney general's reason for not pursuing a trial for Davis seemed weak.

Speed assured President Johnson that Davis could be held "as a prisoner of war" until peace was achieved "in fact, and in law,"[36] again without hinting at what steps needed to be taken in order for peace to be attained. If these hurdles needed to be first overcome before Davis could be tried, the attorney general missed an opportunity to enumerate the steps that needed to be taken. Next, Speed indicated that high treason could not be tried by a military tribunal; instead, Davis would have to be tried in a civil court in the "State or district wherein the crime was committed." It was the position of the attorney general that Davis could not be tried for treason before a military tribunal, but Davis could have faced an indictment for the murder of Union troops. In his letter to the president, Speed ignored the findings of the military tribunal in the Wirz case. Lawyers for Wirz had objected to being tried before the military commission, to no avail. They had also asserted that Wirz was protected by the parole that was part of Joseph Johnston's surrender terms to William Tecumseh Sherman. All of these arguments were litigated and ruled upon. If Wirz could be tried before a military tribunal in the nation's capital for events that occurred in Andersonville, Georgia, then certainly Davis, under indictment for the inhumane treatment of prisoners of war, could be tried in the same venue for the murder of Union prisoners of war. Even if Davis was not to be tried for Andersonville, a favorable venue for a treason trial of Davis could be found in Pennsylvania or Maryland, where invading armies had been sent by his orders.

Speed acknowledged that some well-regarded and scholarly individuals believed that Davis, as commander in chief of the Confederate army, could be found to be constructively present in any district invaded by the Confederate army. If this doctrine was correct, it would have permitted his trial in Maryland, Pennsylvania, and many other locations in the North. Speed did not cite any precedent for his position that this was of "doubtful constitutionality" but simply left this assertion alone. The potential venue of the treason case against Davis was not an academic question. If the law required the case to be tried in Virginia because Davis directed the government from that state during the war, a conviction would be much more difficult to secure. The question became whether that was even possible given the views of most southerners after the war.

Congressional Hearings Begin

Members of Congress were puzzled by the lack of activity in bringing Jefferson Davis to trial, and the Joint Committee on Reconstruction held hearings to try to ascertain the reasons for the delay. Judge John Underwood was brought before the committee in Washington, D.C., and testified on January 31, 1866. The members of the committee harbored great concerns over the viability of trying Davis in the South. What they learned from the judge could not have been reassuring to them. Underwood spoke of a "great bitterness of feeling between those who are loyal and those who adhered to the confederacy; and I think that bitterness has increased within the last two months."[37] Senator Jacob M. Howard of Michigan asked Judge Underwood whether it was possible to get a jury of loyal men. Underwood answered, "Not unless it is what is called a packed jury."

There was another problem that would plague a prosecutor even if there were enough loyal men to sit on a jury—juror intimidation. The judge made the curious assertion that African Americans found more protection under the law than did loyal white men. He explained this by stating that the military shielded African Americans from lawlessness, while since the return of Virginia to civil authorities, several loyal white men had suffered death and other injustices without any protection from the Commonwealth of Virginia. It would be difficult for loyal white men to garner the courage to render guilty verdicts in treason cases if they feared for their safety. Underwood was equally skeptical of finding any Virginia jury that would convict a man of treason. When asked whether a Virginia jury could be found that might convict a man of treason, he answered: "It would be perfectly idle to think of such a thing. They boast of their treason, and ten or eleven out of the twelve on any jury, I think, would say that Lee was almost equal to Washington, and was the noblest man in the State, and they regard every man who has committed treason with more favor than any man in the State who has remained loyal to the government."[38]

The attitude of southerners that the judge described to the committee reinforced the fear of congressional leaders that the people of the South were merely catching their breath before again attempting to break away from the Union. They drew the judge's attention to the topic. Underwood did not share their concern or see a possibility of reopening the rebellion. But his years of residence in Virginia gave him an insight that would prove deadly accurate. The long war that had decimated the southern population and devastated the southern economy was not to be repeated. He did not believe that southern leaders would again try to secede. His belief was not based on a perception on his part that state leaders had undergone a change of heart; they simply did not have the ability to rebel again. Instead, he perceived the intentions of the leading men of Virginia to regain control of the state through the ballot box. What they had lost as a result of the war, they would take back through the political process. These men could not be relied upon to fairly judge their former leader in a treason trial.

The judge was not entirely negative about trying the case, though. Significantly, from the standpoint of a prosecution of Davis for treason, Underwood testified that Davis "is not as popular a man as General Lee by any means. He is regarded as their representative man, but I know that he is not really as highly esteemed as some others at the south. There are those who are strongly opposed to him at Richmond; some of the newspapers there were very hostile, particularly the Richmond Examiner." Underwood explained his perception of why Davis was not well regarded in the South. The former rebel leader was thought of as lacking firmness, being selfish, and displaying leniency toward prisoners during the war. But when asked, "Could either [Lee or Davis] be convicted of treason in Virginia?" Underwood responded, "Oh, no; unless you had a packed jury."[39] Packing a jury was unpalatable to men like Thaddeus Stevens, who called that prospect nothing less than "judicial murder."[40]

The Joint Committee on Reconstruction continued probing the policy questions raised by trying to reunite the two sections of the country, calling Robert E. Lee to testify on February 17, 1866. His testimony touched on a wide-ranging variety of subjects, from war debt to the freedman. On many of the subjects, he did not have a strong opinion. He professed, "rather disingenuously, since he had been in constant communication with such men,"[41] to have little contact with politicians or to have a feel for the pulse of Virginians so as to be able to give the committee an idea of how secessionists in his state felt toward the federal government. Lee dodged many of the questions by claiming to simply not know the general sentiment of the people he had led in battle. He stated that his retirement was so complete that, he claimed, "I scarcely ever read a paper." One fascinating point was that he could not recall whether he had taken an oath of allegiance to the Confederacy. If one had been required, he testified, he would have taken it; however, he could not remember whether an oath was required.[42] Lee did offer opinions that Virginia would be better off if "she could get rid of" African Americans. In his view, the future of the state was impaired by the presence of the black population.

Senator Howard returned to the subject of treason trials with a series of questions for Lee.

> *Question [Senator Howard].* Do you think that it would be practicable to convict a man in Virginia of treason for having taken part in this rebellion against the government, by a Virginia jury, without packing it with direct reference to a verdict of guilty?
>
> *Answer [Robert E. Lee, witness].* On that point I have no knowledge, and I do not know what they would consider treason against the United States. If you mean past acts—
>
> *Mr. Howard.* Yes, sir.
>
> *Witness.* I have no knowledge as to what their views on that subject in the past are.
>
> *Question.* You understand my question: Suppose a jury was impanelled in your own neighborhood, taken up by lot; would it be practicable to convict,

for instance, Jefferson Davis for having levied war upon the United States, and thus having committed the crime of treason?

Answer. I think it is very probable that they would not consider he had committed treason.

Question. Suppose the jury should be clearly and plainly instructed by the court that such an act of war upon the United States, on the part of Mr. Davis, or any other leading man, constituted in itself the crime of treason under the Constitution of the United States; would the jury be likely to heed that instruction, and if the facts were plainly in proof before them, convict the offender?

Answer. I do not know, sir, what they would do on that question.

Question. They do not generally suppose that it was treason against the United States, do they?

Answer. I do not think that they so consider it.

Question. In what light would they view it? What would be their excuse or justification? How would they escape in their own mind? I refer to the past.

Answer. I am referring to the past and as to the feelings they would have. So far as I know, they look upon the action of the State, in withdrawing itself from the government of the United States, as carrying the individuals of the State along with it; that the State was responsible for the act, not the individual.

Question. And that the ordinance of secession, so-called, or those acts of the State which recognized a condition of war between the State and the general government, stood as their justification for their bearing arms against the government of the United States?

Answer. Yes, sir. I think they considered the act of the State as legitimate; that they were merely using the reserved right which they had a right to do.

Question. State, if you please, (and if you are disinclined to answer the question you need not do so,) what your own personal views on that question were?

Answer. That was my view; that the act of Virginia, in withdrawing herself from the United States, carried me along as a citizen of Virginia, and that her laws and her acts were binding on me.

Question. And that you felt to be your justification in taking the course you did?

Answer. Yes, sir.[43]

Given the angst that Lee underwent in making the decision to resign from the United States Army, his testimony after the Civil War to the Joint Committee on Reconstruction reflects a remarkably passive view of fidelity owed to the government by a U.S. military officer.

Lee had expressed his sense of duty and how a strict adherence to principle might result in seemingly inconsistent responses in a letter to Gen. P.G.T. Beauregard written in October 1865. "I need not tell you," he said, "that true patriotism sometimes requires of men to act contrary, at one period, to that which it does at another, and the motive which impels them—the desire to do right—is precisely the same." He recounted how George Washington had once fought with the British against the French and yet, later, fought with the French against the British: "He has not been branded by the world with reproach for this; but his course has been applauded."[44]

What is astonishing is that the members of the committee felt comfortable asking Lee, who had been indicted for treason, about the prospects of securing a conviction against a defendant like him, who would surely fit the definition of "leading man," and Jefferson Davis. Lee's demeanor during the questioning must have been very open. It led to the issue of cruelty toward Union prisoners. Asked, once again with the caveat that he did not have to answer, whether while in command at Richmond, he was privy to knowledge of the cruelties practiced toward Union prisoners, Lee categorically denied any knowledge. However, Lee went further than simply denying whether he knew such practices had occurred. Despite widespread proof of the systematic mistreatment of Union prisoners of war, Lee stated: "I never knew that any cruelty was practiced, and I have no reason to believe that it was practiced. I can believe, and I had reason to believe, that privations may have been experienced among the prisoners, because I know that provisions and shelter could not be provided them."[45] He pointed out to the committee that prisoners of war were entirely the province of the Confederate War Department. Under follow-up questions, Lee admitted to having heard what he described as "mere hearsay" that mistreatment had been reported to the War Department during the rebellion and to having learned after the war that Henry Wirz had been arrested for the crimes at Andersonville. By virtue of Lee's testimony before the Joint Committee on Reconstruction, the attorney general and his staff now possessed the defense of Lee, and perhaps Davis, to the charge of treason and maltreatment of Union prisoners.

10

THE FIRST TRIAL DATE IN 1866

All loyal men desire to see Jefferson Davis suffer in some way.

—*New-York Commercial Advertiser*

The Davis Prosecution Proceeds

ON APRIL 6, 1866, James Speed wrote to John H. Clifford, asking him to contact William M. Evarts and to come to Washington, D.C. "The time has come for action, and I desire consultation with you on the preliminaries," the attorney general told Clifford.[1] The two men met with Speed to discuss the Jefferson Davis treason prosecution. The talk was of a practical nature, and the men exchanged views on venue with an eye toward determining a location that "would result in a proper verdict."[2] They shared a belief that they had a political duty to try the case in a suitable location that fit easily within any constitutional mandate. It was resolved to try him in Richmond, Virginia. They subsequently met with President Andrew Johnson in Washington to discuss Davis's case.[3]

The defense had other issues to resolve in addition to trial preparation. With a client who had been sitting in a prison since May 1865 and an outspoken wife urging his release, Charles O'Conor assigned an associate in his office to work on getting Davis out of prison. He picked George Shea, a forty-year-old lawyer, to manage that part of the case. Shea, like O'Conor, had Irish roots, having been born in Cork, Ireland, before being brought to America as an infant. He was a formidable attorney in his own right who would serve as chief justice of the marine court of New York. A devout Christian, Shea would later write a book about Alexander Hamilton and a short manuscript entitled "The Nature and Form of the American Government Founded on the Christian Religion."[4] In the spring of 1866, O'Conor may have believed that Shea was uniquely qualified to try to gain the release of Davis because of Shea's old intimate friendship with Horace Greeley, editor of the *New York Tribune* and a highly influential Republican voice. The defense hoped that the alliance with Greeley in urging the release of Davis on bail might prove effective. Greeley's support for Chief Justice Salmon P. Chase during the 1864 presidential nominating process could not have hurt his association with the Davis defense team either.[5]

Shea decided on a direct approach to the attorney general about having Davis released on bond. He secured a meeting with Speed to talk about Davis and asked Greeley to go with him to Washington for the meeting. The newspaper editor agreed. Perhaps more remarkably, Speed agreed to meet with an attorney for Jefferson Davis in the presence of the *Tribune* editor. As Greeley recalled, the conversation was between Shea, who was an attorney for Davis, and Speed, with Greeley merely being present. Shea wasted no time in turning to the object of the talk. Would Speed oppose Davis being granted a bond pending trial? As it turned out, the attorney general was so reluctant to express a view that Greeley later claimed to have no idea what Speed might do if presented with an application for bail. Neither did Speed give the two men any idea of what official position the Johnson administration might take on such a motion.[6]

It is not completely clear whether Greeley was prepared to post bail on behalf of Davis, as he would do in 1867. He professed to have never spoken to Davis or had any communication with him about bail, but he certainly espoused that result. Whether or not he had the immediate means and backing to secure Davis's release, especially since the setting of the bond amount was within the discretion of the judge, Greeley's object was well known in Washington. Republican senators Benjamin Wade, Zachariah Chandler, and John Creswell were strongly opposed to bail being posted. The senators met with Greeley in an attempt to dissuade him from going forward with his plan. During an animated half-hour conversation, Greeley became convinced that the three senators feared that Davis's release through the publisher's assistance would injure the Republican Party. Everyone concerned recognized that the political stakes were high in the matter of the *United States of America v. Jefferson Davis.*[7]

A grand jury in Richmond, Virginia, finally returned an indictment against Jefferson Davis on the charge of treason in May 1866, one year after his detention.[8] The true bill was based on the testimony of several individuals who placed Davis at the helm of the Confederate government during the war. One witness, J. F. Milligan, told prosecutors that he was in Richmond during the war and "saw Jeff Davis when he was President in 1863 at the Custom House, when a War was in operation against the United States Government." His testimony was not much different than that which thousands of southerners could have offered. He said that he received his commission from Judah Benjamin in Benjamin's capacity as secretary of war and that he knew John Breckinridge as secretary of war in 1865. He claimed to have heard Davis's inaugural address in 1862 "influencing the people to take up arms against the U.S. government."[9]

Judge George P. Scarbourg offered evidence that he knew "Jeff Davis for many years as President of the Confederate States by common report."[10] The judge then refused to answer many other questions by invoking his Fifth Amendment privilege. Other witnesses testified that John Breckinridge was in Confederate uniform during the rebellion and that Davis had conducted personal interviews on official business while holding himself out as president of the Confederacy. Although this evidence might permit the indictment of Davis and Breckinridge, it would not be very useful at a trial of the case. From a practical standpoint, the government would need to distinguish Davis from the dozens of high-ranking Confederate officials in order to get an impartial jury to convict him of treason. Failure to do so could leave the jury skeptical about the government singling out Davis for punishment. The grave stakes involved in a death penalty case made the need to draw a distinction between Davis and others who arguably had committed treason even more important. Simply proving that he was the president of the Confederacy would not differentiate him from the hundreds of other officials and military officers who had engaged in war against the United States government. Prosecutors must have worried that a jury would not be able to be convinced to sentence Davis to death for simply being the face of the Confederacy.

As the U.S. attorney, Lucius Chandler should have been deeply involved in the grand jury investigation of Davis. Instead, he expressed surprise when he was told by members of the grand jury that a true bill had been found against Davis. Chandler had expected to wait for the circuit court to organize a grand jury to seek an indictment against Davis, but Judge John C. Underwood believed that the district court grand jury should make the decision. As a result of this miscommunication, Chandler had not prepared an indictment beforehand. He found himself taken aback by the news that a true bill had been returned. Underwood caused further problems for the prosecutor when he told Chandler that court would adjourn promptly at three in the afternoon so that the judge could travel to Norfolk. This gave Chandler only two or three hours to prepare the indictment. As a result, the "indictment was very hurriedly prepared by me," Chandler later admitted.[11] It is impossible to explain how a federal prosecutor failed to realize that his most important criminal case was being reviewed by a grand jury. Yet Chandler did not know.

The indictment that Chandler drafted was an identical copy of the language of those indictments returned earlier against other Confederate leaders, merely substituting the name of Jefferson Davis where appropriate.[12] So, while he may have said that it was very hurriedly prepared, in truth, it was very hurriedly copied. His admissions revealed another troubling reality. In the year since the indictments against Robert E. Lee and others had been returned, the federal attorney had done no work to prepare for the coming Davis indictment. Indeed, not even the first indictments returned a year earlier were a product of Chandler's pen: Chandler had copied the indictment brought against Aaron Burr over a half-century earlier almost word for word. Not content to use the Burr indictment as a roadmap for a treason indictment against the former rebel, Chandler lazily copied even the bizarrely antiquated language, accusing Davis of "not having the fear of God before his eyes" but, instead, "being moved and seduced by the instigation of the devil" as the motivation for Davis's treason. This language was lifted precisely from that in the Burr charge.

Astonishingly, the charging instrument brought against the former president of the Confederacy was not, in any way, contoured to the acts that Davis had taken during the Civil War that arguably could constitute treason. Chandler had no help from the attorney general or anyone associated with the administration. The allegations that Chandler drafted were general and vague and, perhaps most important, unclear as to whether the charge of treason was being brought pursuant to the Treason Act of 1862 or the prior statute governing treason, passed on April 30, 1790. This was significant because of the different potential punishment available under each statute. Under the Act of 1790, treason was punishable only by death. The Treason Act of 1862, however, permitted imprisonment and other sanctions less than death.[13]

The grand jury indictment drafted by Chandler charged, in part, that Davis had incited "insurrection, rebellion, and war" against the United States of America.[14] The language was stilted and poorly thought out, if any thought was given to it at all, but clearly charged that Davis had engaged in rebellion and insurrection, allegations that arguably were made under section 2 of the

Treason Act of 1862.[15] If he was found guilty of treason under that section, his punishment would be limited to a prison sentence of a minimum of ten years. The indictment also included language alleging that Davis "did ordain, prepare, levy, and carry on war against the said United States, contrary to the duty of the allegiance and fidelity of the said Jefferson Davis, against the Constitution, government, peace and dignity of the said United States of America, and against the form of the statute of the said United States of America in such case made and provided." Within this sentence, it could be argued that Davis had been charged with levying war against the United States, a crime under the Constitution and under the act of April 30, 1790. Unfortunately, he did not reference either statute in the indictment. Chandler later stated that the indictment was framed so as to meet either the statute of 1862 or the original treason statute from 1790.[16] His explanation was a poor one, indeed. What conceivable reason would Chandler have to draft an indictment charging a crime that left uncertain whether the accused faced a prison sentence or death as the maximum punishment? To say that it met both statutes was to say that it left open to the Davis team the argument that punishment was capped at imprisonment. If Chandler intended for Davis to face the death penalty, the indictment he presented to the grand jury was woefully inadequate.

It cannot be known with certainty today why Lucius Chandler failed in his duties as a prosecutor in the treason trials. It could be that he was simply intimidated by the magnitude and importance of the cases. It could also be—and likely is—that his legal skills were not up to the task. Chandler had not come to the job because he was a preeminent lawyer in Virginia. He had been given the post because he was the only lawyer licensed in the federal district who had remained loyal to the Union. Whatever the reasons, it became clear, even as the case was being prosecuted, that his role as the lead prosecutor in the case carried with it many risks. The problems that arose because of his shortcomings became evident immediately, and nothing that he did, as time progressed, indicated that he would rise to the challenges presented by this major prosecution.

Chief Justice Salmon Chase and the Jefferson Davis Trial

With the treason indictment returned against Davis, a trial date was set for early the following month of June 1866. It was an unrealistically quick date, but it had to be set. Jefferson Davis had been languishing in custody for a year. He could not be held indefinitely without trial. But the government had made no preparation for a trial. Putting together the documentary evidence and interviewing witnesses in advance are critical to success in a case. None of this groundwork had been laid. Jefferson Davis's lawyer also faced an immense amount of work that had not been done, but the position of a defense counsel is different from that of a prosecutor, and O'Conor was well aware of this. Despite all the problems associated with preparing the case, he knew that Chandler was ill prepared and clamored to get the case before a jury. If challenged, O'Conor might have proven to be engaged in a false bravado, but he was willing to take that chance. The case was placed on the court's docket.

The defense team and its allies were actively promoting sympathetic publicity for their client too. On May 24, 1866, the *New York Tribune* published a lengthy report on its front page from George E. Cooper, the military doctor charged by President Johnson with examining Jefferson Davis, detailing the health of the famous prisoner. Horace Greeley's influential newspaper was operating in parallel with the interests of O'Conor's client. The report was dated two weeks previous. Dr. Cooper found Davis to be "quite weak and debilitated." The primary problem that the doctor reported revolved around Davis's failing nervous system. It was stated, for instance, that even "slight noises, which are scarcely perceptible to a man in robust health, cause him much pain," while Davis said that he was very sleep deprived, complaining that he rarely slept for more than two hours at a time. "Should he be attacked by any of the severe forms of disease to which the tide water region of Virginia is subject, I, with reason, fear for the result," the doctor wrote.[17]

The question of his health was much tied by the nation's press to allegations of harsh treatment at the hands of his Union captors. By late May 1866, Nelson Miles was so upset over newspaper reports of Davis's maltreatment at his hands that he wrote to the War Department, claiming that "the gross misrepresentations made by the press infringes severely upon my honor and humanity and I am unwilling to allow such statements to go unnoticed." He enclosed several newspaper clippings and asked to be allowed to reply to the newspaper accounts, since he was "averse to making any communication publically without the permission of the Department."[18]

It did not help that the personal acrimony between Davis and Miles was intense. Some months earlier, Miles had ordered red tape to be removed from Davis's cell because it was of such a length that it might reach well down the wall outside the casement. Davis had flown off the handle at the order, calling Miles "a damned ass" and a "miserable ass."[19] In his own defense, Miles wrote that "every consideration which would promote the health and comfort of the prisoners has been given as far as my instructions would permit." He indicated that Davis's food was "as good and better than officers in the fort" and his housing "second to none save the bars and bolts." Miles conceded, "It is true I have not made him my associate and confidant or toadied to his fancy."[20]

Several of the articles enclosed by Miles did falsely portray Davis's physical state. The *New York World,* on May 24, 1866, reported that "it is no longer a matter of newspaper rumor that the treatment which Jefferson Davis has received during his incarceration in Fortress Monroe has been such as to break down his constitution and to put him, after twelve months of protracted suffering, in imminent peril of death." The *New York News* of the same date told its readers that "his life hangs, as it were, by a thread." The *Richmond Times* alarmed readers by referring to "his judicial murder."[21]

The timing of the articles was suspect for two reasons. They appeared just as Varina Davis arrived in Washington, D.C., reportedly "for the purpose of attaining some modification of the stringent orders in relation to her husband's confinement," according to another clipping that Miles sent to Washington. The reports also came a day after Miles had been told that Charles O'Conor and George Shea would be allowed to visit their prominent client, in person, and have private discussions with him about the case. Miles indicated that he believed the press was being orchestrated: "I am confident this is an effort of Mr. Davis' friends to influence public opinion preparatory to his trial."[22] Whether these dire reports of Davis's failing health were planted or not, they were very useful to his lawyers. Davis's defense team quickly filed an application for his release on bail.

Horace Greeley took up his pen and wrote to his friend Chief Justice Chase to try to influence the judge in attaining either of two goals: first, actually holding the trial of the case; failing that, he asked that a date certain be set for the trial. Informing Chase that both Charles O'Conor and George Shea would be appearing in Richmond on June 4, Greeley implored the chief justice to personally appear to preside over the court. Greeley sought to influence without appearing overtly to be doing so. He wrote Chase, "I am confident that an intimation from yourself to the Attorney General will secure the requisite action." The editor also wanted to try to neutralize the influence of Judge Underwood, who the defense feared would not be nearly sympathetic enough to Davis. "You know, dear Sir, that our friend Judge Underwood will be out of his depth on such an occasion and that it is indispensable that the bearing as well as the action of the Court shall be such as will command respect even where it fails to secure approval." Then, catching himself, he penned, "I will say no more, but profoundly trust that the proceedings to be had on this occasion will be guided to a fit issue by yourself."[23]

Salmon Chase replied in a lengthy letter to Greeley immediately upon receipt of the correspondence. He began by claiming to "know nothing of what is proposed either by the Govt. or by the Counsel for Mr. Davis in respect to his trial." He then explained to Greeley why he would not be attending the session: "In the Districts, in rebel states, I have not held courts, because in such states, as it seems to me, all courts must be either military or quasi-military until complete restoration under legislative action, or, at least, until restoration of the Writ of Habeas Corpus and abrogation of Martial law by Executive action." He complained that there was no settled policy during the Civil War on when a civil court might resume complete control over the jurisdictional questions that would normally fall within the scope of its powers. Even when some courts attempted to reestablish jurisdictional authority, Chase told Greeley, "instances are not wanting where their acts have been nullified by military orders; and even in the late Charge to the Grand Jury, at Norfolk, Judge Underwood referred to the President and General Grant as, in some sort, authority for his action."[24]

Chase admitted that he had consistently directed civil district and circuit judges to yield to military authority or refer the matter to the president when the two found themselves in conflict: "In flagrant war and until restoration of peace, in districts or states where military control is essential to the accomplishment of the objects of the War, the civil must needs be subordinate to the Military authority." But he saw a distinction when the issue of subordination came to the United States Supreme Court, ignoring his earlier assertion about the need for all courts to be open: "The Chief Justice and Justices of the Supreme Court of the United States represent the HIGHEST JUDICIAL POWER of the Nation, which cannot, with propriety or decency, be subordinated to any military authority."[25] His position was that the highest judges of one of the three main branches of government should not defer to military authority. How, then, could the practical question involving the treason trial of Davis be solved?

This is where the chief justice's words begin to convey a sense of avoidance. Of course, a state's complete restoration and federal legislative acceptance of the state would reestablish proper civil judicial authority. Short of that, however, Chase thought that a presidential proclamation ending martial law and restoring habeas corpus in all cases where federal courts had jurisdiction was necessary. He acknowledged that the Peace Proclamation, dated April 2, 1866, was said to have done just that. He wrote Greeley that he had "no opinion concerning the effect of that proclamation,"[26] but because the military continued to operate in a fashion contrary to the construction of the Peace Proclamation, he was unwilling to construe it as having ended martial law and having restored habeas corpus. He enclosed a draft proclamation that he had given to President Johnson weeks earlier, which he believed would clearly permit him to preside over a court in Virginia, and told the editor that Johnson had apparently taken it under advisement. Nonetheless, the most revealing portion of Chase's correspondence were the words: "I desire to avoid all causes of irritation or controversy. There is enough and too much division right now."[27] A treason trial of Davis could not be held without "irritation or controversy."

Four days later, evidently having read the *New York Tribune* article about Davis's health, Chase wrote Greeley that "the 'Anxious' man can have a trial before Judge Underwood."[28] The chief justice did not assert that federal courts in Virginia could not try Davis; he merely indicated that if the rebel was tried, it would only be before Underwood. Chase's desire to avoid being associated with the trial was unmistakable. He was true to his word. When the June trial date arrived, Chase sat at his desk in the corner of his library in Washington, D.C., penning a letter to his daughter, Nettie, and recounted to her the "newsboy cries 'Dai-l-y Chron-i-cle!, full account of' something I don't understand what and 'trial of Jeff Davis!' The sun is under a cloud; but we can dispense with his smiles."[29] Even on a gloomy day, Chase was happy to be away from Richmond.

The First Trial Date

Even if Chase had decided to stay away from the courtroom in Richmond, the defense team had work to do. Davis's popularity had risen in the South during his yearlong incarceration. Newspapers reported that the people of Richmond believed that "Davis is no traitor unless all the late rebels are, and that no one should be tried and punished unless all are subjected to the same ordeal." Reports in the North reflected what every sophisticated person knew: "The difficulty of procuring a jury is manifest."[30] The *New York Tribune* offered a more succinct opinion on the problem confronting a jury: "A loyal jury cannot be collected here to try a case of treason without being threatened with martyrdom, social or otherwise."[31] The threat of violence against jurors could not be overlooked by Judge Underwood, who had been the target of threats and violence from white southerners before the war. He arrived from Alexandria, Virginia, in the early morning of June 5, 1866, and spent most of the morning at the headquarters of the military occupation force. Many of the grand jurors who had indicted Davis on treason were to arrive to present the indictment. The hearing would be held in the old Customs House on Main Street in Richmond, a location literally down the hill from the Virginia State Capitol. A courtroom had been beautifully refitted and would serve as the trial courtroom for all the appearances in the case.

Shortly before noon, several of the lesser-known lawyers working on the case for the accused arrived. William B. Reed, James T. Brady, and George William Brown milled around the courtroom, chatting with local Richmond attorneys. Others on the Davis team, including Edwin Van Sickle and Thomas Edsall, associates in the law firm of Charles O'Conor, and Charles N. Gross of Philadelphia, simply waited around the oblong defense table for court to begin. Robert Ould was present for the Davis team but stood away from the main group of defense lawyers. Ould, as the former agent of exchange of prisoners of war for the Confederacy, was a controversial figure, currently under indictment for treason himself. It did not seem to hurt his popularity in Virginia. The defense team would likely want Ould to be present because of his knowledge of Richmond and its citizens but would not want him to be front and center before Judge Underwood, who doubtless considered Ould a notorious traitor.

Burton N. Harrison, the erstwhile secretary of Confederate president Davis who had played such a large role in assisting Varina Davis and her husband in their flight from Richmond, circulated freely in the courtroom. Harrison was in buoyant spirits, "chatting with nearly everybody" and making himself a conspicuous figure. There appears to have been a nervous energy in the room as the lawyers waited for court to begin. Rumors circulated that Charles O'Conor was in Washington waiting to determine what action, if any, might be taken by President Johnson and was intending to telegraph the defense team to urge either a speedy trial or the release of their client.[32] O'Conor later admitted, "I had positive information that the government would not prosecute at that time and that consequently I did not attend myself."[33] From whom he acquired that positive information, he did not say. However, the government appeared to be a sieve that regularly spilled information to the defense during the course of the case.

Back in the Richmond courtroom, one reporter noted only fifteen or twenty spectators, a number that included two women from New York, attributing the lack of interest to the general belief that the case would be passed on the trial docket.[34] The judge took the bench at one o'clock. As the courtroom came to order, Underwood had the names of the grand jurors called. Fourteen responded as being present, but this was not a quorum. As court personnel were sent out to find the stragglers, Judge Underwood began to read a newspaper from the bench. He then turned his attention to a law book before beginning to write. The courtroom was in recess, despite the presence of the judge, and the lawyers continued chatting informally during the break. Finally, the judge called two other men to the clerk's desk to be sworn in as grand jurors. One potential grand juror refused to take the oath. After a delay of an hour to determine what should be done because of the man's refusal, he was excused for not being able to subscribe to the test oath required for service. When another juror entered the courtroom, after a delay of two hours and forty-five minutes, Underwood undertook to begin work. The judge then spoke to the members of the grand jury, at length, about the intimidation to which they may find themselves subjected, before appointing a foreman because the previously named foreman had not appeared in court. Then Underwood allowed them to retire to a conference room to work.[35]

Underwood's words would become fodder for those who accused him of bias against Davis. The judge said:

> We ought not to be surprised that the treasonable and licentious press of this State and city should wince and rage and become furious when treason and licentiousness are exposed and arraigned for trial and punishment; nor should we be surprised at the enormity and desperation exhibited when we remember that this city has long been the centre and seat of the greatest traffic in human beings that has ever disgraced the world. . . .

> The complaints of threatened violence and intimidation which have been forwarded to me by several of your number for your late heroic and patriotic actions have been submitted to the highest legal and military authorities of the Government, and I can assure you of the earnest sympathy and firm support of all the officers of the law, not excepting the President, whom the treasonable now flatter and fawn upon, but whom they will probably soon curse as heartily as they did two years ago.

Likely more as a warning to the Davis supporters present in the audience, Underwood informed the jurors that a federal statute made it a serious crime to attempt to intimidate a federal juror. His remarks may have been warranted, although harsh, had he stopped at this point. Instead, he ill-advisedly launched into a tirade against the Richmond press:

> You will thus have it in your power to exercise a wholesome restraint upon licentious tongues and pens, and upon a press which, as a blind leader of the blind, has been and still is one of the chief causes of past, present, and prospective calumny and misfortune. The murders, duels, assassinations, violent and ungoverned passions, ending in self-conflagration and self-immolation unparalleled in any heathen country, the poverty, suffering, agony and degradation which have given this city, of almost unparalleled natural capabilities, its bad eminence, are the legitimate fruit of the teachings of the public press; and anything that you can be able to contribute toward reformation will in the highest degree be serviceable to the cause of the country and of humanity. But, gentlemen, let us act with moderation and discrimination, for, though a prostituted press is one of the greatest calamities, a free and virtuous press is one of the greatest public blessings—the greatest ornament and the support of public virtue.[36]

Northern newspapers reported "that the Grand Jurors who found the bill against Davis for treason are subject to much persecution in the South," and speculated that any jury who "dared convict him on the bill and in accordance with law and evidence" would find it "too hot for them down there."[37] Underwood's concern for the grand jurors was understandable, but the resentment of his past treatment in the South now spilled out and made its way across the country in the nation's press. It is hard to imagine any fair-minded person reading his remarks and believing that he could act as an impartial judge in the Davis case.

Even sympathetic northern newspapers found his words to be of concern. The *Commercial Advertiser* of New York emphasized that "all loyal men desire to see Jefferson Davis suffer in some way for his offences" and editorialized that it was the leader of the Confederacy, and not Richmond's editors, who were being arraigned in federal court in Virginia. Underwood's utterances, they feared, would do nothing but bring sympathy to the rebel leader. Most important, however, Underwood's words raised "a doubt whether a Judge who thus gives way to his private griefs, is a fit person to sit in judgment upon the dethroned leader."[38] Jurors who voted their conscience in returning the indictment against Davis undoubtedly faced the threat of violence and intimidation in Richmond. The federal judge, in whose courtroom the case would be assigned, had faced the same type of physical and emotional abuse for his efforts against slavery prior to the war. Underwood certainly felt a strong need to reassure those who would participate in the federal criminal system that they should not feel bullied, but his words reasonably put his judicial temperament into question. Underwood's initial appearance in the Davis case bruised the public's perception of the impartiality of the justice system. To those who believed that Underwood was not up to the task of trying such a high-profile case, his intemperate remarks reinforced that view. The inclusion of Chief Justice Salmon Chase as the trial judge now took on an even greater importance, with unforeseen consequences attendant to this necessity.

Significantly for the prosecution, Lucius Chandler, the federal district attorney charged with the lead role in the Davis prosecution, was said to be in Norfolk, Virginia, confined to his room, too ill to travel to the state capital. With the grand jury now working in an adjoining room, Underwood had no more formal business before the court. He engaged counsel for the defense in an informal, conversational manner, which created an opening that resulted in some confusion in the courtroom. "We shall be happy to hear from members of the bar," he said, "always giving preference to members from a distance." William B. Reed, O'Conor's cocounsel from Philadelphia, rose in response to the judge's invitation to speak. He introduced himself as if Underwood did not know who he was: "I beg to present myself in conjunction with my colleagues as the counsel of Jefferson Davis, a prisoner of state at Fortress Monroe, and under indictment for high treason in your Honor's court."[39]

Reed launched into the concerns of the defense team: "We find in the records of your Honor's court an indictment charging Mr. Davis with this high offence, and it has seemed to us due to the cause of justice, due to this tribunal, due to the feelings of one sort or another which may be described as crystalizing around the unfortunate man, that we should come at the very earliest day to this tribunal, and ask of your Honor, or more properly, the gentleman who represents the United States, the simple question: What is proposed to be done with this indictment?" The actions of the defense would be dependent upon the answer to this question. "Is it to be tried, is it to be withdrawn, or is it to be suspended?" he asked. Reed then dramatically made an assertion to the court. He was now certain that the government was not in the least prepared to try the case, and this knowledge made it easy for him to assert next: "I say with emphasis, I say it with earnestness, that we come here prepared instantly to try that case, and we shall ask no delay at your Honor's hands further than is necessary to bring the prisoner to face the Court."[40]

There could have been no greater bluff made by the defense, since O'Conor was not even in the city. Even without Charles O'Conor, though, the defense made a compelling argument that was full of confidence in their case. Reed continued in his questions about the indictment: "Is it to be withdrawn? If so, justice and humanity seem to us to prompt that we should know it." Then Reed made the argument that would be urged over and over again by the defense: "We ask a speedy trial on any charges that may be brought against Mr. Davis, here or in any other civil tribunal in the land."[41] Without Chandler, who was the lead prosecutor, Maj. John L. Hennessy, the assistant United States district attorney, was forced to admit that he was caught unaware by the defense demand for a speedy trial. He did not know whether the case would go forward or not. Hennessy explained that Lucius Chandler was expected in Richmond later in the day. Once here, obviously, Chandler would be able to tell the court if the defense demand could be honored. If he did not arrive, then, Hennessy told Judge Underwood, he would inform the court about the plans to try Davis by the next morning. However, the prosecution argued, somewhat ironically given that the government sought the death penalty, Davis was in delicate health and a protracted trial in the Richmond heat would be a cruelty to him.[42]

The next day, the court drew to order just before eleven o'clock in the morning. The courtroom was full of spectators interested in hearing what the government prosecutors planned to do with Davis. Judge Underwood soon addressed Hennessy, the assistant prosecutor, and asked to hear from him. Hennessy's address to the court revealed a strange nervousness on his part. If grand jurors faced a hostile public in Richmond for their part in the Davis prosecution, government attorneys must have found themselves very unpopular. Whether fear played a role in his demeanor cannot be determined, but he acted as if he wanted to be considered nothing more than a messenger to the court. He told Judge Underwood, "As the questions propounded by Mr. Reed yesterday are considered of some importance, I have written them out, and propose to read them to the Court."[43] This was an inauspicious beginning.

All that William Reed had demanded the day before was a speedy trial for Davis. He put the prosecution on the spot by asking whether the government intended to try the case, but this hardly should have been taken as a serious question to the men chosen to prosecute it. A federal grand jury had just returned a treason indictment against Davis a month earlier. It alleged that the president of the Confederacy had violated the duty of his allegiance to the United States and waged a war against it that had resulted in the deaths of hundreds of thousands of its citizens. Surely an indictment would not have been sought if the government did not intend to prosecute it. Hennessy might have retorted, without hesitation, that since an indictment had been returned on a heinous, capital offense, the case would be prosecuted to the full extent of the law. Instead, he was so far out of the loop that he did not believe himself to be competent to respond until the next day. And worse, now standing before the court, Hennessy felt compelled to read the answers to the questions rather than respond forcefully to the strange query of whether the charge would be pursued. The defense team must have been pleased with the unprofessional response of the prosecutor. It only got worse for the government.

"Mr. Chandler is still absent, being, I regret to say, entirely prostrated by a recent severe domestic calamity, but as I promised that I would proceed today to reply to the questions of the learned gentleman, I shall do so," Hennessy announced. He then read the questions that Reed had propounded. In reply, he said, "So far as I am instructed, I believe it is to be tried."[44] Hennessy then listed several reasons why it could not be immediately tried. First, he stated, Davis was in military custody and not subject to the jurisdiction of the court. Second, Attorney General Speed was too busy to try the case at this session of the court. Finally, Davis's health precluded a trial in the summer heat.

Hennessy tried to offer assurances to the defense team: "Neither this Court nor any of its officers have any present control over the person of Mr. Davis, and until they have, it becomes impossible for the District Attorney to say where he will be tried—but I assure the gentlemen who represent Mr. Davis here that the moment he comes into the custody of this Court they shall have full and prompt notice when it is intended to try him. So far as the District Attorney and his associates are concerned, they may feel assured that their case will have a just and speedy trial, without further barrier, let or hindrance. This I say for the special department of the Court which I represent. But what the intentions of the Government are with regard to the disposition of Mr. Davis, I am no further instructed than I have said."[45] Hennessy then requested that the case be moved to the fall term of the court.

James T. Brady, another lawyer for Davis, pounced on the weak argument of the prosecutor. He emphasized to Judge Underwood that Davis had not been served with a copy of the indictment nor with a list of witnesses, both prerequisites for a felony trial. But, he said, "Mr. Davis is not claiming the benefits of any of these wants of forms."[46] Despite these irregularities, Brady told the court that the defense was anxious for a speedy trial. Responding to the prosecution's newfound concern for Davis's health, Brady asserted that the heat at Fort Monroe was worse than that in Richmond. Underwood tried to deflect the salient part of the argument—that the defense was ready for trial—and addressed, instead, the comfort of the prisoner. On that point, he disagreed with Brady. "I think counsel are mistaken," he said, "in supposing that Fortress Monroe is not as comfortable a place as Richmond. When I have been there in the summer I have found the sea breeze very refreshing." Brady responded, "But very limited society, your Honor," causing laughter to break out in the courtroom. He continued, "We, the counsel of Mr. Davis, can only say that we are entirely ready" for trial. "We know that we cannot control the action of the District Attorney. We thank him for his polite response." Judge Underwood listened to the arguments and then revealed in his remarks that he and Chase had already discussed and decided the trial schedule. Chief Justice Chase had named the first Tuesday in October as convenient for him to try the case. The Davis trial was then adjourned until that day.[47]

The aggressive tone of the argument from defense counsel underscored the shifting moral high ground from the government to the defense. Never would the government claim that ground during a court proceeding. The defense demanded for Davis only that to which every American citizen was constitutionally entitled: namely, a fair and speedy trial. In return for being granted that, the defense claimed to be ready to waive notice of the indictment and all other procedural rights due their client. The prosecutor was relegated to assuring the court that they, too, were intent on bringing Davis to trial quickly and would do so, if only granted this one continuance.

The federal prosecutor missed an excellent opportunity to respond pointedly to the defense. Hennessy could have advanced facts that would have placed the government and the defendant in a different light. He could have argued that Davis had betrayed the very government that he had served for decades. His treason had extended over four years of brutal warfare and resulted in the deaths of hundreds of thousands of Americans. Even conceding that Davis had been held in custody for a year, the adequate presentation of a case of this magnitude required careful and thorough preparation. For a man who allowed Union soldiers to wither and die from exposure at Andersonville, his warm quarters, whether uncomfortable or not, should not prove too hard a burden to bear, Hennessy could have responded. And the delay in trial was not so great an inconvenience that it warranted making a martyr of Davis. Hennessy missed the opportunity to make these arguments. Instead, he allowed the defense lawyers to champion their client's interests without striking a blow in return. Somehow the momentum for the prosecution needed to be regenerated. As it stood in June 1866, the defense appeared to be gaining control.

11

HENRY STANBERY BECOMES ATTORNEY GENERAL

> Here he exclaimed with much sarcasm that Davis would never be punished, simply because Mr. Johnson had determined to have him tried in the one way that he could not be tried, and had determined not to have him tried in the only way he could be tried.
>
> —Report of an Address by Frederick Douglass, March 1866

SWINGS IN THE MOMENTUM of a lawsuit are often not felt by lawyers or parties. Too often, the day-to-day work obscures an attorney from this occurrence, while clients are too close to the case to see any side but their own. The activity surrounding the Jefferson Davis trial was revealing some rather small, but important, steps that needed to be accomplished before Davis could be tried. Attorney General James Speed met with Charles O'Conor and followed up on their interview with a request to the president to permit Davis to have his attorneys visit him. President Johnson wrote Secretary of War Edwin Stanton, asking for an order to be issued to Gen. Nelson A. Miles at Fort Monroe allowing counsel to meet with Davis. Among the men authorized to see Davis was Burton N. Harrison, Davis's private secretary during the war, who had been accepted into the New York bar as an attorney following his release from prison.[1]

On Thursday, June 8, 1866, Davis was visited by some of his defense team—William B. Reed, Edwin A. Van Sickle, and Thomas Henry Edsall—along with Harrison. Van Sickle and Edsall were young associates in O'Conor's office. Their boss had not made the trek to Fort Monroe. Instead, he remained in Washington, D.C., in hopes of having a meeting to discuss the case with President Johnson and Attorney General Speed. Davis had just acquired, on May 25, the privilege of access to the entire grounds of Fort Monroe during daylight hours. He was granted this concession after he signed a document pledging that he would "make no attempt to, nor take any advantage of any opportunity that may be offered to effect my escape" by virtue of this liberty. Varina Davis, able now to visit her husband, prepared dinner for the men in Davis's casement, using goods for which local merchants refused payment, insisting that the honor of helping Davis was compensation enough. Amid Davis's newfound popularity, the lawyers worked on his defense. Reporters who waited for them outside the fort found the defense team confident that Davis would be released within a week.[2] Davis would be bitterly disappointed.

George Shea brought the application for the release of Jefferson Davis to Judge John C. Underwood while the judge was in Washington. O'Conor was also present, and Attorney General James Speed represented the prosecution when Underwood considered the application. It was an awkward legal position in which the judge found himself. The Constitution guaranteed a speedy trial. Davis had been incarcerated for a year, and the federal government had conceded at the trial date just passed that the case was not ready to be presented to a jury. A delay of six months was now required. Fairness appeared to weigh on the side of granting Davis's release on bond. There was a way, though, to avoid deciding the merits of the application altogether. The defense request was denied by Underwood on the grounds that Davis was in military custody and outside the reach of the civil courts. This appeared to be strange logic to the defense team. After all, the court had set the case for trial. How that could have been done if the defendant was outside the reach of the court was a question that perplexed Davis's lawyers.

O'Conor asked that Underwood put his ruling in writing so that the issue could be presented to the president. The defense lawyer was convinced that Johnson would remove this impediment to Davis's release. Underwood had no qualms about giving the defense a written ruling. In a brief order dated June 11, 1866, addressing the application, he lent credibility to the concerns raised earlier by Chief Justice Salmon Chase. Underwood recounted that Davis had been arrested under a proclamation signed by President Johnson charging Davis with complicity in the assassination of the late President Lincoln. Davis, Underwood noted, was then being held as a military prisoner in Virginia, a state still under military jurisdiction and martial law. Davis "is not and never has been in the custody of the marshal for the District of Virginia, and he is not therefore, within the power of the court. While this condition remains, no proposition for bail can be properly entertained, and I do not wish to indicate any probable action under the circumstances."[3] Underwood could have simply denied the application without comment. By stating the reasons for his denial, however, he very openly shifted the controversy to the executive branch.

The U.S. House of Representatives weighed in on the Davis question on the very day that Underwood denied the application for release of the famous prisoner. George S. Boutwell, a Republican from Massachusetts and a member of the Committee on the Assassination of Lincoln, issued a report finding that "it is notorious that Jefferson Davis was the leader of the late rebellion, and is guilty of treason under the laws of the United States."[4] Boutwell also referred to the presidential proclamation of May 1865, in which President Johnson linked Davis with complicity in Lincoln's murder. The resolution offered the opinion of the House that Davis should be held in custody pending trial. The allegation that Davis was tied, somehow, to the Lincoln assassination prompted Andrew Rogers, a Democrat from New Jersey, to leap to his feet and yell, "The proof is that he had nothing," before being drowned out by cries of "Order! Order!" by other House members. Despite the efforts to debate the resolution, the rules were suspended and a vote taken. The resolution passed 105 to 19.[5] The House made clear that it was unified on the question—Davis should remain a prisoner until his trial. If President Johnson decided to take the initiative to release Davis, his decision would be in direct contradiction to the will of the Radical Republicans in the House.

The defense was not solely reliant upon the judicial track in attempting to secure Davis's release. As with any highly publicized trial, attorneys can attempt to leverage the case on many different fronts. O'Conor began to publicly put pressure on President Johnson to release Davis pretrial. On June 13, 1866, he and another attorney, Thomas G. Pratt, addressed a letter to the president, writing that "the State of Mr. Davis' health renders his further imprisonment detrimental, and probably dangerous to his life."[6] Facing the public relations disaster that would explode if the famous prisoner died in custody while awaiting trial, Johnson agreed to meet with the two men. On that afternoon, the three sat in the White House for a lengthy meeting, during which the lawyers argued that the military detention of Davis and the rules under which it was administered deprived him of sleep and were ruining his health. Pratt and O'Conor pledged to honor the terms of any parole under which Johnson might order Davis released.[7] Johnson, a hard man, was unmoved by their pleas and promises.

Also working hard to secure Davis's release was Horace Greeley, who had made the trip from New York City to Washington, D.C., reportedly seeking to meet with Underwood and, otherwise, to try to persuade the government to parole Davis. Greeley met with Senator Zachariah Chandler of Michigan, Senator Henry Wilson of Massachusetts, and other Radical Republicans, looking to secure Davis's release.[8] He pushed the politicians to use their influence to give Davis his freedom while awaiting trial. Greeley had no more success with them than the lawyers had with Johnson.

Days after this meeting came the publication of *The Prison Life of Jefferson Davis,* ostensibly written by John J. Craven, the Union army surgeon assigned to care for Davis from the date of his confinement at Fort Monroe through December 1865. In fact, the doctor allowed a friend, Charles G. Halpine, to borrow his notes in late March 1866 and ghostwrite the book. Halpine wrote to Andrew Johnson after reviewing the doctor's diary. He told the president that Craven was "an old and active member of the Republican party,"[9] which would render the sympathetic view of Davis immune to criticism. William Hanchett wrote in 1969 that the book "was about as subtle and truthful as the burlesques and hoaxes of Miles O'Reilly," two of Halpine's well-known works of fiction.[10] In his 1987 book detailing the handwritten annotations by Jefferson Davis on his copy of *Prison Life,* Edward K. Eckert took the name of his book from a note that Davis wrote in a margin: "fiction distorting fact."[11] But it was not meant to be a work of history; instead, it was written to soften the views of those who hated Davis.

Davis, as portrayed by Halpine, was kindly and considerate, with a brilliant intellect. According to the book, Davis possessed a reserve of knowledge that "was immense and detailed. He was an expert on history, literature, geology, botany, and human anatomy; on navigation and ship design; on ordinance, industry, and engineering; on birds, dogs, and the Bible; and he liked to recite long passages of Milton."[12] As befitting a southern gentleman, according to Halpine, Davis refused to speak ill of any man. Nor did the rebel waver in his desire to vindicate himself. "In regard to attempts at escape," wrote Halpine, "General Miles might give himself no uneasiness. Mr. Davis desired trial both for himself and cause, and if all the doors and gates of the fort were thrown open he would not leave."[13] Always cognizant of his honor and responsibility,

Davis found "the only duty left to him—his only remaining object—was to vindicate the action of his people, and his own action as their representative, by a fair and public trial."[14]

Halpine, writing as Dr. Craven, ended the book by claiming, "It was not my intention to have published this narrative until after the trial of the prisoner; but on submitting the matter to friends, whose judgment I relied upon, it was decided that there was no material in these pages which could bias or improperly interfere with public opinion, or the due course of justice." Yet within two pages, Halpine urged Americans to "let a great nation show the truest quality of greatness—magnanimity—by including him in the wide folds of that act of amnesty and oblivion, in which all his minor partners, civil and military, in the late Confederacy are now so wisely enveloped."[15] Halpine's objective comes clearly into focus in the final pages of his book: "Make him a martyr and his memory is dangerous; treat him with the generosity of liberation, and he both can and, we think, will be a power for good in the future of peace and restored prosperity which we hope for the Southern States."[16] The public image of Davis was shifting from that of him being the disdained architect of a failed war effort that devastated the entire South to a nearly perfect gentleman suffering at the hands of a bloodthirsty government bent on revenge.

Ironically, Davis found the book distasteful. George William Brown, a southern sympathizer from Maryland who had spent over a year in prison during the war, wrote to former president Franklin Pierce that "Dr. Craven's book is doing a great deal of good, but it contains a great deal that annoys Mr. Davis very much. It is, he says, sensational in parts and that is particularly disagreeable to him, and in some things is incorrect."[17] But the Davises recognized the value of the book. Neither Jefferson nor Varina ever publicly criticized the work. As Hanchett pointed out, "Considering the extent to which the book rehabilitated his reputation in the South and won him friends among his former enemies in the North, even a proper Victorian like Davis might have forgiven an admiring friend whose only offense was overly colorful writing and a few minor indiscretions."[18] At least one member of the Davis family believed that the work succeeded in making him a sympathetic character. Joseph E. Davis, Jefferson's brother, wrote to the imprisoned rebel leader that "the prison life by Dr. Craven is I think exerting an influence greater than expected."[19] Public opinion plays an important role in the prosecution of criminal cases. While many individuals recognized that the work was a political tract, it did sway public opinion against the prosecution. Halpine's work of fiction, ostensibly authored by a Union military doctor who had unique access to Davis and who grew to admire his character immensely, diminished the popularity of the prosecution's case.

James Speed Leaves the Cabinet

Attorney General James Speed was rapidly becoming disillusioned with the Johnson presidency. He had been appointed by his friend Abraham Lincoln to the cabinet post, and the fourteen months following Lincoln's assassination had not been happy ones for Speed. While his legal skills might be wanting, no one had ever accused Speed of lacking physical courage. He continued to listen to his own conscience on matters of politics and wrote that "still each individual man must diligently seek to find out what is right and fearlessly pursue it."[20] The attorney general was politically much closer to the Radical Republicans than to the conservative Johnson.[21] Perfectly aligned on the need to prosecute Davis, he found himself at odds with the new president on many other important issues. Struggling with what to do in this situation, he turned to his brother, Joshua, in the early months of 1866, and talked of quitting the cabinet. Joshua Speed offered advice against stepping down. On April 1, 1866, he wrote his brother: "You were appointed by the late President, as a representative man of the party for freedom in the slave States. The country and the party are both satisfied with the appointment. It would grieve those with whose political fortunes our political destiny is linked, for you to quit. While what is still worse, it would gladden the hearts of your enemies. So long as you can with honor, which I know you will never sacrifice, I would advise you to remain; when that cannot be done, I know you will quit."[22] The attorney general hung on to his post, but the breach between he and Johnson began to widen even further.

Speed was not alone among the members of the administration in his opposition to Johnson's policies. Reconstruction was an extremely divisive issue facing the nation, and Johnson's proposed policy about it formed the foundation for the split in the president's cabinet. Newspapers began attacking the attorney general. The *Daily National Intelligencer,* located in Washington, D.C., published a letter to the editor, ostensibly from Lexington, Kentucky, that Speed "is universally regarded by the Union men of Kentucky, and, doubtless, of the whole country, as being thoroughly identified in sentiment with the Radical party, whose leaders in Congress are waging a relentless warfare upon the Administration of President Johnson."[23] Speed was only one of several members of the cabinet said to be either close to resigning or near being pushed out of the Johnson cabinet. It was serious enough that the *New York Tribune* termed the upheaval "the Cabinet crisis."[24] Clear information was difficult to come by because, in July 1866, Washington was "full of rumors of Cabinet changes, but there is nothing definite about them."[25] Along with Speed, Secretary of War Edwin Stanton, Secretary of the Interior James Harlan, and William Dennison Jr., the postmaster general, were rumored to be leaving the cabinet. As if this was not enough, Secretary of the Navy Gideon Welles noted in his diary in mid-July that Illinois senator Lyman Trumbull had "introduced another of his revolutionary bills to deprive the President of his Constitutional right of removing from office."[26]

Amid the chaos in the cabinet, Speed's attention—understandably—was not on the Davis prosecution. By mid-July, under increasing pressure, Speed met with the president and offered his resignation. He wrote his brother about the July 12, 1866, meeting: "I had a full and frank talk with the President, the result of which was that I am to resign. I would have done so at once, but preferred to give him a day or two to look around for my successor."[27] Speed told Joshua that the conversation had been as kind and courteous, on both sides, as he could have wanted, but their differences made continued collaboration impossible. The immediate crux of their differences revolved around the wisdom of the Fourteenth Amendment to the Constitution, which Speed supported and Johnson opposed. When the dust settled, Harlan and Dennison had also left the cabinet. Stanton, described by Welles as "selfish, insincere, a dissembler, and treacherous,"[28] remained in the cabinet, ultimately forming the basis for the Johnson impeachment when the president forced him from office. Headlines trumpeted the news as: "Cabinet Break-Up" and the "Disruption Complete."[29]

The consequences of Speed's resignation on the Davis prosecution could not be gauged at the time of his leaving the post of attorney general. Speed had intended to personally prosecute Davis. Whether he was a lawyer up to that task can be debated; however, he lent the prestige of the office to the prosecution. He also brought with him to trial that moral certainty of the principled basis for the prosecution of a man he considered a traitor. This self-assurance fuels prosecutors during the long hours of preparation in a major case and girds them against the questioning of their motives and judgment as they pursue convictions. Perhaps what was irreplaceable was Speed's courage. A man like Speed, who had entered a rally for secession in the red-hot times before the war and who had replaced the American flag on the stage and then spoken down the secessionists who filled the packed hall, would be fearless enough to try Jefferson Davis for treason in Virginia. Of that, there was no doubt. It remained to be seen whether Speed's successor would be as courageous.

Henry Stanbery Takes the Helm

No sooner had Speed resigned than Johnson offered the post to Henry Stanbery. On July 17, 1866, the *Cincinnati Enquirer* printed Speed's terse letter of resignation, dated July 16, and reported that "the President immediately telegraphed to Hon. Henry S. Stanbery, of Kentucky, proffering him the appointment."[30] The man to whom Johnson offered the cabinet seat was considered a highly accomplished lawyer. Although Stanbery lived in Covington, Kentucky, his practice was located right across the Ohio River, in Cincinnati. He was sixty-three at the time of his appointment and not in the best of health. Politically, however, he differed significantly from the man he would replace.

On July 23, the Senate confirmed his nomination. If his confirmation breezed through the Senate, it was not because his politics were obscured from the public eye. The *Cleveland Plain Dealer* editorialized that "other changes, demanded no less by a decent self-respect and regard to consistency on the part of the President, than by the imperative exigencies of the times, will doubtless soon be made, and the places now occupied by men of narrow views and intensely radical proclivities, will doubtless be filled by those who will honestly and faithfully co-operate with the Chief Executive in efforts to restore and preserve the Union."[31] Replacing Speed with Stanbery gave the cabinet a much more conservative bent. It was well known that Johnson had turned to Stanbery for assistance in justifying Johnson's veto of the Civil Rights Act of 1866, prior to Stanbery's appointment to the attorney generalship. The *Daily Inter Ocean* from Chicago wrote that Stanbery "has been very conservative in his opinions, and has had the credit of preparing the legal part of the President's first veto upon the Freedmen's Bureau bill."[32] It would come as no surprise that Stanbery would have a different approach to the treason charge pending against Jefferson Davis.

William M. Evarts and John H. Clifford, lawyers hired by Stanbery's predecessor, were cognizant that Stanbery might want to forge his own path in the case. On August 14, Evarts penned a letter to Stanbery about the matter: "We had the honor, about a year ago, to be retained by the late Atty. Genl., Mr. Speed, for the Government in the matter of the public prosecution which it was thought might be instituted for the trial of Jefferson Davis and other leaders of the Rebellion. In consequence of this we have had several deliberate consultations with Mr. Speed and the President on the general subject of these prosecutions, but have had no occasion to proceed further." Then he got to the point of his letter: "You should feel entirely free to dispense with associate counsel, or to select from the profession of the Country, such as in your own choice, should seem most suitable to the public interests in your charge. We beg, therefore, to place wholly at your own disposal the question whether we shall longer consider ourselves of counsel for the Government in these prosecutions, assuring you that as we were governed only by a sense of public duty in acceding to the wishes of the Government, as communicated to us by Atty. Genl. Speed, so, now we have no personal views or feelings in surrendering to his successor the trust with which we have been honored." Evarts signed the letter and sent it to Clifford for the Boston lawyer to consider and then transmit to Stanbery.

Clifford added his own thoughts to the letter, agreeing with Evarts that it was appropriate for the two men to offer Stanbery the option of keeping counsel retained by his predecessor. But Clifford had been struggling for some time with the more basic question of whether treason prosecutions were wise for the federal government to undertake at all. His heart was not in the effort, and his head told him that it was unwise to attempt to prosecute rebel leaders. He told Stanbery of his feelings: "If it is the purpose of the Government to proceed with the trial of Jefferson Davis upon the Indictment pending against him in Virginia, I do not feel that any public or professional duty would require me to take a part in the proceedings." He then added his reason for resigning from the case: "Under existing circumstances I can see no reasonable probability of any other result of such a trial, than the re-opening of a question which has already been solemnly determined by the highest tribunal to which it can ever be submitted, with almost certain impunity to the prisoner, and to the consequent humiliation of the Govt. and the Country."[33]

Clifford had come to the point that he no longer believed the trial of Davis would serve the Union cause. That he had not come to it quickly was evidenced by a clipping that he had kept from the *Chicago Tribune,* dated November 15, 1865, entitled "Object of Jeff. Davis' Trial." The editorial echoed his concerns. The newspaper had written that no decision reached by a trial would "add weight to the letter of the Constitution, or settle a question which has been sealed by the blood of half a million men."[34] When Clifford wrote Stanbery of a trial reopening a question that had already been decided by the "highest tribunal to which it could ever be submitted," he was referring to the war itself and how the outcome of the struggle had determined that secession was not constitutionally permissible.

Clifford foresaw that Davis's legal position would be that states had the right to secede. If this was correct, Davis could not be guilty of treason because he would owe no loyalty to a government from which he had legally separated. If Davis was found "not guilty" of treason, the acquittal would give rise to the argument that the war had not finally determined this issue. If that possibility were not reason enough to not prosecute, Clifford considered that the indictment would be heard in Richmond, Virginia, formerly the capital of the Confederacy. Unable to reconcile his thoughts that a treason trial held in the former Confederacy was anything but foolish, Clifford resigned from the prosecution.

To friends, the Boston attorney was even blunter about his reasoning. Congressman George S. Boutwell wrote Clifford, asking, "If there is no controlling reason to the contrary I wish to know why you resigned from the Davis case."[35] "I withdrew from the Davis case," Clifford replied, "with the consent of Atty. Genl. Stanbery simply because I was satisfied that his trial before any Jury in Virginia would only result in the humiliation of the Govt., with entire impunity to the prisoner. And as I was under no official or professional obligation to do so, I was not disposed to participate in the enactment of a judicial farce, the result of which was a foregone conclusion."[36]

With Clifford off the case and only two months into his tenure as attorney general, Stanbery recognized that direction needed to be given on the question of what to do with the rebel president. The case had been set for trial in early October, but newspapers reported that Underwood realized he might not have authority to hold court in Richmond, where the trial was to be held. The Fourth Circuit Court had met in Richmond until the war, when Congress removed it from the rebel-held city to Norfolk, Virginia, which was within Union lines. Despite having held court in Richmond in June, no real action had been taken on the Davis case. Underwood adjourned the case at that time until October 1866 because, as he announced in court, "the Chief Justice, who is expected to preside on this trial, has named the first Tuesday in October as the time that will be most convenient to him."[37] Now Underwood was hesitant to proceed on the case until a new term began, when new congressional authorization could clearly permit him to preside over cases in Richmond. No one was certain whether the scheduled trial would proceed.

Stanbery was determined to press the issue before the cabinet to get some direction of what to do with the case. Over the next several weeks, he sought to gain an understanding of the course to be taken against Davis. So, when President Johnson and the full cabinet met on October 1, 1866, the attorney general brought up Davis. By then, Jefferson Davis had been in custody for sixteen months. Stanbery, shifting about-face from the legal position held by his predecessor, Speed, explained that he saw no legal basis to hold the former Confederate president in military confinement. If he was a prisoner of war, the lawyer reasoned, the war was over and he should not be held by the military. If he was not a prisoner of war, then the only other avenue to proceed against him was as a criminal through the courts, yet that process was not being pursued vigorously.

Both William Seward and Stanton responded to the new attorney general and left no doubt of the ill feelings they harbored toward Davis. The war had taken a toll on the two Union leaders, and they viewed Davis as a traitor who had forfeited all of his civil rights by his actions. They began their discussion by pointing out the position set out by Stanbery's predecessor. According to James Speed, they said, Davis was not a military prisoner but was only being held in military custody for his own safety. Very early in 1866, Speed had determined that Davis could not be tried by a military tribunal for the crime of treason. However, since Davis was under indictment for treason, he was subject to trial by the federal courts. The two powerful cabinet members argued that Davis could be held in military custody for his own safety, even though he was subject to a civil tribunal. Since Davis was held outside the power of the civil court, the speed at which he could be bought to trial was, by necessity, a bit slower. His presence at trial would have to be made by moving him from Fort Monroe to Richmond, a process that could not have been difficult. But at stake in the discussion was not only the speed at which Davis could be tried for treason but also the department under which he was held. At the time of this discussion, he was held by the military, which was under the War Department and Stanton. If Davis were moved, Stanton would no longer oversee Davis's treatment or custody. Stanton was loath to lose that control.

Stanbery remarked that the federal district attorney should then be directed to have Davis brought into the custody of the United States marshal for confinement. Doing so would place the prisoner under the control of the court and allow the court to dispose of any issues in the case. Edwin Stanton became visibly agitated at the suggestion. He heatedly argued to Stanbery "that Davis had forfeited all his rights—that he had no right to demand anything—we could hold him as long as we pleased—we ought to hold him, and he was opposed to any action in the case at present."[38] Seward indicated that while he had been in favor of Davis being tried by a military tribunal, he was, at present, opposed to any action being taken. Orville Browning, confirmed as secretary of the interior as of September 1, 1866, came to Stanbery's defense and said that he thought Davis should be transferred to civilian custody. Having heard from four cabinet members voicing opposing views, President Johnson stepped in and said that he agreed with Stanbery and Browning. Davis "should be brought to trial for treason as soon as possible," according to the president. Even after Johnson told Stanbery what he wanted done in the Davis case, Seward and Stanton argued that although lawful authority was lacking to keep Davis in custody indefinitely, the president had the power to do so and should exercise that power.[39] The new members of the cabinet reflected Johnson's views much closer than did the two men held over from the Lincoln administration.

The division on whether Davis should be held in military or civilian custody reflected fears deeper than merely putting the former Confederate president to trial. As a backdrop of the times, the president and some members of the cabinet still feared another armed conflict was brewing. Conspiracies to overthrow the government were seriously discussed by the president and cabinet. The prospect of transferring Davis from military custody worried Stanton, who feared another outbreak of violence, a possibility that was acknowledged by many in the administration. But an important point to remember regarding the decision to try Davis is that Henry Stanbery and Andrew Johnson did not differ in their views. Since Stanbery drew his direction from the president and Johnson wanted Davis prosecuted as quickly as possible, any delay in getting the case to trial cannot be attributed to hesitation or equivocation on the part of the president.

O'Conor did his best to find out if Chase would be in Richmond in October but had no success. He wrote to Varina Davis that "the Chief Justice declines to state whether he will attend that term or not and intimates that no previous announcement of his intentions need be expected." The New York lawyer gauged Chase insightfully: "He is bent upon running for the Presidency. Mr. Johnson and he thus being rivals for the succession Mr. Davis is the subject of a regular game between them. How to deal with Mr. Davis is an embarrassing problem. Each wishes to avoid any mischief to himself and to work all possible mischief to his opponent. Hence the delay and indecision of both."[40]

As these meetings were being held, Jefferson Davis's lawyers were trying to determine if the trial would take place. Three of his attorneys were in Richmond. William B. Reed, J. Randolph Tucker, and Robert Ould issued a letter for publication, expressing their frustration. Over their three signatures, they wrote that "the counsel of Mr. Davis, now in attendance at Richmond, deem it their duty to lay before the public the following brief statements of facts." The press release pointed out how Judge Underwood had, in June, continued the case "until the first Tuesday in October, which is preferred by the Chief Justice and Attorney General. The case will then, if not before disposed of, be taken up." The three lawyers wrote that "in accordance with this order of the Court the undersigned are in attendance here. They find no Court." Frustrated, the men released their telegraphed message to Underwood in Alexandria, dated September 29, indicating they were in Richmond and asking if court was to be held. The terse reply that they received from Underwood was also published: "There will be no United States Court in Richmond next week."[41]

Just days after the cabinet meeting, President Johnson noted that "a special term of the Circuit Court of the United States was appointed for the first Tuesday of October, 1866, at Richmond, Va., for the trial of Jefferson Davis on the charge of treason."[42] This seemed to be a hopeful sign. Johnson had met with Charles O'Conor very early in October as O'Conor attempted to find out if the case would be tried. Only after the meeting was O'Conor apprised that the defense attorneys in Richmond had been told that no court would be held.

President Johnson must have been frustrated at the lack of professionalism being exhibited by federal officials. He voiced his concern that it was now clear that the court would not be in session in October at all and that there was some doubt as to whether November's term would even be held. The delay in the trial troubled the president. According to Johnson, there was "no good reason why the civil courts of the United States are not competent to exercise adequate jurisdiction" over the case. He asked the new attorney general to give his opinion if any further action was necessary from the executive branch to have the case proceed to trial.[43]

Conversations about the Davis trial between Attorney General Henry Stanbery and Lucius H. Chandler, the federal attorney in Virginia, also continued. Stanbery met with Chandler near the beginning of October 1866 and asked why Chandler had not requested Davis's transfer from military to civilian custody. Stanbery listened to Chandler's answer and then instructed him to put the response in writing. The attorney general likely perceived a need to nail down on paper the reluctant prosecutor about the inexplicable slowness in the prosecution. Several days later, Chandler responded in a rather formal reply: "In compliance with your request, I submit, herewith, the substance of the verbal statement I made you, a few days since, in answer to your question, 'Why no demand had been made upon the military authorities for the surrender of Jefferson Davis, in order that he might be tried upon the Indictment found against him in the United States Circuit Court, at the term held at Norfolk, in May last.'"[44] Having answered Stanbery in conversation, Chandler now tried to explain his reasoning in writing. The effort could not have been an easy one, since Stanbery's request that Chandler respond in writing must have carried with it the implication that his earlier explanation had not been quite acceptable. Still, he tried to justify his procrastination.

"Two reasons have influenced me in not taking any steps for removing him from their custody," Chandler wrote. "The one relates to his safekeeping, the other to his own personal comfort and health. I have never had any doubt but that he would be delivered to the United States Marshal for the District whenever he should have demanded him on a 'capias' [a court order directing an officer to take a defendant to a place as directed by the court], or any other civil process. But you can readily understand that so soon as he goes into the hands of that officer, upon any action had by me, his place of confinement would be one of the state jails of Virginia. At Fortress Monroe all necessary precautions can be, and are taken to protect his escape. Over the internal police of a state jail, the Marshal has no authority, and the safe custody of the prisoner could not be secured save at a very great expense." Safe custody of the prisoner was not Chandler's only reason. "Mr. Davis is now in as comfortable quarters as the mass of those occupied by the Army officers at the Fort," Chandler maintained. "The location is a healthy one. His family has free access to him. He has full opportunity for exercise in the open air. If his health be feeble, remove him to one of the state jails, and his condition, instead of being bettered, would, in all these respects, be much for the worse. His counsel probably understand all this, and, I think, will not be likely to take any steps which would decrease the personal comforts, or endanger the life of their client."[45]

The attorney general must have been surprised at Chandler's lack of initiative. In October 1866, there was no greater criminal charge pending in the entire country than that against Davis. Yet the prosecutor in the case had not asked for his transfer to a facility where he could be prosecuted for the capital offense of treason because of expense and inconvenience to the accused. The only reason advanced by Chandler that might have made sense to the attorney general was that a Virginia jail might prove incapable of keeping Davis from escaping without a significant expenditure.

Stanbery revisited the issue at the cabinet meeting a week later. Now armed with Chandler's reply to his questions, he advised President Johnson to order the commandant of Fort Monroe to honor a demand for Davis's transfer to the civilian authorities in Virginia. Predictably, Stanton opposed this move and argued that it was a mistake to announce to the public that Davis would be transferred to civilian authorities. Stanbery countered by pointing out that the public was being given the perception that the Johnson administration was blocking the trial of Davis and thereby shielding him from punishment. Politically, it made sense to clear this misperception up for the public. Stanbery maintained that he "wanted the case placed in its true light, and the courts and the Country informed that Mr. Davis was held subject to the order of the Court whenever it chose to call for him."[46]

Three days later, during another cabinet meeting, Stanbery read a letter from the president asking whether there was anything that he needed to do to bring Davis to trial and, if so, for direction as to what steps were necessary. Stanbery let the cabinet know that Johnson need do nothing more than what he had already done. Following Johnson's directions, all the military restraints upon the civil courts proceeding against Davis in Virginia had been withdrawn, and it was Stanbery's understanding that Davis was now being held at Fort Monroe simply awaiting an order from the District Court in Virginia to be brought before it to answer the pending indictment.[47]

On October 12, 1866, the attorney general issued a written opinion that "there is nothing in the present condition of Virginia to prevent the full exercise of the jurisdiction of the civil courts."[48] He went on to address the inaction of the legislative branch: "Mr. Davis remains in custody at Fortress Monroe precisely as he was held in January last, when, in answer to a resolution of the Congress, you reported communications from the Secretary of War and the Attorney General, showing that he was held to await trial in the civil courts. No action was then taken by Congress in reference to the place of custody."[49] In a passage that must have frustrated congressional leaders who sought to have Davis tried and hung, Stanbery wrote that Lucius Chandler had "been notified that the prisoner would be surrendered to the United States marshal upon a *capias* under the indictment, but the district attorney declines to have the *capias* issued because there is no other place where the prisoner could be so safely kept."[50] Stanbery also deftly pointed out that Charles O'Conor had not formally applied to the trial court to have Davis transferred to civil custody. Stanbery's opinion ignored the fact that Chandler had been looking to Washington for guidance and that the local district attorney did not consider himself competent to decide matters involving the trial of Jefferson Davis without specific orders from Johnson and Stanbery. It also paid no attention to the clearly articulated demand by Davis's trial team for a speedy trial.

Stanton noticed the distance that Stanbery sought to place between the Washington office of the attorney general and the district attorney in Virginia. Sensing that Stanbery would not want to be involved in the trial itself and knowing that the hesitancy of a lead attorney to try a case might delay the proceedings, Stanton insisted that it was Stanbery's duty as attorney general to conduct the trial in person himself. Stanton also pointed out, as any fine attorney would, that the indictment needed to be amended to specify the acts of Davis that constituted treason. The secretary of war held it to be Stanbery's duty to draft a proper indictment, subpoena and secure the attendance of witnesses, and present the case against Davis in Richmond. Stanbery responded with a long discussion of his view of the office he held. He believed himself to be the legal advisor of the president and the cabinet, not a prosecutor. The only court that he needed to appear before was the United States Supreme Court. Davis's indictment was no more important, and no less so, than any indictment pending before federal courts, and he believed it would be improper for him to appear to prosecute Davis personally. Stanton did not hesitate to try to intervene in the business of other cabinet members, and the tension between him and Stanbery over the Davis case came out in the open.[51] The impassioned argument exposed a terribly troubling view, held by Stanbery, of the Davis treason indictment. It was just another criminal case to Stanbery. As a result of that opinion, Stanbery would not bring the power of his personal presence to the courtroom for the trial. Chandler was further out on his own than he would have been under Speed, and he needed close supervision if he was to successfully prepare the case for trial. As it now stood, he would not get that essential management.

Davis Awaits Trial

As tension rose within the administration on how to proceed against Davis, the former rebel's defense team continued its efforts to lobby individuals in the cabinet about the case. William B. Reed, a defense lawyer for Davis, stopped in Washington on his way back from Fort Monroe to Philadelphia in order to talk to Orville Browning, Johnson's newly confirmed secretary of the interior. Reed warned Browning that Davis's health was precarious and that Davis, if he continued in confinement, would not live to see the spring. This claim was made so often by members of Davis's family, friends, and defense team that it soon lost its credibility. Reed, however, also lobbied for a general amnesty to be issued by the president on Thanksgiving Day. He found a sympathetic ear in Browning, who nonetheless told him that he did not believe it would be best for a general amnesty to be issued. Browning recorded a different view in the privacy of his diary: "I have no doubt it would be the best possible thing for the Country, if the Country was prepared to receive it, but it is not."[52]

Reed also sought help for more practical issues. He asked that Davis be given access to the entire fort, day and night, rather than being confined to a cell from sundown to sunrise. Browning told Reed that he agreed that the confinement throughout the night was unnecessary and then broached an unlikely subject. Browning told the defense attorney that he wished Davis would escape, claiming that "it would be the best thing for us—would relieve us of a great embarrassment."[53] As Davis's attorney, Reed could not advocate his client's escape and told Browning that the Confederate president would not escape if he could. Browning committed to Reed that he would bring the subjects of Davis's continued confinement and a general amnesty to the cabinet. He did so the very next day. After a discussion, the entire cabinet voted unanimously to have orders sent to the commandant of Fort Monroe "to extend to Mr. Davis all the liberty, day and night, compatible with his safe keeping."[54] No action was taken on the request for amnesty.

It did not take long for the cabinet discussions to be leaked to the newspapers. Ten days after Attorney General Stanbery replied to President Johnson, the entire correspondence on the issue was published on the front page of the *New York Herald*.[55] The controversy that Stanton wanted to keep under wraps was now known to the American public. The fissure within the cabinet became deeper. Stanton often found himself at odds with the attorney general and secretary of the interior, who also had the support of the president. Browning began to believe that the secretary of war "manifestly wanted to do the President an injury" through his advice to Johnson. Browning, for one, had no faith in Stanton, writing in his diary that "he has no sincerity of character, but is hypocritical and malicious."[56] While the fracturing of the Johnson cabinet would eventually affect the Davis prosecution, the work that needed to be done to prepare for the case did not slow.

Underwood Prepares for the Trial

Judge Underwood undertook an examination of the law of treason in the interim. In late 1866, he wrote to George S. Boutwell, a Radical member of the Joint Committee on Reconstruction in the House of Representatives and a former abolitionist governor of Massachusetts,[57] asking Boutwell's opinion about the punishment for treason. Underwood struggled with the two federal statutes on treason, the Act of 1789 (or 1790, as it is sometimes called) and the Act of 1862. Since the Constitution permitted the legislature to set the punishment for treason, Underwood believed it important to reconcile the two statutes.

In the very first Congress, in 1789, legislators passed an act setting punishment for various crimes. Section 1 of that act provided that any person found guilty of treason "shall suffer death."[58] In 1862, however, Congress expanded the range of punishment for crimes associated with the rebellion. Entitled "An Act to Suppress Insurrection, to Punish Treason and Rebellion, to Seize and Confiscate the Property of Rebels and for Other Purposes," it stated "that every person who shall hereafter commit the crime of treason against the United States, and shall be adjudged guilty thereof, shall suffer death, and all his slaves, if any, shall be declared and made free; or, at the discretion of the court, he shall be imprisoned for not less than five years and fined not less than ten thousand dollars."[59] The second section of the act set a maximum punishment at ten years imprisonment for inciting, assisting, or engaging in any rebellion or insurrection against the United States or giving aid or comfort thereto. Section 4 reflected the poor drafting of the law. It provided "that this act shall not be construed in any way to affect or alter the prosecution, conviction, or punishment of any person or persons guilty of treason against the United States before the passage of this act, unless such person is convicted under this act."[60] Inexplicably, the law provided that a person convicted before the passage of the act would not have the punishment assessed under that conviction altered, unless the person was convicted under the act. It is no wonder that Underwood sought the thoughts of a legislator in interpreting the statute.

Congressman Boutwell answered Underwood's letter from Boston on October 30, 1866. Underwood had expressed a concern that the Act of 1789 providing death to be the exclusive punishment for treason may have been repealed by the Act of 1862. Boutwell did not think it mattered. "The first section of the act of 1862 authorizes the death penalty in the case of treason and it is entirely immaterial whether the act of 1789 is repealed or not," he wrote. "The circumstance that the court may impose a milder sentence under the second paragraph of said section, does not limit the power of the court to proscribe or impose the highest penalty—death."[61] Of course, Underwood may have been hesitant to be in the position of determining whether Davis should be executed or his life spared by a term of imprisonment. Under the Act of 1789, that question did not arise; a person convicted of treason would die.

Boutwell urged Underwood to interpret the statutes in combination. The earlier law, he wrote, "defines the proof necessary" for a conviction under the law of treason, while a conviction under the latter act would permit either the death penalty or a term of imprisonment. He closed by writing, "Considering the case of Davis, I see no reason why he may not be indicted under the act of 1790 by virtue of the 4th section of the act of 1862."[62] Unfortunately for the court, the indictment made mention of neither statute while containing language that could arguably limit the punishment to a term of imprisonment. Proceeding under the indictment as drafted by Chandler put Underwood in a precarious legal position, but he had no ability to alter the charging instrument on his own initiative.

The November Term Arrives

On November 1, 1866, the federal court in Norfolk began its regular term. John Underwood presided, but there was a glaring absence: Lucius Chandler was not in court. Underwood announced that Chandler had "been summoned by the Attorney General of the United States, and is therefore unable to wait upon you to-day." The judge continued: "There now seems a strong probability that the United States Circuit Court will be held on the fourth Monday of this month in Richmond—perhaps merely to meet and then adjourn. Chief Justice Chase has given his opinion that there is no impediment in the way of holding the court, and it's being presided over by the District Judge."[63] The news that Chase would once again avoid being present for trial was not what either party wanted to hear. However, Chase had excused himself from attendance because the Supreme Court would meet in early December and assign, at that time, judges to circuit courts. There was a chance that he would not retain the Fourth Circuit Court of Appeals. Whether this was correct or not, Chase presided over that court in November 1866. It seemed that nothing could make him appear for the Davis trial. Underwood was relegated to trying the case alone, if it was to be tried.

The politically ambitious Salmon Chase was wise to dodge the trial. Underwood faced terrible abuse for his past statements and his presiding over the Davis prosecution. The *Norfolk Virginian* wrote that "Jury-Packing Underwood arrived in the city yesterday morning and stopped at the National. From his declaration that he can pack a jury to hang Jefferson Davis, we shouldn't wonder if he was in Norfolk on the look out for fitting jurors, picking them from the gutters of society with a hook, as a rag-picking beggar picks the dirty, pestiferous rags. Pity but that the hirsute appendage of Jury-Packing Underwood's phiz was of fuller growth, that it might cover up his face, and with it the shame that he must feel, if human still, and not a monster damned."[64] It did not take much political astuteness for Chase to recognize that he did not want to be associated with the prosecution of Jefferson Davis, even as a judge.

November 26 was the fourth Monday of the month. Despite Underwood's announcement, the *Baltimore Sun* reported that "the United States Circuit Court was to hold its November term to-day, but neither Judges Chase nor Underwood have arrived, and nothing has been heard from them."[65] J. Randolph Tucker covered the setting for the Davis defense team, since the lawyers had not received notice of whether the case would proceed to trial. Despite the strong probability that the court would meet, according to Underwood's earlier statements, it did not. A question that needed to be asked by the defense was whether the Johnson administration was losing interest in prosecuting the former rebel.

Jefferson Davis, his family—especially Varina—and his supporters were understandably upset with the continued incarceration. If he could just be released on bond, his life would be much better. O'Conor's belief that Davis would be released and the prosecution ended did not materialize. However, his confidence in his case was not shaken in the least. "A trial is not probable; a conviction is scarcely within the range of possibility," he wrote Varina. "Mr. Davis and yourself should keep your minds free from any anxiety as to ultimate results. There is no danger. The only thing to be considered is how to prevent mischief to Mr. Davis from the privations to be inflicted during that limited term of imprisonment which must yet be endured. The term can not be long."[66] But a year had come and gone with no resolution to the treason charge.

12

A SECOND TRIAL DATE

It certainly does not lie in the mouth of rebels to deny the rights to try prisoners of war for crimes against [civil] laws, committed either prior to or during the war.

—Benjamin Butler

HENRY STANBERY was known to be a man of conservative opinions that reflected those of his boss, Andrew Johnson. The president, of course, had enunciated a tough stance against traitors. As his presidency progressed and Johnson faced stiff opposition from the Radical Republicans, he fell back for support on the men whose views he shared: conservative Democrats, the largest number of whom were to be found in the South. This did not necessarily mean that his position on trying Jefferson Davis for treason was forced to change—and publicly, it did not. So far as the nation knew, Johnson fully intended to have Davis prosecuted. But Stanbery's intentions, privately conveyed to Davis's defense attorneys, reveal a disturbing shift of the administration's plan toward the prosecution.

It would have been troubling to any person hoping to see Jefferson Davis tried for treason to know that the attorney general was revealing confidences to Davis's lawyers. Even more disconcerting would have been the knowledge that he was advising them on how to pilot their case. Thomas Pratt, one of the lawyers for Davis and a former governor of Maryland, was in Washington, D.C., at Charles O'Conor's direction, testing the waters on the questions of a presidential pardon for their client. On November 24, 1866, just two days before the critical fourth Monday in November, Pratt wrote to O'Conor to tell him of a meeting with Stanbery. "The Attorney General tells me," he related, "that the President will issue in a few days a proclamation of general amnesty and he advised that no application should be made in Mr. Davis' case until you have seen this proclamation. He said that everything was working as favorably as we could wish for Mr. D."[1] Pratt admitted that he hesitated to act when faced with the advice of Stanbery and asked for direction from O'Conor.

O'Conor was ecstatic. Immediately upon receipt, O'Conor wrote a letter to Varina Davis on the blank lines of the Pratt letter. She had been pushing the defense to try to have her husband released. O'Conor now believed he had something positive to offer her. He informed her that Governor Pratt had met with Stanbery and William M. Evarts, the leading counsel for the prosecution. Their discussions made it "certain that no good could result from a display of force at Richmond. It seems to me that we cannot be mistaken in relying confidently on a speedy release and an end of all prosecutions."[2]

Jefferson Davis was a man prone to discouragement, and the past year and a half had been difficult on him. Varina, his fierce defender, proved a relentless correspondent to anyone, especially his lawyers. O'Conor dealt with his high-maintenance client as best he could, but he was aware that neither of them was convinced that the case was going as it should. When he wrote to Varina, knowing that she would share the information with her husband, he knew that he was not telling them what they wanted to hear. The couple wanted a display of force in Richmond. O'Conor relied upon what he heard from Pratt and what he read between the lines. His reading was too optimistic, but he tried to bolster the spirits of his client and his client's wife, writing, "I can say nothing more that would be of interest and have only to add my sincere desire and earnest hope that the depression of spirits much spoken of lately has passed off, and that Mr. Davis and yourself will be prepared to meet the enemy with a resolute and cheerful front. This is very desirable as the eyes of the world will be upon you."[3]

O'Conor must have been bitterly disappointed that there was no change in the posture of the case after Pratt's meeting with Stanbery and Evarts. It did not take him long to admit that he was incorrect. On November 19, he wrote again to Varina Davis, stating, "When I last had this pleasure I announced briefly my apprehension of an almost immediate parole." No matter his source, he had been incorrect. Now he told Varina, "It appears, however, that the difficulties of his own position produce vacillation in the president's views; and it is in doubt whether the President will take any action before the assembling of Congress." This bad news was not all. O'Conor told the couple that "Chief Justice Chase will not attend the Richmond court on Monday, and Mr. Stanbery, the Attorney General[,] has signified as much as that the government has no desire to proceed to a trial before Judge Underwood."[4]

The lawyer attributed the change to national politics: "I am quite clear that there is to be a patch-up of their difficulties between the President and Congress. The moment this or any thing else of a decisive nature occurs Mr. Davis will be discharged by the free will of both parties or of the party in power." O'Conor saw the indictment not so much in terms of a criminal case as a struggle of party politics. "The only question on which I have any doubt," he wrote to Varina, "is whether we ought to urge action in a preemptory way by praying [filing] a Hab[eas] Cor[pus] on Monday with a view to bringing Mr. Davis before the Court and demanding his discharge on bail if a trial be not accorded immediately. If this be desired, let me know by telegram instantly." O'Conor advised against filing the writ, calling it "a vain display not likely to advance our interests in any quarter."[5]

His reasoning for this belief was simple. He told Varina Davis: "I incline to let the Court pass by without more than a simple appearance by counsel. I think it will merely open and close with an announcement that no business will be transacted in consequence of the absence of the Chief Justice. Our cause of complaint by reason of the delay in according a speedy trial as required by the Constitution will be as perfect in this case as if we made an outcry before Judge Underwood. Every one knows that a trial before him is not desired by either party."[6] But the filing of an application for a writ of habeas corpus was a legal step that he was eventually forced to take.

O'Conor was right in believing that the trial would not occur in December 1866. Chief Justice Salmon P. Chase remained silent on the business before the court but was corresponding freely on political matters. He told Horace Greeley, in a letter dated November 21, 1866, of "the facts of my interviews with the President. He has indicated, on several occasion, within this month & the last days of October that he would like free comparison of views with me, and I have seen him several times." The talks that he related to Greeley had to do with the proposed passage of Fourteenth Amendment to the Constitution and Johnson's opposition to the amendment with twelve southern states still being unrepresented. Johnson also backed the "immediate restoration of political participation in the Government to the ex rebel States."[7] Chase was busy in Washington but did not find the time to travel to Richmond for Davis's December trial. The news was a mere sideline in most papers. The *New York Herald* noted, "It is uncertain when the United States

Circuit Court will meet, as Chief Justice Chase has not yet made known his intentions respecting a special session."[8] The trial was held over until the May term of the court in 1867.

The Captivity of Davis

Davis's confinement made it difficult to meet with his attorneys to prepare his defense. The problem was exacerbated by O'Conor's office being in New York while his client was incarcerated in Virginia. Whether O'Conor's assessment is credible, he certainly was "not altogether willing to trust our mail" and often found different methods of communicating with Davis.[9] O'Conor preferred to have mail sent to him by Davis addressed to a third party in New York City. Even the letter from O'Conor informing his client that he should use this method of communication was cryptic. The lawyer did not wish to reveal the name of the trusted person in the letter. All that O'Conor told Davis was that "Mrs. Davis has the name of a gentleman in New York to whom letters may be safely enveloped for me." O'Conor did not believe that the federal government was above opening mail to him from the former Confederate president. Still, the system proved less than satisfactory, with O'Conor complaining that he was uncertain whether letters sent through a third party in Montreal actually reached Davis, despite the system having been set up by the former Confederate leader's trusted advisor Burton Harrison.[10] A reluctance to communicate freely via letters, which did not end when Davis was eventually released on bail, hampered his attorneys' ability to prepare a defense and formed another reason why the defense team hoped to have Jefferson Davis released. If Davis was out on bond, he could meet with his lawyers at any place of their choosing.

As late as December 1865, Davis was still not allowed to write freely, even to his attorneys. "The restrictions heretofore imposed in regard to correspondence have not been removed as you had been led to suppose," Davis wrote to his Philadelphia lawyer, William B. Reed.[11] The idea that Davis's letters were still being sent through and opened by the commanding officer at Fort Monroe appeared to be news to Reed. Reed wrote back to Davis, acknowledging his "letter, the content of which I have communicated to Mr. O'Conor."[12] The truthfulness of Davis's statement is borne out by the signature of attorney general James Speed on Reed's reply to Davis. The stress that Davis was under because of his incarceration and his inability to freely communicate, even with his lawyers, was heightened even further by the mystery surrounding the basis for his prosecution. He told Reed that "no information has been furnished to me as to the charge on which it is proposed to prosecute me."[13]

Even his letters to his wife were read and censored. She complained to her husband in a letter dated November 27, 1865, about the number of erasures in his letter to her. She wondered what Davis was hiding from her, since "Mr. Speed attached a note to your letter showing that he did not" erase any of its contents. Davis complained that his "days drag heavily on."[14] The prisoner dealt with censorship that he found unnecessary and harassing. He told his wife that the erasures were the result of Gen. Nelson Miles returning a letter as having unacceptable content, which was marked through by Davis but subsequently returned again as still being legible. Davis groused, quite understandably, about the close confinement in which he was held and told Varina about Clement C. Clay's sickness, which he linked to his own maladies, writing, "Like myself he no doubt suffers from food unsuited to him."[15]

Suffering from neuralgia of the head, inflamed eyes, and dyspepsia, Davis tried to reassure Varina that he was getting better physically, although he missed Dr. John J. Craven, the post physician, who, by February 1866, had been relieved of his duties at Fort Monroe. Davis had always been a loving father to his children, and he missed them terribly. His longing for them was a constant thread through his letters to Varina. The yearning played strange games on his mind, as he told his wife in early February 1866: "On the night of the thirtieth [of January 1866] I was sitting before the fire because I could not sleep and had a startling optical illusion, such you know as were common in fever; but to my vision, I saw little Pollie walk across the floor and kneel down between me and the fire in the attitude of prayer, I moved from consequent excitement and the sweet vision melted away. I have not called it a dream because not conscious of being asleep, but sleep has many stages, and that only is perfect sleep which we call Death."[16] As any caring father would, he worried that his children would not even recognize him, and he thanked Varina for showing them photographs of him. Varina and Jefferson maintained a strong bond throughout their separation because of his incarceration, but it was extremely difficult for them.

Varina's letters, probably written in an effort to keep his spirits from lagging too much, also serve as evidence of the shifting opinion of Davis in the

South. From New Orleans, she wrote, "It is impossible to tell you the love which has been expressed here for you." It was difficult for Varina to bear the sympathetic thoughts being voiced about her husband without breaking down herself. "People sit and cry until I am almost choked with effort to be quiet—but it is a great consolation to know that a nation mourns your suffering with me," she told him.[17] Doubtless, the nation of which she spoke was the Confederate States of America.

By April 1866, Davis was heartened by the federal proclamation that restored the authority of the civil courts in Virginia. Although he admitted to Varina that "there has been no important change in my condition and the future action to be taken in my case has not been in any wise revealed to me," he thought that he might now be transferred from military to civilian custody. No matter what happened, "it is hardly possible that any change should not be for the better." His wife was constantly maneuvering to be able to visit her husband, but he warned her against it. "You evince a purpose to seek for permission to visit me here, but I think you had better wait for further developments," he told her.[18] "You would probably be disappointed and your grief thereby rendered more poignant, but worse than even that, you would be exposed to the prying curiosity and heartless vulgarity of the scavengers of the press, who cater to the unmanly malice which has so long and unscrupulously assailed me."[19] Davis, having been beaten down by the press accounts of having been captured in women's clothing, was loath to be subjected to new accounts of his emotional and strong-willed wife demanding the right to visit him.

On April 18, a very positive development occurred for Davis—Clement C. Clay was released. Clay has been arrested for being a coconspirator in the assassination of Lincoln. He was being held in Fort Monroe along with Davis. Joseph Holt and Edwin Stanton had been focused on putting together the evidence that would serve to convict Clay and Davis. The testimony unraveled, however, and the main witness for the prosecution, Sanford Conover, was discredited and eventually indicted for perjury. With Clay's release, the idea that Davis was complicit in the murder of the late president collapsed. This turn of events could only help Davis because evidence that the allegation against him on the heinous killing was false would lessen the anger many in the North felt toward him. The grounds for complaint about the lack of civility with which Davis was being treated only strengthened when Clay was discharged from Fort Monroe but not allowed to say goodbye to Davis.

Varina Davis's efforts to be allowed to visit her husband finally paid off when, on April 26, 1866, she was informed that the government had granted her permission. She was in Montreal, Canada, at the time and arrived at Fort Monroe on May 3, with her daughter Winnie. When she arrived at her hotel, she was so anxious to see Davis that she did not change from her traveling clothes but immediately flew to the fort. Once there, she was escorted to Nelson Miles's office and, after promising not to furnish her husband with a deadly weapon or assist him in escaping, within fifteen minutes was reunited with her husband. It was a glorious day for them both, but Varina was upset at the debilitated state that she claimed her husband was in.

For the next six months, Mrs. Davis was restricted to visiting her husband during daylight hours. During the evenings, she was exhausted by the steady stream of visitors and well-wishers who approached her at her living quarters, a casement in the fort that had been outfitted for the wives of officers. Within three weeks, Varina had made her way to Washington, D.C., to try to gain an audience with the president. Johnson refused to see her at first. However, as the pressure built against him for this refusal, he eventually relented. On May 25, Johnson met with Varina and gave her some news that would cheer her: based upon the recommendation of James Speed, Johnson was granting Davis the freedom of the entire post at Fort Monroe. Lifting the close confinement of the rebel was one of Varina's main goals, and she hoped that it would lead to other good tidings—like a bond on the treason charge. Varina found Johnson to be courteous and reassuring. According to her account of their meeting, the president told her that he did not give any weight to the accusation that Davis was complicit in Lincoln's assassination but admitted to being besieged by men who did believe it, making life difficult for the president.

True to her nature, Varina Davis did not quit after gaining the concession from the president. In the middle of August, she traveled to New York City to visit with O'Conor. She met with Thomas G. Pratt, one of the many Davis defense attorneys, who was a delegate to the National Union convention, the conservative party of many, both North and South, including Democrats, who met in opposition to Radical Republican plans for Reconstruction. The delegates included former Confederate vice president Alexander H. Stephens and other prominent Confederates. Varina urged that "a remonstrance against [Davis's] imprisonment . . . be made by the delegations."[20] After waiting two days, she was able to write to her husband about her meeting with O'Conor, in the process misspelling the names of her husband's lead counsel and the U.S. attorney general: "Mr. O'Connor is here . . . . He had a most satisfactory interview with a man he considers very satisfactory—Mr. Stanbery—*S. is no longer* 'against us' but Stanbery and 'J. are our friends.'"[21] The "S." referred to was likely Stanton, but could be Seward, while the "J." was Johnson. Jefferson Davis did not believe that Johnson had the political courage to order his release, no matter what O'Conor indicated to Varina. Moreover, he did not believe that he would be tried in October. He was proved right on both counts.

The minor successes that Varina Davis had in 1866 seemed to fuel her efforts in the new year. She found herself writing to her husband from Baltimore in late March 1867, telling him of her exertions on his behalf. She hoped to meet with Pennsylvania representative Thaddeus Stevens, the outspoken Radical Republican, who she thought might help her secure her goals. She was unsuccessful in getting in to see the man because of his failing health. She made more progress on other fronts. Her encounter with William B. Reed, the Philadelphia defense counsel for Davis, had produced a hopeful feeling in her. Apparently, Reed was privy to information from a reliable source, John Work Garrett, the wealthy president of the B&O Railroad, who had spoken to the secretary of war and found that Stanton was no longer opposed to Davis being released on a bond. While Garrett admitted that Stanton had made no explicit promises, Garrett believed from his talk with Stanton that Davis would find out if he could be unconditionally released within two weeks. It was clear that everyone involved on Davis's behalf was working as one to gain his release. No stone was left unturned as they applied political pressure to gain a legal victory.

Jefferson Davis's close confinement in Fort Monroe was no more, but he was still a prisoner. He now felt free to give his opinion to visitors and, presumably, permitted them to publicize his judgments. In April 1867, the *New York Herald* printed an account of a conversation that Professor Thomas Chenoweth had with Davis while the professor was teaching Davis and several women to paint. Davis reassured Chenoweth that "he had no complaint to make of what appeared to be the strict measures of the government to prevent his escape and that he entertained towards all the officers of the fort none but the most kindly and friendly feelings as they had ever been ready and willing to promote his comfort. He said he was under many obligations to the citizens of Baltimore. As to his trial he would express no opinion—he was in the hands of the government and patiently awaited the decision which would either place him before the courts of justice or release him."[22] Davis was, in fact, terribly embittered by his treatment and incarceration, but he was also a seasoned politician. He knew what would play well in the press.

The Prosecution and Defense Lawyers Prepare for Trial

In early May 1867, with the trial looming, Lucius Chandler went to Washington to try to determine whether Chief Justice Chase would be present for the trial. He met Chase on a sidewalk and accompanied him to the banking house of Jay Cooke & Company, where the former Treasury secretary needed to transact some business. As they walked, Chandler told the chief justice of his objection to trying the case without Chase presiding over the trial. If Chandler's sudden appearance and prying into Chase's intentions caught the chief justice by surprise, he did not betray his intentions to the prosecutor.[23] Chase did not give him any indication of whether he would appear for the trial setting.

Chandler had approached Chase on this very subject several times in the past, including once the previous year in Baltimore, as Chase sat on the bench. On that occasion, Chandler went into the courtroom, and Chase motioned the attorney to the bench, where they held a short discussion. When Chandler asked him whether he would be present for Davis's trial, the judge told Chandler that he had no intention of holding court in Virginia so long as the military was in control there. Since President Johnson had removed that impediment, Chase did not use this excuse as he and Chandler strolled from the bank to the Capitol. The best that Chandler could ascertain from his conversation with Chase was that the chief justice could not be in attendance in Virginia before May 20, because the Supreme Court would not adjourn until just before that date.[24] Chandler's preoccupation with Chief Justice Chase's schedule probably signaled Chandler's realization that the prosecution was unprepared for trial. He appeared to be trying to gauge whether the case would advance at the next setting.

Meanwhile, the defense lawyers were intent on securing the release of their client, and they now tried to force the hand of the government prosecutors. George Shea filed an affidavit with the court in Alexandria, Virginia, on May 1, 1867, to accompany a writ of habeas corpus seeking the release of Jefferson Davis that indicated he had last seen the accused in March. Besides the obvious ground for the writ—that of the length of detention and failure of the government to bring Davis to trial were grounds enough for his release on bail—Shea also argued that the incarceration had greatly impaired the health of his client and that his continued incarceration "through the ensuing summer would involve serious danger to his life."[25] Davis had been imprisoned for two years. Despite Shea's having already sworn to the pleading, Judge John C. Underwood took the unusual step of personally administering the oath to Shea, who then reswore to the facts in the affidavit.

The next day, Charles O'Conor gave formal notice to Henry Stanbery that the writ of habeas corpus had been allowed by Underwood. O'Conor indicated that Brig. Gen. Henry S. Burton, the commanding officer at Fort Monroe, was required to bring Davis to the Court, "together with the cause of his imprisonment." Although the writ demanded that Burton be required to show the basis for Davis's detention, that burden would fall on the United States district attorney for the District of Virginia. The notice that O'Conor delivered to Stanbery did not request Davis's release but merely stated that the court would be requested "to do and receive what shall then and there be considered concerning the said Jefferson Davis."[26] Given that Chandler had seven months earlier told Stanbery that he had left Davis at Fort Monroe for Davis's health and comfort, Stanbery must have realized that the strength of the argument for transfer was with the defense.

There was no way for O'Conor to know whether the writ of habeas corpus would be obeyed. Each of the previous times when he had spoken optimistically about the possible release of his client, he had been wrong. Lucius Chandler suggested to Stanbery that they seek Edwin Stanton's involvement.[27] Davis was in military custody, and the decision on whether to comply with the order was up to President Johnson. Stanton, as head of the War Department, held Davis. If the writ was issued by a civil judge and the military refused to honor it, a constitutional crisis would ensue. Andrew Johnson held the power to force a crisis if he chose to refuse obedience to the writ.

On May 4, 1867, Chandler wrote to Secretary of War Stanton, informing him that the circuit court would meet in Richmond in May and asking him to issue an order to the commandant at Fort Monroe to "surrender Jefferson Davis to the United States Marshal" on the writ issued by the court.[28] Now two members of the Johnson cabinet were aware of the writ ordering the transfer of Davis to civilian custody. This movement by the district attorney, slight as it was, signaled the government's intention to at least attempt to procure the presence of the defendant in Richmond for his trial date. Without his attendance, no trial could be had; with it, the defense needed to be ready for trial. But the filing of the writ held greater significance—it signified the intention of the defense to get Davis released from custody. Two years into Davis's incarceration, it appeared that a trial might be held. If the case was not tried, Chandler knew that an application would be made for bail. It would be up to the prosecution team to either acquiesce in that request or argue against the application.

In the meantime, Chandler was in Washington trying to determine whether Davis was legally permitted to post a bond on the charge of treason. The United States Constitution provides that "the Congress shall have power to declare the punishment of treason."[29] As stated earlier, when the punishment for treason was initially codified by the First Congress in the late 1700s, the law stated that a person adjudged guilty of treason against the United States "shall suffer death."[30] In 1862, the Thirty-Seventh Congress revisited the punishment for treason by passage of "An Act to Suppress Insurrection, to Punish Treason and Rebellion, to Seize and Confiscate the Property of Rebels, and for Other Purposes." Under Section 1 of the Act of 1862, treason was still punishable by death. The sentencing court, however, had the discretion to sentence the traitor to imprisonment for not less than five years and assess a fine of no less than ten thousand dollars.[31] The indictment that Chandler had hurriedly drafted did not specify under which statute Davis was charged, so conceivably, Davis was subject to imprisonment or death. In Chandler's view, the 1862 law did not supersede the prior act, so the Davis prosecution might proceed under either statute.

That did not answer the question regarding bond. Just days before the court setting, Chandler met with Attorney General Henry Stanbery and William Evarts on the question of the legality of Davis being released on bond. The three men talked about the law on admitting a person to bail. After Chandler produced a copy of *Conkling's Treatise,* turned to the chapter on bail in criminal cases, and read the paragraph on the subject, Evarts agreed with Chandler's take. "The right to bail, I apprehend," he later said, "is confined to cases where death cannot be the penalty. There, I suppose, in all cases the prisoner has a right to be admitted to bail; but where death may be the penalty, it is within the discretion of the court, on the evidence, under the usages of law, and under all the circumstances of the case."[32] If the prosecution intended to keep Davis in custody during the pendency of the case, they would necessarily be forced to argue that the court should, in its discretion, deny Davis a bond because of the potential for the death penalty.

According to Chandler, the court's discretion on whether to admit Davis to bail would hinge upon three factors. First, the court would have to consider the evidence. The defense might argue that Davis did not commit treason by acting as president of the Confederacy, but a grand jury had found probable cause to bind him over for trial on the charge. Judge Underwood could be depended upon to rule that his actions, if true, did constitute treason. A ruling to the contrary would bar the case from being tried, so it would be reasonable to presume that the judge, a Radical Republican, would not make that finding. The second factor was the usage of law. In this, the prosecution would have a much more difficult burden. Treason was not a common charge in civilian court. The most prominent man tried for treason was Aaron Burr, who had been released on bond by Chief Justice John Marshall,[33] a fact that would make the defense argument for a bond weigh heavier with a judge than a prosecutor's argument against it. The third factor, that which allowed the court to consider all the circumstances of the case, would have proven a compelling argument for the prosecution.

The government's goal in any bond hearing would be to educate the judge on the seriousness of the offense, which, in Davis's case, was well-known to the court, and to put on evidence regarding the inadequacy of a bond to compel the appearance of the defendant for trial. Davis faced the death penalty if convicted of treason. Chandler might have considered producing witnesses who would be able to testify about the large number of prominent rebels who had fled the United States after the war and who now lived abroad. The argument that Davis might refuse to return for trial was compelling. The argument would have been further bolstered by the fact that Davis was caught trying to flee the country at the end of the war. Unlike Clement C. Clay—who, upon learning that he had been accused of conspiring in the assassination of President Lincoln, stopped his flight and immediately turned himself in to a Union military officer—Davis had only been captured after a long and intensive manhunt. If he was inclined to flee then, why would a court believe that he would return to face a hangman's noose if released on a bond? Add to that the fact that Varina Davis had family in Montreal, Canada, and that some of the Davis children resided there, and the risk of flight and foreign connection would cause a judge to pause in granting a bond. The prosecution, if it had chosen, could have produced evidence that would have made it extraordinarily difficult for Judge Underwood to release Davis on bond. The question that loomed unanswered was whether the prosecution would either try Davis or fight his release.

Events now began to move quickly. On Monday, May 6, 1867, Charles O'Conor summoned Burton Harrison to his office and sent him immediately to Richmond. Traveling through a driving rainstorm, Harrison carried with him the writ of habeas corpus for Davis to be brought to Richmond. On Wednesday, May 8, the writ was filed with the U.S. District Clerk's Office in Richmond. The next day, Harrison, Robert Ould, and the federal marshal began the eighty-mile journey to Fort Monroe to serve the writ on Gen. Henry S. Burton, the commander of the fort. On that Thursday, former president Franklin Pierce visited Davis at the fort. By Friday, Harrison was reunited with the person he called "Chief." Although the reunion took place in Davis's casement, the awareness that this was the second anniversary of Davis's capture and that he might soon be released was a cause for hope for those present.[34] General Burton received the writ on Friday morning, May 10, and made plans to travel to Richmond the following day, taking Davis with him.

The Writ Is Obeyed and Davis Leaves Fort Monroe

On Saturday, Davis and his family spent his last hour at Fort Monroe cheerfully meeting with the people who had come to bid him farewell. At last able to smile serenely, he walked leisurely among the citizens of Norfolk to the boat. Instead of utilizing a naval vessel, the erstwhile prisoner was loaded into the steamer *John Sylvester,* an ordinary riverboat that provided service between the coast and Richmond. Security was not lax—it was nonexistent. There were no guards on board, a fact that would belie any claim by prosecutors that Davis posed a continuing danger to the government, and regular passengers mingled with the famous prisoner. Word spread that the former rebel was being transported to the capital of Virginia, and small groups of Virginians waited to get a glimpse of Davis. At Brandon, Virginia, a reception was prepared for him, and "ladies came on the boat, embracing and kissing him, weeping, praying and asking God's blessing on him, until we were all overcome with the scene."[35] Many of the women who met with him had been friends of his family during the war.

The wharf at Richmond was crowded with hundreds of people, despite the morning paper having published a request by authorities that no demonstration be made upon his arrival. From an early hour, a detachment of Union soldiers had been stationed on the avenues leading to the wharf in an attempt to discourage people who had no business at the dock from crowding it for his arrival, and many people stayed in town to await his arrival. But those who were determined to see the former president of the Confederacy got around the soldiers anyway. The officer in command was relegated to clearing a large square of the wharf around which the people gathered. As the steamer came into sight and the American flag became evident, just after five o'clock in the afternoon, the onlookers became noticeably anxious and tried unsuccessfully to crowd the cleared area. After the steamer was docked, James Lyons, a former Confederate congressman, went aboard and greeted Jefferson Davis affectionately, before escorting Varina Davis, who was attended by two servants, off the boat and into his carriage. After a few minutes, Jefferson Davis, wearing a heavy black overcoat, walked down the gangplank holding on to Harrison's arm. His countenance was much older and feebler to those who had not seen him in two years. Apparently, a full gray beard contributed to the changed look. Harrison complained that the crowd was composed mostly of African Americans, "some of whom had been instructed, by the vicious Yankee emissaries who are among them, to show their insolence to us."[36]

The hills surrounding the wharves were covered with curious spectators, but the fifty mounted artillery soldiers who escorted the group ensured that nothing unseemly occurred. Davis, General Burton, Fort Monroe surgeon Dr. George Cooper, and Burton Harrison were taken by open carriage at a rapid pace to the Spotswood Hotel, leaving all behind them in a cloud of dust. Along the way, men and women stood in the street with uncovered heads, while women waved handkerchiefs at him from the windows along Main Street. Once at the hotel, Davis found that the proprietors had prepared the same suite of rooms for him that he had occupied in 1861, when he came to Richmond as the newly elected president of the Confederate States of America. Again, there were no guards or other constraints on him. That night, he received nearly a hundred of Richmond's most prominent citizens. Davis's activities on Sunday resembled, in no way, those of a man facing—the very next day—a capital trial. Instead, he spent it indoors receiving more people and several bouquets of flowers. Harrison described parts of the day, "The parlor was crowded with pretty women—he kissed every one of them—and I observed that he took delight in kissing the prettiest when they went out as well as when they came in."[37] Elsewhere in Richmond, several prominent men, including Horace Greeley, editor of the *New York Tribune,* had arrived to assist Davis in posting a bond, if one was granted.[38]

A Schism Develops in the Prosecution Team

A couple of weeks before the trial date, Lucius Chandler wrote to William Evarts, in New York, telling him about the writ of habeas corpus. The writ was set to be argued to the court on May 13, 1867. Chandler stressed the importance of Evarts being in Richmond for the hearing. Chandler also asked for a meeting with the New York lawyer before the hearing. Evarts quickly replied that he could meet in Washington the weekend before the Monday hearing but told Chandler that, because of his schedule, he would request that he not be asked to go to Richmond on the thirteenth. Chandler needed to see Evarts sooner than was proposed and hurriedly traveled to New York City. To his surprise, Evarts found himself face to face with Lucius Chandler in Evarts's New York City office. Despite being cocounsel on the Davis case for nearly two years, they had never met.[39]

Chandler explained to the astonished Evarts that, having time on his hands, he had decided to travel to New York City to confer with Evarts about the writ hearing. They sat in Evarts's office talking about the writ. Chandler told Evarts that no new indictment had been presented against Davis. During the discussion, Evarts found out that Chandler had not drafted a superseding indictment to present to the grand jury then sitting in Virginia. This could only mean that Davis would go to trial on the year-old indictment, except that Chandler informed Evarts that he did not expect to try Davis on that indictment. Instead, the federal attorney indicated to Evarts that if Davis was to be tried, Chandler would prefer to try him under a new indictment. The Virginia lawyer said he was not prepared to try the case. Evarts could not have been pleased to hear this. The man who was in charge of prosecuting Davis still seemed oddly uncertain of whether the former Confederate president would actually go to trial, even at this late date.

Something needed to be done. Either Chandler needed to be replaced by an attorney who would proceed immediately with the aggressive preparation for the trial or Chandler needed to be informed that his only job was to prepare for Davis's imminent prosecution. Chandler told Evarts that he was convinced that the trial would not go forward during this term of the court for the same reasons that Chief Justice Chase had given in the past—namely, that a civil trial could not be held in Virginia while the state was still under military occupation. Uncertainty about if or when a case will be tried can often lead to unpreparedness on the part of a lawyer. An attorney who believes that a case will not be tried will find it exceptionally difficult to prepare with the intensity necessary for the proper arrangement of pleadings, witnesses, documentary evidence, and argument. Chandler clearly was not utilizing his time to prepare for the trial of Davis in May 1867.[40]

The Jefferson Davis treason file had been on the desk of Lucius Chandler for precisely two years. During that time, he had not amended the indictment to clearly set out the facts that he asserted would prove Davis was guilty of treason. Even Chandler admitted that a new indictment was desirable. Without an indictment, Chandler could not possibly know what witnesses, physical evidence, and documentary evidence needed to be organized for presentation to the jury to support the allegation of treason. That was why the document was so critical for the government and perhaps why Evarts was so appalled at the lack of preparation. Of course, the prosecution needed to prepare the new indictment far enough in advance of trial so that the defense was deprived of the argument that they were not given proper notice of the amended allegations. For Chandler to have not addressed the indictment during the previous two years was a sign that he should not be leading the prosecution. Even if he was waiting to amend the indictment to put the defense at a disadvantage, he could have been assembling the evidence necessary to form the foundation of a conviction. He had done none of this. Evarts was stunned at the lack of preparedness.

Evarts later described their exchange as "there being some matters of professional opinion between us regarding the indictment."[41] In fact, the conversation appears to have become very pointed on the issue. But even Evarts was not without blame. He admitted that he had probably not read the indictment at the time he met Chandler in New York; certainly, he had never closely studied the indictment that accused Davis of treason. For a prominent lawyer who had been retained to assist in the prosecution, this is a damning admission.[42]

Chandler viewed the Davis prosecution from the lens of a politician, rather than that of a lawyer. Since he lived in Virginia and had run for political office from the state, he was concerned with his popularity. His constant need for direction from the administration, while laudable if he was intent on pursuing the case as diligently as he could, was, instead, a reflection of his unwillingness to take the blame for the prosecution. Chandler did not view the case as an opportunity. He saw it as a burden. Given his constant need of supervision and his inability to motivate himself to work on the case, it is puzzling that the attorney general, if he intended to see Davis tried for treason, did not replace Chandler as lead attorney for the prosecution.

On Saturday, May 11, 1867, Chandler traveled to Washington, D.C., to meet with his cocounsel William Evarts and the attorney general about the case.[43] The subjects discussed make obvious that the prosecution team was in disarray. Evarts, who assumed that Attorney General Stanbery would take the lead in prosecuting Davis, was informed that he had no such intention. It was his view, he told Evarts, that his post did not require him to prosecute any criminal case. This, of course, ignored the fact that the Davis treason trial was no ordinary case but would be, in all likelihood, the trial of the century. Evarts took exception to Stanbery's decision not to lead the prosecution. Whether the duties of the office required the attorney general to take the lead in the case, Evarts told Stanbery "that public opinion, and the duty of the government, in a trial of this nature, will require the Attorney General to [take the] lead for it when the trial takes place."[44]

Evarts did not persuade Stanbery to change his view. For the first time since accepting a retainer to assist in the case, Evarts now learned that the attorney general of the United States did not even expect to be in attendance when the trial commenced. The New York attorney did not believe that he had been hired to substitute as first chair for the attorney general in the prosecution of Davis and would decline to take the role of lead attorney now. He believed that he had been retained to be an associate counsel for the government, rendering "the best advice I could to the government on questions either of policy or of law."[45] It must have been a shocking realization for Evarts that Chandler was the lead attorney for the government.[46]

The meeting took a strange twist for the United States attorney for Virginia too. Chandler had told Judge Underwood the day before that the prosecution was arranging for the trial of Davis. The meeting in Washington, however, did not go well for Chandler. Evarts and Chandler discussed the same issues with Attorney General Stanbery that they had already discussed in Evarts's office. Evarts told Stanbery that he did not see any way that Davis could be tried in in the coming week. Too much had not been done that was necessary for the trial of a case. Instead of finalizing the preparation for the trial, it was determined that Chandler had not prepared the case well enough to present to a jury. A decision was made to announce that the government was not ready for trial.

The three lawyers recognized the probable consequences of such an announcement, one of which was that Davis would make a motion for a bond. Evarts examined the question of whether Davis, being under indictment for a charge carrying a possible death sentence, was subject to bond. He began by looking at the statute and decided that, unless Davis was subject exclusively to the death penalty, he would be legally entitled to a bond. Evarts was told that Davis had been indicted under the Treason Act of 1862, which permitted the punishment of treason to include imprisonment or death. With this understanding, the three believed that Davis would be subject to bail at the judge's discretion. Chandler pointed out that two men indicted for high treason after the Whiskey Rebellion had been granted bail. He thought that the judge would consider the evidence, the usages of the law, and all the circumstances surrounding the case.

After discussing this issue at length, they made a serious decision—the three lawyers decided to acquiesce in Davis being bonded out of jail. The question then came up of what the proper bond amount should be for the crime of treason in the Davis case. It was a capital crime, and an argument could be made that bond was not permissible; moreover, the risk of flight could be articulated convincingly. The prosecution might easily argue for an extremely high bond. They expected Judge Underwood to listen intently to their points on the amount and sufficiency of the bond. The question became what amount the government should request. Evarts showed himself to be a savvy lawyer. He told the attorney general that it was his impression that supporters of Davis could raise any amount required to secure his release. If he was correct in that presumption, Evarts contended that the bail should be set at a significant figure but not an extravagant amount. Successfully arguing for a bail amount that was unreasonable and then having Davis's supporters produce citizens willing to meet that bail would only make Davis appear to have more support than the prosecutors would want the public to believe he had. Somehow, the figure of $100,000 seemed high enough to make the charge gravely serious without being so great as to appear oppressive.[47] Two days before the trial was to begin, the government had decided not to try the case and not fight a defense motion for a bond.

Despite this case's being the most high-profile case in the United States, and now with the knowledge that it was not being competently handled, Attorney General Stanbery had not, and would not, personally take charge of overseeing the prosecution. Evarts believed that Stanbery thought the case was the responsibility of Lucius Chandler and did not warrant personal involvement by the attorney general.[48] He was too kind in his assessment. Evarts and Chandler were likely in the dark about the conversations that Stanbery had engaged in with O'Conor and other representatives and supporters of Jefferson Davis. Stanbery was not so much leaving the prosecution to Chandler and Evarts as washing his hands of it.

13

JEFFERSON DAVIS IS RELEASED ON BOND

I was not certain whether Mr. Davis would be tried or not. If he was not tried, I knew, weeks before, that an application would be made for bail.

—Lucius Chandler

VIEWED IN HINDSIGHT, there is an inevitability to almost every historical event. To the individuals involved, such certainty does not exist. Neither Jefferson Davis nor his defense team knew precisely what to expect at the trial date that Monday. Charles O'Conor exuded confidence, but his confidence had been misplaced before. The coming days would be terribly stressful for Davis and his family.

James Lyons, the man who had escorted Davis onto the wharf in Richmond, foresaw disaster in the manner that O'Conor was handling the case and tried to warn the former Confederate president. On May 5, 1867, Lyons wrote Davis:

> When the President first announced the purpose to try you, I wrote him and asked permission to visit you and act as one of your Counsel—To that I received no reply—When in the next annual message he again announced the purpose to try you I wrote again referring to my first letter, and in reply was informed by the Atty Genl, Speed, that the question of Counsel was one with which the Government had nothing to do—that your Counsel were selected by yourself—I mention these facts to explain why I made no offer to you, and as probably excusing me for what I am about to say, not as one of your counsel, but as one of your warmest personal friends. The papers say that you are to be brought before Judge Underwood in a few days upon a writ of Habeas Corpus—To be tried, bailed or committed as he may decide—My object now is to implore you to withdraw this application,

> I urged one of your leading counsel when he was here not to permit such a step to be taken, and I understood he concurred with me, and if you have seen Underwoods late charge to the Grand Jury, and the composition of that Jury you will I am sure concur with me also, in the opinion that the step will be fatal to you—If tried you will be tried before a Jury composed of negros and the worst kind of white men, and your conviction is inevitable, and what hope there is of pardon then, which is withheld now?[1]

Jefferson Davis knew that there existed the possibility that Lyons was correct in his predicted result, if not for the reasons that Lyons feared. Davis had, in the minds of thousands, committed treason. A loyal jury, guided by a Unionist judge, could render a just verdict of guilty in the case. The death penalty could be imposed on Davis. The former Confederate could hang for his crime. Davis had to have been apprehensive about the coming days.

An Assemblage in Richmond

William M. Evarts traveled to Richmond on Sunday, May 12, 1867, with no expectation that the treason trial of Davis would begin on Monday. He spent part of the day huddled with Lucius Chandler on the case. Gen. Henry S. Burton, to whom the writ of habeas corpus had been addressed, met with the two lawyers that night. Burton, who likely had no experience with writs, allowed Evarts to draft the return for him. Come the next day, Davis would be transferred from military custody to civilian, and Burton would be rid of his most famous prisoner. Evarts, in drafting the return, made no mention of any basis for Davis to be returned to military custody after he was turned over to the federal judge in Richmond. This effectively ended the possibility, unless further action was taken by military authorities, for Davis to be returned to be tried by a military commission for complicity in the assassination of Abraham Lincoln, an allegation that had previously been considered a basis for his detention by the military. That explosive contention had long since crumbled beneath an embarrassing acknowledgment that the evidence upon which the claim was made had been perjured.[2]

Judge Underwood was in Richmond for the case and, that Sunday, spoke to both Evarts, on behalf of the government, and George Shea, who acted as counsel to Davis. Just an hour before midnight on the Sunday evening before the Monday court session, Underwood was visited in his room by Chandler and Evarts. The government was in an embarrassing position. Putting on a brave face, Chandler told the judge that he was ready to try the case and had no doubt but that he would be able to convict Davis. His certainty was not shared by the rest of the government team. Evarts, despite Chandler's confidence, did not contradict Chandler's assertion that a conviction could be gained but told the judge that the government was not ready for trial. Judge Underwood, unaware that no trial preparation had been done by Chandler, told the prosecutors that he thought a jury would render a fair verdict according to the evidence presented. But the conduct of Evarts, an experienced and skilled lawyer, in pushing for a delay betrayed the prosecution's concern that Davis might not be convicted or might not, if convicted, receive a severe enough penalty.[3] The meeting broke up, leaving Underwood perplexed at the prospect for the coming day.

Chief Justice Salmon P. Chase, whose presence as presiding judge in this trial was hoped for by both the government and defense, had already decided that he could not attend the Richmond court if the trial was held on May 13. He wrote to Judge Underwood that the business of the Supreme Court would detain him in Washington for at least the first two weeks of Davis's trial. Chase did not request that Underwood delay the start of the trial. The chief justice had no interest and showed no intention of appearing for the trial. It was not for a lack of trying to induce the judge to Richmond.

Underwood had gone so far as to suggest lodging for Chase. The justice found the lodging less than adequate. After thanking him for finding the accommodations, Chase wrote, "I do not know that I should care to be in the same house with Mr. Davis, while he and I occupy unpleasant relative positions." Instead, he indicated, "I will thank to request Mr. Chandler to procure suitable quarters for me." The tension between Underwood and Chase was evident by Chase's admonition in a postscript that "I see that the newspapers are well informed as usual. Their correspondent seems to know too much. I take it for granted that you keep your own counsel."[4] That was an ironic statement for Chase, always trying to work the press in his favor, to make against Underwood.

If Supreme Court business detained Chase in Washington, D.C., for several weeks in May, it certainly did not keep him longer. By the beginning of June, the chief justice found himself in Raleigh, North Carolina, opening a circuit court.

His trip south, described in a letter as "a very pleasant journey,"[5] sounded leisurely and relaxing. In Richmond, he "rode out and visited Gamble Hill, the old residence of the Cabells and thought of pleasant days in Richmond long, long ago." He wrote of going to "Libby Prison and all through it and remembered our brave officers who were confined there," before he went "to the Davis House—the Presidents House of the Confederacy, which Mr. Davis left one Sunday and Mr. Lincoln entered the next Tuesday."[6] Finally, in a month when the *Cleveland Plain Dealer* chastised Chase for his "intrigues for the Presidency," he remarked that "almost all the leading men of the state are here."[7] Chase did not wish to be in the courtroom when Davis appeared. There was no political capital to be gained by being involved in the trial of Jefferson Davis.

Davis Finally Appears in Federal Court

The excitement of having Davis in the midst of the city had not died down when the federal court opened on Monday, May 13, 1867, in Richmond, Virginia. A military guard was placed around the U.S. courthouse, while a strong police presence was inside the building maintaining order. The courtroom was packed with interested spectators, many of them women and many of them African Americans, waiting for the hearing to begin. The treason trial of Davis could not have meant the same thing to these people coming from diverse backgrounds and having lived so many different experiences. This much is undeniable, however: the trial was an important drama playing out in the old capital of the Confederacy. Judge Underwood had denied Davis bail a year earlier, and many of Davis's supporters feared the worst. Members of the defense counsel were concerned that Davis would be brought from relative comfort at Fort Monroe only to be ordered held in a local jail awaiting trial. If he was denied bail, he could conceivably be held at Libby Prison or the Virginia Penitentiary, neither of which was a place that any person would want to be confined. The two jails would not have allowed Davis the comforts permitted by the military at Fort Monroe near the end of his confinement there. While Davis's supporters dreaded such a result, many northerners could not conceive of him being released on bond.[8]

The *New York Herald* reported that "much is conjectured and little known as to what will be done in the case of Mr. Davis. It does not seem probable that Chief Justice Chase and President Johnson should be playing an idle game of cross purposes in a matter so likely to attract general attention, and so the common notion that they fully understand each other in this matter is doubtless correct. Their understanding will result in bringing Mr. Davis into court—and what then?"[9] The newspaper made the point that an important hurdle had been overcome by transferring Davis from military to civilian custody. Now the constitutional right of habeas corpus was reestablished, and he was subject to the same laws as any person accused of a crime in the United States. But this was as much as was known. The writer speculated that several questions remained. What if Judge Underwood, who, the *Herald* claimed, was "known to entertain opinions in this case," was to deny Davis bail and the prisoner's defense team turned to the Reconstruction governor, Gen. John Schofield, to enforce a right of speedy trial? While the newspaper denied that the court had the power to deny bail since the Treason Act of 1862 did not make the crime exclusively a capital offense, Judge Underwood might not agree that the indictment stemmed only from the Act of 1862 but might rule that the indictment stemmed from the 1790 act, under which death was the only penalty. In that case, the government could argue that Davis could not be admitted to bail. All speculation would soon be put to rest, but the anxiety revolving around the case buzzed through the courtroom.

At 11:00 a.m., the prisoner was brought into the courtroom by Gen. Henry S. Burton, who was in full uniform, and a United States marshal who, coincidentally, like the judge, was named Underwood. The spectators were noticeably anxious, but according to one person, "kept their excitement under control, [only] however, because everybody felt that an outburst would only compromise Mr. Davis."[10] Davis proceeded to sit next to the prisoner's box. His face was flushed, and he looked nervous. The marshal invited Burton Harrison to sit next to Davis so that Davis might have a friend nearby. The return to the writ of habeas corpus was read aloud, and Judge Underwood complimented General Burton for complying with the writ. He then relieved the commander of Fort Monroe of the custody of Davis. The marshal immediately served the warrant on Davis and took custody of him. Davis and Harrison were then moved to the defense counsel table.[11]

Unknown to the spectators, the lawyers in the case had spoken extensively about how the hearing would proceed. They had agreed that there would be no speeches made and that the arguments of counsel would be kept to a minimum. The prosecution team had assured the defense that the hearing would go well for them, but Underwood made the defense nervous, since he still had to render a decision on whether Davis would be granted bail or simply handed over to the jailers to be held in custody pending trial. The Radical judge was so despised by the defense that they considered him malicious in his attitude toward the defendant. O'Conor rose to address the court and spoke briefly of Davis's long confinement and unstable health. He asked the judge to grant a bail. It is a long-standing tradition in American law that a person may not be held indefinitely awaiting trial. For two years, Davis had languished in custody awaiting his fate. Now the prosecution again was not prepared for trial. It would have been very difficult for the government to argue that Davis should continue to be held without bail. True to their agreement in Washington, the prosecutors did not attempt to make that argument.[12]

The prosecution, as inept as it had been to this point, perhaps took the smart path in not opposing the defense motion for bond. Arguing against Davis being freed would have potentially exposed them to the judge chastising them for their slow movement in the case. It would have been very difficult for any judge to rule that Davis, after being confined for two years, should be jailed while the government continued to prepare the case against him. But by not opposing a bond being set, the prosecution acquiesced in the release of a man against whom the public believed the death penalty was sought. In this death penalty case, the community had to be convinced that the accused posed a real threat that should result in his death, rather than imprisonment. Permitting him to walk free in a death penalty case was an implicit admission by the government that Davis no longer posed a threat to the government.

Underwood believed that there was an agreement between Evarts and O'Conor on the question of bail. Nonetheless, by the time of the hearing, he knew that a bail had been arranged in the amount of $100,000 for Davis's release. William Evarts rose and addressed the court. He said that as a representative of the prosecution, he did not intend to proceed with the trial of the prisoner during the present term of the court. The defense team had been made aware shortly before then that the government would announce it was not ready for trial. Davis's team had a request for bail ready for Underwood's consideration. Lucius Chandler consented to the judge setting bail for Davis. Evarts, while not consenting, did not object to the request either. Instead, he indicated that the judge would first have to decide whether the charge was one for which bail could be admitted. If it was, then the question of the appropriateness of bail would have to be decided.[13] From the government's viewpoint, this at least put the onus of setting a bond on the judge. Chandler did not have instructions from Attorney General Henry Stanbery to consent to the taking of bail but apparently was not ordered to argue against it either.

This was a remarkably acquiescent tone for a prosecutor. Certainly, the government could have argued that the delay in trying Davis was reasonable, given the seriousness of the charge and the vast amount of evidence that would have to be reviewed for presentation at trial. But the government made no argument that Davis should remain confined pending trial. While the judge seemed surprised the night before that the prosecution was not ready to try the case, especially given that he had been repeatedly assured by Chandler that the case would proceed in the May term, he likely was influenced in his decision to grant bail by the fact that the government offered no objection to it being granted. Ultimately, Underwood was satisfied that the $100,000 bond would secure Davis's appearance whenever the trial was held.[14]

But before he entered an order on the bail, Judge Underwood took up the important topic of setting a firm trial date. He announced to the attorneys that he had received a letter from Salmon P. Chase telling him that the chief justice would be in Richmond in the first week of June 1867, after the close of the term of the U.S. Supreme Court. This was significant for two reasons. All parties had expected that a trial of the former Confederate president should be presided over by both Judge Underwood and Chief Justice Chase. This would give the trial a legitimacy and gravitas necessary for a treason trial of a man like Davis. But Underwood's announcement also gave the prosecution the notice that they might be able to procure a superseding indictment with the grand jury that was then in session in the Virginia district. If they could get the indictment, there was a possibility that the trial would only have to be postponed a couple of weeks, instead of moved to a new term of the court.[15] When the prosecution made no effort to urge the early June trial date, the judge set the case for the fourth Monday in November 1867.[16] If Davis was to be incarcerated pending trial, the jailing would last at least five and half months.

Judge Underwood now addressed the motion for bond. It was his opinion that bail could be set in a treason case. Since the government voiced no opposition to bail being set and because the case was yet again delayed because of the failure of the prosecution to announce it was ready for trial, he ordered that bail be set in the amount of $100,000. Underwood specified that

$50,000 must be posted by persons residing in Virginia. He would allow out-of-state persons to post the other half. There must have been rustling among the spectators in the courtroom at the knowledge that Davis would soon be released. There was no report of an outburst from the gallery, though. At this time, Horace Greeley and Augustus Schell of New York came forward to act as sureties, along with other northern men. After Greeley affixed his name to the bond, Jefferson Davis, to the Republican editor's apparent surprise and delight, approached him and grasped Greeley's hand in thanks.[17] A number of Virginians then came forward to match the amount posted by their former enemies.

Davis was free on bail, his only condition being his promise to return for a November trial date. There is no evidence that either the prosecution or the judge expressed a concern about Davis's remaining within the boundaries of the United States. It was well known that Varina Davis, after her husband had been imprisoned at Fort Monroe, had been ordered by the War Department to Savannah, Georgia. Despite her protests, she had been required to remain there, but, in July 1865, she had sent all of her children, except her baby, to Canada to live with her mother. In the ensuing months, she had kept up her efforts to get authorization to join either her husband or her family in Canada. Finally, in January 1866, she was given permission to live with her family. In April of that year, she was reunited with her children in Montreal.[18] It was apparent to everyone that Jefferson Davis would, in all likelihood, immediately leave for Canada, and yet there was no provision in his bond that he remain in the United States. This lack of concern was a reflection of how dramatically the perception of Davis had changed in the two years since his arrest. In mid-1865, even his wife, who faced no allegations of criminal wrongdoing, was restricted in her ability to travel. Now the defendant himself, still facing the prospect of a capital trial, was released on a bond with no condition imposed that reflected a concern on the part of the government that he be restricted in his movements in any way.

Accounts differ of how those in the courtroom reacted to the news. Newspaper accounts indicate that "there was no noise or demonstration of any kind," while Burton Harrison wrote to his mother that "the courtroom, which had been as still almost as a death chamber, resounded with shouts."[19] What is certain is that several people congratulated Davis, and he quickly exited the courthouse to a waiting carriage. There he was met by an enthusiastic crowd of people, cheering him and wishing him well. He pushed through the crowd to the carriage and returned to the hotel, where he was again faced with a great number of people wanting to greet him. According to Harrison, Jefferson Davis, Harrison, and others, including Davis's pastor, made their way into the parlor, closed the door, and knelt to pray. "We were all sobbing with tears of joyful emotion," Harrison recalled.[20] Davis would leave for Canada that night, stopping off first in New York City to stay with his attorney at O'Conor's suburban home.[21]

The Nation Reacts

The news of Jefferson Davis being released on bail struck many Union men as a travesty of justice, and Underwood began to hear that almost immediately. One man, identified only as "a New Yorker," wrote the federal judge that "there are 10,000 graves of soldiers crying for revenge and he (Davis), a traitor, [is] allowed to walk the streets on his own recognizance. Revenge. Revenge, deep and complete will be carried out on his soul. A traitors doom is Slavery or death."[22] Underwood likely believed that he was required to grant bail to a man who had been held in custody for two years awaiting trial, when the government conceded that it was not ready to try him. The realization that the duty existed could not have made the decision any easier for the judge, given the understanding that he would be seen as the person who released Davis from jail. Despite the years of intimidation that Underwood had experienced as a principled man advocating emancipation in the South, he had rendered a decision, based on the law, that freed the man who represented those who had made the life of the abolitionist miserable. Underwood did his magisterial duty.

Others could not believe that northern men, once stalwarts of the antislavery movement, would combine with secessionists from the South to secure Davis's release. William Lloyd Garrison, the longtime abolitionist, voiced what many felt. "Americans here feel very indignant that Horace Greeley should have gone bail for Jefferson Davis. What next?" he asked.[23]

African American leaders betrayed no surprise at the development. Many had not expected Davis to suffer any penalty for his leadership of the Confederacy. Frederick Douglass claimed in an address in Washington, D.C., that he "had nothing to say even in regard to Jeff Davis, no objection to raise against the mitigation of punishment." But the dynamic speaker went on to say that "Mr. Davis had evinced great qualities; he was a great criminal, he was a wolf, but not a wolf in sheep's clothing, although he was once found with certain other clothing on," a witty statement that would result in great laughter.[24] Not lost in the sarcasm, however, was the clear belief that Davis was a criminal and would escape justice. African Americans, along with thousands of white Americans, wondered at a criminal justice system that set free the most prominent traitor of the South. The release of Davis, this "great criminal," came as no surprise to Douglass.

The House Judiciary Committee Expands the Investigation of President Johnson

The Radical Republicans investigating Andrew Johnson immediately shifted the inquiry into the administration's handling of the Davis treason trial. Less than three weeks after Davis's release, U.S. District Attorney Lucius H. Chandler appeared before the House Judiciary Committee to testify about the government's acquiescence in the request for a writ of habeas corpus and granting of bail. Upset that Davis had been released, several members of the committee grilled the lawyer about his role in having allowed it to occur. Chandler faced the hostile questioning with some deftness not found in his legal work. The members were interested in why Davis had been transferred from military to civilian custody. "Were you not aware," asked one representative, "of the fact that [Davis] had been arrested in pursuance of a proclamation of the President, charging him with complicity in the assassination of President Lincoln?" The question was critical because the attorney general had issued an opinion that persons involved in the murder of Lincoln could be legally tried before a military commission. If Johnson had reliable information that Davis had been complicit in the assassination, why was he being moved to civilian custody to be tried for treason? Chandler was evasive in his answer. "I had supposed that was one of the reasons why he was arrested," he explained, "but I did not suppose that it was the only reason. I supposed that, apart from the assassination of President Lincoln, Mr. Davis would have been placed precisely where he was on the general ground that he was a traitor."[25]

During the hearing, Chandler testified about three very brief conversations that he had had with the president about Davis. The federal prosecutor said that he could "never get from him anything other than that the Attorney General had that whole matter in his charge." Chandler explained to the committee, "I know that on one occasion I was a little persistent in the matter, but still all the answer that I could get was that the matter was entirely within the jurisdiction of the Attorney General, and that I must see him in reference to it." According to Chandler, Andrew Johnson had delegated the prosecution to the proper department head—the attorney general—and expected that officer to manage the case. When asked if the administration had ever given him "definite, positive, and precise instructions" regarding a trial for Davis, he simply answered: "Never. The whole matter has been left to me."[26] Chandler's testimony illuminated the strange lack of direction that plagued the prosecution of Jefferson Davis.

When the questioning turned to the issue of a bond being granted to Davis, Chandler admitted that he had no "instructions" from the attorney general to acquiesce in Davis being given a bond but answered, "I thought the Attorney General did acquiesce in his being admitted to bail," remarkably testifying that "this, however, was an inference of mine, not drawn from any language actually used, or any remark made by him." Asked, "Were you consenting to the taking of bail?" he replied directly, "I was consenting to the taking of bail; had I not been, I certainly should have objected."[27]

Other aspects of Chandler's testimony revealed his deepest thoughts about being placed in the position of trying Jefferson Davis for treason. "I have been exceedingly desirous, at all times, to know fully what were the views of the administration in reference to that matter [admitting Davis to bail]," he professed. "I deemed it to be a matter of public concernment. I believed the trial, if it came off, would be one of the most important trials which the world ever saw. I did not think it right that the whole onus of the matter should be placed on my shoulders. I thought it right that the administration should give me definite, positive, and precise instructions."[28] Chandler believed that he was being saddled with a political trial that hampered him and his future while those who decided that the charge should be brought escaped as much responsibility for it as they could.

The next day, Attorney General Stanbery appeared before the committee. He was questioned about his suspension of the treason case against Clement C. Clay as well as the dismissal of confiscation suits against Clay. He justified the suspension by stating that treason cases had been indicted in too many states and this was an effort to manage the prosecutions. As to the dismissal of the confiscation case against Clay, Stanbery claimed that the Confiscation Act had been a wartime measure and implied that it would not be utilized once peace was established. This was a conservative's view of the act but an interpretation with which Andrew Johnson agreed.

Stanbery testified to the committee later that he had never spoken to the president about the Davis treason trial, except during cabinet meetings. He narrowed the subject of their conversation, in that setting, to the question of where Davis should be held. "I frequently stated," he said, "that we were in a wrong position in reference to Mr. Davis being held in military custody without any charge being preferred against him by the military, and that it was desirable some way or other that we should get out of what I considered a very false position." The attorney general told the committee that he had held this view since his appointment to the cabinet and had urged this action at every relevant discussion within the cabinet. Jumping on this point, a committee member asked Stanbery the basis, then, for not having transferred Davis to civil authorities earlier. Stanbery answered with a familiar refrain: "I should think it was a matter of very doubtful expediency at that time voluntarily to take him from custody where he was perfectly safe, and hand him over to be put in a jail in Virginia." Neither did he take any responsibility for the two years that Davis had languished in custody. "When I came into office," he told the committee members, "he had been under indictment a long time. The government had employed the most eminent counsel to assist the district attorney. The case was in the hands of competent parties so far as the prosecution was concerned, and I do not know that anything ever occurred to me as necessary to be done that was not done, so far as I myself was concerned as Attorney General. I have heretofore stated, and I now repeat, that it was not any part of my duty to attend the trial of Jefferson Davis." Then he added emphatically, "It is not my duty to attend treason cases, no matter where they are."[29]

Having established that Stanbery saw himself as nothing more than a resource for Chandler, he was finally asked directly by Representative George Boutwell the question everyone must have wanted answered: "Why then did you not give directions to the district attorney to bring Jefferson Davis to trial?" Stanbery did not back down from the query. "When the Chief Justice stated that the condition of Virginia was such that he did not consider it proper for him to hold court there," he explained, "I felt it was a matter of great delicacy to proceed under those circumstances, and to direct him to be tried with or without the Chief Justice. It would be a trial of very great consequence, and it occurred to me that it would be proper to have the presence of the Chief Justice, or of some Justice of the Supreme Court of the United States. When the Chief Justice took that ground I did not feel authorized myself to order the district attorney to go on and try Davis before the district judge. I understood, also, from the district attorney that he was unwilling to do it, and that he thought it was not proper to bring the case to trial before the district judge."[30] There was no chance of a trial being held without Chase presiding over it, and Chase refused to be involved with the matter. The Radical Republicans on the committee must have wondered at the Gordian knot obstructing the trial of Davis.

Stanbery's testimony deeply hurt the government's case against Jefferson Davis. He admitted: "I never have been myself able to see how, if called upon to justify Davis's imprisonment, it could be done. The government has always in that matter stood in a false position." This was a stunning position for the man whose job it was to ultimately oversee the prosecution of Davis. Davis's military imprisonment had been, in the opinion of the attorney general, illegal. He could concede no point of greater substance to conservatives in the nation, and southern whites in particular, other than to state that he did not believe Davis had committed treason. He came close to making that statement. When pressed about why he had ended all treason prosecutions except for Davis's, he stated: "I considered that no one certainly was expecting that those trials for treason should go on. If it was our duty to try parties indicted for treason who had taken part in the rebellion, then it was our duty not only to try them, but to prosecute every one else who had been guilty of the same offence. We could not 'make fish of one and fowl of the other.'"[31] In words that could have been uttered by Charles O'Conor on his client's behalf, Stanbery testified that he saw no difference between Davis and others who could have been charged with treason.

Judge Underwood followed Stanbery in the witness chair that day. Asked whether he would have granted bail for Jefferson Davis if the prosecution had objected, Underwood answered, "I do not think I had made up my mind in advance." He admitted that he had not expected an application for bail to be made but that he "thought that where the government had refused or neglected to proceed with the case for so long, it was a proper case for bail." Asked if he thought the government was in default on the case, he answered simply, "I did." Further, it was his testimony that the government had offered no good reason being unready to proceed to trial, making it "a proper case for bail." Underwood contrasted the recent conduct of the government on the application for bail with the motion made by O'Conor a year earlier for bail. In that instance, the "Attorney General, Mr. Speed, took an interest in it . . . and came before me when the application was made." The appearance and argument against granting bond to Davis worked on that occasion. "I refused the application," Underwood testified.[32]

It was the judge's belief that the $100,000 bail "seemed to have been arranged between the government and Mr. O'Conor." Underwood indicated that William Evarts had informed him of the decision the previous night: "The first I knew of it was about 11 o'clock the night before, Sunday night." He later modified his testimony to indicate that if Evarts "did not tell me on Sunday night he told me so the next morning."[33] Nonetheless, the government and the defense had agreed on the amount of bail.

The federal judge also indicated that he no longer feared that an impartial jury could be found in Virginia to convict Jefferson Davis, or any other man, of treason, given the proper evidence. A year earlier, he said, "many men [had] told me that it would cost them their lives to act upon a jury." However, "there is no danger now, and has not been for some time."

The Myth of the Lost Cause Is Bolstered

White southerners reacted joyfully at the release of a man they once had considered responsible for the destruction of their cause. If the two-year incarceration had turned the hair of Jefferson Davis gray and noticeably aged him, it had also worked a turn in the way former rebels in the South viewed him. The release also played a role in building the myth of the Lost Cause. Many began to view the federal government's hesitancy to try Davis for treason as a vindication of their cause. Stephen R. Mallory, the Confederate secretary of the navy, wrote to Davis on May 14, 1867, exclaiming, "We never believed that the Conquerors would hazard the consequences of trying you for treason, a cause which would place the Government itself upon trial, and subject it to the condemnation of the civilized world; and, though not unprepared for your release, we find, mingled with our inexpressible relief and gladness, a certain feeling of triumph."[34]

John H. Reagan, Davis's postmaster general, wrote his old boss in language comparing the struggles of Davis to the Messiah that Davis could not have missed: "It will no doubt be a great consolation to you to know that the great mass of our people regard you as suffering in your own person for and on account of them."[35] Howell Cobb added his perception that "the people of the South still regard you as their representative, in all the sufferings and persecutions, to which you are subjected."[36] The bitter expatriate former Confederate general Jubal A. Early wrote from Toronto, Canada, stating, "I do not call that imprisonment [of Davis] unconstitutional or illegal, for these are now unmeaning terms, as there exists in our once happy country no constitution or law, except the will of an unprincipled and utterly shameless faction."[37]

One of Davis's lawyers, William B. Reed, urged Davis to begin writing a history of the war. "I attach great importance to what we talked about in Richmond—History—your History," he told Davis. "It is due to the South and to your friends every where that it should be told as you can tell it."[38] Joseph E. Davis wrote his brother that Jefferson should consider writing a book about the war. Jefferson Davis effortlessly assumed the mantle of a hero wronged. He replied to Early, who had just published a book about the last year of the war, and made his intention known that he would likely be writing his own book. He told his former general its purpose: "To vindicate the struggle of the South to preserve their political and social inheritance, by truthfully stating events was alike due to those who suffered for that sacred cause and to those to whom its regeneration must be confided."[39] Writing a book that vindicated the South would also likely help with another problem by adding some much needed income to the Davis household.

Davis received a letter from Bernard J. Sage, a Confederate naval veteran, who had spoken to Charles O'Conor about the issue of secession being incorporated into Davis's defense. Sage believed that "it would redound to your credit as a far-seeing statesman, and have much more moral weight with the jury and the country at large, to prove that while the right of secession was an article of your faith, you thought the time and manner of attempting it was impolitic" before the war.[40] From the southern point of view, if secession was not unconstitutional, then Davis could not be guilty of treason. As time went on, those who identified with the unreconstructed South began to argue that the failure of the federal government to bring Davis to trial was a result of its fear that the South had been right about secession all along and were unwilling to gamble on a verdict of not guilty, which would prove that point.

New Plans for a Trial

Davis was able to write in September, "I am still at a loss as to the purpose of the U. S. Govt. in relation to myself and therefore look forward to an appearance before the District court in Richmond next Nov."[41] It was not long before the day of trial was set. In early October, Charles O'Conor wrote his client that "the appointed day is Nov. 25th."[42] At long last, the trial appeared to be imminent. The lawyer did not lack in confidence; however, every trial carries risk with it. What must have been going through O'Conor's mind at this time? A loss could mean that Davis would be incarcerated for a long time, perhaps the rest of his life, or worse, executed. Varina Davis, always a difficult person to handle, could be depended upon to attribute blame on the lawyer for the loss. If a conviction did occur, O'Conor might go down in history as having lost the single most important case in American history. Yet there existed no room for negotiation. A settlement could not be reached in the case as it might be in many other criminal cases. Davis could not be asked to offer a plea bargain of any sort. The case must be tried, or the federal government must be forced into a position of abandoning the prosecution. Did Davis truly understand the risk involved? No trial lawyer reading the letter by O'Conor to Davis can fail to recognize the undertone of the correspondence and the angst being felt by the lawyer as he wrote.

The tone of O'Conor's letter reflected the deep concern that he felt. He discussed the problems with the case. Many problems existed with it, from the standpoint of the defense counsel. The first involved the trial judge and the trial date being so late in November: "Chief Justice [Chase] must be in Washington Dec. 2. Therefore if a trial shall take place at the appointed term it will be before Judge Underwood." O'Conor assessed Chase very accurately: "Chase is an eager candidate for the Presidency and is quite anxious to get rid of the case. Forcing it on before Underwood seems good policy for him." Insofar as the government wanting Chase to be present for the trial, O'Conor believed the prosecution team to be at cross-purposes. He did not dispute that Lucius Chandler would want Chase to preside over the trial, but O'Conor did not believe that Evarts wanted Chase to do so because it would diminish Chase's presidential prospects. "Evarts desires to help him [Chase] in the hope of being selected for the judicial seat which his [Chase's] translation would leave vacant," he wrote Davis.[43] O'Conor thought that Evarts was looking past the Davis prosecution and wanted to help Chase win the presidency so that Evarts could be named to the Supreme Court. With Chase not desiring to preside over the trial and Evarts not pushing him to do so, O'Conor believed that the trial would proceed before Underwood as the sole judge. This arrangement did not favor the defense.

O'Conor gauged John Underwood to lack confidence in his powers, although he thought him to be a Radical in the mold of Thaddeus Stevens. Here O'Conor made a stunning prediction: "Of course, he believes that the seceding States read themselves out of the Union and have been conquered. He sees that these premises lead inevitably to your acquittal. It is highly probable that on the opening he would direct an acquittal, laying down formally and sententiously the Thad Stevens law." How could O'Conor believe it to be "highly probable" that John Underwood or any federal judge would direct an acquittal on the opening of the trial? It is instructive that O'Conor appeared to have such accurate information on Chase and Chandler and yet precious little information on or understanding of Underwood. O'Conor would not have made such a bold prediction had he known that Underwood had engaged in research, less than a year earlier, attempting to determine whether Davis could face the death penalty as indicted. Far from considering the summary dismissal of the case after the government opened, Underwood was determining the court's range of punishment under the law, including whether his authority extended to sentencing O'Conor's client to death if Davis was convicted. This would have been a wasted exercise on the part of Judge Underwood if he was convinced that he must summarily acquit Davis.[44]

The second issue was the jury. "The jury," according to O'Conor, "will be composed of 8 or 9 negroes and 3 or 4 of the meanest whites who can be found in Richmond."[45] Davis must have blanched at the first two issues addressed by O'Conor. Varina Davis, if she was shown the letter, must have been beside herself with fear. O'Conor would write Varina in the middle of October about the racial makeup of the potential jury to say that "Chandler professes the kindest disposition and says he will try to get a White jury. But this is impossible. Underwood is a devoted courtier at the feet of Sambo and there is no appeal from his decisions."[46] The New York defense attorney, as we have seen, was an avowed racist and made no effort in his correspondence to hide the fact. This lack of restraint in his language must be coupled with his knowledge that the recipients of his letters would find no fault with his words. William B. Reed referred to the possibility of trying the case before Underwood by saying that "he and his negroes will be grotesque."[47] But the point to be borne in mind is that Davis and his supporters were terrified of being judged by the people whom they had enslaved just over two years earlier. It was not an unjustified terror.

In spite of O'Conor's ability to garner concessions from the prosecutor Lucius Chandler, even to the detriment of Chandler's own case, not to mention justice itself, O'Conor knew that Chandler did not carry enough weight to outright dismiss the case against Davis. And all efforts of the defense team and its supporters to influence the president or attorney general to dismiss the prosecution had failed. "I am satisfied that neither the President nor his Attorney General can be induced to do any act or to utter a word bearing upon the subject," O'Conor wrote. "The Statute devolves upon District Attorney Chandler the duty of conducting the case, and those at headquarters will not interfere with him!" One of the ironies of the Jefferson Davis case was exposed at this time. O'Conor did not find his opponent, Lucius Chandler, intimidating. He regarded him as a lightweight in the courtroom. But Chandler was not being directed by either Andrew Johnson or Henry Stanbery. In O'Conor's view, they had yielded the direction of the case to the district attorney: "Chandler, poor fellow, does not know what to do and is very anxious. He is to be in New York shortly in order to consult Evarts. No doubt we shall meet." Having Chandler make the decision on whether to proceed with the trial of the case increased the potential for a trial for the very reason that Chandler did not believe that he had the authority to dismiss the case.[48]

If the case proceeded to trial, the defense advantage of Chandler being the lead prosecutor in the case was heavily diminished by the inclusion of William M. Evarts on the prosecution team. Evarts, O'Conor informed Davis, "is deemed the great legal gun of the radicals and who really is as good a lawyer as any to be found in the party if indeed he be not decidedly the best." Evarts's skill as a trial attorney made the case much tougher for the defense. O'Conor knew that Evarts was ambitious and would perform well in trial if the case proceeded. Evarts, either through a Chase victory in the presidential race or by acquitting himself well during the treason trial, hoped to advance into a judicial seat for himself.[49]

O'Conor closed his letter with an acknowledgment that he was not in control of events: "Here is a chapter of uncertainties. The future is absolutely impenetrable; and we can do nothing but prepare our minds and our materials for a confrontation of the enemy at Richmond on the 25th of November. We must be ready to receive his fire and to return it. A man can always guess even when it is impossible to assign a reason in support of his conjecture. So I will add my guesses: their value must be judged of by the reader. 1. I guess the case will not be pushed to trial in November. 2. I guess when Chandler visits New York a stipulation will be entered into for a continuation of the case to the May term and dispensing with your personal presence at the November term. I must acknowledge, however, that I have not absolute confidence in either of these conjectures. And we must govern ourselves with reference to an entirely opposite event."[50]

As the year drew to a close, Davis's attorney had no more idea of what would happen to his client than he had when he was initially retained. Davis, predisposed to being nervous anyway, could not have been pleased with this opaque analysis of his future.

14

A PROSECUTION IN DISARRAY

Reports are multiplying that the Democracy will adopt Chief Justice Chase as its candidate. . . . I have held them incredible, and do so still.

—George Templeton Strong

ON OCTOBER 19, 1867, Lucius Chandler wrote to Attorney General Henry Stanbery that he had "notified Messrs. O'Conor and Shea of counsel for the accused that the government would be ready for trial" at the next court date, scheduled for November 25.[1] In the meantime, William M. Evarts brought Richard Henry Dana Jr., his former Harvard Law School classmate, aboard the prosecution team. Evarts and Dana must have been amazed that Chandler suggested that the case was ready for presentation to a jury. How could Chandler have thought that a case could proceed on the indictment presently pending? In light of Chandler's view of what constituted proper case workup, Evarts took the unusual step of suggesting to Attorney General Stanbery that "it would be proper to have an associate counsel in Virginia of ability" retained on the case to handle the day-to-day activity in Davis's prosecution.[2]

Richard Henry Dana Jr. Is Retained

When John H. Clifford quit the prosecution, it left Evarts in a bind. Evarts was the only highly regarded attorney on the prosecution and had a trial date approaching rapidly. In addition to wanting a well-qualified Virginia attorney on the prosecution, he wanted to replace Clifford. He quickly set about trying to remedy that shortcoming. It is not surprising that when he did, he looked to his friend Richard Henry Dana Jr., from Boston. Dana was a former U.S. district attorney who knew his way around a federal courtroom and would be an immense help in a major prosecution. Evarts first cleared the hire with Stanbery and, by late October, was able to write Dana that he had spoken to

Stanbery and received "notice that you would be associated with me as counsel for the Government in the prosecution of Mr. Davis." In the letter, Evarts wasted no time in telling Dana of the critical issues. A decision needed to be made regarding when the prosecution would be ready for trial and whether they would try to insist that Chief Justice Chase be part of a two-judge panel presiding over the case. "Next," he told Dana, "the indictment must be looked at" and care taken that they had lined up evidence to prove each allegation. Dana likely knew of these looming issues with the case before agreeing to join the prosecution, but reading that they existed could not have been reassuring, since the case had been pending for nearly two years. Evarts ended by saying that "the whole responsibility of the thing legal and political will be upon *us*."[3] The pressure on the prosecution team could not have been more succinctly stated. Despite these warnings, Dana agreed to help with the case.

If Evarts had a rocky relationship with Chandler, he was getting along well with his opposing counsel. Charles O'Conor and Evarts had long known each other socially and professionally. As experienced lawyers, they discussed the issues involved in the Davis trial to determine whether they might be able to agree on issues facing the adversaries. As the November trial date approached, Evarts and O'Conor met in New York and conferred. Ten days before the trial date, Evarts told Dana about the conversation: "I informed him that we should be ready for trial at some time during the term, if the attendance of the Ch. Justice could be had, and that we should not expect to proceed with the case in the absence of the Ch. J[ustice]. He concurs." O'Conor told Evarts that Davis would be in Richmond on November 25 "and will be ready to renew the recognizance" bond. If a trial was to be held, there would have been no need for Davis to renew his bond, so it was clear that the lawyers did not believe that the case would proceed to trial on that day.

Still, Evarts was working diligently on the case. He wrote to Dana, "In the meantime I have arrived at the fact that J. D. [Jefferson Davis] used to wear a confederate uniform on great occasions, and have a witness who can prove it in the person of a colored witness who came to me last evening to see whether he could do for my service." Evarts questioned the man about his knowledge and found that he had been a slave of the former Confederate president "until he concluded to do what his master put off till it was too late, run away!" Evarts then took a swipe at the local U.S. attorney: "So, you see, I am ahead of Chandler on [the proof of] overt acts [necessary in a treason trial] and witnesses to prove them."[4]

Evarts was not the only lawyer looking for help for Chandler in Virginia. Less than a month and a half before trial, Chandler himself asked Stanbery for permission to retain Gen. Henry H. Wells, an attorney from Alexandria, Virginia, to assist in the prosecution. Chandler assured the attorney general that Wells was a good Union man who had entered the United States Army at the beginning of the war. More important, however, Chandler emphasized that Wells was knowledgeable on the law, "a good advocate and one of the best men I have ever known in the preparation of a case. I can see him at all times and thus have the benefit of his advice where it would be out of my power to have an interview with Mr. Evarts. I have no question that the interests of the government would be truly subserved by having the General in the case and should regard it as a great personal favor."[5] In any major trial, there is a great deal of work to be done in the six weeks leading up to it. However, Chandler's letter is a remarkable document because it has to do with assembling the trial team only six weeks before trial. This aspect of his request makes clear that the prosecution continued to be in disarray.

Stanbery replied to Chandler on October 25, saying that he had written a letter to General Wells of Alexandria, offering to engage him as assistant special counsel in the prosecution against Davis. Stanbery also told Chandler that Evarts had requested, and been permitted, to retain Richard H. Dana Jr. as counsel on the case. Stanbery urged Chandler to prepare well for the case. "I need not urge upon you," he wrote, "the necessity of thorough preparation for the trial of this case now so near at hand. If you should desire consultation here, you will advise me in due time, so that I may notify the other counsel to be present."[6] Stanbery's concerns about Chandler's ability to properly prosecute the case jump off the page. The need to exhort an attorney to be properly prepared for the Davis trial cannot be interpreted in any way other than as revealing Stanbery's deep-seated fear that the case was not being managed properly. His anxiety must have been heightened by the requests for new and additional counsel only days before the commencement of trial.

A week later, in early November, a meeting was held in Richmond involving the prosecution team.[7] Evarts and Dana recounted the discussion in a letter to Stanbery, who had been in attendance. This was the first concrete evidence that the prosecution was not ready for trial. Evarts stated, "We now understand that it is the purpose of the Government that this trial shall be proceeded with when the case can be properly prepared, and the Court having jurisdiction shall be ready to hear the cause."[8] With three weeks left before the trial date, the counsel for the United States indicated that the case would be presented when it could be properly prepared. The attorneys asked the court for a delay to be able to prepare their case. This was a damning admission that the past two years had been wasted by the government.

What followed in the letter caused Stanbery grave concern. Evarts wrote that "the first point to which we think attention should be given, as of the greatest importance and responsibility, is the preparation of an indictment, in view of the evidence upon which, and the witnesses by whom, it is to be supported at the trial."[9] Obviously, an indictment is the charging instrument in a felony criminal trial. The Fifth Amendment to the United States Constitution mandates that "no person shall be held to answer for a capital, or otherwise infamous crime, unless on a presentment or indictment of a grand jury."[10] Besides being a distressingly elementary statement of criminal law, it must have raised questions to Stanbery about the government seeking a new indictment against Davis at this late stage.

Because the indictment sets out the crime alleged to have been committed by a defendant, a new indictment describing the manner by which Davis committed treason or another crime would likely result in the defense requesting a continuance of the case in order to investigate the new factual allegations in the indictment. Since Davis had languished in prison for over two years awaiting trial, questions from the court would arise about why the government had waited so long to seek a new indictment. How could it possibly be argued that the prosecution needed more time now to prepare the initial pleading in a criminal case? The other question that would arise is how the public would perceive this new delay.

Stanbery would not feel any better as he read through the letter. Evarts wrote: "Although, as we understand, an indictment has heretofore been found, yet neither in framing it as a pleading, nor in selecting the overt acts as the body of the crime, nor in the scrutiny of the evidence by which the averments are to be maintained, has the matter been submitted to the attention of the counsel specially retained for the prosecution. Indeed, so far as this pending indictment has ever been suggested in consultations in which such special counsel have taken part, according to Mr. Evarts' knowledge on the subject, it has always been assumed that whenever the actual prosecution was definitively determined on, the subject of the indictment would need to be taken up, substantially as an original question."[11] This paragraph is simply stunning.

What could Evarts have meant by the phrase "whenever the actual prosecution was definitively determined on"? Did the lawyers for the government believe that the decision on whether to try Davis or not had still not been made? Why did Evarts not bring this issue up prior to November 1867? Drafting a new indictment and presenting it to another grand jury would require time that might not, at this late hour, be available.

Evarts informed Stanbery that he and Dana were not aware of what steps Chandler had taken to draft and present a new indictment. Clearly, there was a communication failure between the local district attorney and the attorneys hired to assist him. Evarts's tone was aloof: "We cannot but think . . . that the approaching term of the Circuit Court to be held at Richmond will require as the preliminary step towards a trial, the preparation of an indictment and its finding by the Grand Jury. Whenever the District Attorney shall advise us that he is ready to take up this subject we shall give the matter the proper attention." Evarts's letter strikes the reader as odd in other ways as well. He both deflected blame away from himself and dampened hope that Davis could be tried even in early 1868. "Supposing that an indictment is procured, upon which the counsel of the Government will be ready to proceed to trial, and the presence of the witnesses and documentary evidence is assured, we have to consider no other condition in respect of the time or Term of the Court at which the trial can be brought on, except such as arises in respect of the Court's being able to proceed with the trial," he told Stanbery.[12] His opinions reflected no urgency to get the case to trial.

Chase Faces a Problem with the Trial Date

Chief Justice Salmon P. Chase, meanwhile, made it clear that if the trial date remained at the very end of November, he would not be able to attend. He offered what most judges would realize that trial lawyers would not want—to begin the trial two weeks earlier, on November 13. Already, Charles O'Conor was not planning to be in Richmond until November 15 and had advised Davis that "it does not seem necessary to me or even desirable that you should appear until the day of trial," November 25.[13] If Davis wished to meet with counsel prior to trial, O'Conor suggested that they meet at O'Conor's home in Fort Washington, New York, rather than Richmond. Only five days after writing this letter to his client, O'Conor hurriedly penned a short note to Davis: "You must not come until you hear from me again."[14] O'Conor had gotten wind that Chase might not be present for trial, which would ensure another delay if it was up to the defense.

O'Conor had not received any official information from the court about a potential delay but had read about the issue in the newspapers. By October 29, he felt that he could no longer wait to tell Davis about the turn of events. "Chase has written a letter to Underwood suggesting that Chandler should ask our assent to an earlier day for appearance to stand trial i.e. the 13th of November," he wrote Davis. "He says he could not preside throughout a trial commencing as late as the 25th." O'Conor remarked that since Chandler had not notified him as requested, "we are not required to respond until an application is made to us by that officer [Chandler]." O'Conor was frank in his assessment of Chase's request: "Everyone having any knowledge of business knows that after having made our arrangements for a later day we would not be likely to acquiesce in the suggested change; and consequently Chase's letter is regarded as rather a stupid *dodge* on the part of that electioneering aspirant."[15]

The defense attorney believed that William Evarts would see through Chase's proposal and not even communicate the offer to O'Conor, recognizing it as an effort by Chase to once again avoid association with the Davis trial. However, O'Conor was prepared if Evarts or Chandler did send Chase's proposition to him. He revealed the simple strategy that he would employ in responding to the missive: "If he should I will defer answering until I can communicate with you and with my associates scattered about in sundry States. This, of course, will practically operate as a refusal."[16] O'Conor's tactic would allow the defense attorneys to maintain their stance that they were in favor of an immediate trial, something they had urged somewhat falsely since the initial court appearance years earlier, while assuring themselves that their delay in responding to the request would pose no danger to having the case actually proceed to trial.

If O'Conor was not willing to push the trial date forward, it was inconceivable that the prosecution, scrambling to even appear ready for the case, would agree to it. Chase was making an offer that he recognized gave him political cover in his quest to become president—and not face criticism that he had neglected his duties as chief justice—while having no chance of being accepted. As with many of Chase's political moves, it was embarrassingly transparent.

By the middle of November, O'Conor was working under the impression that the case would not go forward. He wrote to Davis to tell him that "as there is a possibility that I may be able to relieve you from the visit, let it be understood that if such an event at all occurs, at however late a period, I will telegraph Rev. Mr. Ellegood of Montreal, as if for himself this: 'It is not necessary at present. Stone.'"[17] There is no indication why O'Conor felt compelled to telegraph in code, but by the next day, he was able to write again and give Davis a better idea of what would occur. With some relief, he wrote his client: "I am at last fully advised of the course resolved upon by the Government. Counsel will appear for the prosecution on the 25th instant and announce to the Court that they are prepared to proceed at this term, but consider the presence of the Chief Justice indispensable or at least so desirable that they will not proceed without him." O'Conor was certain that "it will not be the 25th but some other convenient day during the winter. Some weeks must elapse first."[18]

O'Conor predicted that Chief Justice Chase "cannot and will not promise to attend at any time during the winter. If we are right in this, the case will go over to the May term." Now O'Conor changed his mind about Davis traveling to Richmond. "Your presence cannot be dispensed with," he wrote. The defense counsel knew that Davis needed to be in Richmond to allow the argument to be made that the trial should proceed against the wishes of the prosecution. Only in this way could Davis's right to a speedy trial be asserted and protected. If the government wanted more time, the defense had to argue that the defendant did not. It was a false argument but one that legally needed to be urged.

The Prosecution in Disarray

The involvement of Richard Henry Dana Jr. on the case seemed to incline Evarts to initiate questions more openly about how the prosecution was being handled. Evarts and Dana soon interjected their political opinion on how the case should be tried. Their position on Davis's trial might raise the question of whether they were privy to a changing political landscape in the White House in Washington. In early November 1867, they coauthored a letter to Stanbery. "We feel quite sure that, upon every possible consideration applicable to this question, it is the general judgment of the country, as it is certainly our own, that the Chief Justice should preside in this Circuit at the trial," they wrote.

"As his public duties at the Term of the Supreme Court at Washington preclude him from holding Circuit at Richmond at the approaching November term in that City, unless at an adjourned day in the following Spring, we cannot hope that a trial can actually be had until such adjourned day, or at the May Term. We have not heard that the counsel of Mr. Davis have any expectation of anticipating the obligation of his recognizance by desiring a trial on the 13th instant, and we presume that no obstacle will be interposed on their part to the trial being reserved until the Chief Justice will be at liberty to hold the Circuit."[19]

This letter prompted the attorney general to immediately write to Chandler in Richmond. He sent a copy of their letter, along with the admonition that Chandler should pay "special attention to the first point referred to in their letter, viz., the preparation of the indictment, and I would suggest that, without delay, you frame such an indictment as you think necessary, and submit it to your associate counsel for revision, and, if deemed necessary by you or them, to arrange for a consultation here either as to the indictment or any other matter which you deem necessary."[20] Chandler's professional ability must have been in extremely low standing in Stanbery's opinion. While the tone of the letter was civil, his suggestions could have been seen as nothing less than insulting to an experienced litigator.

"It would be well," he wrote, "besides preparing the indictment, to prepare carefully, an abstract of the proofs necessary to be made out, and of the evidence, or written, which you expect to adduce, and to furnish your associates with such an abstract also for their consideration. The time fixed for the trial being so near at hand, I deem it proper again to call your early attention to this important subject, and to ask you to acknowledge promptly the receipt of this communication, and advise me what steps you have taken towards the preparation of the case."[21]

This correspondence signaled a number of problems. Stanbery believed that Chandler lacked a basic understanding about how to prepare a case for trial. This letter came after Chandler had spent two years as chief prosecutor in the case. The question must be asked, then, whether Stanbery should have removed him from the prosecution team. At the very least, if the case demanded it, why did Stanbery not put Evarts or Dana in charge of the day-to-day preparation of the case? Stanbery recognized Chandler's ill-preparedness yet still retained him in the role of lead counsel.

Chandler responded, as instructed, in a letter to Stanbery. He told the attorney general that after meeting with his new associate counsel, General Wells, on the subject, "the preparation of the indictment has been commenced." Chandler intended to have a copy of the proposed indictment to Stanbery within a week and hoped to have the suggestions of Evarts and Dana soon after that. He closed with the promise that he would "also attend to the abstract of the proofs and the necessary evidence."[22] From all appearances, Chandler had found Stanbery's letter to be motivational. There is no hint of displeasure on Chandler's part at having received a letter lecturing him about elementary aspects of trial work.

The Davis Defense Team Prepares for Trial

The prosecution was plagued by leaks that assisted the defense. No sooner had Henry H. Wells been brought on to help the prosecution than he told Robert Ould, who was working for the defense, that Judge John C. Underwood intended to try Davis at the November term. Chandler was aware that the trial date was firm as well, so the defense could expect the prosecution to be prepared for trial. Confirming his insider's knowledge, Wells let Ould know that "Underwood has ordered a panel of 72 [potential jurors], being double the usual number [of jurors]." Seasoned trial lawyers like Charles O'Conor knew that once a jury panel was ordered to be summoned, a case was likely to be tried. And as an attorney who had been involved in many high-profile cases, O'Conor knew that summoning an unusually large number of potential jurors meant that a high-profile case was meant to be heard, since many prospective jurors would have formed opinions that would disqualify them from sitting on a widely publicized case. Ould was also able to determine that "Chandler has gone to New York, it is said and believed, to confer with Evarts."[23]

Privately, the defense team was preparing for trial and expecting the worst. Robert Ould wrote to William Corcoran, one of Davis's backers, that "it seems now to be definitely settled that the trial of Mr. Davis will take place about the last of next month before Judge Underwood alone and a jury composed almost entirely, if not exclusively, of negroes." Ould, the former Confederate in charge of prisoner exchanges, found Davis's situation unfathomable. "It is almost impossible to conceive that the Government of the U.S. could descend to such an abyss of baseness as to allow such a proceeding," he complained.

"My opinion that is that we should demand a continuance of the case until Chase will agree to attend. In that matter however I shall have to follow the lead of Mr. O'Conor. The trial will be a very long one." Even if the jury pool was poor and the judge believed to be biased against Davis, Ould was not prepared to give in. "I am in favor of contesting fiercely every point, beginning with a challenge of the Grand Jury that found the indictment," he wrote Corcoran. "What will Europe think of trying ten imperial States on the law before Underwood, and on the fact before twelve negroes? Will it not make the name of American a badge of abasement in every circle where honor is reverenced?" Recognizing that the venom in the letter was so poisonous, Ould apologized near the end of the correspondence: "The events however are so recent and our feelings so deep, that you must pardon me."[24] His letter also revealed that he believed that the righteousness of the southern cause was on trial.

O'Conor wrote to Varina Davis, scarcely able to believe that the case might actually proceed to trial: "I find it impossible to believe that we are destined to play parts in a farce so contemptible as a trial before Underwood and a set of recently emancipated Negroes, but it is equally impossible to assert with confidence that the thing will not happen." Still, despite sounding a bit nervous about the prospect of a trial in November, O'Conor tried to reassure his client's worried wife. He wrote, "You may rest assured that no effort will be left untried to ward off anticipated evil. I cannot think that life is in danger; nor has it come within my calculation of possibilities that imprisonment can be renewed. You must dispel apprehensions on this subject. I trust we will be able to avert all such misfortunes."[25] It is doubtful that Varina's fears were assuaged, but the defense attorney did tell Jefferson Davis not to appear in Richmond unless he was called by O'Conor. This could only mean that O'Conor doubted that the trial would take place. At the end of October, the defense lawyer would write to Davis that "certain disclosures have been made to me which indicate a total want of readiness on the part of the enemy at this time." He thought that the trial would go over to May 1868. "Unless otherwise instructed I shall acquiesce," he told Davis.[26]

The Prosecution Begins to Issue Subpoenas

The prosecution requested the issuance of two subpoenas on Thursday, November 20, 1867, for the trial five days later. Gen. Horace Porter, the Medal of

Honor–winning aide-de-camp to General Grant's staff, had a subpoena issued for his appearance. There was no evidence that it was served. Gen. George G. Parke accepted service of the second subpoena a day later in Washington. Newspapers reported other witnesses being summoned and appearing on the court date. Robert E. Lee; his eldest son, Custis Lee; and his nephew, Fitzhugh Lee, were all reported to be in Richmond pursuant to summons from the government. Jefferson Davis was said to be staying at the home of his counsel, Robert Ould, but he did not travel to the federal courthouse. According to the *New York Herald,* Davis was "in excellent health and is quite cheerful. Many friends are calling on him tonight."[27]

On the day long anticipated and seemingly now about to arrive, Underwood never took the bench. Uncertain whether Chase intended to appear, the district judge waited until the train from Washington, D.C., got to Richmond. When it was found that Chase was not on board, Underwood had his deputy marshal announce to those waiting outside that because of Chase's absence, the court would be adjourned until the next day at 11:00 a.m. The expectant crowd, said by the *Daily National Republican* of Washington to be "consisting chiefly of blacks, quietly dispersed."[28] Newspapers also reported that Davis's failure to come to the courthouse was challenged by some, who insisted that it was a violation of his bond condition. Underwood did not agree. As Dana told his wife, Sarah, "Today, when the great drama was expected, nothing happened." It was not as if they had believed that anything would happen. Dana and Evarts did not even bother to go to the courthouse but spent the day in their hotel, "making preparations on the case and the evidence."[29] Their preparation was not put to use. That evening, the two prosecutors and Judge Underwood strolled through Richmond, viewing, among other sites, the John Marshall house.

Upon the public indication that Chase would come into Richmond on Tuesday, the courtroom was opened. It was densely crowded with people. Outside the courthouse, in a nearby park, a detachment of federal cavalry stood watch. There would be no mischief allowed during the trial. Davis was not present, nor were any of the witnesses who had been subpoenaed by the prosecution. The time set for the opening of court came, and everyone waited for Underwood to take the bench. Underwood waited to see if Chase would finally come to court. At 11:30, Underwood came into the courtroom from his chambers alone. Taking his seat, he announced to the parties that he regretted that Chief Justice Chase was absent. The members of the grand jury, several of them African American, were brought into the courtroom and sworn. Underwood issued verbal instructions for them to investigate treason.

After the grand jury was excused from the courtroom, Underwood called the Davis case. William Evarts rose for the prosecution. He told the court that it was the intention of the government to try the Davis case at some point during the current court's term. But, he said, the prosecutors hoped to name a day after the adjournment of the Supreme Court for the trial so that Chief Justice Chase could preside over the case. Underwood agreed with the proposal because he also believed that it would be beneficial, to both parties, for there to be two sitting judges. Evarts suggested the fourth Wednesday in March 1868.

O'Conor rose from the defense table. If he was to take into account the interests of his client, he would not agree to the postponement of the trial, he told Judge Underwood. O'Conor said that the case should have been heard the previous May. It would benefit Davis the most for the case to begin that day, he said. The New York litigator was making a record to preserve Davis's right to a speedy trial, and it is likely that everyone present in the courtroom with knowledge of the law recognized that fact. Evarts and Underwood certainly would have realized the reason for O'Conor's words. The lawyer was making an appellate record in the event of his client's conviction, but he did not, as we have seen, truly want the case to go to trial on that day. The posture of the government and the judiciary, however, played into O'Conor's tactics. However, despite the postponement being personally inconvenient to his client, O'Conor told the court he would acquiesce in the government's desire to delay the trial again, as the defense agreed that "the presence of Chief Justice Chase would be beneficial, not alone to the interests of the accused, but to the interest of all."[30] The case was moved to March 1868.

Evarts Begins to Direct the Prosecution

Evarts expected that Chandler and Wells would use the continuance to draft an indictment, present evidence to a grand jury, and search through the archives in Washington for documentary evidence of Davis's guilt. He also hoped that Chandler would forward to him and Dana allegations to be offered as the overt acts of treason by Davis and the proof that would be introduced at the trial to prove the crime alleged in the indictment. Evarts waited impatiently for Chandler's work to reach him. On January 7, 1868, he wrote a letter to Dana about the Virginia lawyers that revealed an uncharacteristic irritability. He had not heard from them, he said, "nor have I any confidence that they have done or are doing anything."[31] He told Dana that his next step would be to write to the attorney general directly to complain of the inaction. When he received no word, by January 11, 1868, from Chandler or Wells, he wrote to Chandler, expressing his uneasiness in not having heard from the U.S. attorney. His "somewhat pointed letter" spurred Chandler to take a hurried visit to New York in the middle of January.[32] During the visit, Chandler left Evarts with a mass of documents, which Evarts claimed to be in no good order and which Evarts and Dana had previously seen in Richmond in early November. Evarts feared the worst and voiced his concerns to Chandler in a letter that was copied to Stanbery: "We are now within four weeks of the day assigned for the attendance of Mr. Davis for trial, and as far as I am aware, we are in precisely the same position as to preparation that we were in November last."[33] Of paramount importance was the looming three-year statute of limitations. If a true bill was not returned before the end of the limitations period, the government would be forced to go to trial on the indictment issued in 1866. Since the instrument was one that everyone believed had been poorly drafted, it was essential that it be amended. In a letter to Dana, Evarts asked the Boston lawyer to travel to New York to work on the case, then asked, "What do you say to a demonstration to the Atty. Genl. against trying [the case] at all?"[34] While they did not put into writing any suggestion to Stanbery that the case be dismissed, this is the first hard evidence that Evarts was beginning to doubt the wisdom of the prosecution.

Instead, Evarts wrote to Attorney General Stanbery, enclosing a copy of a letter that he addressed to "Chandler in the subject of the pending prosecution against Jefferson Davis and the delays which have occurred in procuring an indictment."[35] He told the attorney general that "Mr. Chandler will probably confer with you" about the postponement that the procurement of the new indictment would entail.[36] As the most prominent attorney for the United States in the Davis prosecution, Evarts likely had little time to personally prepare the case for trial. But he was becoming reconciled to the idea that he would have to take over the reins. By this time, he was acutely aware that Lucius Chandler was over his head on the case and, perhaps, also unwilling to take responsibility for prosecuting it. Evarts still did not attempt to have Chandler removed from the prosecution team or, failing that, try to minimize the role that the local district attorney would have in the case. Acknowledging that he knew Dana was "annoyed at the position of the Davis matter," Evarts counseled: "There is no help for it. If he is tried, we must try him, and we must have a sufficient indictment." He admitted that this could result in another delay in the trial until the May term of the court. But this was better than proceeding on a faulty indictment. "Can you come here and draw an indictment with me?" he finally asked.[37]

Dana responded with a letter that likely spoke of the uselessness of proceeding any further in the prosecution because Evarts wrote in response, "I approve of the spirit of your letter." He wanted Dana to make the first draft of a letter to Stanbery on that issue. "If you will draft a letter to the Attorney Genl." that expressed their reasoned belief that the government should "proceed no further in the case and send it to me with your signature," he asked Dana, "I will add mine to it." He also promised to "put the matter of Dist. Atty. Chandler and Genl. Wells before the Atty. Genl."[38]

Two days later, on February 16, Evarts had not heard from Dana. He wrote him another letter. "I await your letter," he said, "in which I am to join, to the Atty. Genl. on the principal question" of whether the prosecution should proceed. Evarts wrote to Chandler and Wells as he had promised to do. Wells replied immediately. He admitted that "there has been most unpardonable neglect in the preparation of the Davis case." Wells explained to Evarts that "after the departure of yourself and Mr. Dana from Richmond [in November 1867], Mr. Chandler was before the Grand Jury for more than a week taking testimony in the case, and that he might be uninterrupted, I took charge of his court business." Wells said that he had read through the transcripts of the testimony and thought that it was satisfactory. "I impressed upon Mr. Chandler the necessity of forwarding to you the draft of an indictment and also of a properly digested copy of the oral testimony, supposing you already had the documentary proofs," he told Evarts. Chandler and Wells were supposed to meet in Richmond on January 21, 1868, after the U.S. district attorney had gone to New York and met with Evarts. Instead, when Wells arrived in Richmond, he waited for three weeks because Chandler "was not well and did not come to Richmond" until the end of that time. Wells wrote that he "delivered the indictment to Mr. Chandler about the 20th of December and have not seen it since." He suggested that he would take "the sole responsibility of preparing a full brief of the evidence so digested as to meet the overt acts charged in the indictment and forward the same to [Evarts]." However, he ended the letter on an ominous note. "If he does not come or send the papers," he told Evarts, "then it cannot be done."[39]

A second letter that was enclosed was a copy of the correspondence from Wells to Chandler, drawing his attention to the fact that Chandler had failed to send either a copy of the indictment back to Wells or the "abstract of the oral and documentary evidence so digested as to show its application to the facts charged."[40] Evarts responded immediately that "the main thing *now,* is to act with promptness and diligence." In the letter, he acknowledged that the work that needed to be done would only come with another delay in the trial. The letter also implied that Dana and Evarts would take the case over at trial. However, the letter raised another topic that Evarts did not directly address. "I shall be glad to hear from you in advance when we may expect to receive the results of your and Mr. Chandler's examination of the matter, that we may be prepared to give it our attention," he told Wells. Finally, Evarts directed that "notice be given at once to Mr. Davis' counsel of the postponed day of his attendance." He was not willing to leave Davis or his counsel in the dark about the inability of the government to proceed in the case. "It is very undesirable that Mr. Davis and his counsel should be called to Richmond only to acquire a further notice that we are not ready to proceed," he wrote.[41] Evarts immediately wrote to Dana that "we must be prepared to take the matter over as soon as the materials are placed before us."[42]

Evarts's letter to Wells set out the expectation that Wells and Chandler would examine some issue in the case and send their results to Evarts and Dana for their independent study. This could have meant a review of something as mundane as the evidence that would be presented at trial, but since this letter was written in 1868, well into the case, it might also have presaged an opinion that the case was being analyzed with questions being asked whether it should be tried at all.

On February 26, 1868, Dana finally sent Evarts the letter setting out the case against trying Davis. The draft letter stated, "Our minds have been moved from the first by doubts of the expediency of trying [Davis] at all which have so ripened into convictions that we assume the responsibility of offering to you, unasked, our opinion upon the subject." They explained their motivations, which were identical to the reasons given by John H. Clifford when he resigned from the case. It had nothing to do with Jefferson Davis. "We cannot see any good reason why the government should make a question whether the late war was treason and submit it to the decision of a petit jury of the vicinage of Richmond," Dana had written. The question they believed they would be arguing in Richmond would profoundly influence the history of the war. "The legal issue," Dana said, "was whether secession by a state was a constitutional right which made legal what would otherwise have been treason." The Boston lawyer was not certain that the question would be answered in a way satisfactory to the government. Further, "we feel also assured that the public interest in this trial has very much abated, if not ceased. And as to the direct result of a conviction, the sentence of death for Mr. Davis, we suppose we shall have your concurrence when we express our belief, that after this lapse of time and all that has occurred in the interval, the people of the United States will not desire to see it carried into execution." Dana finally came to the point. "In short," he said, "we feel it our duty to suggest to you the consideration in which we cannot but think you will concur, that the point of law which the government can desire to have mooted and ruled upon, is one already sufficiently settled, and that the only matter of fact to be submitted to the jury is one of those events of history to which no doubt can ever be attached. Under such circumstances we cannot but think that the dignity of our republic will be lowered and the adequacy of our political system to deal judicially with such cases brought into doubt, by making a question of the law and of these established facts, and putting in the power of any one man on a petit jury, at Nisi Prius, to give a triumph to the chief traitor and his favorers, and a defeat to the government which will not be much the less humiliating because it will be absurd."[43] Evarts pocketed the letter that he had requested, admitting to Dana, "I cannot make up my mind to send it."[44]

Evarts's fear, which he first expressed in late 1867, was thus proved correct: the government was not able to proceed to trial in March 1868. Judge Underwood approved an agreement between William Evarts and Charles O'Conor, permitting Davis to depart while they attempted to hammer out a new trial date. Evarts and O'Conor signed an agreement on March 6, 1868. It permitted Chandler and either Robert Ould or James Lyons, associate counsel for Davis, to fill in a trial date, allowing both Evarts and O'Conor to escape Richmond. The court ordered that Davis personally appear at the next trial date "according to the condition of his recognizance."[45]

Finally on March 26, 1868, a second indictment for treason was returned against Davis. The grand jury that issued this indictment had African Americans as part of the panel. This was unheard of in the South, and the defense team would attempt to use the fact to question the validity of the indictment itself. However, the African Americans on the grand jury were well-educated and sophisticated men. John Oliver, for instance, was a free black carpenter who had studied at Oberlin College and Folsom's Commercial College in Cleveland, before teaching school in Massachusetts. He had prepared himself for the ministry in Boston, but near the end of the 1850s, he became involved in the antislavery movement. In 1865, he moved to Richmond, intending only to stay until his work as a postwar observer was done. But the maltreatment that he received and witnessed prompted him to stay on in the city. He would later serve as a deputy United States marshal.[46] Nevertheless, to Ould and O'Conor, his presence on the panel delegitimized the charging instrument.

Andrew Johnson Is Impeached

Two days earlier, the eleven Articles of Impeachment had been delivered to the United States Senate by the managers of the impeachment proceedings from the House of Representatives. Evarts was summoned to Washington, D.C. On March 8, he had been asked by Secretary of State William Seward to determine his interest in assisting in the representation of Andrew Johnson in the upcoming impeachment trial. Secretary of the Navy Gideon Welles, for one, was not pleased with the prospect of Evarts joining the defense team. Welles believed that Evarts had recently "abandoned the Administration," with cause, and was a "cold, calculating, selfish man."[47] Two days later, at a cabinet meeting, Evarts was announced as part of the impeachment defense team. There is no indication that anyone discussed how pulling Evarts away from the Davis treason case, only weeks before its scheduled trial, would affect that prosecution. Andrew Johnson's sole focus now was understandably on his own fate. It was incumbent upon Evarts to advise the government that one consequence of him being diverted from the Davis prosecution would be that the trial of the treason case might be hindered. There is no evidence that he did. Perhaps it was so obvious that no notice needed to be given. There is also the possibility that no one cared. His full attention now would be on his role as counsel for the president. Evarts, the most well-regarded advocate for the Davis treason prosecution, set aside that case and signed on as counsel for

President Johnson in the impeachment proceeding. Until the Senate vote on May 16, 1868, failed to convict Johnson and remove him from office, Evarts would work full-time on that case.

Henry Stanbery resigned his post as attorney general "to stifle any grumbling that he could not faithfully serve both as attorney general and as the president's chief defender."[48] He joined Evarts on March 11, 1868. Within days, Stanbery was appearing before Chief Justice Chase to argue against the impeachment of the American president. The loss of Evarts as part of the prosecution team against Davis appeared to coincide with, if not directly cause, the acceleration of the downward spiral of the effort to actually try the Confederate leader.

By this time, Andrew Johnson was much reviled by the Radical Republicans and focused on fighting the attempt to remove him from office. Benjamin F. Butler, of Massachusetts, the hated "Beast" Butler—detested in the South as Johnson was by his political opposition—was one of the House managers of the impeachment proceedings. Describing Johnson as unfit for the office of the presidency, Butler was not satisfied with that description. He gave a lengthy opening statement that challenged the very legitimacy of the Johnson presidency: "We can say this man was not the choice of the people for the President of the United States. He was thrown to the surface by the whirlpool of civil war, and carelessly, we grant, elected to the second place in government, without thought that he might ever fill the first. By murder most foul he succeeded to the Presidency, and is the elect of an assassin to that high office, and not of the people."[49] His was an extraordinarily vicious attack on Johnson.

The impeachment trial of Johnson almost certainly killed the prospect of a Davis treason trial, although it was likely not evident to the individuals involved at the time. Edwin Stanton, once the firmest of advocates for a trial, no longer was in the Johnson cabinet. The nation watched as a seemingly dysfunctional government tumbled into open warfare between the branches of government. While the momentum of the prosecution had slowed, if it ever had reached a speed that would allow diminution, what was once going to be the trial of the century now took a back seat to the Johnson impeachment trial. With Evarts diverted, Stanbery resigned from his supervisory post, and Chase now presiding over the president's trial, it is not surprising that the Davis prosecution slid into insignificance.

In February 1868, O'Conor admitted to his client: "I am as yet certain of nothing except that a trial cannot be had sooner than April 6th. It is believed that the Chief Justice will not consent to attend to the trial in April because his whole attention is likely to be taken up with preparations for the Republican Nominating Convention." The convention was scheduled to begin in early May. O'Conor had spoken to William Evarts about the scheduling of the case. The two New York lawyers shared the concern that the case might not get tried in April, and Evarts promised to "go to Washington and strive to get things placed on a definite footing at once."[50] All that O'Conor could tell Davis was that he hoped to know something in a week or ten days about the scheduling of the case. Adding to the pressures of trial preparation was the indictment that was handed down against Davis on March 26, 1868. O'Conor did not receive a copy of the new indictment until April 9 and had not yet been able to do more that give it a cursory look.[51]

The Defense Team Comes under Pressure

On the very day that the new indictment came down, Senator Lyman Trumbull introduced Senate Bill 464.[52] The bill proposed that the qualification of jurors in crimes against the United States be changed to allow that a potential juror could not be struck for cause, or be held to be incompetent to sit as a juror, because the person had formed or expressed an opinion on the matters to be investigated by the grand jury if that opinion had been formed by the person's reading of newspapers and knowledge of history. The bill contained the caveat that the potential juror (all male at that time) had to state, to the satisfaction of the judge, that he could act impartially in his decision. Likewise, a person sitting on a petit jury would not be disqualified from service on the trial of a criminal case simply because he had formed or expressed an opinion, which was not based upon personal knowledge, as to the guilt of the person charged, so long as he could render a verdict based upon the evidence produced in court. Under this law, a judge would have the discretion to disqualify a potential juror if the court was not satisfied that the juror could set aside his opinion.[53]

Senator James A. Bayard Jr., of Delaware, whose son, Thomas Bayard, was a member of the Davis defense team, thought the bill "dangerous in its principles" because "a man who has formed and expressed an opinion for or against an accused person ought not to sit as a juror in the trial of his cause."[54] The bill passed the Senate by a vote of 37 to 9. Bayard's criticism neatly encapsulated the argument from the Davis defense team that the government would go to any lengths to ensure a conviction. That was not a surprise. There was little doubt that this bill would be seen by the Davis defense team as an effort by the government to pack a jury against Davis, especially since Underwood had testified to Congress that a conviction could not be had without improperly tampering with the makeup of the jury. The very next day, O'Conor wrote to Davis: "It is announced that a bill has passed the Senate to facilitate packing the jury. This measure was initiated more than a year ago. I have long expected it. It is no doubt, unconstitutional; but Chase and Underwood will decide otherwise."[55] Davis himself thought that "the prospect of any thing approaching a fair trial is certainly bad."[56]

Meanwhile, the nation's press began to circulate rumors that southerners were urging Davis to stay in Canada and not appear on his bond. Henry A. Wise, former governor of Virginia, found the suggestion absurd. "No man dare to approach Davis with any such proposition," Wise was reported to have remarked, since "his great pride of character and a high sense of honor would scorn the idea."[57] If the idea of Davis jumping bail appeared ridiculous to Wise, Charles O'Conor worried that Davis just might do that. He cautioned the former Confederate president against forfeiting the bond: "Nothing would so much delight the enemy as your failure to appear. This is so desirable to them that they would be very sure to add their whispers if they thought you could be deterred from coming by such means. I cannot say that I impute to them anything that has been said, for I sincerely believe that the meanest among them does not suspect you of capacity to do a dishonorable act or of any inclination to shirk from personal hazard."[58] O'Conor raised the issue again in April 1868, as the trial approached: "The Herald is vehemently urging that you pay the $110,000 and keep out [of] their way. I presume you get it and need no advice from any quarter on a point like that."[59] Despite later assertions that the Confederate leader was anxious to be tried, his attorney sensed the need to write to him about not forfeiting his bond by refusing to appear for a trial setting. O'Conor's messages to him about this subject make much more sense in the immediacy of the moment; it is difficult to imagine that Davis wanted to attend a trial that might result in his hanging.

As the latest trial date approached, O'Conor began to show the tension associated with the trial of a major case. Much of the aggravation stemmed from the seeming inability to get a firm trial date. After being set for April 14, 1868, Judge Underwood told defense counsel in mid-March that the case would not begin on that day. Instead, Underwood entered an order on April 2 continuing the case until the last day of the court's term, Saturday, May 2, 1868. Unable to contain himself, O'Conor wrote to Evarts, asking for an update on the schedule. On April 10, O'Conor wrote to Davis, giving him "positive information that Saturday, May 2, is the day. No doubt you get the papers and you may think it strange that whilst the Herald of Apr. 6 contained a copy of the order of the Court purporting to be entered on the 2nd I should remain uncertain until the 9th that the fact is so."[60] O'Conor tried to glean accurate information before he conveyed it to his client, but the notoriety of the case oftentimes resulted in publication of information that the lawyer did not believe trustworthy enough to rely on. His letters to Davis began to take on a slightly different tone, which may reflect a concern on his part that his client might not have complete confidence in him after all the delay.

Months earlier, William Evarts had told his New York opponent that he would try to figure out when the case would actually begin. Now he was in the midst of Johnson's impeachment trial but was still concerned with the pending Davis treason trial. He had spoken to Chase about the scheduling but gleaned nothing from their conversation. In mid-April, he wrote to O'Conor, admitting, "I am not able to give any very trustworthy impressions as to what may need to be done in the Richmond case, but I will try for my own comfort as well as yours to form some judgment on the subject and give you early information of the expectation."[61] He did admit to O'Conor that he did not want to be forced into the treason trial immediately on the heels of the impeachment trial. If that consideration came into play, then Davis's trial would be postponed even further into 1868. O'Conor wrote his own note to Davis on Evarts's letter and forwarded it to him. This odd manner of communicating with his client revealed O'Conor's fear that Davis might be skeptical about his attorney's ability to know, with certainty, when his trial was to begin. Davis continued to be a very nervous client, and his wife, Varina, was not only a high-maintenance client's wife but at times attempted to take matters into her own hands, a lawyer's worst nightmare. By sending Davis the Evarts letter, O'Conor must have hoped that his client would be satisfied that nothing else might be found out about the trial date: "It's not likely that we shall be any better informed until we meet in Richmond on Saturday, May 2. I will probably send you a printed copy of the new indictment in a day or two."[62]

The case was now nearly three years old. Whatever momentum the prosecution possessed after the war to prosecute rebel leaders was almost completely gone. "We no longer desire to hang Jefferson Davis, or even John Surratt," declared the *Atlantic Monthly* in the May 1868 issue, in an article half-humorously pointing out how the nation had changed since the end of the great war.[63] Indeed, the country's attention was now gripped by the collision between the executive and legislative branches in the impeachment proceedings initiated against President Johnson. Chief Justice Chase, moreover, found the spotlight that he would have overseeing the president's impeachment trial much more alluring than that of a treason trial of the former southern chieftain and the potential that his involvement might alienate southern voters, hampering his anticipated run for the presidency.

Salmon Chase had never lost his zeal for the presidency, even after he was appointed to the Supreme Court. In the midst of this election year, notice was taken that he had begun politicking for that office. The potential that a presidential bid might call into question Chase's judicial impartiality did not escape scrutiny from a major periodical. *The Nation* mused that "judges have not simply to consider the effects of their conduct on their own character—they have to consider also the effect of it on the popular confidence in the administration of justice. It make little difference how pure a judge is if people do not think him pure, and people will not think the Chief-Justice or any other judge pure who, while on the bench, is working for a nomination. It is not necessary, and not desirable, that a man should always act with a view to promoting the general weal; but it is well established that the effect on the general weal of a particular line of conduct, if generally followed under similar circumstances, is a proper test of its quality; and if the Chief-Justice will ask himself what would be the effect on the community of all judges doing what he is doing, we feel sure he would be at least inclined to leave it off. Whether he would leave it off, depends on other circumstances."[64] Adding to the ethical question surrounding his quest for the nomination was that Chase sought the Democratic Party nomination after years of being a Republican. Since the litigators on the Davis defense team were Democrats and the vast majority of the white South was Democratic, the question of whether politics would play a role in Chase's handling of the treason trial became a concern for those seeking a conviction.

Although the case could not be started on the last day of the court's term,

Underwood's order required that Davis "appear personally before this court, according to the condition of his recognizance."[65] Late in the year, Davis and Varina boarded the *Cuba* and sailed south, stopping at Key West, Havana, and finally, New Orleans. They traveled from there to Vicksburg, Mississippi, and then to Jackson. Davis was greeted enthusiastically. He wrote a friend that "the political events of the summer and fall, with the natural subsidence of the feeling created by my liberation, emboldened me to return to my friends and the land with which alone I associate the feeling of home."[66] The return to Mississippi heartened Davis.

Davis could not remain in his home state for long. Another trial date was looming, although he understood that this date, too, would likely not result in a trial. By this time, the trial dates were less threatening and more of an inconvenience to Davis. "Though it is sufficiently apparent that Chief Justice Chase cannot attend the adjourned session of the Court at Richmond, yet the promised notice has not been given to me which would relieve me from attendance," he wrote his nephew Hugh Davis.[67] Charles O'Conor had written to Davis a month earlier, telling his client, "I am as yet certain of nothing except that a trial cannot be had sooner than April 6th," but no official word had arrived from the court postponing the session. To O'Conor, even an April trial date appeared unrealistic. He wrote that "it is believed that the Chief Justice will not consent to attend to a trial in April because his whole attention is likely to be taken up with preparations for the Republican Nominating Convention. This body is to assemble in early May."[68]

Undoubtedly, O'Conor had kept his calendar clear for the March trial date and must have begun his final preparation in the days ahead of that trial. Now, facing a new indictment and a client who he may have feared was losing faith in him, he had to clear the month of May. His opposing counsel, William Evarts, was assuring O'Conor that he would be notified as soon as Evarts knew of a firm trial date. Evarts promised to travel to Washington to "strive to get things on a definite footing at once."[69] Rearranging his calendar based on the latest new development was horribly disruptive to O'Conor's practice. For the busy lawyer, the trial preparation and change in scheduling of the case drove him to the brink of explosion.

The trial was set for March 12. In the first two weeks of March, there were a flurry of telegrams to Davis about the trial date. Robert Ould telegraphed Davis that "the trial will be continued the day will be fixed on the twelfth."[70]

Two days later, Ould again telegraphed his client, stating that the case "will certainly be continued to fourteenth April perhaps later."[71] O'Conor had remained in New York City and, on March 11, telegraphed Davis that the trial would "certainly not [proceed] this month [and] probably not until May or June." Although O'Conor had promised to "soon notify" him,[72] Davis must have wondered about his counsel not having any greater influence on setting a firm trial date than that of a messenger. Defense counsel was correct in one respect: Underwood postponed the trial until April 14, 1868. On April 2, however, the judge once again permitted the parties to delay the case further and move the setting to May 2, 1868.

The pressure of the case was immense, and pretrial details that escaped the public's eye had the attention of Davis's defense counsel. Robert Ould, of Richmond, acting somewhat in a role as local counsel for Davis, took on the task of evaluating potential members of the Davis jury, because neither O'Conor nor Thomas Bayard, from a family in Delaware prominent in Democratic politics, hailed from Virginia. Since a summons to potential jurors needed to be sent to them to appear in federal court well before the trial date, the names of the persons in the jury pool became available to counsel before that date. Information about the men who would be called to sit on the jury was immensely valuable. Ould sent Bayard a list of forty-seven men from whom the jury would be drawn. Of particular concern to the Davis lawyers was that nineteen of the men were African Americans. O'Conor's public defense of slavery before the war, his virulent racism, combined with the obvious problem of having African Americans sit in judgment of a man who had led eleven states in a war to preserve the rights of slaveholders, made the anticipation of trying the case before a jury that included African Americans a very unfavorable prospect to the defense.

The Richmond lawyer noted three characteristics of the potential jurors that might be of assistance to O'Conor. First, Ould carefully divided the men by city. Since this was a federal case, the jurors would be drawn from well outside of Richmond. Second, he made a mark "opposite to such as are known to be conservative, with a cross as to such as are well known to be to decidedly such." Ould did not know anyone listed from outside of Richmond but indicated that he would inquire about the other men so as to be able to recognize "our friends." Third, "the whites are marked 'W' and negroes 'C,'" he told Bayard.[73] Jury selection is critical in any trial. Since each individual brings a unique point of view and personal experiences to the jury box, getting an idea of the background of the individual prior to the jury selection is important.

As Charles O'Conor departed New York City, he stopped by the offices of the *New York Tribune* to talk to Horace Greeley. Unable to find him, O'Conor penned a quick letter to the publisher. He admitted that despite being set for May 2, the trial of the case was likely to be postponed because of the Johnson impeachment trial. His anger spilled over. "There is something very contemptible in the way this case is treated by those who direct the prosecution," he wrote. "It is abuse, oppressive and humiliating, to me to be left playing tail to the kite of some persons of little significance who have control over it. I am pretty patient always, have been extremely so in this case, but my patience is exhausted." He then got to the point of his letter. He asked Greeley to "give me an introduction to any influential persons on your side and *effectively* advise them to give me and my reasons a favorable audience." With the prospect for a trial slipping away, once again, O'Conor was willing to turn to anyone he believed might be able to assist him in getting a resolution to the Davis treason charge, even a man of opposing political views like Horace Greeley. As if to cement his reputation for social awkwardness and a remarkable lack of tact, he tried to explain to Greeley why he had taken the unusual step of writing to him: "I write because you and Gerrit Smith have behaved like men of high and honorable sentiments. For any other member of your party, I have nothing to say touching this affair that is in any degree creditable."[74]

Arriving in Washington at the very end of April, O'Conor immediately set out to see if the trial would actually begin in early May. He met with his cocounsel Thomas Bayard. O'Conor must have still been in an agitated state because he later complained to Bayard that they were not able to openly discuss the Davis case because of the presence of a stranger. The two lawyers set an appointment and agreed to meet later in the day. O'Conor then left in his quest to talk to someone who could give him an answer about whether the trial would actually begin. Within a half-hour of leaving Bayard, O'Conor encountered William Evarts and found that the trial would not take place in May. They hammered out several important agreements. First, the trial would be postponed until June, with the understanding that even that date would be moved to November 1868. Second, new sureties would be permitted to be posted on behalf of Davis. And finally, Davis would not have to personally appear for court.

O'Conor left the city without even telling Bayard, who waited for a scheduled meeting with O'Conor, unaware that the New York lawyer had left town. In his typical fashion, O'Conor wrote to Bayard from New York, explaining to him: "It then appeared that by starting within the hour I could return immediately to New York and save much time. Hence my non-appearance at the appointed hour when I hoped to have the pleasure of seeing you and explaining many things while participating in your hospitality. A multitude of details had to be despatched and the most important were prevented, i.e. a letter to you excusing my failure to call and a telegram to Mr. Davis."[75] O'Conor's lack of manners did accurately convey his impression of himself. His time was more valuable than anyone else's, and Bayard would have to comfort himself knowing that he played second fiddle to the much more important defense lawyer from New York City. In O'Conor's eyes, the opportunity to work with O'Conor and help try the Davis case undoubtedly should be adequate compensation to Bayard for the aggravating slights he had to endure.

But the prospect for trial slipped away once again, and O'Conor wrote to his client to explain that the case was reset until the November court term. Davis was in England. His absence would have potentially created problems, since his presence would have been mandated by the bond conditions, if the trial had gone forward. However, the likelihood of a trial was apparently very slim. O'Conor confessed that "it is not probable that I shall be able to learn anything about the course to be adopted by the prosecution until we are on the verge of the term."[76] The leader of the Davis defense team had no better idea of when his client would go to trial than anyone else. The former president of the Confederacy remained in legal limbo. Still, with Davis out of jail, delay did not hurt the defense.

15

THE TREASON CHARGE IS DISMISSED

> The epithets that have been heaped upon us of "Rebels" and "traitors" have no just meaning, nor are they believed in by those who understand the subject even at the North.
>
> —Robert E. Lee

The Prosecution Team Dissolves

Lucius Chandler's term as United States attorney for Virginia was set to expire on June 30, 1868.[1] He had been nominated for Congress by the Republican Party earlier in April and apparently had no intention of seeking another term as the federal district attorney.[2] In addition to his term's expiring at the end of June, his wife, Susan, died early that month.[3] The death of his wife and his run for Congress likely left him little time to concentrate on the Davis trial, which was now set outside the term of his office anyway. President Johnson would have to find another attorney to prosecute the former Confederate president. The change could not have hurt. Chandler's popularity with the non-Radical white population of Virginia had sunk to new lows. Shortly after leaving office, he attempted to get a drink at a hotel in Jerusalem, Virginia, and "was accosted by an ugly crowd shouting insults, groans, hoots, and hisses at the 'white negro' who allegedly favored 'political, civil and social equality' for blacks."[4] The office of U.S. attorney for Virginia would remain vacant for a month after Chandler left it. It was difficult to find a willing aspirant.

The prosecution suffered a major setback in June 1868, when President Johnson offered the office of attorney general to William Maxwell Evarts. On June 3, after Johnson had narrowly avoided removal from office, the Senate rejected Stanbery's nomination to return as attorney general. Johnson would be unable to get him back into his cabinet.[5] After Johnson's next choice, Benjamin R. Curtis, declined, the president asked Secretary of State William Seward to meet with Evarts in New York City and tender the post to him. Evarts considered the offer for over a week before writing to Johnson to accept.[6] Despite Evarts's immense prestige as a lawyer, not everyone was pleased with the nomination. *The Nation* opined that "the nomination of Mr. Evarts for the Attorney-Generalship, though good for the country—for we know of no one who would make a better Attorney-General—will hardly help Mr. Evarts's reputation. The office has not gained in dignity under Mr. Johnson, and nearly every reason which warranted Mr. Evarts in acting as his counsel in the recent [impeachment] trial militates against his accepting office at his hands."[7]

From the standpoint of the Davis prosecution, with Evarts undertaking the new responsibilities of the office of the attorney general, the ultimate responsibility for the prosecution devolved upon him. The question remained whether he would pick up the work, once again, on the case. What was certain was that his new duties as attorney general, especially if he chose to involve himself personally in the prosecution, would surely reduce the time that he would have to work on the treason trial. Organizing the office, getting up-to-date on the issues confronting the attorney general, and keeping up with the immense workload of that position almost ensured that the Davis prosecution team would lose the top lawyer on the government side.

The potential loss of Evarts to the prosecution did not mean that the case would not be tried. Certainly, the defense was convinced that the case would proceed to a verdict. Through his conversations with Evarts prior to Evarts's moving to Washington to assume the duties of attorney general, Charles O'Conor had come to the conclusion that Evarts hoped to abandon the prosecution. O'Conor noticed a dramatic shift in Evarts's attitude on this point after the move. He surmised that Evarts had been unaware of the strong feelings of William Seward, Evarts's close supporter and friend, that the Davis treason indictment should be prosecuted. In the last talk that O'Conor had with Evarts prior to the scheduled November hearing, Evarts admonished the Irish American defense lawyer "that there was no just ground to hope for a voluntary abandonment of the prosecution." O'Conor replied that he had never expected leniency so long as "a particular individual to whom my evidences pointed, had power to keep it on foot." The person to whom O'Conor obliquely referred was Seward. Evarts reminded O'Conor that the president had famously pledged to make treason odious, to which O'Conor replied with his belief that "the prosecution was not attributable to Mr. Johnson's personal wishes nor to his pledges or outgivings concerning treason."[8]

On July 1, 1868, the cabinet met and listened to a draft proclamation for general amnesty. The document had been prepared by William Seward. It excluded persons under indictment. Secretary of the Navy Gideon Welles was perplexed by this exclusion and "asked how many there were under indictment."[9] Only John Surratt and Jefferson Davis were remaining under indictment, according to Seward. "Why prolong this unhappy controversy?" Welles inquired, pointing out that Surratt had been charged with a crime involving the conspiracy to murder the late president. Only Davis was now under indictment for treason.[10] Andrew Johnson agreed that only Davis was left out of the proposed amnesty proclamation. The president asked for his cabinet members to "consider the subject of an unqualified amnesty to all, without any exception."[11] By the very next day, Johnson met with Welles and Secretary of the Interior Orville Browning to discuss the unqualified amnesty. Following the meeting, Welles noted in his diary: "Browning thought this was a mistake, said they would try again to impeach. The President wished to know if they would frame an article based on his amnesty."[12] He told Johnson that the question of amnesty, and the risks associated with it, could only be answered by the president himself. The question was whether it was expedient. In asking this, however, Welles made the point that "there was this fact: if Jeff Davis was tried and not convicted, we should have a strange and unsatisfactory result."[13] Then Welles posed a final question: "could he be convicted by any jury where he can be legally tried?"[14] Johnson was on the precipice of granting a general amnesty but hesitated, in part, because of his fear of retaliation by the Radical Republicans.

Political events began to move quickly. By July 9, 1868, Chief Justice Salmon P. Chase's bid for the Democratic Party presidential nomination was over. While it may have disappointed Chase, it surprised no one else. The party that Chase had opposed for decades could not bring itself to nominate him. Instead, the party nominated Horatio Seymour. The election of 1868 pitted Ulysses S. Grant as the Republican nominee against Seymour. Andrew Johnson had only eight months left as president. On July 21, Evarts made his first appearance as attorney general at a cabinet meeting. It was unclear whether he would consider it his duty to try Davis personally or permit Richard Henry Dana Jr. to do so. Discussions within the administration reveal that the motivation to try Davis was slowly coming to a halt. Edwin Stanton was no longer present to urge the personal involvement of the attorney general in the trial.[15]

When it became evident that Chandler was not to seek, or receive, a reappointment, forty members of the Richmond bar wrote the president seeking to influence him in his appointment. They wanted him to appoint Thomas R. Bowden, then attorney general of Virginia, to the post.[16] President Johnson declined to follow their recommendation. Instead, he chose to nominate S. Ferguson Beach, described by the *Alexandria Gazette* as "an able lawyer, in this city, where he has resided since early manhood, [and] has always been a Union man."[17] With the congressional session coming to an end, Beach was confirmed on July 26, 1868, just days after his nomination.[18]

The Republican Congress recessed for two months the next day. Ordinarily, Congress would have adjourned *sine die,* or without a specific day to reconvene, and then come back into session only at the regular session in December. Instead, the leaders called a prolonged recess until September 21, 1868. Welles believed it had been done as an encroachment on the president's right "to convene Congress, if public necessity requires."[19] As support for his opinion, Welles noted in his diary that the Radicals "signed a paper to the purport that they would not convene in September unless called together by E[dwin] D. Morgan, Senator, and [Robert] Schenck, Representative. These two men are chairmen of the Radical party committees of their respective houses, and on them was conferred the executive authority of calling an extra session for party purposes. Such is Radical legislation—and Radical government."[20] Radical Republicans would not trust Johnson enough to give him four months without legislative oversight.

Near the end of August, Richard Henry Dana Jr. penned a letter to Evarts from Boston. The letter expressed the sentiments that both men felt—a deep ambivalence toward the trial of the case. Evarts was not surprised to receive it, as he had asked Dana to write just such a letter to Stanbery months earlier. And on August 10, 1868, he had written Dana indicating, "I think you had better write a spontaneous letter in regard to the case of Davis, and I will give the matter prompt attention."[21] There could not be anything spontaneous about it. Evarts simply needed to be able to submit a letter urging dismissal that was not months old.

So, just two months away from trial, Dana wrote as requested and confessed in the letter that the doubts he harbored about trying Jefferson Davis "have so ripened into conviction, that I feel it my duty to lay them before you in form as you now hold a post of official responsibility for the proceeding."[22]

Evarts did not let on that he had earlier urged the drafting of this letter or that he had had anything to do with this latest version of the opinion. The two lawyers had talked privately about whether Davis should be tried at all from the time when Dana was first brought aboard to assist in the trial. Now Dana set forth the reasons why a trial was not in the interest of the federal government. While contrived because of the timing, his letter forms the best evidence of what the lead prosecutors of Davis thought, in late 1868, about the legal and practical sides of the litigation.

As a practical matter, Dana pointed out "that these indictments are to be tried in what was for five years enemy's territory, which is not yet restored to the exercise of all its political functions, and where the fires are not extinct. We know that it only requires one dissentient juror to defeat the Government and give Jefferson Davis and his favorers a triumph. Now, is not such a result one which we must include in our calculation of possibilities?" Richmond, the capital of the Confederacy, was a very unfavorable venue for the case. Even if no rebel sympathizer ended up on the jury, Dana worried that "a fear of personal violence or social ostracism may be enough to induce one man to withhold his assent from the verdict especially as he need not come forward personally, nor give a reason, even in the jury-room."[23]

Dana also addressed the potential legal pitfalls. Judge John C. Underwood would certainly instruct the jury "that the late attempt to establish and sustain by war an independent empire within the United States was treason." What troubled Dana was that "the only question of fact submitted to the jury will be, whether Jefferson Davis took any part in the war. As it is one of the great facts of history that he was its head, civil and military, why should we desire to make a question of it and refer its decision to a jury, with power to find in the negative or affirmative, or to disagree? It is not an appropriate question for the decision of a jury; certainly it is not a fact which a Government should, without great cause, give a jury a chance to ignore." If the trial resulted in a hung jury, or worse, in an acquittal, the "result would be most humiliating to the Government and people of this country, and none the less so from the fact that it would be absurd. The Government would be stopped in its judicial course because it could neither assume nor judicially determine that Jefferson Davis took part in the late civil war. Such a result would also bring into doubt the adequacy of our penal system to deal with such cases as this."[24]

The Boston lawyer might have urged a trial "if it were important to secure a verdict as a means of punishing the defendant." But Dana knew that the passage of time had worked against the prosecution. Davis had now been out on bond for over a year. He had committed no crimes. He had attempted no rebellion. Dana argued that "it would be beneath the dignity of the Government, and of the issue, to inflict upon him a minor punishment; and, as to a sentence of death, I am sure that, after this lapse of time and after all that has occurred in the interval, the people of the United States would not desire to see it enforced."[25]

Having set forth these points, Dana questioned the point of the trial. He concluded with a warning that "the risks of such absurd and discreditable issues of a great state trial, are assumed for the sake of a verdict which, if obtained, will settle nothing in law or national practice not now settled, and nothing in fact not now history, while no judgment rendered thereon do we think will be ever executed. Besides these reasons, and perhaps because of them, I think that the public interest in the trial has ceased among the most earnest and loyal citizens."[26]

Dana was willing to try the case and believed that, if undertaken, a victory for the federal government was critical. Despite his reservations, he told Evarts: "I am confident that I can do my duty as counsel to the utmost of my ability and with all zeal. For my doubts are not what the verdict ought to be. On the contrary, I should feel all the more strongly, if the trial is begun, the importance of a victory to the Government, and the necessity of putting forth all powers and using all lawful means to secure it. Still, I feel it my duty to say that if the President should judge otherwise, my position in the case is at his disposal."[27]

If it had been unexpected, the content of the letter would have been considered a bombshell. But Evarts clearly believed that the time had come to bring to the president's attention his own concerns over trying Davis. Now that he was attorney general, Evarts had the authority over the case and whether it should be prosecuted. What he had to do, however, was convince Johnson that the case should not be tried. Remarkably, he still could not bring himself to submit the letter to Johnson. He pocketed Dana's letter for six weeks.

While the defense remained unaware, the prosecution was quickly losing steam. On October 9, 1868, Attorney General Evarts wrote to President Johnson about the case. He finally enclosed a copy of the letter from Dana. He did not explain why it had taken him six weeks to get a copy to the president, but he stated that Dana had expressed "views, in a careful and deliberate form, as to the propriety of the Government's remitting further prosecution of the pending indictment." Evarts confessed that his view of the case was in line with Dana's letter, saying, "Had I remained in a private professional relation to the case and to the Government, his communication probably would have borne my signature also."[28]

Gideon Welles noted in his diary at the end of October 1868 that Evarts had gone back to New York to vote and "to attend to his immense private business."[29] Evarts had only been to one cabinet meeting in the past five weeks, and Welles complained that "important opinions are consequently postponed and action delayed."[30] The attorney general addressed the entire cabinet on November 6, 1868, and informed them that "he did not think, and had not for the last two years thought any good end was to be attained by trying him [Davis]—that if tried there was no likelihood whatever, and if convicted he would not be, and at this day ought not to be punished." He claimed that the trial was but a meaningless prosecution and that he never supported actions of that character. Since the Supreme Court would begin its term in the first week of December, Chase could not be present for the Davis trial, Evarts told the cabinet. Neither he nor his associate, Richard Henry Dana Jr., were willing to proceed with the case before Judge Underwood alone.[31]

Looking at the case as a whole, Evarts told President Johnson and the cabinet, the time had come for a dismissal of the indictment. The attorney general advised the president to issue a final proclamation of amnesty and pardon without delay. The proclamation that Evarts proposed should encompass all cases that had not been addressed through previous amnesty proclamations. He urged Johnson to "close-out," once and forever, the rebellion. After the president issued such a proclamation, Evarts would be free to dismiss the case against Davis. The suggestion by Evarts was not well received by everyone in the cabinet. Gideon Welles and William Seward, the last remaining holdovers from the Lincoln administration, opposed this idea. Johnson, however, expressed his support and asked Evarts to prepare a proclamation for consideration during the next cabinet meeting.[32]

When November began, with the charges still pending against Davis, overtures were made to President Johnson through an "intimate friend of the President" about obtaining a pardon for Davis. Johnson replied without equivocation that "he would let the law take its course" and that "there was nothing in his power except a pardon, and that he would *never* grant one."[33] Clearly, Johnson was not prepared to reveal to the supporters of Davis that he was considering a general amnesty. Nor was he inclined to tell them of the cabinet discussions about dismissing the case against Davis. The cause was again set late in the month of November 1868. This was not a trial setting, and Davis would not be required to be present. However, he was not even to be found in Canada. Davis was touring England in November 1868, offering opinions about the holy city of Jerusalem and the unique fitness that Englishmen had for the task of exploring the city.[34] Being tried for treason did not seem to be one of his immediate concerns.

In the interim, O'Conor wrote to his cocounsel, Robert Ould, informing him that the case would be tried. O'Conor now wanted the defense team to shift tactics. If the defense had once attempted to get along with the prosecutors in the hope that the government might be persuaded to dismiss the case, after four years, O'Conor no longer felt bound to pursue that tack. He told Ould that the defense needed to take a hard-nosed approach to the case, even to the point of embarrassing the prosecution, if possible. Further, O'Conor had information that Chief Justice Chase might be receptive to the argument that the Fourteenth Amendment was a punishment that precluded any criminal charge against the leaders of the Confederacy. In other words, Chase might believe that the passage of the constitutional amendment, which disenfranchised rebel leaders because it constituted a punishment for their involvement in the war, might bar prosecution seeking other sanctions, such as for criminal treason. Ould took the information and was able to confirm that Chase did indeed consider this to be a correct interpretation of the new amendment. O'Conor told Ould to press the position. No other member of the defense team was even aware of the argument that was to be made, and Davis himself was not informed.[35]

Just two weeks before the Davis treason trial was scheduled to begin in Richmond, the two opposing lawyers met at a bar function in New York City. William M. Evarts, now the U.S. attorney general, entered the banquet room of the Astor House alongside his opposing counsel in the Davis case, Charles O'Conor, to thunderous applause from nearly 250 members of the New York bar. O'Conor, as president of the bar, escorted Evarts to the banquet table of the patriotically decorated room. O'Conor sat at the center of the table, with the new attorney general to his right and President-Elect Ulysses S. Grant to his left. Also joining them at the table were Adm. David Farragut, the governor of New York, the mayor of New York City, and Richard H. Dana Jr. In attendance were all of the most distinguished lawyers and jurists of the state, who stood until O'Conor and his guests were seated. At the close of the dinner, toasts were proposed for the president-elect, which were met with prolonged applause. Charles O'Conor then rose from his seat and offered a toast to "our guest," William M. Evarts. When Evarts rose to reply, he was met with three cheers from the guests. Grant left at eleven o'clock in the evening, but the banquet continued into the late hours of the night.[36]

Three days later, on November 20, 1868, Evarts attended a cabinet meeting in Washington, D.C. A proclamation granting a general amnesty and pardon for former rebels had been under consideration for some time. Evarts told the president that if an amnesty was not to be issued, then he needed to immediately instruct prosecutors in the Davis case to postpone the trial, which was set for the following Monday. Johnson admitted that he continued to grapple with the question of whether to issue such a proclamation and had not decided to do so. A reading of this entry in Browning's diary makes it appear very improbable that the government ever intended to try Davis in November. Davis was out of the country, and William Evarts was waiting for a decision to be made on the amnesty proclamation that, depending on its scope, might pardon Davis himself. It is also clear, however, given that Davis was not present, that the prosecution did not expect the Davis defense team to go on the offensive come the court date.[37] Evarts wrote to S. Ferguson Beach, the U.S. attorney in Richmond, ordering him to "arrange with such counsel as may represent the defendant for an assignment of the trial for such day in the latter part of March or early in April, as you shall learn will be acceptable to the honorable judges of the court."[38]

A delay of the trial would not prove so easy this time. Two days before court, O'Conor informed Evarts that the defense intended to try to quash the indictment. Evarts promptly informed Dana. On Monday, November 30, the U.S. circuit court convened in Richmond, with both Salmon Chase and John Underwood sitting as judges. Once again, Chief Justice Chase announced that he would not be able to preside over a trial, citing the upcoming Supreme Court term. And as before, the federal government requested a continuance so that the case could be tried before the chief justice in the coming year. For the first time in months, the defense team showed a shift in its tactics by indicating that it had other matters to press. Robert Ould urged a motion to quash the indictment against Davis on the grounds that the recent passage of the Fourteenth Amendment to the Constitution, ratified on July 9, 1868, operated as a bar to further prosecution of any person who engaged in insurrection or rebellion against the United States. Ould submitted an affidavit swearing that Davis served as a representative from Mississippi in 1845 and had taken an oath to support the Constitution of the United States on December 8, 1845.

Section 3 denied civil or military office to former Confederates who had previously served as a federal or state official who had sworn to uphold the United States Constitution. Ould argued that these disqualifications were the constitutional punishment for engaging in the rebellion and that no other sanction, even for the constitutional crime of treason, could be added for participation in the Civil War. The argument was bolstered by the fact that the amendment did specifically impose unique sanctions on the rebels. Ould attempted to make the sanction into a double jeopardy claim by asserting that the civil sanctions imposed by the amendment constituted a criminal punishment that prohibited further prosecution against Davis because a treason trial exposed the former rebel to a second punishment. The prosecution was caught flat-footed by Ould's assertions and asked the court to postpone a decision on the issue until it was able to fully prepare a rebuttal. Prosecutors suggested that a hearing on the motion to quash be delayed until after the end of the Supreme Court session. Defense attorneys challenged such a long delay and asked that it be heard as soon as possible. Chief Justice Chase, perhaps sensing the opportunity through this novel legal position to rid himself of having to preside over the trial, postponed the argument three days.[39]

By this point, the nation's newspapers were openly questioning whether the case should be dropped by the prosecution. The *New York Evening Post* reported that William Evarts stated that the case would have been tried in the previous year but for the impeachment proceedings against Johnson.[40] If Evarts did say that, his remark flew in the face of the obstacles that he knew existed to trying the case, even a year earlier. Referring to the prosecution as a "farce," the *Springfield Republican* asked its readers how long the prosecution would be maintained. Asserting that very few people cared whether he was tried and that no one expected him to be, the editors argued that he should "be at once relieved of all legal liabilities and allowed to sink into merited obscurity."[41] A newspaper in Connecticut, the *New London Democrat,* sarcastically noted that "the distinguished criminal has gone abroad and occupies his leisure moments in lecturing about Jerusalem."[42] It was becoming much more difficult to maintain the posture that the case had any momentum that would lead it to be tried.

Lawyers for both sides arrived in court on December 3, 1868, prepared to argue the defense motion to quash the indictment against Davis. The biggest name, and most important lawyer for the government, Attorney General Evarts, did not attend, reportedly because of other, more pressing engagements. Robert Ould took the lead on behalf of Davis. The arguments that he made simply elaborated upon those that he had broached with the court the previous Monday. Boiling the argument down to its essence, he asserted that the passage of the Fourteenth Amendment imposed punishment upon those who engaged in the rebellion and barred the government from seeking further sanctions against Davis, including criminal sanctions for the crime of treason. Richard Henry Dana Jr. rose to address the court on behalf of the government, remarking, once again, that the argument had been unexpected to both the prosecutors and the court. Chase responded that it was not unexpected to the court since the defense had set out the basis of the motion to quash on Monday. O'Conor, playing both to the court and the audience, offered that the defense would not oppose any amount of time for the prosecution to prepare its response so long as Chief Justice Chase was able to hear the argument.

Given the government's position that it was unprepared to respond, Chase took a recess until afternoon to hear the government's response. When the court reconvened, H. H. Wells, the military governor of Virginia, and S. Ferguson Beach, the new U.S. attorney for the Eastern District of Virginia, took the lead on arguing the motion. Beach argued first. He remarked, correctly, that the defense motion rested upon the proposition that the effect of the constitutional amendment was to repeal the treason acts of 1790 and 1862 under which the indictment of Davis was framed by asserting that the punishment for treason had been changed by the amendment. The Fourteenth Amendment, he told the court, operated only to disenfranchise former rebels; it did not punish them for crimes. This was a collateral and incidental disability that was attached to the commission of the offense but not a change of punishment. There was nothing in the language of the amendment that would indicate that it was intended to act as a bar against a treason prosecution. Governor Wells then offered his take on the defense motion. The intent of the passage of the Fourteenth Amendment was not to change the criminal code of the United States; instead, it was to protect places of public trust from those who have previously violated that trust by engaging in the rebellion. He acknowledged that one statute may repeal another; under the rules of statutory construction, that may be done if the two statutes were so incompatible as to be mutually exclusive.[43] Wells could not fathom how the two were incompatible.

Wells finished his argument at three in the afternoon. His cocounsel, Dana, rose and told the court that he requested that his argument be postponed, overnight, for him to prepare. He also asked the court to be allowed to close the arguments, intending to force O'Conor to speak first so that he might answer any issue raised by the New York defense attorney. In other words, he was requesting that the traditional sequence of argument be taken out of order, since ordinarily it is the party with the burden of proof, in this case the defense because it was their motion to quash, that retains the right to close arguments.

At ten o'clock the next morning, Chief Justice Chase drew the court to order. The federal courthouse, which sat just down the hill from the Virginia State Capitol, was packed with spectators anxious to hear Davis's attorney, Charles O'Conor, and the government's attorney, Richard Henry Dana Jr., argue the motion to quash. There was no spare seat to be found in the courtroom itself. Chase had the bearing and deep dignity of a man in a high place. He asked the defense whether there was anything further that needed to be added before the prosecution responded to the motion. Two lawyers had already argued the motion the day before. James Lyons was scheduled to be the third. He responded to the court by saying that he had determined not to argue the motion in the hope that the two defense arguments would prove sufficient and that the ruling might be expedited by his decision not to take any more of the court's time.

Dana spoke on behalf of the government in a hearing covered closely by the nation's press. He acknowledged the momentous decision that the two judges would shortly render. "The Fourteenth Amendment," he argued, "is not a provision of criminal law, looking to the punishment of individuals by depriving them of office, but is an organic measure, having for its object the securing of trustworthy persons for administration. It has, therefore, no effect to repeal the laws against treason, on which this indictment rests."[44] The amendment "was a measure of precaution to secure the country against filling offices with persons who had once before filled them and broken their oaths." Dana urged the court to see the amendment for what it was: "an expression only of the public will as to the fitness of those who engaged in the rebellion after breaking their oaths to hold office again." He closed with the observation that, viewed from the defense perspective, the Fourteenth Amendment would actually encourage rebellion since it would bar participants from any penalty except disfranchisement.[45] Characterizing the defense position as "absurd," Dana asserted that it was indeed the position of the case now before the court, with the defense acknowledging "that the defendant did commit treason, and, admitting that he held office and took the oath" of allegiance to the United States but cloaking Davis with the Fourteenth Amendment and claiming that the newly ratified constitutional amendment exempted him from punishment. The powerful argument by Dana confidently maintained that there existed no evidence that Congress intended this interpretation of the amendment or that the people, by accepting it, envisioned this strange interpretation.[46]

It is apparent from the reaction of the prosecutors that they were surprised by the novel defense argument, first raised on Monday, about the legal effect of the Fourteenth Amendment on Davis's treason prosecution. By Thursday, however, this surprise should have been overcome. Why would the U.S. attorney have asked the court, on Thursday, for more time to consider the motion to quash? Clearly, Dana was prepared to respond to the defense motion, which he mocked and treated as specious. Of course, the Fourteenth Amendment did not mean to bar the criminal prosecution of traitors. Either Dana should have responded to the motion at the opening of the court on Thursday morning, or he should have prepared his cocounsel to respond as he did after lunch so that the defense motion could be turned aside immediately at the opening of the day. But by its hesitancy to address the motion directly and forcefully, the government permitted the defense motion to appear to have some merit. As Charles O'Conor rose to address the court, it was yet unknown whether either Chase or Underwood would see the motion as meritorious.

O'Conor took an interesting tack in his argument by addressing Chief Justice Chase almost to the exclusion of Judge Underwood. He began his presentation by subtly reminding the court that this was a case of great importance. Almost immediately, he remarked that the chief justice was now linked to the great John Marshall, who had famously tried the Aaron Burr treason case in Richmond at the beginning of the century and had first interpreted the constitutional provision on treason. Without directly stating the proposition, O'Conor then attempted to broaden the question to include not only Jefferson Davis but the entire southern people. In O'Conor's view, the great chief justice had, by his rulings in the Burr trial, done much "to give practical explanations and interpretations of those provisions of the Constitution which provide for the punishment of citizens for alleged treason, and to decide whether cases of this nature are to be proceeded with farther to vex and annoy and inspire with terror a whole people." Now, O'Conor stated, Chase possessed the ability to interpret this new amendment. The only question was whether Chase would "be found ready to do as much to comfort the people as his illustrious predecessor had been in his day."[47] O'Conor urged Chase to view this prosecution in the context of the greater political question facing the nation. Without directly stating it, the question that O'Conor wanted Chase to answer was whether the prosecution of Davis served the nation well. This was, of course, a question of policy not for a judge to decide but urged nonetheless.

O'Conor then read the court section 3 of the Fourteenth Amendment.[48] He argued that the amendment was self-enforcing and needed no judicial interpretation, which was his way of arguing that the only way to interpret the section was to find that it provided for the only punishment to be inflicted upon people who engaged in the rebellion. There was no need for the court to look at the intent of the framers of the amendment, he asserted; "we find upon its face that the framers contemplated its operation on the individual, and looked upon it as the infliction of a punishment." Now O'Conor engaged in a sleight of hand, stating, "It is a familiar fact, that the terms disability and penalty indicate punishment for crime."[49] The problem with O'Conor's argument was that section 3 does not contain the word *penalty;* it only uses the word *disability.* But O'Conor wanted the court to conflate the words *disability* and *penalty.*

O'Conor never claimed that the framers of the amendment sought to limit the punishment of rebel leaders. Instead, he phrased his argument differently: "If the framer of this section, instead of being willing to have them hung to satisfy the vengeance of those who demanded blood, intended by it to bind up the wounds of the nation, to let the past be the dead past, he is not a traitor, but a statesman, a patriot and a benefactor of his race and country."[50] The nuances of this argument were brilliant, yet a judge as capable as Chase could see through the legal weaknesses of O'Conor's presentation. Whether he wished to is another matter. The amendment would only help the Davis defense if it barred the treason prosecution. If it reflected the legislature's desire to reconcile the two warring sections of the nation had no bearing on the ability of the government to proceed with the treason trial.

O'Conor then shifted his argument once again. Southern leaders, he stated, were also punished by social stigma, referring to them as "pariahs in the land of their birth."[51] He ignored the overwhelming evidence that rebel leaders were considered heroes in the white South. Whatever social stigma they suffered was limited to that which they may face in the North and then only among those who considered their actions dishonorable. He also took no notice that social stigma often accompanies criminal acts but has rarely been viewed as a substitute for the penal sanctions provided by law. The New York lawyer did not want the court to view this case as only involving Davis, despite the fact that the statute of limitations had run out for all others on the crime of treason at the time of his argument, in December 1868, and the accompanying fact that many of the leaders of the rebellion had be pardoned for their actions during the war.

O'Conor reasoned that the punishment of the removal of civil rights was adequate for the "object in view," that of chastising the former leaders of the South: "The bravest of those who led the Southern armies to battle are now disqualified from holding any office whatever" and moreover, "in point of civil rights, [are] below the humblest of their former slaves."[52] He made no mention of whether this punishment was adequate for the crime of treason. The amendment inflicted a new punishment, according to O'Conor, that was substituted for that to which they were liable under the existing law at the time of their actions. By this time, the arguments had been going for five and a half hours. Chase ordered a forty-five-minute break.

When the defense continued after the break, O'Conor raised a new question: How could fair trials for treason be had after a war so great as the one just ended? The only answer, of course, was that fair trials could not be held in such an atmosphere as existed in the country in the latter part of the 1860s. He found it repugnant to humanity that the Confederate leaders would be treated as equals by their Union counterparts during the war but then put on trial for their lives after the war. Surely, he argued, this was not what either the government or the people intended to be done. This, he maintained, was why the Fourteenth Amendment was adopted. Acknowledging that it was a great and beneficial act of mercy by the American people, he nonetheless asked Chase and Underwood to give the amendment the expression that he claimed it was meant to bear. Universal suffrage, something that he would never have accepted, "should be accompanied, hand in hand, with universal amnesty of supposed offenses arising out of the unfortunate controversy, in which universal suffrage may be said to have had its origin and establishment."[53] His arguments now drifted even further from the facts. What if the war had lasted several generations? Would the great-grandson of Davis have faced a treason charge? O'Conor's argument now bore little relevance to the motion to quash, but he was not arguing a criminal motion; he was arguing for Judge Chase to make a radical change in national policy. The Fourteenth Amendment did not act as a guard against the further political rule by the men who had pushed the Union into war; it was an amendment designed to minimize the consequences to those men for their actions in bringing the war. O'Conor then made his boldest assertions, beginning with the proposition "that indictments for treason or other prosecutions for belligerent acts in the due and orderly prosecution of a civil war on the rebel side, are not properly the subjects of criminal prosecutions or civil action." Instead, he argued, if the rebel conduct during the war warranted vengeance, the victors should inflict it immediately without resort to the judicial system. He suggested that the punishment "might be inflicted by refusing quarter, it might be inflicted by decimating those in the ranks and executing, in some military form, the leaders." It was almost absurd for the defense to avow that the lawlessness brought on by raising a black flag to indicate no quarter would be given or decimating by execution prisoners of war was a fitting substitute for a treason trial conducted under the rules of law after the war, but that did not stop O'Conor from making the argument. "If the vanquished had demeaned themselves in a manner so criminal as to justify such extreme severity, extreme severity may be safely employed," he asserted. "If they have not so conducted themselves, it ought not to be employed."[54]

Having set up the straw man, O'Conor now proceeded to attempt to knock it down: "It will be seen, therefore, that there is no occasion, at the close of a civil war, for resorting to the aid of the civil magistrate, through an indictment and trial by jury, to punish traitors for warring against the Government. The only motive that could induce the victorious General to turn his vanquished adversary over to the civil law and seek his destruction by the verdict of a jury condemning for treason, is his unwillingness to brave the common sentiment of mankind by condemning him, of his own authority, to a military execution. It is a very mean and unworthy office to assign to the judiciary, and it is to be regretted if, under any circumstances, the judiciary is not at liberty to refuse compliance."

His was a bizarre and irrational argument based entirely on an emotional plea to Chief Justice Chase to reject the treason charge against Jefferson Davis because the military had not summarily executed the former Confederate president immediately after the war. O'Conor's words implied that the federal government was asking the judiciary to bloody the hands of justice by trying Davis for treason for no reason other than revenge. He ignored the constitutional definition that clearly stated that "treason against the United States, shall consist only in levying war against them."[55] He also disregarded the constitutional mandate that spoke of convictions, witnesses, and courts clearly indicating that treason would be the proper subject of a civil trial after the person levied war. It was an argument that O'Conor may have thought played well to the white southerners in the gallery and felt compelled to articulate. O'Conor was an attorney with a violent temperament. He had made impassioned arguments like these many, many times. He could not have believed that a cool-minded judge would be swayed by them.

Then he turned to another strange point. He asserted the position that

> in the cases of such civil war, a trial in the ordinary course of the law is entirely inappropriate to dealing with the case of the leaders. Their acts are so notorious and have been so open, that they do not form a legitimate subject of proof in a court of justice. They are actually known to the Government in all of its departments. They are actually and officially known to the court, and cannot be properly the subject of proof or disproof. To obtain an impartial jury is utterly impossible, for the jurors must all themselves have actual personal knowledge of all the facts which, upon an indictment and plea, would be formally put in issue. Gravely submitting, on testimony formally taken, to twelve jurors in the county of Henrico, the question whether an open and public war against the United States was

> here maintained and waged, and whether Jefferson Davis was the leader of it, would be a mockery and a farce.[56]

O'Conor then made an argument that only an attorney caught up in his own rhetoric and faced with a case involving overwhelming evidence of the guilt of his client could make with a straight face. The Sixth Amendment to the Constitution grants an accused the right to an impartial jury. With all the evidence of Davis's guilt, it was utterly impossible for him to be judged by an impartial jury.

The New York litigator then began to wind down. Losing none of his passion but ending his long argument on a calmer note, O'Conor asked the court to "give peace and the vast assurances of peace to a vast section of this country." Not quite satisfied, O'Conor pointed out to the court the "great and beneficent act of grace and mercy in the construction which we have put upon it, and which tends to advance that which all good men who are believers in universal suffrage so much admire—that universal suffrage should be accompanied, hand in hand, with a universal amnesty of all supposed offenses arising out of the unfortunate controversy in which universal suffrage may be said to have had its origin and establishment."[57] O'Conor, harnessed so long with the highly pressurized case of Jefferson Davis, finally vented his feelings and emotions in the packed courtroom.

The *New York World* found O'Conor's reasoning to be a "masterful argument."[58] The *New York Tribune* was more insightful in reporting that O'Conor made no "satisfactory reply" to Dana's argument. O'Conor did "press a strong point against the Government by holding it up as repugnant to the world's idea of humanity to deal for four years with the leaders in a war as men in all respects equal in official rank, and honorable enough to be treated with, and then, with the coming of peace, to hang these same men as traitors."[59] Whether he convinced the judges or not, it must have come as a tremendous relief to finally be able to put his famous oratorical skills to use in the case.

A Divided Trial Court

Chase adjourned the court until the next day, but the prosecutors and defense attorneys were recalled by him to the courtroom that evening. Once all were assembled, Chase announced that he and Judge Underwood had considered the motion to quash and disagreed on what constituted the proper ruling. Chase told the lawyers that he was in favor of granting the motion to quash, while Underwood thought it should be denied. Because there was a split on the issue, Chase stated that the question would be certified to the United States Supreme Court for review and decision. Then, having dropped this bombshell, Chase decided to leave Richmond for Washington, D.C., the next day.[60]

Davis's defense team advanced an argument that, they conceded, requested the court to construe the Fourteenth Amendment as the defense construed it. There was ample evidence that their construction was incorrect. The intentions of the authors of the amendment and the plain language of the amendment made the defense's proposed construction a difficult one to conceive. O'Conor had gone even further and urged the court to ignore the law and find that a treason indictment was not in the best interest of the nation after the war. His argument proposed that the court legislate an outcome on a question that was clearly outside the province of the judiciary. He unmistakably was appealing to Chief Justice Salmon Chase.

The question is how the defense team came to think that Chase might be open to such an odd argument. The answer is stunning. O'Conor revealed to his client that Robert Ould had been tipped off that Chase "was inclined to consider the disfranchisement of the leaders by the late amendment of the Constitution as a punishment which precluded the infliction of any other penalty for the same offence, i.e. engaging in 'the rebellion.'" Acting on this information, O'Conor was "determined at once to give him a chance of making a judicial determination accordingly."[61] The news that Chase would be open to this argument arrived so near the court date that O'Conor did not have time to even apprise his client of the position that he would be taking. Apparently, Ould and O'Conor had only a single conversation about the chief justice's inclination before they put it forward.

O'Conor, however, relied upon more than just this tip. After the argument, he conversed with the chief justice and was able to report to Davis that "the Chief Justice is thoroughly enlisted. His judgment is with you; his fancy is excited; he says a judicial determination of this point in your favor would furnish a magnificent chapter in our history and sundry things of that sort."[62] As a judge, Chase should not have told O'Conor that his judgment was with Davis. Indeed, it was unethical for him to do so. Certainly, O'Conor knew after the decision was announced that Chase had voted to quash the indictment. The question was certified to the U.S. Supreme Court. Since it still needed to be litigated before the Supreme Court and because Chase would be the presiding judge, he should not have reassured O'Conor that he was in Davis's corner.

Why, then, would Chase tell O'Conor this? Likely, he did because it served his political ambitions to let O'Conor know his feelings. According to O'Conor, Chase even mentioned to O'Conor his concern that the defense lawyer had conceded a disputable point. O'Conor wrote to Davis that Chase "twice returned to this topic," making clear that the chief justice was attempting to help O'Conor refine the argument that he might make before the Supreme Court. It must be understood that appellate judges argue with their colleagues about the outcome of cases pending in their courts. By Chase admonishing O'Conor not to concede a disputable point, it makes it that much easier for Chase to prevail in chambers on the point. If Chase wanted to argue that a particular point was indisputable, all that another Supreme Court justice would have to do to counter would be to point out that even the counsel for the party itself conceded that the point was disputable. The excitement that O'Conor felt by hearing Chase give him pointers on polishing his argument is palpable in his letter to Davis. Chase was on Davis's side and had told them so. The defense lawyer, in his exhilaration, wrote Davis, "I mention these things to shew you the state of his mind."[63]

Even in his delight, though, O'Conor betrayed a suspicion of Chase's purpose by telling Davis that "what may be the real objects of this practised politician I know not. Various motives may be imputed to him. Only one of them involves any thing unpleasant."[64] Apparently, the lack of ethics was not considered unpleasant by O'Conor; however, his suspicion that Chase, ever the abolitionist in the minds of the Democrats, might have thought that the Fourteenth Amendment had not been legally ratified and was looking for an opportunity for the Supreme Court to render a decision to affirm its legality, concerned the New York lawyer. No matter how pliable Chase was in an effort to advance his political ambitions, even the recipients of his favors distrusted his motives. Another question, whether O'Conor intentionally addressed his argument to Chief Justice Chase almost to the exclusion of Judge Underwood, became clear when he told Davis that Underwood's opposition to granting the motion to quash constituted only a "formal impediment."[65] His vote was not the one that mattered.

On Monday, December 7, 1868, Congress assembled in Washington, D.C. Two days later, President Johnson's annual message was read to the combined houses. Tracing Reconstruction from December 1865, when Johnson claimed that "civil strife had ceased, the spirit of rebellion had spent its entire force, in the Southern States the people had warmed to national life,"[66] the president claimed that congressional legislation had left the country in agitation and strife. Johnson called for the repeal of much of the Radicals' enacted agenda and a shrinking of the federal government. He made no mention, however, of the pending case against Davis, despite its occupying center stage only days earlier. Nor did he mention any intention on his part of issuing an amnesty proclamation.[67] Having permitted the message to be read in the House of Representatives, members then "denounced it as infamous, abominable, wicked."[68] The Senate, aware of its content, did not initially permit it to be read; the senators relented a bit later. The enmity between the legislative and executive branches of government would continue through the end of Johnson's administration.

The president alone, however, held the power to pardon. On Christmas Day 1868, he utilized it. Johnson issued a proclamation granting "universal amnesty and pardon for participation in said rebellion extended to all who have borne any part therein." The edict extended the amnesty to "every person who, directly or indirectly, participated in the late insurrection or rebellion a full pardon and amnesty for the offense of treason against the United States."[69] By this issuance, the Davis case was effectively over.

O'Conor wrote Davis early in January 1869, "Of course you have read the Christmas-day proclamation." O'Conor then recounted how, just shortly before the last trial date in November, the president had stated that he would never consider granting a pardon to Davis. "Yet on the heel of this came a general amnesty," he said in wonder. His letter explained that "this act supersedes the necessity of arguing the question presented to the Supreme Court by the certificate of division" on the motion to quash the treason indictment. "Nothing remains to be done except some mere formal details."[70] The case was over.

Less than two months remained in the Johnson presidency. On Friday, January 8, 1869, a cabinet meeting was held. All the members of the Johnson cabinet were in attendance. William Evarts gave a copy of instructions that he had sent to all government prosecutors. In it, he directed that United States district attorneys file a nolle prosequi, a formal entry by the prosecutor giving notice that prosecution in the case will cease, in all pending treason indictments arising out of the rebellion, including—most notably—the Jefferson Davis treason prosecution. The diary of Secretary of the Interior Orville

Browning, which references Evarts's telling the entire cabinet of his decision, does not indicate that the decision warranted any discussion.[71]

The following evening, Evarts dined with all the justices of the Supreme Court except the frail Associate Justice Robert Cooper Grier. Whether he told them of his decision to end the treason prosecution against Davis is not recorded, but the appeal from the divided trial court was pending. The government's efforts to punish rebels was quickly winding down. Two days after this dinner, Evarts presented the full cabinet with his plan to end all pending confiscation cases. Only William Seward and Secretary of the Treasury Hugh McCulloch even hesitated to accept his proposal. After only a short discussion, the president and his cabinet voiced unanimous support for the move.[72] The Davis treason charge would be dismissed, and the confiscation suits against the former rebels would be ended.

Despite the decision being reached, it was not until Thursday, February 11, 1869, that the United States district attorney entered a nolle prosequi in the treason prosecution against Davis. Both indictments were dismissed. Almost as an afterthought, since no action had ever been taken on the other treason indictments found in 1865, long-standing but unprosecuted indictments against Robert E. Lee, Wade Hampton, Henry Wise, William Mahone, Jubal Early, and nearly thirty others were dismissed. Robert Ould, attorney for Davis, moved that the court order that the men acting as sureties on Davis's bond be discharged from further obligation to the bond.[73] Ironically, one of the nolle prosequi entered on that day was in relation to the treason indictment against Ould himself.[74]

The end of the prosecution did not generate headlines but was, instead, buried far from the front page. Northern papers treated it with disdain. The *Elkhart Weekly Review* of Indiana noted the dismissal in the case of "Davis and other traitors," while the *Portsmouth (N.H.) Journal of Literature and Politics* headlined the news as simply "the farce ends."[75] Davis was not present in the Richmond courtroom. He was touring Paris.[76]

CONCLUSION

The Jefferson Davis Trial in American Memory

> To be pardoned for a great crime, as for instance treason or piracy, is the next thing to being punished for it.
>
> —Gerrit Smith

ON MAY 9, 1865, Gideon Welles confided to his diary that "the President in the exercise of the pardoning power may limit or make condition, and, while granting life and liberty to traitors, deny them the right of holding office or voting."[1] Little did he know, about a month after Lee's surrender, how prescient his entry would prove. Five years after the war ended, no Confederate had been hanged for treason. The only rebel seriously prosecuted had escaped with his life and liberty. All that was left to be determined was whether the narrative of the case could be rewritten. Jefferson Davis was intent on doing just that. In the decades following the war, a fierce battle was fought over the memory of men like Davis and Lee. While Lee did little to publicly attempt to shape history, Jefferson and Varina Davis took an active role in it, at once portraying the former Confederate president as a martyr and hero of the Confederacy.

After the case was dropped, Davis carefully cultivated the image of a fearless man, wrongfully accused of a heinous crime who, during his confinement, had wanted nothing more than a public trial to prove the legality of secession and his own innocence. That image resonated with southerners, who were already becoming deeply immersed in the myth of the Lost Cause. The truth is much different and much more human. While he was imprisoned, Davis proved to be a nervous, difficult client. His flight from Richmond, when many other rebel leaders were disregarding personal danger and submitting to federal authority, began the long road through the latter half of the decade of the 1860s that often exposed Davis's human fears and frailties. The humiliation of his capture, his transfer to solitary confinement, and his lengthy imprisonment and isolation from his family resulted in him becoming deeply depressed and anxious over his future. His wife, Varina, wrote letter after letter pleading for his release while citing the toll that the confinement took on him physically and mentally. Once he was released but still under indictment, his lawyer fretted over his fragile mental and physical constitution, not knowing when, if ever, Davis would appear to answer the charges in Richmond.

In mid-January 1876, Davis wrote from New Orleans to James Proctor Knott, the Democratic chairman of the Committee on Amnesty for the United States House of Representatives. Congress was taking up the thorny question of amnesty for those few remaining rebels who had not had their rights fully restored. Several members of Congress were willing to legislatively grant amnesty to virtually everyone, but they adamantly opposed the inclusion of Davis. The former rebel president made his unrepentant views clear to the congressman. He did not seek amnesty and did not desire it. He maintained that he had committed no wrongdoing and regretted nothing that he had done: "As it appears from the published proceedings of Congress that the passage of a general amnesty bill is obstructed by the objection to including me in its provisions, I write to express my regret that any of my compatriots should suffer by identification with me, and to request that you will not allow the objection to prevent others from enjoying whatever benefits may be accorded to them, on the condition of my exclusion. Further it may be proper to state that I have no claim to pardon, not having in any wise repented, or changed the convictions on which my political course was founded, as well before, as during, and since the war between the States."[2]

His words mirrored his public position after the federal government failed to bring him to trial but was much different than what he and his supports sought for him during his incarceration. While the treason charge was pending against him, the subject of pardon was broached with President Johnson through Davis's intermediaries, despite Johnson sternly disavowing the possibility of a pardon being granted to Davis even as late as November 1868. No rebuff slowed the attempts by lawyers for Davis to secure a pardon for their client while he stood charged in the case. Both Jefferson and Varina Davis were aware of the endeavors to secure his release through pardon and did not object to those efforts, but after the threat of a hangman's noose was lifted, they began to claim that he had wanted a trial all along.

Davis's effort to rewrite history stretched to the end of his life. Nearly a quarter-century after the end of the war, he publicly defended his role in the

Civil War in an article he authored and had published in the *North American Review.* He had, he stated, "no excuses to make and no apology to offer." Neither the loss of life nor the destruction of his beloved South chastened him. "Instead of being 'traitors,' we were loyal to our States; instead of being rebels against the Union, we were defenders of the Constitution as framed by its founders and as expounded by them," he claimed.[3]

The controversy revolving around the mistreatment of Union prisoners continued to haunt Davis until the end of his life. When amnesty was discussed in Congress in 1875, the proposed act erupted in contentious debate surrounding Davis's role in the deaths of Union prisoners of war. Democrats and southerners believed that the Republicans were merely waiving the bloody shirt once again and were not genuine in their opposition to granting Davis amnesty. But Andersonville and other southern prisoner of war camps haunted northerners, who believed that someone in the rebel leadership—Davis, specifically—should pay for the crimes committed in those camps. The horrors there were real. The lives lost and the health destroyed of the many thousands of northern men who were in those camps could not be forgotten or forgiven so soon after the war. Southern leaders might deny their knowledge of the extent of the suffering at these camps; they might deny that the suffering was worse than that experienced by southern men in Union prisons; they might claim that the suffering was exaggerated; however, what they could not deny was that the North did not forgive them for the misery of their compatriots, sons, and husbands in the camps.

George Shea wrote a letter to the editor for publication in the *New York Tribune* that appeared on January 24, 1876. In it, he addressed the accusation still in circulation that Davis had "conducted the war in a manner not permitted by the rules of civilized nations, especially in the treatment of prisoners." As proof of the innocence of Davis on the charge, Shea pointed out that "the Government, by its conduct, having tacitly abandoned those special charges of inhumanity" when it transferred him from Fort Monroe to Richmond for trial on the treason indictment, essentially admitted that Davis had no complicity in the crime. "The apparent unwillingness of the Government to prosecute, under every incentive of pride and honour to prosecute, was accepted" as a confirmation that Davis was not guilty of the mistreatment of prisoners. Lack of proof sufficient to proceed to trial does not equate to innocence, nor does the lack of will to proceed to trial equate to it. But the argument was simply too tempting for Shea to resist.[4] His protestations satisfied no one.

As Davis neared the end of his life, he wrote two lengthy articles for publication in *Belford's Magazine* that were subsequently published in pamphlet form. The first article appeared in January 1890, just after his death the month before. Varina Davis claimed that "it should be a complete vindication of the Confederate authorities before all fair-minded men."[5] The articles could do no such thing. Varina Davis's own actions taken after this "complete vindication" reflected her fears that more needed to be done to convince history that her husband did not approve of the mistreatment of Union prisoners.

At his death, the relentlessly loyal and dogmatic woman was finishing a book about her husband that she hoped would shape the memory of his life and presidency. In 1890, Varina Davis published *Jefferson Davis, Ex-President of the Confederate States of America: A Memoir,* an apologia for her beloved husband. The second volume contained a chapter entitled "The Exchange of Prisoners and Andersonville," in which she revisited the tired Confederate mantra holding the Union responsible for the end of prisoner exchanges after the Confederate Congress had passed a law differentiating the treatment of African American Union soldiers from that of white Union soldiers captured and held prisoner of war. Complete with charts and statistics and the ever-present comparisons between the death rates in northern and southern prisoner of war camps, Mrs. Davis conducted a spirited defense of her husband's policy toward Union prisoners of war. Meanwhile, she admitted that men at Andersonville had died from heat and exposure, as well as a lack of medicine, while maintaining that many of the soldiers who were captured by the Confederate army were deserters, African American soldiers, bowery roughs, and gamblers, which apparently mitigated the guilt of their captors and the subsequent treatment by the South.[6]

It is apparent that Varina Davis, in writing her memoirs, wanted to address the war crimes issue that had haunted her husband. She wrote that "Mr. Davis was so painfully affected by the death-rate and suffering of the prisoners at Andersonville, that even in the few hours he spent at home their condition weighed dreadfully upon his spirits."[7] She then recounted an incident she had witnessed between Davis and the commanding general of the Army of Northern Virginia: "One day I found General Lee there. Both were very grave, and the subject of their conference was the want and suffering at Andersonville, as portrayed by General Winder's private letter to the President. Mr. Davis said, 'If I could only get them across the trans-Mississippi, there beef and supplies of all kinds are abundant, but what can we do for them here?' General Lee answered quickly to this effect, 'Our men are in the same case, except that they are free. Their sufferings are the result of our necessities not of our policy. Do not distress yourself.'"[8]

In one simple paragraph of her memoirs, Varina Davis admitted that Davis and Lee were perfectly aware of the "want and suffering at Andersonville" and the decision by Davis not to do anything about it. Even with the damning knowledge of large-scale starvation, there is no record that Davis had considered the unilateral release and return of the Union soldiers to the North. Jefferson Davis prided himself on his Christian virtue and manliness. The decades after the war that he spent haunted by the specter of these men being systematically murdered were not spent that way because he was entirely innocent of their deaths.

Those on the Union side viewed the failure to bring Davis to trial on the treason charge differently. Attorney General James Speed spoke to the Society of the Loyal Legion in Cincinnati, Ohio, in late spring 1887 about the character of Abraham Lincoln. He touched on the issue of the punishment of the rebels and how Lincoln's generous influence was felt long after his death: "The nation imbibed his magnanimity. The spectacle of so vast a collision, with none brought to punishment, stands alone in history. Only that group of fiends who stilled the pulsations of Lincoln's great heart paid the penalty of crime."[9]

Jefferson Davis was not tried because the leaders of the United States were noble, principled men not bent on vengeance. That group of northern men and women looked at the Confederate leadership and saw unvarnished traitors. They harbored no doubt that Davis deserved to hang for the treason he had committed. But in their eyes, the United States was imbued with an exceptionalism in many regards, not least of which was the penchant for mercy, when societies in other nations would have sought revenge.

Other northerners disagreed with this decision. Predictably, Democrats and Republicans had differences of opinion, but more telling was the split among Republican and former abolitionist ranks. Men like Horace Greeley and Gerrit Smith joined the chorus of voices decrying the treatment of Davis and arguing that he should not be tried for treason. They were so certain of this position that they signed his bond to have him released from custody.

The failure to bring Davis to trial for treason did not arise from a Union concern that the results of battle would be overturned by the courts. By the blood drawn by the sword, secession had been rendered unconstitutional once and for all. The failure to bring him to trial did not proceed from a fear that he would be acquitted, although there was that concern. Until the very end of the time that he faced indictment, Union officials were concerned about the possibility of an acquittal but not cowed by it. Andrew Johnson never wavered in his belief that Davis was guilty of treason and should be punished for it. Nevertheless, he consistently placed his trust in the subordinates whom he believed to be experts in the field of law and deferred to their recommendations regarding every aspect of the prosecution.

There were, of course, the constitutional hurdles that had to be overcome by the prosecution. Members of the Johnson administration grappled with the question of venue from the start but ultimately came to the correct conclusion that the Constitution required that the treason trial of Davis be held in the former capital of the Confederacy. Once the issue of venue had been decided and the location of a trial set at Richmond, the prosecution was understandably saddled with the worst possible location for a trial, excepting, perhaps, South Carolina. The prosecution might be able to "pack" a jury, as Judge Underwood suggested was a possibility, but that would be a very poor, and dangerous, precedent to set. The prosecution would be terribly unpopular among the white southerners who still held significant power in the South, and even if enough loyal men might be found to serve on the jury, the acknowledged danger of sitting as a juror would be that it would subject jurors to intimidation in Richmond. That the lives of jurors would be in jeopardy was a significant risk.

If the reason cannot be fully explained by these constitutional concerns, then why did Jefferson Davis avoid trial? The motivations, including the political aspirations, of the men involved in the case forced this conclusion. The convergence of constitutional hurdles, events, personalities, ambitions, and skills operated to deny a courtroom confrontation to those who believed Davis should be brought to trial. The blame for the botched prosecution may be clearly assessed.

Lucius Chandler bore the primary responsibility for the failure to bring Davis to bar. As the United States attorney for Virginia, it was initially his duty to bring the case against Davis. He lacked the confidence and the skill to do so. Frustratingly slow in his decision making, he looked for reassurance that he should bring Davis to trial even after the attorney general had authorized the indictment of the former rebel. Since he was not a trial lawyer, he did not understand how to draft a proper indictment or prepare a case for trial. And because of his political ambition—he ran for Congress on several occasions—the question will always arise whether he slowed the progress of bringing Davis to trial because he believed that his involvement in the prosecution would turn many Virginian voters against him politically.

Chandler never gained election to the House of Representatives, although he ran for the office on three occasions. Nor did his life end happily. In 1876, he was accused of misusing funds during, among other times, his tenure as federal attorney. The allegation took a serious toll on his spirit, but he enlisted help to get his name cleared of the charge. Finally, at the beginning of April 1876, while in Washington, D.C., he was told that there was no evidence to support the accusation. Reportedly, he appeared to be deeply comforted by the news. He returned to Norfolk immediately and the next day spent writing out a deed conveying property to one of his daughters. Early the next morning, he rose very early, dressed in a black suit, filled his pockets with rocks, and drowned himself in the Elizabeth River. His body was not recovered for some days.[10]

The political ambition of Salmon Chase motivated him to have nothing to do with allowing Davis to be brought to trial. Immediately after the war, he found reason in the Union military occupation of Virginia to avoid holding court in the state, in spite of the civil courts being open and presided over by John C. Underwood. His position was justifiable but was undercut when he acknowledged that the situation in Virginia legally permitted a district court judge to hold court but maintained that, so long as the military occupied Virginia, a Supreme Court justice could not attend. Chase did not want to preside over Davis's trial and used every reason to avoid the Richmond bench.

Recently, a scholar has characterized Chase as approaching "the business of the judiciary with reservation and humility."[11] Chase's protestations of being an impartial judge and his refusal to speak to Andrew Johnson about the Davis prosecution are pointed to as being evidence of his strict judicial bearing. This ignores, however, the clear evidence that Chase met with lawyers for Davis about the charge and gave them advice on how to proceed—three times going so far as to suggest avenues of approach to prevail against the government. And on one of those occasions, Chase obliquely referred to his political aspirations. Even Chase's biographer and editor of his papers, John Niven, admitted that Chase's positions in the case "was in part at least motivated by political as well as practical considerations."[12] Frederick J. Blue, a biographer of Chase, wrote that "the trial might easily be an embarrassment to Chase, whether or not a guilty verdict was returned."[13] Chase's political ambition drove his actions in the Davis trial. Other than Lucius H. Chandler, Salmon Chase bore the greatest responsibility for Jefferson Davis not being tried for treason.

Andrew Johnson cannot escape scrutiny and bears the accountability for any failures of his administration, including the failure to bring Davis to trial for treason. Johnson never did change his conviction that rebel leaders should pay a price for their treason. The reason that Davis was not brought to trial, despite Johnson's desire—at least until the very end of his administration, when he recognized the futility of putting Davis to trial—was that Johnson delegated the task to men he considered professionals in their field and allowed them to pursue the object without direct involvement from the president. One cannot help wondering what the outcome of the trial would have been had Thomas Jefferson been president and wanted Davis to face the charge, as Jefferson had pushed the Aaron Burr treason trial. Davis certainly would have heard a verdict rendered by the jury. But Andrew Johnson was not Jefferson, and his participation in the Davis prosecution was limited to his clear direction to his cabinet members that he wanted the case tried. None of his three attorneys general could get the case to bar. While the treason indictments would be dismissed and Davis freed from that millstone, he lived out his life continuing to address a storm that would not cease.

The work of Charles O'Conor in the defense of Jefferson Davis was hard-nosed, innovative, and patient. It contributed greatly to the case not being brought to trial. O'Conor used his political connections, the national news media, and his reputation as a fearless advocate to make the trial of the treason case appear daunting. His use of the media to garner sympathy for his client was critical to the shift in the public sentiment away from holding a trial. He accomplished this while consistently maintaining a posture of being ready to try the case at a moment's notice. His client did not want a trial. O'Conor did not want a trial. But being able to convince the prosecution that he was ready to try the case at any time also has the effect of diminishing the zeal of a prosecutor to bring the case to bar. The work of this eccentric, angry lawyer cannot be underestimated in having brought about the result that was attained for his client.

The failure of the Union leadership to bring anyone to trial for treason lent itself to the incorrect argument that they *could not* have brought them to trial. Thaddeus K. Oglesby, a noted southern defender and frequent speaker at Confederate veteran reunions, availed himself of this tack. He had served as personal secretary to Alexander H. Stephens and spent his life attempting to rewrite the history of the Confederacy. On March 20, 1899, he appeared before the Atlanta Camp of Confederate Veterans to read a lengthy address to them presenting the southern view that Davis had been mistreated at Fort Monroe during his imprisonment after the end of the Civil War. His talk was entitled "The Shackling of Jefferson Davis." Union general Nelson Miles, whose duty it was to ensure that Davis did not escape, was the object of particular scorn during the lecture, with much of the evidence of Davis's martyrdom having been furnished by Varina Davis. As the speech began to wind down, Oglesby turned to the charge of treason that had been brought against Davis: "The barbarous treatment of Jefferson Davis was due . . . to the fact that he was the leader of the vanquished side." The treason charge had no foundation in fact "as one State cannot commit treason against another State," he claimed. "The absurdity of the charge is apparent."[14]

Oglesby summed up his position by adopting the southern myth that had been nurtured by him and many others throughout the South—Davis was charged with treason merely for being on the losing side of the war. Oglesby reached back, past the United States Constitution, which was the foundational document that not only defined treason but which formed the Union, to the Declaration of Independence as the underpinning of his argument for secession and vindication of Davis on the treason charge. The people's right to alter or abolish any form of government that has become destructive to the ends of life, liberty, and the pursuit of happiness was made clear by Jefferson's language, he argued. But he was not content to let the argument rest on the principles enunciated in the Declaration of Independence. Instead, as he stood before the Georgia veterans and their families, he took a further step of asserting that the right of secession did exist and that a trial of Davis would have vindicated that right. He held that Davis

> was never brought to trial for "treason" or anything else, though he eagerly wished and constantly urged a trial. The United States Government would never put to the test of an investigation, in accordance with the constitution and laws of the land, the question whether or not he had committed treason against that government. It was a test he greatly desired, and he

> was greatly disappointed at the government's declining it. Had he been tried for treason the issue presented to the Supreme Court of the United States would have been precisely the same which was argued by Calhoun and Webster, precisely the same which was fought by Lee and Grant. That issue required an answer to the question: Did the States have a right to secede? For if the States had no right to secede, Jefferson Davis was a traitor. If they had a right to secede, he was a patriot. This question the political heads of the government feared to submit to its own tribunal, well remembering that in the Dred Scott decision that tribunal itself had placed the seal of constitutionality upon the principles for which the Southern statesmen and people stood. By the release, without a trial, of Mr. Davis, the world was informed that the United States government feared to imperil in the courts of reason what it had gained in the field of battle, and the result was a judgment by default, against the United States, that whereas the right of secession now no longer exists, nevertheless, and notwithstanding, the right of secession *did* exist, and Mr. Davis was not a traitor, but a patriot.[15]

The speech perpetuated a myth that was taught and retaught in the decades following the Civil War.

Confederate veterans and their families were taught a deeply flawed course on constitutional history by Oglesby on that spring day in 1899. They learned that the Union, by not trying Davis for treason, had tacitly acknowledged that the South had been legally justified in breaking from the Union in 1861. The listeners found that *Dred Scott* would not have been overturned by the United States Supreme Court but would have been upheld in principle. Those present for the reunion were given a defiant, and incorrect, view of the reasons why Davis was not tried for treason. It sowed the seed of resentment against the North that pervaded the South in those years.

The southern view of why Davis was not tried has continued, in many circles, to be based upon a mistaken belief that he was not tried because he was correct in his constitutional beliefs. Well into the twentieth century, historians wrote of the harsh treatment of southerners after the war. Reconstruction was treated as a retributive era of the nation's history. "Certain it is that only a few besides President Davis dimly foresaw the vindictiveness of the conquerors" is a typical statement involving the years following the American Civil War and the treatment of Davis.[16] The Union victors of the war did not treat the rebel leaders harshly. Henry Wirz was hanged for Andersonville. Jefferson Davis was imprisoned for two years and then set free. Across the Atlantic, there was a recognition that the treatment of the South after the war was anything but punitive. One author for an English journal wrote that at the end of the rebellion, "no life was forfeited, excepting that of those who were proved to be accomplices in Mr. Lincoln's murder, and that of a certain Wirz convicted of heinous cruelty towards Northern prisoners incarcerated at Andersonville. Such lenient conduct was but right, yet rarely, if ever, has it marked the close of those civil strifes which have desolated in turn every country of the Old World."[17]

Even though the Johnson administration never decided that treason prosecutions of rebel leaders violated a basic American policy that this crime should only be sparingly brought to bar, the long-term consequence was just that. The significance of there being no treason prosecution after the Civil War that resulted in the conviction or execution of any leader of the Confederacy is typically understated or ignored altogether. The four years of the rebellion had tested the federal government in a manner never before experienced. By the time that the indictment against Davis was dismissed, Article III, Section 3, of the Constitution was implicitly acknowledged to not represent a primary protection of the security of the American government. This was a positive development in the law. Since breaking from England, Americans had recognized the ability to misuse the treason statute. The Aaron Burr prosecution confirmed that understanding. The failure to try Davis after the war, when the clearest possibility existed of credibly taking the constitutional crime to a jury, came to herald the hesitancy of the American government to use the law. By 1945, Associate Justice Robert Jackson of the Supreme Court, writing the majority opinion in *Cramer v. United States,* stated that "after constitutional requirements have been satisfied, and after juries have convicted and courts have sentenced, Presidents again and again have intervened to mitigate judicial severity or to pardon entirely. We have managed to do without treason prosecutions to a degree that probably would be impossible except while a people was singularly confident of external security and internal stability."[18] If this was the ultimate legacy of the failure to try Jefferson Davis for treason, it can only be viewed as a triumph of American jurisprudence.

NOTES

Preface

1. Burgess, *Reconstruction and the Constitution.*

2. Fleming, *Confederacy and Reconstruction,* pt. 2, 88.

3. Dunning, *American Nation,* 22:22–23.

4. Bowers, *Tragic Era,* 43–44.

5. Milton, *Age of Hate,* 245.

6. Coulter, *History of the South,* 8:176–77.

7. Foner, *Reconstruction,* 190.

8. Findings and Sentence by Lew Wallace, *Trial of Henry Wirz,* H.R. Ex. Doc. No. 23, 40th Cong., 2d sess., 805–7.

9. Phillips, "Lincoln's Grasp of War," 185.

10. Freeman, *Calendar of Confederate Papers,* 439 n. 509.

11. Nicoletti, "Did Secession Really Die at Appomattox," 588.

12. Nicoletti, *Secession on Trial,* 5.

13. Nichols, "United States vs. Jefferson Davis," 267.

14. Forgie, *Patricide in the House Divided,* 152.

15. William Blair offered a very short, well-reasoned overview of the multiple issues involved in the potential prosecution of Confederate leaders in Blair, *Why Didn't the North Hang Some Rebels.*

16. Brands, *Man Who Saved the Union,* 381.

17. Blair, *Why Didn't the North Hang Some Rebels,* 13.

18. Roland, *Reflections on Lee,* 103.

19. Simon, *Papers of Ulysses S. Grant,* vol. 15: *May 1–December 31, 1865,* 149.

20. Blair, *Why Didn't the North Hang Some Rebels,* 21.

Chapter One

Epigraph: Burke, "Speech of Edmund Burke," 36.

1. Davis, *Rise and Fall of the Confederate Government,* 2:701.

2. Ibid.

3. For details of the capture of Jefferson Davis, see Cooper, *Jefferson Davis,* 534.

4. Davis, *Rise and Fall of the Confederate Government,* 1:183.

5. *Chicago Copperhead Convention,* 1.

6. Ibid., 7.

7. Webster, *Works of Daniel Webster,* 1:68–69.

8. McPherson, *War That Forged a Nation,* 152.

9. Welles, *Diary,* 2:181.

10. Bates, *Diary,* 428.

11. This resignation, coupled with the death of U.S. Supreme Court chief justice Roger Taney six weeks earlier, opened up two of the nation's most prominent legal positions. Intrigue swirled around Washington, D.C., as men actively sought the Supreme Court bench or put their names forward as possible candidates for attorney general. One of the names brought to Lincoln's attention to fill Taney's seat was that of William M. Evarts of New York. He was proposed by Gideon Welles, among others, who believed that Evarts "stood among the foremost at the New York bar; perhaps no one was more prominent as a lawyer." Welles recorded Lincoln's assessment of Evarts as "a good lawyer" (Welles, *Diary,* 2:181). Evarts lost the job to Lincoln's former secretary of the Treasury, Salmon P. Chase, but emerged as a top prosecutor on the Jefferson Davis treason indictment.

12. First Cong., 1st sess., chap. 20, 1789, 93.

13. Bloch, "Early Role of the Attorney General," 561–653.

14. Quoted in Cummings and McFarland, *Federal Justice,* 192–93.

15. Welles, *Diary,* 2:183.

16. Leonard, *Lincoln's Forgotten Ally,* 2–3.

17. Nicolay and Hay, *Abraham Lincoln,* 9:346–47.

18. *New York Times,* December 1, 1864.

19. Joseph Holt to Abraham Lincoln, December 1, 1864, Lincoln, *Collected Works,* 8:127.

20. Testimony of James Speed, Judiciary Committee of the House of Representatives, 39th Cong., 2d sess., and 40th Cong., 1st sess., *Impeachment Investigation,* 794.

21. Richards, *Who Freed the Slaves,* 92.

22. Abraham Lincoln to James Speed, December 1, 1864, Lincoln, *Collected Works,* 8:126.

23. Speed, *James Speed,* 52. The author is the grandson of Attorney General Speed.

24. Testimony of James Speed, 794; *Trenton (N.J.) Daily State Gazette,* December 9, 1864.

25. *New York Times,* December 9, 1864.

26. *New-Hampshire Sentinel,* December 29, 1864.

27. *New Orleans Tribune,* December 15, 1864.

28. Speed to his mother, December 11, 1864, in Speed, *James Speed,* 53.

29. Waugh, "'I Only Knew What Was in My Mind,'" 317. Waugh's brilliant analysis of the evolution of the terms of surrender crafted by Grant is great reading and was relied upon by the author in this discussion.

30. Ulysses S. Grant to Robert E. Lee, April 9, 1865, in *War of the Rebellion,* ser. 1, 95:58 (hereafter cited as *OR,* for *Official Records*).

31. Parole of Gen. Robert E. Lee and Staff, endorsed by George H. Sharpe, assistant provost marshal general, *OR,* ser. 1, 97:667.

32. Ibid.

33. Ulysses S. Grant to Abraham Lincoln, March 20, 1865, *OR,* ser. 1, 97:50.

34. Abraham Lincoln to Ulysses S. Grant, March 20, 1865, *OR,* ser. 1, 97:50.

35. Abraham Lincoln to Ulysses S. Grant, April 6, 1865, *OR,* ser. 1, 97:593.

36. David B. Lyman to Richard Henry Dana Jr., April 9, 1865, Dana Family Papers, Massachusetts Historical Society.

37. Testimony of John Minor Botts, in Kendrick, *Journal,* 287.

Chapter Two

Epigraph: Welles, *Diary,* 2:286.

1. Sherman, *Memoirs,* 2:326.

2. Ibid., 326–27. The *New York Times,* on July 4, 1865, repeated Sherman's rendition of this meeting. He told the *Times* that Lincoln said, after the story of the temperance man, "I'm bound to oppose the escape of Jeff. Davis; but if you could manage to let him slip out unbeknownst-like, I guess it wouldn't hurt me much." This version seeks to have the Union army play a slightly more active role by managing "to let him slip out."

3. Testimony of James Speed, *Impeachment Investigation,* 798.

4. Grant, *Personal Memoirs,* 2:522.

5. Abraham Lincoln, First Inaugural Address, March 4, 1861, Lincoln, *Collected Works,* 4:265.

6. Witt, *Lincoln's Code,* 142.

7. Forgie, *Patricide in the House Divided,* 273.

8. Abraham Lincoln's Reply to Emancipation Memorial Presented by Chicago Christians of All Denominations, September 13, 1862, Lincoln, *Collected Works,* 5:423.

9. Abraham Lincoln to Erastus Corning and Others, June 12, 1863, Lincoln, *Collected Works,* 6:266.

10. Ibid., 6:265.

11. Gallagher, "Another Look at the Generalship of R. E. Lee," 286.

12. Lincoln to Corning, June 12, 1863, Lincoln, *Collected Works,* 6:264.

13. Winik, *April 1865,* 253.

14. Abraham Lincoln to Fernando Wood, December 12, 1862, Lincoln, *Collected Works,* 5:553.

15. Abraham Lincoln to Reverdy Johnson, July 26, 1862, Lincoln, *Collected Works,* 5:343.

16. Abraham Lincoln to John W. Crisfield, June 26, 1862, Lincoln, *Collected Works,* 5:285.

17. *Hartford (Conn.) Daily Courant,* April 14, 1865.

18. *New York Tribune,* April 17, 1865.

19. Keckley, *Behind the Scenes,* 190.

20. Hodes, *Mourning Lincoln,* 56.

21. Quoted in Trefousse, *Radical Republicans,* 307.

22. Freidel, *Francis Lieber,* 360.

23. Richard Henry Dana Jr. to R. H. Dana, Easter Sunday 1865, Dana Family Papers, Massachusetts Historical Society.

24. Hodes, *Mourning Lincoln,* 132.

25. Emmie Sublett to Emily Anderson, April 29, 1865, in Sublett, *Ladies of Richmond,* 291–92.

26. Welles, *Civil War Diary,* 627–28.

27. Welles, *Diary,* 2:287–88.

28. Ibid., 2:289.

29. Trefousse, *Andrew Johnson,* 192.

30. Testimony of John Minor Botts, *Journal of the Joint Committee on Reconstruction,* 287.

31. Ulysses S. Grant to Edward O. C. Ord, April 15, 1865, in *OR,* ser. 1, 97:762.

32. Ord to Grant, April 15, 1865, *OR,* ser. 1, 97:762.

33. Grant to Ord, April 15, 1865, *OR,* ser. 1, 97:762.

34. Ulysses S. Grant to Julia Dent Grant, April 16, 1865, in Grant, *Papers,* , 14:396.

35. Brands, *Man Who Saved the Union,* 378.

36. Welles, *Diary,* 2:291.

37. Testimony of James Speed, 798.

38. Edwin M. Stanton to John A. Dix, April 15, 1865, *OR,* ser. 1, 97:780.

39. Edwin M. Stanton to Winfield S. Hancock, April 16, 1865, *OR,* ser. 1, 97:799.

40. Henry W. Halleck to Christopher C. Augur, April 15, 1865, *OR,* ser. 1, 97:766.

41. Richard S. Ewell to Ulysses S. Grant, April 16, 1865, *OR,* ser. 1, 97:787.

42. *Macon (Ga.) Telegraph,* May 17, 1865.

43. John Appleton to William Hoffman, April 16, 1865, *OR,* ser. 1, 97:787.

44. *Macon (Ga.) Telegraph,* May 14, 1865.

45. James M. Mason, letter to the *London Index,* April 27, 1865, reprinted in the *Augusta (Ga.) Daily Constitutionalist,* May 27, 1865.

46. *Charleston (S.C.) Courier,* April 20, 1865.

47. *Augusta (Ga.) Chronicle,* April 27, 1865.

48. Edward O. C. Ord to Ulysses S. Grant, April 17, 1865, *OR,* ser. 1, 97:814.

49. General Orders, No. 27, *OR,* ser. 1, 97:816.

50. C. H. Morgan to C. C. Augur, May 6, 1865, *OR,* ser. 1, 97:1103.

51. C. H. Morgan to William H. Emory, May 6, 1865, *OR,* ser. 1, 97:1104.

52. White, *Abraham Lincoln and Treason,* 77–80.

53. Edwin M. Stanton, August 8, 1862, *OR,* ser. 3, 123:321.

54. Lincoln, "Proclamation Suspending the Writ of Habeas Corpus," September 24, 1862, Lincoln, *Collected Works,* 5:436–37; Neely, *Fate of Liberty,* 233–34.

55. See, e.g., *OR,* ser. 2, 115:250–52.

56. J. W. Walker, May 9, 1865, General Orders, No. 27, *OR,* ser. 2, 121:543–49, ordering the hanging of Milligan and others after trial by a military commission.

57. Lambdin Milligan's case was appealed to the U.S. Supreme Court. As *Ex parte Milligan,* 71 U.S. 2, 18 L.Ed. 281, 4 Wall. 2 (1866), the case formed the basis of a seminal opinion holding that it was unconstitutional to try civilians in military courts if civilian courts were still in operation. But in May 1865, the government prosecuted civilians before military commissions without hindrance.

Chapter Three

Epigraph: William T. Sherman to Judson Kilpatrick, April 14, 1865, *Sherman's Civil War,* 861.

1. Eckert, *"Fiction Distorting Fact,"* 47.

2. Conroy, *Our One Common Country,* 250.

3. Varina Davis to Jefferson Davis, May 2, 1865, Davis, *Papers of Jefferson Davis,* 11:576.

4. Davis, *Rise and Fall of the Confederate Government,* 2:718.

5. Harrison, "Capture of Jefferson Davis," 131.

6. Ibid.

7. Kean, *Inside the Confederate Government,* 206.

8. W. T. Sherman to Judson Kilpatrick, April 13, 1865, in *OR,* ser. 1, 100:198.

9. Johnston, *Narrative of Military Operations,* 396–97.

10. Mallory, "Last Days of the Confederate Government," 240–41.

11. Alfred Iverson to John M. Otey, April 14, 1865, *OR,* ser. 1, 47:799.

12. John H. Reagan to Jefferson Davis, April 22, 1865, *OR,* ser. 1, 47:825–26.

13. Jefferson Davis to Varina Davis, April 14, 1865, Davis, *Papers of Jefferson Davis,* 11:541.

14. J. E. Johnston to W. T. Sherman, April 14, 1865, *OR,* ser. 1, 100:206–7.

15. W. T. Sherman to J. E. Johnston, April 14, 1865, *OR,* ser. 1, 100:207.

16. W. T. Sherman to Kilpatrick, April 14, 1865, *OR,* ser. 1, 100:215.

17. J. Kilpatrick to W. T. Sherman, April 16, 1865, *OR,* ser. 1, 100:233.

18. W. T. Sherman to J. Kilpatrick, April 16, 1865, *OR,* ser. 1, 100:234.

19. W. T. Sherman to U. S. Grant and Secretary of War Stanton, April 15, 1865, *OR,* ser. 1, 100:221.

20. Edwin M. Stanton to W. T. Sherman, April 15, 1865, *OR,* ser. 1, 100:220–21.

21. W. T. Sherman to Wade Hampton, February 24, 1865, *OR,* ser. 1, 100:546.

22. Sherman, *Memoirs,* 2:349.

23. R. M. Sawyer (from Sherman) to U. S. Grant, April 17, 1865, *OR,* ser. 1, 100:237.

24. Special Field Orders, No. 56, April 17, 1865, *OR,* ser. 1, 100:238–39.

25. John H. Reagan, April 17, 1865, *OR,* ser. 1, 100:806–7.

26. Sherman, *Memoirs,* 2:353–54.

27. Jefferson Davis to J. C. Breckinridge, April 18, 1865, *OR,* ser. 1, 100:809.

28. U. S. Grant to E. M. Stanton, April 21, 1865, *OR,* ser. 1, 100:263.

29. W. T. Sherman to U. S. Grant, April 18, 1865, *OR,* ser. 1, 100:243.

30. Edwin M. Stanton to Lieutenant-General Grant, April 23, 1865, *OR,* ser. 1, 100:263.

31. *New York Times,* November 18, 1865.

32. Welles, *Diary,* 3:295.

33. *New York Herald,* April 23, 1865.

34. Welles, *Diary,* 3:296.

35. Davis, *Papers of Jefferson Davis,* 11:558.

36. Jefferson Davis to Howell Cobb, April 21, 1865, *OR,* ser. 1, 49:1257.

37. Wade Hampton to Jefferson Davis, April 19, 1865, *OR,* ser. 1, 47:813–14.

38. Judah Benjamin to Jefferson Davis, April 21, 1865, *OR,* ser. 1, 47:821–23.

39. John H. Reagan to Jefferson Davis, April 22, 1865, *OR,* ser. 1, 47:823.

40. Thomas T. Munford, Special Orders, No. 6, April 21, 1865, *OR,* ser. 1, 97:1395.

41. Ibid. Jefferson Davis to Zebulon B. Vance, April 11, 1865, *OR,* ser. 1, 97:1393.

42. Davis, "Speech at Charlotte," April 19, 1865, Davis, *Papers of Jefferson Davis,* 11:550.

43. Ibid.

44. Jefferson Davis to Braxton Bragg, April 20, 1865, Davis, *Papers of Jefferson Davis,* 11:551.

45. Mallory, "Last Days of the Confederate Government," 244.

46. Davis, *Jefferson Davis,* 620.

47. Harrison, "Capture of Jefferson Davis," 137.

48. Davis, *Papers of Jefferson Davis,* 11:559.

49. J. E. Johnston to M. Lovell, May 2, 1865, *OR,* ser. 1, 100:892.

Chapter Four

Epigraph: Charles Sumner to Salmon P. Chase, June 25, 1865, *Selected Letters of Charles Sumner,* 2:311–12.

1. The attorney general, James Speed, had given Johnson a written opinion on April 30, 1865, that any person implicated in Lincoln's murder "not only can, but ought to be tried before a military commission." "Opinion on the Constitutional Power of the Military," 16; "Order for Military Trial of Presidential Assassins," May 1, 1865, *Papers of Andrew Johnson,* 8:12.

2. Johnson, "A Proclamation," May 2, 1865, *OR,* ser. 1, 104:566–67.

3. Clay's missive was included verbatim in J. H. Wilson to E. M. Stanton, May 12, 1865, *OR,* ser. 1, 104:733.

4. Hess, *Braxton Bragg,* 248–49.

5. David Pierson to William H. Pierson, May 9, 1865, Pierson, *Brothers in Gray,* 259.

6. Wade Hampton to J. E. Johnston, April 26, 1865, *OR,* ser. 1, 100:841.

7. Archer Anderson to Wade Hampton, April 27, 1865, *OR,* ser. 1, 100:846.

8. Wade Hampton to J. E. Johnston, April 27, 1865, *OR,* ser. 1, 100:846.

9. Wheeler, "Effort to Rescue Jefferson Davis," 86.

10. Ibid., 85.

11. Ibid.; Thomas W. Scott to Horace N. Howland, May 8, 1865, *OR,* ser. 1, 104:665.

12. Christopher C. Washburn to Otto Funke, May 8, 1865, *OR,* ser. 1, 104:677.

13. Harrison, "Capture of Jefferson Davis," 138.

14. Varina Davis to Jefferson Davis, May 1, 1865, *Papers of Jefferson Davis,* 11:573.

15. H. S. Doggett to Isaac H. Carrington, January 13, 1865, *OR,* ser. 2, 121:68–69.

16. Andrew Johnson to Edwin M. Stanton, May 4, 1865, *OR,* ser. 2, 121:526.

17. John A. Dix to Edwin M. Stanton, May 16, 1865, *OR,* ser. 2, 121:557.

18. Joseph E. Brown to Andrew Johnson, May 6, 1865, *OR,* ser. 1, 104:630.

19. Edwin M. Stanton to J. H. Wilson, May 7, 1865, *OR,* ser. 1, 104:646–47.

20. R.M.T. Hunter to H. W. Halleck, May 11, 1865, *OR,* ser. 2, 121:551.

21. H. W. Halleck to Edwin M. Stanton, May 11, 1865, *OR,* ser. 2, 121:550.

22. Edwin M. Stanton to H. W. Halleck, May 11, 1865, *OR,* ser. 2, 121:551.

23. Edwin M. Stanton to H. W. Halleck, May 11, 1865, ser. 2, 121:551.

24. George C. Gibbs to Edward M. McCook, May 12, 1865, *OR,* ser. 2, 121:552–53.

25. James H. Wilson to John M. Schofield, May 7, 1865, *OR,* ser. 1, 104:648.

26. James H. Wilson to Beroth B. Eggleston, May 7, 1865, *OR,* ser. 1, 104:654.

27. William T. Sherman to U. S. Grant, May 8, 1865, *OR,* ser. 1, 104:662.

28. James H. Wilson to Edwin M. Stanton, May 9, 1865, *OR,* ser. 1, 104:680.

29. James H. Wilson to William T. Sherman, May 8, 1865, *OR,* ser. 1, 104:663.

30. James H. Wilson to Beroth B. Eggleston, May 8, 1865, *OR,* ser. 1, 104:666.

31. James H. Wilson to John M. Palmer, May 9, 1865, *OR,* ser. 1, 104:690.
32. Gideon Welles to Henry K. Thatcher, May 9, 1865, *OR,* ser. 1, 104:694.
33. Wheeler, "Effort to Rescue Jefferson Davis," 88.
34. Benjamin D. Pritchard to Thomas W. Scott, May 11, 1865, *OR,* ser. 1, 104:721–22.
35. James H. Wilson to Edwin M. Stanton, May 13, 1865, *OR,* ser. 1, 104:743.
36. Jones, "'Your Left Arm,'" 241.
37. Chestnut, *Mary Chestnut's Civil War,* 817.
38. Wilson, *Under the Old Flag,* 1:336.
39. Jones, "'Your Left Arm,'" 243.
40. Ibid., 243–44.
41. Wilson, *Under the Old Flag,* 1:337.
42. Jones, "'Your Left Arm,'" 244.
43. Ibid., 243.
44. Clay-Clopton, *Belle of the Fifties,* 256.
45. Ibid., 258.
46. Report of Lt. Col. Benjamin D. Pritchard, Fourth Michigan Cavalry, May 25, 1865, *OR,* ser. 1, 103:536–37.
47. Edwin M. Stanton to Benjamin D. Pritchard, May 14, 1865, *OR,* ser. 1, 104:761–62.
48. "Alexander H. Stephens' Prison Life," 169.
49. Clay-Clopton, *Belle of the Fifties,* 261.
50. Wheeler, "Effort to Rescue Jefferson Davis," 89.
51. "Alexander H. Stephens' Prison Life," 169.
52. Ibid.
53. Reagan, *Memoirs,* 223.
54. *Confederate Veteran* 1, no. 5 (May 1893): 145.
55. Wheeler, "Effort to Rescue Jefferson Davis," 90.

5. Chapter Five

Epigraph: Charles Sumner to John Bright, August 8, 1865, *Selected Letters,* 2:321.

1. Charles P. Washburn to William M. Wherry, May 14, 1865, *OR,* ser. 1, 100:497.
2. Edwin M. Stanton to Henry W. Halleck, May 15, 1865, *OR,* ser. 1, 100:505.
3. Edwin M. Stanton to Henry W. Halleck, May 14, 1865, *OR,* ser. 1, 100:494.
4. Henry W. Halleck to Edwin M. Stanton, May 13, 1865, *OR,* ser. 1, 104:741.
5. Edwin M. Stanton to Quincy A. Gillmore, May 15, 1865, *OR,* ser. 1, 100:505.
6. Ibid., 505–6.
7. Lieber, *Lieber on Guerrilla Parties,* 20–21.
8. Ibid., 22.
9. Edwin M. Stanton to Henry W. Halleck, May 14, 1865, *OR,* ser. 1, 104:759.
10. Henry W. Halleck to Richard Delafield, May 15, 1865, *OR,* ser. 1, 104:773.
11. Edwin M. Stanton to Henry W. Halleck, May 19, 1865, *OR,* ser. 1, 104:837.
12. Edwin M. Stanton to Henry Halleck, May 19, 1865, *OR,* ser. 2, 121:560.
13. Charles A. Dana to Edwin M. Stanton, May 22, 1865, *OR,* 121:564.

14. Ibid.

15. Wilson, *Life of Charles A. Dana,* 364.

16. Charles A. Dana to Edwin M. Stanton, May 22, 1865, *OR,* ser. 2, 121:564.

17. Ibid.

18. Charles A. Dana to Nelson A. Miles, May 22, 1865, *OR,* ser. 2, 121:565.

19. Nelson A. Miles to Charles A. Dana, May 24, 1865, *OR,* ser. 2, 121:571.

20. *Daily National Intelligencer* (Washington, D.C.), May 26, 1865.

21. *New York Herald,* May 27, 1865.

22. Edwin M. Stanton to Nelson A. Miles, May 28, 1865, *OR,* ser. 2, 121:577.

23. Nelson A. Miles to Edwin M. Stanton, May 28, 1865, *OR,* ser. 2, 121:577.

24. Henry W. Halleck to Nelson A. Miles, May 28, 1865, *OR,* ser. 2, 121:577–78.

25. Winthrop, *Digest of Opinions,* 328–30.

26. Hannibal Hamlin to Andrew Johnson, May 3, 1865, Johnson, *Papers of Andrew Johnson,* 8:20.

27. Andrew Johnson, "Interview with Pennsylvania Delegation," May 3, 1865, Johnson, *Papers of Andrew Johnson,* 8:21–22.

28. Johnson, *Reports of Cases,* 6.

29. *New York Tribune,* June 5, 1865.

30. Ibid.

31. *Daily Age* (Philadelphia), June 15, 1865, quoting *Petersburg (Va.) News.*

32. Ibid.

33. *Philadelphia Inquirer,* June 8, 1865.

34. *New York Tribune,* June 5, 1865.

35. Ulysses S. Grant to Robert E. Lee, April 9, 1865, *OR,* ser. 1, 95:58.

36. Charles H. Morgan to Christopher C. Augur, May 6, 1865, *OR,* ser. 1, 97:1103.

37. *New York Tribune,* May 29, 1865.

38. Johnson, *Reports of Cases,* 13–14.

39. *Alexandria (Va.) Gazette,* June 12, 1865.

40. James Speed to Lucius H. Chandler, June 20, 1866, in *Impeachment Investigation,* 512.

41. Thaddeus Stevens to William D. Kelley, May 30, 1865, Stevens, *Selected Papers,* 2:6.

42. Thaddeus Stevens to Andrew Johnson, July 6, 1865, Stevens, *Selected Papers,* 2:7.

43. McPherson, *Embattled Rebel,* 3.

44. John (LNU) to Thomas F. Bayard, June 15, 1865, Thomas Francis Bayard Papers, Library of Congress.

45. James H. Wilson to William D. Whipple, May 15, 1865, *OR,* ser. 1, 104:783.

46. Greeley, *Recollections,* 412.

47. *Evening Star* (Washington, D.C.), May 26, 1865.

48. *Camden (N.J.) Democrat,* June 3, 1865.

49. U.S. Const., Art. III, Sec. 2.

50. Edwin B. Stanton to Joseph P. Holt, June 7, 1865, Joseph Holt Papers, Library of Congress.

51. Ibid.

52. "Loyalty of Clerks and Other Persons Employed by Government," 80.

53. The other conspirators were Lewis Powell (often called Lewis Payne), David Herold, Samuel Arnold, Michael O'Laughlin, Edman Spangler, George Atzerodt, and Samuel Mudd. John

Surratt, Mary's son, fled the United States and was not tried in 1865. Samuel Mudd, a doctor who treated John Wilkes Booth's broken leg, and Samuel Arnold and Michael O'Laughlin escaped a death sentence, whereas Booth was killed while being captured.

54. E. D. Townsend, General Court-Martial Order No. 356, July 5, 1865, *OR,* ser. 2, 121:696–98.

55. George, "Conspiracy Trial's 'Suppressed Testimony,'" 120.

56. Marvel, *Lincoln's Autocrat,* 378.

57. Trefousse, *Radical Republicans,* 309.

Chapter Six

Epigraph: Quoted in Burlingame, *Abraham Lincoln,* 1:347.

1. V. Davis, *Memoir,* 2:647.
2. Hill, "Decisive Battles of the Law," 560.
3. Smith, *Stormy Present,* 151.
4. V. Davis, *Memoir,* 2:647.
5. Daly, "Charles O'Conor," 513–35.
6. Bigelow, "American Lawyer," 6–7.
7. *Charles O'Conor Memorials,* 7.
8. Daly, "Charles O'Conor," 527.
9. Ibid., 524.
10. *Charles O'Conor Memorials,* 75.
11. Remarks of William M. Evarts, in ibid., 44.
12. Remarks of James C. Carter, in *Charles O'Conor Memorials,* 30–31.
13. Remarks of Charles A. Peabody, in *Charles O'Conor Memorials,* 14.
14. Daly, "Charles O'Conor," 526.
15. Ibid., 529.
16. S. J. Tilden to unknown recipient, Charles O'Conor file, January 15, 1853, New York Public Library.
17. See Strong, *Diary,* 435.
18. O'Conor, *Negro Slavery Not Unjust.* O'Conor was wealthy enough to have his cases self-published in a single edition of nearly one hundred leather-bound volumes. This pamphlet is found contained in vol. 34, which includes the Lemmon slave case, referred to later in this book, and the slavery question generally. Also found in that volume is a copy of Abraham Lincoln's Cooper Union speech. Unfortunately for this study, O'Conor's volume—which would chronologically contain the Jefferson Davis case—has been missing for years, according to the New York Law Institute archivists.
19. *New York Bar Magazine* (June 1865): 89.
20. Daly, "Charles O'Conor," 532.
21. Strong, *Diary,* 84–85.
22. Charles O'Conor to Franklin Pierce, July 5, 1865, Franklin Pierce Papers, Library of Congress.
23. Ibid.

24. Davis, *Jefferson Davis,* 655.

25. Franklin Pierce to Jeremiah Black, June 21, 1865, Jeremiah Black Papers, Manuscript Division, Library of Congress, Washington, D.C.

26. Charles O'Conor to Franklin Pierce, July 15, 1865, Franklin Pierce Papers, Library of Congress.

27. James Mason to Charles O'Conor, June 19, 1865, James M. Mason Papers, vol. 8, Library of Congress.

28. *New York Times,* June 7, 1866.

29. *New York Herald,* August 28, 1865.

30. Testimony of James Speed, in *Impeachment Investigation,* 800.

31. Welles, *Diary,* 2:365–66.

32. Testimony of William M. Evarts, in *Impeachment Investigation,* 645.

33. Cooper, *Jefferson Davis,* 541.

34. Testimony of James Speed, in *Impeachment Investigation,* 798.

35. Dougherty, "William M. Evarts," 4.

36. Dana, *Journal,* 1:39–40.

37. Evarts remarks, in *Charles O'Conor Memorials,* 41.

38. Ibid., 44.

39. Dougherty, "William M. Evarts," 5.

40. *New York Herald,* January 26, 1860.

41. Ibid., January 26, 1860.

42. *New York Tribune,* February 26, 1857.

43. *New York Herald,* January 26, 1860.

44. Dougherty, "William M. Evarts," 6.

45. O'Conor, *My Own Cases,* 22. Interestingly enough, also found in the volume compiled and bound by O'Conor is a pamphlet containing the Cooper Union speech by Abraham Lincoln.

46. *New York Herald,* January 26, 1860.

47. Daly, "Charles O'Conor," 524.

48. O'Conor, *My Own Cases,* 34:31.

49. O'Conor remarked to the Court that it was easy to argue points that were well received by onlookers but that arguing a position that might be subjected to gasps from the audience took courage.

50. *New York Herald,* January 27, 1860.

51. O'Conor, *My Own Cases,* 34:69.

52. *New York Herald,* January 27, 1860.

53. Burlingame, *Abraham Lincoln,* 1:605.

54. Dyer, *Public Career,* 62–77.

55. Welles, *Diary,* 2:367–68.

56. *Boston Journal,* July 26, 1876.

57. United States Census for the City of Norfolk, Va., 1860, 69; *Daily Eastern Argus,* April 20, 1863.

58. *New York Tribune,* October 24, 1861.

59. *Alexandria Gazette,* April 16, 1861.

60. House of Representatives, Report No. 59, 38th Cong., 1st sess., April 25, 1864.

61. *Cases of Contested Elections in Congress from 1834 to 1865, Inclusive,* House of Representatives.

62. *Richmond Whig,* September 22, 1865. See also Speech of Hon. Lucius H. Chandler of Virginia, in the House of Representatives of the United States, in Defence of His Claim to a Seat in That Body for the Thirty-Eighth Congress (reprinted from the Cong. Globe, May 21, 1864).

63. *Daily Eastern Argus* (Portland, Me.), April 20, 1863.

64. *Journal of the Proceedings of the Senate of the United States in Executive Session,* 37th Cong., 2d sess., December 23, 1861, 27; and *Philadelphia Inquirer,* February 20, 1862.

65. *Journal of the Proceedings of the Senate of the United States in Executive Session,* 38th Cong., 1st sess., June 20, 1864, 590; June 27, 1864, 626; June 30, 1864, 636.

66. *Cleveland Leader,* November 17, 1865; and *New York Herald,* November 16, 1865.

67. Testimony of Lucius H. Chandler, in *Impeachment Investigation,* 503.

68. John C. Underwood to Andrew Johnson, July 10, 1865, *Papers of Andrew Johnson,* 8:387.

Chapter Seven

Epigraph: Welles, *Civil War Diary,* 543.

1. Malone, *Jefferson and His Time,* 5:335.

2. Newmyer, *John Marshall,* 199.

3. Robertson, *Burr's Trial,* 2:424. Newmyer writes that Marshall made this ruling "almost as an afterthought." Newmyer, *John Marshall,* 200. A close reading of Marshall's lengthy ruling supports his conclusion. Newmyer's study, which deals with much more than the Burr trial, is a wonderful resource in understanding the development of the federal judiciary.

4. *Springfield (Mass.) Republican,* July 8, 1856; and *New York Reformer,* July 3, 1856.

5. *Salem (Mass.) Register,* August 20, 1863.

6. *New York Herald-Tribune,* August 25, 1856.

7. Ibid., September 12, 1856, quoting *Winchester Virginian,* August 5, 1856.

8. *New York Tribune,* December 2, 1856; and *Cleveland Leader,* December 6, 1856.

9. *Portland (Me.) Advertiser,* July 8, 1856.

10. *Daily Globe,* January 16, 1857; and *Wooster Republican,* February 5, 1857.

11. Letter to the Editor of the *Evening Post* from Thomas H. Fisher, *New York Evening Post,* March 4, 1857, 3.

12. *Alexandria Gazette,* October 16, 1857; *New York Evening Post,* January 5, 1867.

13. *Massachusetts Spy,* May 13, 1857.

14. *New York Herald,* May 11, 1857.

15. *Daily Advocate* (Baton Rouge, La.), August 27, 1857.

16. See *New York Evening Post,* February 17, 1857; and *St. Albans (Vt.) Messenger,* September 1, 1859.

17. *Liberator,* July 29, 1859.

18. *Charleston (S.C.) Mercury,* January 31, 1859.

19. Reprinted in *New York Herald-Tribune,* December 6, 1859.

20. Ibid.

21. *Alexandria (Va.) Gazette*, April 4, 1863; and *National Intelligencer*, September 2, 1863.

22. *Hartford Daily Courant*, May 29, 1863.

23. Edward Bates to John C. Underwood, March 28, 1863, John C. Underwood Papers, Library of Congress.

24. *New York Herald*, April 3, 1863.

25. Bates to Underwood, March 28, 1863.

26. *Lowell Daily Citizen and News*, April 6, 1863.

27. U.S. Const., Art. III, Sec. 3.

28. *Richmond Examiner*, December 7, 1863; *New York Herald*, November 27, 1863.

29. Kean, *Inside the Confederate Government*, 217–18.

30. *Chicago Legal News: A Journal of Legal Intelligence*, February 3, 1877, 9:162.

31. Kendrick, *Journal*, 283.

32. Testimony of John C. Underwood, in *Impeachment Investigation*, 578.

33. Abraham Lincoln to Salmon P. Chase, June 30, 1864, Lincoln, *Collected Works of Abraham Lincoln*, 7:419.

34. Goodwin, *Team of Rivals*, 634–35.

35. Chase, *Salmon P. Chase Papers*, 5:3–4.

36. Ibid., 5:11.

37. Ibid., 5:12.

38. Ibid., 5:15.

39. Ibid., 5:21.

Chapter Eight

Epigraph: Stephens, *Recollections*, 233.

1. Charles O'Conor to E. D. Townsend, June 2, 1865, *OR*, ser. 2, 121:634.

2. Charles O'Conor to Jefferson Davis, June 2, 1865, *OR*, ser. 2, 121:634.

3. *Illustrated New Age* (taken from the *New York World*), June 5, 1865.

4. *New York Herald*, June 9, 1865.

5. Ibid.

6. Edward D. Townsend to Nelson A. Miles, June 5, 1865, *OR*, ser. 2, 121:639.

7. Nelson A. Miles to Edward D. Townsend, June 6, 1865, *OR*, ser. 2, 121:642.

8. Edward D. Townsend to Nelson A. Miles, June 6, 1865, *OR*, ser. 2, 121:642.

9. Jefferson Davis to Charles O'Conor, June 15, 1865, *OR*, ser. 2, 121:655, enclosing a rewritten letter dated June 7, 1865, which had removed the sentence that was found objectionable by the War Department.

10. Ibid.

11. Charles O'Conor to James Mason, September 6, 1865, James M. Mason Papers, Library of Congress.

12. *Report of the Commission on the Andersonville Monument*, 18.

13. "Statement of the Object and Methods of the Sanitary Commission," *Documents of the Sanitary Commission*, 2:61:95 and 2:69:45.

14. See Isaiah H. White to Daniel T. Chandler, August 4, 1864, *OR*, ser. 2, 120:524.

15. Samuel White to Abraham Lincoln, September 12, 1864, *OR*, ser. 2, 120:816.

16. Ulysses S. Grant to Edwin M. Stanton, November 29, 1864, *OR*, ser. 2, 120:1074–75.

17. *Narrative of Privations and Sufferings.*

18. *Voice from Rebel Prisons*, 8.

19. *Narrative of Privations and Sufferings*, 95.

20. Sherman, *Sherman's Civil War*, 685.

21. Ibid., 690.

22. Isaiah H. White to Daniel T. Chandler, August 2, 1864, *OR*, ser. 2, 120:524–25.

23. Isaiah H. White to John H. Winder, August 4, 1864, *OR*, ser. 2, 120:541–42.

24. Daniel T. Chandler to R. H. Chilton, August 5, 1864, *OR*, ser. 2, 120:546.

25. Ibid., 547.

26. Ibid., 547–48.

27. R. R. Stevenson to John H. Winder, October 31, 1864, *OR*, ser. 2, 120:1076.

28. J. A. Campbell to Secretary of War [James A. Seddon], endorsing the report dated August 5, 1864, of D. T. Chandler, *OR*, ser. 2, 120:551.

29. Chipman, *Tragedy of Andersonville*, 27–28.

30. C. J. McRae to James M. Mason, September 9, 1865, James M. Mason Papers.

31. C. J. McRae to Charles O'Conor, September 9, 1865, James M. Mason Papers. This letter to O'Conor was copied by McRae and sent to Mason.

32. Ibid.

33. *New York Herald*, August 22, 1865.

34. Chipman, *Tragedy of Andersonville*, 28–30.

35. *Boston Daily Advertiser*, August 24, 1865.

36. Testimony of Charles E. Tibbles, in Chipman, *Tragedy of Andersonville*, 347.

37. *Boston Daily Advertiser*, August 24, 1865.

38. Executive Documents of the House of Representatives, 40th Cong., 2d sess., Ex Doc. No. 23, Trial of Henry Wirz (Washington, D.C., 1867), 805.

39. *Hartford Daily Courant*, November 1, 1865.

40. *Daily Constitution Union*, November 6, 1865.

41. Ibid., November 8, 1865; and *New York Herald*, November 9, 1865.

42. *New York Herald*, November 9, 1865.

43. Ibid.

44. Stephens, *Recollections*, 235.

45. Nelson A. Miles to E. D. Townsend, December 25, 1865, *OR*, ser. 2, 121:840.

46. Procter, *Not without Honor*, 174.

Chapter Nine

Epigraph: Thomas Jefferson to Thomas Paine, July 11, 1789, Jefferson, *Writings*, 3:71. The full quotation is: "Another apprehension is, that a majority cannot be induced to adopt the trial by jury; and I consider that as the only anchor ever yet imagined by man, by which a government can be held to the principles of its constitution."

1. Butler, *Butler's Book,* 915.

2. McCulloch, *Men and Measures,* 410.

3. Ibid., 409–10.

4. Varina Davis to Francis P. Blair, July 10, 1865, Andrew Johnson Papers, Library of Congress.

5. Varina Davis to James Steedman, August 6, 1865, Andrew Johnson Papers, Library of Congress.

6. Francis P. Blair to Andrew Johnson, July 18, 1865, Andrew Johnson Papers, Library of Congress.

7. Joseph Holt to Edwin Stanton, July 3, 1866, Joseph Holt Papers, Manuscript Division, Library of Congress.

8. George Shea to Horace Greeley, August 22, 1865, Horace Greeley Papers, New York Public Library.

9. Lathrop, "Bailing of Jefferson Davis," 636–44, 636.

10. *New York Tribune,* August 25, 1865.

11. Varina Davis to Andrew Johnson, August 30, 1865, Andrew Johnson Papers, Library of Congress.

12. Ibid. The letter is published in Davis, *Papers of Jefferson Davis,* 12:22–24. Editorial notes indicate, however, that Davis never acknowledged receiving the letter.

13. *Richmond Whig,* October 17, 1865.

14. Ibid.

15. Reagan, *Memoirs,* 228.

16. Parrish, *Richard Taylor,* 450.

17. Taylor, *Destruction and Reconstruction,* 240.

18. Ibid., 241–42.

19. Ibid., 244.

20. Ibid., 246–47.

21. Lathrop, "Bailing of Jefferson Davis," 638.

22. Ibid., 639. See also Cox, *Union, Disunion, Reunion,* 368–70, for a discussion of this view of treason.

23. Chase's political aspirations were so apparent that even his biographical entry in *The Oxford Companion to the Supreme Court of the United States* remarks that he was "ever ambitious, Chase sought unsuccessfully to become a presidential nominee [in 1868]. (See EXTRAJUDICIAL ACTIVITIES)." Hall, *Oxford Companion to the Supreme Court,* 137.

24. "Message of the President," December 4, 1865, Cong. Globe, 39th Cong., 1st sess., app., 2.

25. *Richmond Whig,* October 17, 1865.

26. Ayers, *Thin Light of Freedom,* 368.

27. Thaddeus Stevens, "Reconstruction," September 6, 1865, *Selected Papers of Thaddeus Stevens,* 2:13.

28. *Report of the Joint Committee on Reconstruction,* pt. 2, viii.

29. *Hartford Daily Courant,* January 11, 1866.

30. James Speed to Andrew Johnson, January 4, 1866, Johnson, *Papers,* 9:570.

31. Ibid.

32. Ibid.

33. Ibid.

34. *Philadelphia Inquirer,* June 10, 1865.

35. *Baltimore Sun,* June 29, 1865.

36. *Hartford Daily Courant,* January 11, 1866.

37. Testimony of Judge John C. Underwood, *Report of the Joint Committee on Reconstruction,* pt. 2, 6.

38. Ibid., 7.

39. Ibid., 10.

40. Stevens, "Reconstruction," 2:15.

41. Fellman, *Making of Robert E. Lee,* 264.

42. Ibid.; testimony of Robert E. Lee, *Report of the Joint Committee on Reconstruction,* pt. 2, 129–36.

43. Ibid., 133.

44. Fellman, *Making of Robert E. Lee,* 281–82.

45. Ibid., 134–35.

Chapter Ten

Epigraph: "Jefferson Davis's Trial," *New-York Commercial Advertiser,* June 6, 1866, 2.

1. James Speed to John H. Clifford, April 6, 1866, John H. Clifford Papers, Massachusetts Historical Society.

2. Testimony of William M. Evarts, in *Impeachment Investigation,* 645, 656.

3. Ibid., 645.

4. Davis, *Constitutionalist,* 7:488.

5. Van Deusen, *Horace Greeley,* 303.

6. Testimony of Horace Greeley, in *Impeachment Investigation,* 779–80.

7. Ibid., 780.

8. Davis Indictment, Jefferson Davis Trial Papers, Library of Virginia, Richmond.

9. Notes on Witnesses, Jefferson Davis Trial Papers, University of Chicago, box 1.

10. Ibid.

11. Testimony of Lucius H. Chandler, in *Impeachment Investigation,* 503.

12. This is true, except for the indictment of John C. Breckinridge, which had language unique to him.

13. Testimony of Chandler, in *Impeachment Investigation,* 503–4.

14. Indictment of Jefferson Davis, May 10, 1866, Library of Virginia.

15. Cong. Globe, 37th Cong., 2d sess., July 16, 1862, 412.

16. Testimony of Chandler, 503.

17. *New York Tribune,* May 24, 1866.

18. Nelson A. Miles to E. D. Townsend, May 26, 1866, *OR,* ser. 2, 121:914.

19. Charles P. Muhlenberg to John S. McEwan, December 29, 1865, *OR,* ser. 2, 121:841; and Miles, *Nelson A. Miles,* 67.

20. Miles to Townsend, May 26, 1866.

21. Ibid., 915–18.

22. Ibid., 914.

23. Horace Greeley to Salmon P. Chase, June 1, 1866, Salmon P. Chase Papers, Library of Congress.

24. Salmon P. Chase to Horace Greeley, June 1, 1866.

25. Ibid.

26. Ibid.

27. Ibid.

28. Salmon P. Chase to Horace Greeley, June 5, 1866, Salmon P. Chase Papers, 5:105.

29. Salmon P. Chase to Janet Chase, June 5, 1866, Salmon P. Chase Papers, 5:103.

30. *New-York Commercial Advertiser,* June 5, 1866.

31. *New York Tribune,* June 5, 1866.

32. *Albany Evening Journal,* June 6, 1866; and *New York Herald,* June 6, 1866.

33. Charles O'Conor to Burton Harrison, June 25, 1866, Burton Harrison Papers, Library of Congress.

34. *Albany Evening Journal,* June 6, 1866; and *New York Herald,* June 6, 1866. The Customs House now serves as the building housing the federal United States Court of Appeals for the Fourth Circuit. It is closed to the public, and my efforts to get a tour of the building were rebuffed until I asked to go to the Office of Attorney Admissions, at which time I was given access to that office to apply for admission to the court. Once inside the building, I spoke to the federal marshals about getting a tour of the building. They contacted Sarah Carr, one of the communications specialists, who was gracious enough to give me a tour of the entire Customs House. Unfortunately, the courtroom itself is no longer there, but Ms. Carr did show me where it once existed.

35. *Albany Evening Journal,* June 6, 1866.

36. *New-York Commercial Advertiser,* June 6, 1866.

37. *Jamestown (N.Y.) Journal,* June 15, 1866.

38. *New-York Commercial Advertiser,* June 6, 1866.

39. *New York Herald,* June 6, 1866.

40. Ibid.

41. Ibid.

42. *New York Tribune,* June 5, 1866, and June 6, 1866; *Albany Evening Journal,* June 7, 1866; and *New York Herald,* June 7 and June 6, 1866.

43. *New-York Commercial Advertiser,* June 6, 1866.

44. Ibid.

45. Ibid.

46. Ibid.

47. Many newspapers observed that "it is axiomatic in the defense of criminal cases that a criminal defense attorney is never so ready to try a case as when the prosecution is obviously unable to do so. Davis' defense team demand for a speedy trial despite not having a copy of the indictment or a list of prosecution witnesses seems to fall squarely within this axiom." *Albany Evening Journal,* June 7, 1866; *Alexandria (Va.) Gazette,* June 7, 1866; and *New-York Commercial Advertiser,* June 6, 1866.

Chapter Eleven

Epigraph: Frederick Douglass, "The Issues of the Day: An Address Delivered in Washington, D.C., on 10 March 1866," *Frederick Douglass Papers,* 4:122.

1. Andrew Johnson to Edwin M. Stanton, June 6, 1866, Johnson, *Papers of Andrew Johnson,* 10:567–68.

2. *New York Herald,* June 9, 1866; and *New York Tribune,* June 9, 1866; Davis, *Papers of Jefferson Davis,* 12:152.

3. *Alexandria (Va.) Gazette,* June 12, 1866; and *New York Tribune,* June 12, 1866.

4. *Assassination of Lincoln: Report,* Committee on the Assassination of Lincoln of the House of Representatives, 39th Cong., 1st sess., Report No. 104, July 1866.

5. Cong. Globe, 39th Cong., 1st sess., June 11, 1866, 3089.

6. Charles O'Conor to Andrew Johnson, June 13, 1866, Johnson, *Papers of Andrew Johnson,* 10:583–84.

7. *New York Herald,* June 14, 1866; and *New York Tribune,* June 14, 1866.

8. *Richmond Whig,* June 12, 1866; and *Daily Albany Argus,* June 15, 1866.

9. Charles H. Halpine to Andrew Johnson, March 20, 1866, Johnson, *Papers of Andrew Johnson,* 10:275.

10. Hanchett, "Reconstruction," 283.

11. Eckert, *"Fiction Distorting Fact,"* 10.

12. Hanchett, "Reconstruction," 284.

13. Craven, *Prison Life,* 359.

14. Ibid., 373.

15. Ibid., 369.

16. Ibid., 374–75.

17. Eckert, *"Fiction Distorting Fact,"* xlviii.

18. Hanchett, "Reconstruction," 286.

19. Joseph E. Davis to Jefferson Davis, July 14, 1866, Davis, *Papers of Jefferson Davis,* 12:153.

20. Speed, *James Speed,* 85.

21. *Daily Albany Argus,* July 23, 1866.

22. Speed, *James Speed,* 89.

23. *Daily National Intelligencer* (Washington, D.C.), July 16, 1866.

24. *New York Tribune,* July 16, 1866.

25. *Albany Evening Journal,* July 14, 1866.

26. Welles, *Diary,* 2:549.

27. Speed, *James Speed,* 93.

28. Welles, *Diary,* 2:552.

29. *Cincinnati Daily Gazette,* July 14, 1866.

30. *Cincinnati Enquirer,* July 17, 1866.

31. *Cleveland Plain Dealer,* July 24, 1866.

32. *Daily Inter Ocean* (Chicago), July 28, 1866.

33. William M. Evarts and John H. Clifford to Henry Stanbery, August 14, 1866 (copy), John H. Clifford Papers, Massachusetts Historical Society.

34. *Chicago Tribune,* November 15, 1865, John H. Clifford Papers, Massachusetts Historical Society.

35. George S. Boutwell to John H. Clifford, June 27, 1867, John H. Clifford Papers, Massachusetts Historical Society.

36. John H. Clifford to George S. Boutwell, June 30, 1867 (copy), John H. Clifford Papers, Massachusetts Historical Society.

37. *Daily National Republican* (Washington, D.C.), October 2, 1866.

38. Browning, *Diary,* 2:97.

39. Ibid.

40. Charles O'Conor to Varina Davis, September 18, 1866, Jefferson Davis Papers, American Civil War Museum, Richmond.

41. *Daily Constitutionalist* (Augusta, Ga.), October 7, 1866.

42. Andrew Johnson to Henry Stanbery, October 6, 1866, Johnson, *Papers of Andrew Johnson,* 16:316.

43. Ibid.

44. L. H. Chandler to Henry Stanbery, October 8, 1866, Jefferson Davis Trial Papers, University of Chicago Library.

45. Ibid.

46. Browning, *Diary,* 2:98–99.

47. Ibid., 2:99.

48. Ashton, *Official Opinions,* 69.

49. Ibid., 71.

50. Ibid.

51. Ibid.

52. Browning, *Diary,* 2:104–5.

53. Ibid., 2:105.

54. Ibid.

55. *New York Herald,* October 22, 1866.

56. Browning, *Diary,* 2:130.

57. *Report of the Joint Committee on Reconstruction,* iii; *Weekly Eagle* (Brattleboro, Vt.), January 15, 1852.

58. Gales, *Debates and Proceedings,* 2:2215.

59. Cong. Globe, 37th Cong., 2d sess., Laws of the United States, approved July 17, 1862, app., 412.

60. Ibid.

61. George S. Boutwell to John C. Underwood, October 20, 1866, Papers of John C. Underwood, Library of Congress.

62. Ibid.

63. *New York Herald,* November 4, 1866.

64. *Augusta (Ga.) Daily Constitutionalist,* November 8, 1866, reprinting the *Norfolk Virginian.*

65. *Baltimore Sun,* November 29, 1866.

66. Charles O'Conor to Varina Davis, September 18, 1866, Jefferson Davis Papers, American Civil War Museum, Richmond.

Chapter Twelve

Epigraph: Benjamin Butler to Andrew Johnson, April 25, 1865, Butler, *Letters,* 5:605.

1. Thomas J. Pratt to Charles O'Conor, November 24, 1866, Jefferson Davis Papers, American Civil War Museum, Richmond.

2. Charles O'Conor to Varina Davis, November 26, 1866, Jefferson Davis Papers, American Civil War Museum.

3. Charles O'Conor to Varina Davis, September 18, 1866, Jefferson Davis Papers, American Civil War Museum.

4. Charles O'Conor to Varina Davis, November 19, 1866, Jefferson Davis Papers, American Civil War Museum.

5. Ibid.

6. Ibid.

7. Salmon P. Chase to Horace Greeley, November 21, 1866, Chase, *Correspondence of Salmon P. Chase,* 5:138.

8. *New York Herald,* December 19, 1866.

9. Charles O'Conor to Jefferson Davis, May 23, 1867, Jefferson Davis Papers, American Civil War Museum.

10. Charles O'Conor to Jefferson Davis, June 15, 1867, Jefferson Davis Papers, American Civil War Museum.

11. Jefferson Davis to William B. Reed, November 26, 1865, Jefferson Davis Papers, 12:62.

12. William B. Reed to Jefferson Davis, December 2, 1865, Jefferson Davis Papers, American Civil War Museum.

13. Jefferson Davis to William B. Reed, November 26, 1865, Jefferson Davis Papers, 12:62.

14. Varina Davis to Jefferson Davis, November 27, 1865; and Jefferson Davis to Varina Davis, December 2–3, 1865, Jefferson Davis Papers, 12:67.

15. Jefferson Davis to Varina Davis, January 24, 1866, Jefferson Davis Papers, 12:102.

16. Jefferson Davis to Varina Davis, February 3, 1866, Jefferson Davis Papers, 12:113–14.

17. Varina Davis to Jefferson Davis, March 18–22, 1866, Jefferson Davis Papers, 12:134.

18. Jefferson Davis to Varina Davis, April 8, 1866, Jefferson Davis Papers, 12:139.

19. Ibid., 12:142.

20. Varina Davis to Jefferson Davis, August 14, 1866, Jefferson Davis Papers, 12:157.

21. Varina Davis to Jefferson Davis, August 16, 1866, Jefferson Davis Papers, 12:158.

22. *New York Herald,* April 9, 1867.

23. Testimony of Lucius H. Chandler, in *Impeachment Investigation,* 508.

24. Ibid., 508–9.

25. Writ of Habeas Corpus, May 1, 1867, Jefferson Davis Papers, University of Chicago Library.

26. Charles O'Conor to Henry Stanbery, May 2, 1867, Jefferson Davis Papers, University of Chicago Library.

27. Testimony of Chandler, 502.

28. Lucius H. Chandler to Edwin Stanton, May 4, 1867, Andrew Johnson Papers, Library of Congress, microfilm.

29. U.S. Const., Art. III, Sec. 3.

30. Peters, *Public Statutes at Large,* April 30, 1790.

31. *United States Statutes at Large,* 12:589–90.

32. Testimony of Chandler, 504–5.

33. Hoffer, *Treason Trials,* 134.

34. Harrison, *Aris Sonis Focisque,* 202–3.

35. Ibid., 203; *Daily Albany Argus,* May 13, 1867; *New York Herald,* May 12, 1867; and *Norwich (Conn.) Aurora,* May 15, 1867.

36. Harrison, *Aris Sonis Focisque,* 203; *New York Herald,* May 12, 1867; and *Norwich (Conn.) Aurora,* May 15, 1867.

37. Harrison, *Aris Sonis Focisque,* 203; and *Norwich (Conn.) Aurora,* May 15, 1867.

38. *Lowell (Mass.) Daily Citizen and News,* May 13, 1867.

39. Testimony of Evarts, 645.

40. Ibid., 646.

41. Ibid., 645.

42. Ibid., 648.

43. Testimony of John C. Underwood, in *Impeachment Investigation,* 579–80.

44. Testimony of Evarts, 658.

45. Ibid., 658–59.

46. Ibid., 658.

47. Testimony of Evarts, 646.

48. Testimony of Chandler, 505; testimony of Underwood, 579–80; testimony of Evarts, 646–47 and 653–54.

Chapter Thirteen

Epigraph: Testimony of Lucius H. Chandler, *Impeachment Investigation,* 504.

1. Lyons to Jefferson Davis, May 5, 1867, Davis, Jefferson Davis Papers, 12:195–96.

2. Ibid., 650–52.

3. Testimony of John C. Underwood, in *Impeachment Investigation,* 579–80; and testimony of William M. Evarts, in *Impeachment Investigation,* 648–49.

4. Salmon P. Chase to John C. Underwood, May 13, 1867, Papers of John C. Underwood, Library of Congress.

5. Salmon P. Chase to Janet Chase, June 7, 1867, Chase, Salmon P. Chase Papers, 5:153.

6. Ibid. 5:153–54.

7. *Cleveland Plain Dealer,* June 11, 1867; Chase, *Salmon P. Chase Papers,* 5:154.

8. Harrison, *Aris Sonis Focisque,* 204; *Norwich (Conn.) Aurora,* May 15, 1867; and *Boston Herald,* May 11, 1867.

9. *New York Herald,* May 12, 1867.

10. Harrison, *Aris Sonis Focisque,* 204; and *Norwich (Conn.) Aurora,* May 15, 1867.

11. Ibid.

12. Harrison, *Aris Sonis Focisque,* 204–5; *Norwich (Conn.) Aurora,* May 15, 1867; testimony of Lucius H. Chandler, in *Impeachment Investigation,* 505.

13. Testimony of Chandler, 505; testimony of Underwood, 579; testimony of Evarts, 652.

14. Testimony of Underwood; and testimony of Evarts, 652.

15. Testimony of Evarts, 656.

16. Cooper, *Jefferson Davis,* 566.

17. Van Deusen, *Horace Greeley,* 353.

18. Cooper, *Jefferson Davis,* 543–45.

19. *Norwich (Conn.) Aurora,* May 15, 1867; Harrison, *Aris Sonis Focisque,* 205.

20. Harrison, *Aris Sonis Focisque,* 206.

21. Cooper, *Jefferson Davis,* 567.

22. A New Yorker to John C. Underwood, May 14, 1867, John C. Underwood Papers, Library of Congress.

23. William Lloyd Garrison to Samuel May Jr., June 11, 1867, *Letters,* 5:508.

24. Frederick Douglass, "The Issues of the Day," March 10, 1866, *Frederick Douglass Papers,* 4:122. Of course, Douglass's reference to being "found with certain other clothing on" was a reference to Davis reportedly having been captured in his wife's clothing.

25. Testimony of Chandler, 502.

26. Ibid., 503.

27. Ibid., 505.

28. Testimony of Chandler, 505.

29. Testimony of Henry Stanbery, *Impeachment Investigation,* 554–56.

30. Ibid., 557.

31. Ibid., 560–61.

32. Testimony of Underwood, 578–79.

33. Ibid., 579.

34. Stephen R. Mallory to Jefferson Davis, May 14, 1867, Davis, *Papers of Jefferson Davis,* 12:198.

35. John H. Reagan to Jefferson Davis, May 21, 1867, Davis, *Papers of Jefferson Davis,* 12:201.

36. Howell Cobb to Jefferson Davis, July 31, 1867, Davis, *Papers of Jefferson Davis,* 12:235.

37. Jubal A. Early to Jefferson Davis, May 24, 1867, Davis, *Papers of Jefferson Davis,* 12:202.

38. William B. Reed, May 18, 1867, Davis, *Papers of Jefferson Davis,* 12:200–201.

39. Jefferson Davis to Jubal A. Early, June 8, 1867, Davis, *Papers of Jefferson Davis,* 12:209.

40. Bernard J. Sage to Jefferson Davis, August 24, 1867, Davis, *Papers of Jefferson Davis,* 12:244.

41. Jefferson Davis to Charles J. Helms, September 15, 1867, Davis, *Papers of Jefferson Davis,* 12:247.

42. Charles O'Conor to Jefferson Davis, October 2, 1867, Jefferson Davis Papers, American Civil War Museum, Richmond.

43. Ibid.

44. Ibid.

45. Ibid.

46. Charles O'Conor to Varina Davis, October 21, 1867, Jefferson Davis Papers, American Civil War Museum.

47. William B. Reed to Jefferson Davis, October 8, 1867, Davis, *Papers of Jefferson Davis,* 12:252.

48. Charles O'Conor to Jefferson Davis, October 2, 1867, Jefferson Davis Papers, American Civil War Museum.

49. Ibid. Evarts later served as Andrew Johnson's chief defense counsel in the president's impeachment trial and was rewarded for his work by being asked to join Johnson's cabinet as United States attorney general. Dyer, *Public Career of William M. Evarts,* 101.

50. Charles O'Conor to Jefferson Davis, October 2, 1867, Jefferson Davis Papers, American Civil War Museum.

Chapter Fourteen

Epigraph: Strong, *Diary,* 213.

1. Lucius H. Chandler to Henry Stanbery, October 19, 1867, Jefferson Davis Trial Papers, box 1, University of Chicago Library.

2. William M. Evarts to L. H. Chandler, February 18, 1868, Jefferson Davis Trial Papers, box 1, University of Chicago Library.

3. William M. Evarts to Richard Henry Dana Jr., October 28, 1867, Dana Family Papers, Massachusetts Historical Society.

4. William M. Evarts to Richard Henry Dana Jr., November 15, 1867, Dana Family Papers, Massachusetts Historical Society.

5. Chandler to Stanbery, October 19, 1867.

6. Henry Stanbery to Lucius H. Chandler, October 25, 1867, Jefferson Davis Trial Papers, box 1, University of Chicago Library.

7. See Evarts to Chandler, February 18, 1868, and October 19, 1867, for a reference to having met in Richmond.

8. William M. Evarts and Richard H. Dana Jr. to Henry Stanbery, November 2, 1867, Jefferson Davis Trial Papers, box 1, University of Chicago Library.

9. Ibid.

10. U.S. Const., Amend. V.

11. Evarts and Dana to Stanbery, November 2, 1867.

12. Ibid.

13. Charles O'Conor to Jefferson Davis, October 18, 1867, Jefferson Davis Papers, American Civil War Museum, Richmond.

14. Charles O'Conor to Jefferson Davis, October 23, 1867, Jefferson Davis Papers, American Civil War Museum.

15. Charles O'Conor to Jefferson Davis, October 29, 1867, Jefferson Davis Papers, American Civil War Museum.

16. Ibid.

17. Charles O'Conor to Jefferson Davis, November 12, 1867, Jefferson Davis Papers, American Civil War Museum.

18. Charles O'Conor to Jefferson Davis, November 13, 1867, Jefferson Davis Papers, American Civil War Museum.

19. Evarts and Dana to Stanbery, November 2, 1867.

20. Henry Stanbery to L. H. Chandler, November 4, 1867, Jefferson Davis Trial Papers, box 1, University of Chicago Library.

21. Ibid.

22. L. H. Chandler to Henry Stanbery, November 6, 1867, Jefferson Davis Trial Papers, box 1, University of Chicago Library.

23. Robert Ould to Jefferson Davis, October 11, 1867, in Davis, *Papers of Jefferson Davis,* 12:253.

24. Robert Ould to William Corcoran, October 25, 1867, William Corcoran Papers, Library of Congress, Washington, D.C.

25. Charles O'Conor to Varina Davis, October 21, 1867, Jefferson Davis Papers, American Civil War Museum.

26. Charles O'Conor to Jefferson Davis, October 29, 1867, Jefferson Davis Papers, American Civil War Museum.

27. *New York Herald,* November 23, 1867.

28. *Daily National Republican* (Washington, D.C.), November 26, 1867.

29. Richard Henry Dana Jr. to Sarah Dana, November 25, 1867, Dana Family Papers, Massachusetts Historical Society.

30. *Cincinnati Daily Gazette,* November 27, 1867.

31. William M. Evarts to Richard Henry Dana Jr., January 7, 1868, Dana Family Papers, Massachusetts Historical Society.

32. William M. Evarts to Richard Henry Dana Jr., January 22, 1868, Dana Family Papers, Massachusetts Historical Society.

33. Ibid.; Evarts to Chandler, February 18, 1868.

34. Evarts to Dana, January 22, 1868.

35. William M. Evarts to Henry Stanbery, February 18, 1868, William M. Evarts Papers, Manuscript Division, Library of Congress.

36. Ibid.

37. William M. Evarts to Richard Henry Dana Jr., February 9, 1868, Dana Family Papers, Massachusetts Historical Society.

38. William M. Evarts to Richard Henry Dana Jr., February 16, 1868, Dana Family Papers, Massachusetts Historical Society.

39. Henry H. Wells to William M. Evarts, February 20, 1868 (copy), Dana Family Papers, Massachusetts Historical Society.

40. Henry H. Wells to L. H. Chandler, February 22, 1868 (copy), Dana Family Papers, Massachusetts Historical Society.

41. William M. Evarts to H. H. Wells, February 24, 1868, William M. Evarts Papers, Library of Congress.

42. William M. Evarts to Richard Henry Dana Jr., February 26, 1868, Dana Family Papers, Massachusetts Historical Society.

43. Richard Henry Dana Jr. and William M. Evarts to Henry Stanbery (draft letter never sent to Stanbery), February 26, 1868, Dana Family Papers, Massachusetts Historical Society.

44. William M. Evarts to Richard Henry Dana Jr., March 3, 1868, Dana Family Papers, Massachusetts Historical Society.

45. Ibid.; Agreement for Postponement of the Trial Set for March 1868, signed by William M. Evarts and Charles O'Conor, March 6, 1868, Jefferson Davis Trial Papers, box 1, University of Chicago Library.

46. Ripley, *Black Abolitionist Papers,* 5:136.

47. Welles, *Diary,* 3:307–8.

48. Stewart, *Impeached,* 173.

49. *Trial of Andrew Johnson,* 1:119.

50. Charles O'Conor to Jefferson Davis, February 14, 1868, Jefferson Davis Papers, American Civil War Museum.

51. Charles O'Conor to Jefferson Davis, April 9, 1868, Jefferson Davis Papers, American Civil War Museum.

52. Cong. Globe, 40th Cong., 2d sess., March 26, 1868, 2114.

53. Cong. Globe, 40th Cong., 2d sess., April 8, 1868, 2275–76.

54. Ibid., 2276.

55. Charles O'Conor to Jefferson Davis, April 10, 1868, Jefferson Davis Papers, American Civil War Museum.

56. Jefferson Davis to James M. Mason, April 16, 1868, Davis, *Papers of Jefferson Davis,* 12:289, Jefferson Davis to James M. Mason, April 16, 1868.

57. *Daily Eastern Argus,* April 24, 1868.

58. Charles O'Conor to Jefferson Davis, November 13, 1867, Jefferson Davis Papers, American Civil War Museum.

59. Charles O'Conor to Jefferson Davis, April 10, 1868, Jefferson Davis Papers, American Civil War Museum.

60. Ibid.

61. William M. Evarts to Charles O'Conor, April 14, 1868, Jefferson Davis Papers, American Civil War Museum.

62. Charles O'Conor to Jefferson Davis, April 17, 1868, Jefferson Davis Papers, American Civil War Museum.

63. *Atlantic Monthly,* May 1868, 629.

64. *The Nation,* July 2, 1868.

65. *New York Herald,* April 6, 1868; and J. H. Carrington to Jefferson Davis, March 24, 1868, Jefferson Davis Papers, American Civil War Museum.

66. Jefferson Davis to James M. Howry, February 8, 1868, Davis, *Papers of Jefferson Davis,* 12:271.

67. Jefferson Davis to Hugh Robert Davis, March 7, 1868, Davis, *Papers of Jefferson Davis,* 12:277.

68. O'Conor to Davis, February 14, 1868.

69. Ibid.

70. Robert Ould to Jefferson Davis, March 9, 1868, Jefferson Davis Papers, American Civil War Museum.

71. Robert Ould to Jefferson Davis, March 11, 1868, Jefferson Davis Papers, American Civil War Museum.

72. Charles O'Conor to Jefferson Davis, March 11, 1868, Jefferson Davis Papers, American Civil War Museum.

73. Robert Ould to Thomas Bayard Jr., April 24, 1868, Thomas Francis Bayard Papers, Library of Congress.

74. Charles O'Conor to Horace Greeley, April 24, 1868, Horace Greeley Papers New York Public Library.

75. Charles O'Conor to Thomas Bayard Jr., April 29, 1868, Thomas Francis Bayard Papers, Library of Congress.

76. Charles O'Conor to Jefferson Davis, August 1, 1868, Jefferson Davis Papers, American Civil War Museum.

Chapter Fifteen

Epigraph: Robert E. Lee to R. S. McCulloh, September 28, 1869, in Rowland, *Jefferson Davis,* 7:258–59.

1. *Richmond Whig,* June 9, 1868.
2. *New York Herald,* April 29, 1868.
3. *Richmond Whig,* June 12, 1868.
4. Crofts, *Old Southampton,* 261.
5. Welles, *Diary,* 3:375.
6. See William H. Seward to Andrew Johnson, June 11, 1868; and William M. Evarts to Andrew Johnson, June 20, 1868, in Johnson, *Papers of Andrew Johnson,* 14:199 and 14:239–40.
7. *Nation,* July 2, 1868.
8. Charles O'Conor to Jefferson Davis, December 7, 1868, Jefferson Davis Papers, American Civil War Museum, Richmond.
9. Welles, *Diary,* 3:394.
10. Ibid., 3:395. This was not quite correct information. The 1865 indictments against Lee and many others were still pending in Richmond. However, there was an understanding that they would never be proceeded upon.
11. Ibid.
12. Ibid.
13. Ibid., 3:395–96.
14. Ibid.
15. Ibid., 3:409.
16. *Alexandria (Va.) Gazette,* June 30, 1868.
17. Ibid., July 25, 1868.
18. Ibid., July 27, 1868.
19. Welles, *Diary,* 3:415.
20. Ibid., 3:415–16.
21. William M. Evarts to Richard Henry Dana Jr., August 24, 1868, Dana Family Papers, Massachusetts Historical Society.
22. Richard Henry Dana Jr. to William M. Evarts, August 24, 1868, Andrew Johnson Papers, Library of Congress.
23. Ibid.
24. Ibid.
25. Ibid.
26. Ibid.
27. Ibid.
28. William M. Evarts to Andrew Johnson, October 9, 1868, Andrew Johnson Papers, Library of Congress.
29. Welles, *Diary,* 3:463.

30. Ibid.

31. Browning, *Diary,* 2:225.

32. Ibid., 2:225–26.

33. Charles O'Conor to Jefferson Davis, January 6, 1869, Jefferson Davis Papers, American Civil War Museum.

34. *Boston Daily Advertiser,* November 28, 1868.

35. Charles O'Conor to Jefferson Davis, December 7, 1868, Jefferson Davis Papers, American Civil War Museum.

36. *Frank Leslie's Illustrated Newspaper,* December 5, 1868. Grant gave a conditional acceptance of the invitation, telling the sponsors that he would not attend if any of the cabinet members attended. See Browning, *Diary,* 2:226–27; and Welles, *Diary,* 3:467.

37. Browning, *Diary,* 2:227.

38. William M. Evarts to S. Ferguson Beach, November 20, 1868 (copy), Dana Family Papers, Massachusetts Historical Society.

39. *Baltimore Sun,* December 3, 1868.

40. *New York Evening Post,* November 28, 1868.

41. *Springfield (Mass.) Republican,* November 28, 1868.

42. *New London (Conn.) Democrat,* December 5, 1868.

43. *Richmond Whig,* December 4, 1868; and *Boston Post,* December 7, 1868.

44. *Richmond Whig,* December 4 and 8, 1868.

45. *Boston Post,* December 7, 1868.

46. *Richmond Whig,* December 8, 1868.

47. Ibid.

48. Sec. 3 reads as follows: "No person shall be a Senator or Representative in Congress, or elector of President or Vice President, or hold any office, civil or military, under the United States, or under any state, who, having previously taken an oath, as a member of Congress, or as an officer of the United States, or as a member of any state legislature, or as an executive or judicial officer of any state, to support the Constitution of the United States, shall have engaged in insurrection or rebellion against the same, or given aid or comfort to the enemies thereof. But Congress may by a vote of two-thirds of each House, remove such disability."

49. *Richmond Whig,* December 8, 1868.

50. Ibid.

51. Ibid.

52. Ibid.

53. *Boston Post,* December 7, 1868.

54. *Richmond Whig,* December 8, 1868.

55. U.S. Const., Art. 3, Sec. 3.

56. *Richmond Whig,* December 8, 1868.

57. Ibid.

58. Davis, *Papers of Jefferson Davis,* 12:335.

59. *New York Tribune,* December 5, 1868.

60. *Daily Eastern Argus* (Portland, Me.), December 5, 1868.

61. Charles O'Conor to Jefferson Davis, December 7, 1868, Jefferson Davis Papers, American Civil War Museum.

62. Ibid.

63. Ibid.

64. Ibid.

65. Ibid.

66. Andrew Johnson, Fourth Annual Message, December 8, 1868, *Papers of Andrew Johnson,* 15:283.

67. Ibid., 15:281–304.

68. Welles, *Diary,* 3:479.

69. Johnson, "Proclamation 179."

70. Charles O'Conor to Jefferson Davis, January 6, 1869, Jefferson Davis Papers, American Civil War Museum.

71. Browning, *Diary,* 2:234; and *Black's Law Dictionary,* 5th ed. (St. Paul: West Publishing Co., 1978), 945.

72. Browning, *Diary,* 2:234–35.

73. *Cincinnati Daily Gazette,* February 12, 1869.

74. *Alexandria (Va.) Gazette,* February 12, 1869.

75. *Elkhart (Ind.) Weekly Review,* February 18, 1869; *Portsmouth (N.H.) Journal of Literature and Politics,* February 20, 1869.

76. *Richmond Whig,* February 9, 1869.

Conclusion

Epigraph: G. Smith, *No Treason,* 7.

1. Welles, *Diary,* 2:301–4.

2. Jefferson Davis to James Proctor Knott, January 22, 1876, in the possession of the author.

3. Davis, "Lord Wolseley's Mistakes," 473.

4. Shea, *Jefferson Davis,* 3–16.

5. V. Davis, *Jefferson Davis,* 2:549.

6. Ibid., 2:537–38.

7. Ibid., 2:573.

8. Ibid., 2:574.

9. Speed, *James Speed,* 133.

10. *Critic-Record* (Washington, D.C.), April 10, 1876; *Evening Star,* (Washington, D.C.), April 17, 1876; and *People's Advocate* (Alexandria, Va.), April 22, 1876.

11. White, "Trial of Jefferson Davis," 124.

12. Niven, *Salmon P. Chase,* 409.

13. Blue, *Salmon P. Chase,* 264.

14. Oglesby, *Shackling of Jefferson Davis.*

15. Ibid.

16. Robinson, *Justice in Grey,* 629.

17. "United States Constitution and the Secessionists," 442.

18. *Cramer v. United States,* 325 U.S. 1, at 25 (1945).

BIBLIOGRAPHY

Manuscript Collections

Thomas Francis Bayard Papers. Manuscript Division. Library of Congress, Washington, D.C.

Jeremiah Black Papers. Manuscript Division. Library of Congress, Washington, D.C.

Salmon P. Chase Papers. Manuscript Division. Library of Congress, Washington, D.C.

John H. Clifford Papers. Massachusetts Historical Society, Boston.

William Corcoran Papers. Manuscript Division. Library of Congress, Washington, D.C.

Dana Family Papers. Massachusetts Historical Society, Boston.

Jefferson Davis Papers. American Civil War Museum, Richmond. (The museum changed its name from the Museum of the Confederacy in 2014.)

Jefferson Davis Trial Papers. Library of Virginia, Richmond.

———. University of Chicago Library, Chicago.

William M. Evarts Papers. Manuscript Division. Library of Congress, Washington, D.C.

Horace Greeley Papers. New York Public Library, New York.

Burton Harrison Papers. Manuscript Division. Library of Congress, Washington, D.C.

Joseph Holt Papers. Manuscript Division. Library of Congress, Washington, D.C.

Andrew Johnson Papers. Library of Congress, Washington, D.C. (microfilm edition).

James M. Mason Papers. Manuscript Division. Library of Congress, Washington, D.C.

Charles O'Conor Miscellaneous Papers. Manuscript Division. New York Public Library, New York.

———. New York Law Institute, New York.

Franklin Pierce Papers. Library of Congress, Washington, D.C. (microfilm edition).

John C. Underwood Papers. Manuscript Division. Library of Congress, Washington, D.C.

Published Primary Sources

Bates, Edward. *The Diary of Edward Bates, 1859–1866.* Edited by Howard K. Beale. Washington, D.C.: Government Printing Office, 1933.

Browning, Orville Hickman. *The Diary of Orville Hickman Browning.* Edited by James G. Randall. 2 vols. Springfield: Illinois State Historical Library, 1933.

Butler, Benjamin F. *Butler's Book.* Boston: A. M. Thayer & Co., 1892.

——. *Private and Official Correspondence of Gen. Benjamin F. Butler during the Period of the Civil War.* 5 vols. Published by author, 1917.

Chase, Salmon P. *The Salmon P. Chase Papers.* Edited by John Niven. 5 vols. Kent, Ohio: Kent State University Press, 1998.

Chestnut, Mary. *Mary Chestnut's Civil War.* Edited by C. Vann Woodward. New Haven: Yale University Press, 1981.

Chipman, N. P. *The Tragedy of Andersonville: Trial of Captain Henry Wirz, the Prison Keeper.* 2d ed. Sacramento, Calif.: published by author, 1911.

Clay-Clopton, Virginia. *A Belle of the Fifties.* New York: Doubleday, Page & Co., 1905.

Cox, Samuel S. *Union, Disunion, Reunion: Three Decades of Federal Legislation 1855 to 1885.* Providence, R.I.: J. A. & R. A. Reid, 1885.

Dana, Richard Henry, Jr. *The Journal of Richard Henry Dana, Jr.* Edited by Robert F. Lucid. 3 vols. Cambridge: Belknap Press of Harvard University Press, 1968.

Davis, Jefferson. *Jefferson Davis: Constitutionalist.* Edited by Dunbar Rowland. 10 vols. Jackson: Mississippi Department of Archives and History, 1923.

——. *The Papers of Jefferson Davis.* Edited by Lynda L. Crist. 13 vols. to date. Baton Rouge: Louisiana State University Press, 1971–.

——. *The Rise and Fall of the Confederate Government.* 2 vols. New York: D. Appleton & Co., 1881.

Davis, Varina. *A Memoir: Jefferson Davis, Ex-President of the Confederate States of America.* 2 vols. New York: Belford Co., 1890.

Douglass, Frederick. *The Frederick Douglass Papers.* Edited by John W. Blassingame and John R. McKivigan. 4 vols. New Haven: Yale University Press, 1991.

Garrison, William Lloyd. *The Letters of William Lloyd Garrison.* Edited by Walter M. Merrill. 6 vols. Cambridge: Belknap Press of Harvard University Press, 1979.

Grant, Ulysses S. *The Papers of Ulysses S. Grant.* Edited by John Y. Simon. 32 vols. Carbondale: Southern Illinois University Press, 1985.

——. *Personal Memoirs of U. S. Grant.* 2 vols. New York: Webster & Co., 1892.

Greeley, Horace. *Recollections of a Busy Life.* New York: J. B. Ford & Co., 1865.

Harrison, Burton N. "The Capture of Jefferson Davis." *Century Illustrated Monthly Magazine* 27 (November 1883).

Jefferson, Thomas. *The Writings of Thomas Jefferson.* Edited by H. A. Washington. 9 vols. Washington, D.C.: Taylor & Maury, 1853.

Johnson, Andrew. *The Papers of Andrew Johnson.* Edited by Paul H. Bergeron. 16 vols. Knoxville: University of Tennessee Press, 1992.

Johnson, Bradley T. *Reports of Cases Decided by Chief Justice Chase in the Circuit Court of the United States for the Fourth Circuit, 1865–1869.* New York: Diossy & Co., 1876. Reprint, Book Renaissance (printed on demand).

Johnston, Joseph E. *Narrative of Military Operations.* New York: D. Appleton & Co., 1874.

Jones, James P. "'Your Left Arm': James H. Wilson's Letters to Adam Badeau." *Civil War History* 12, no. 3 (September 1966): 230–45.

Kean, Robert Garlick Hill. *Inside the Confederate Government: The Diary of Robert Garlick Hill Kean.* Edited by Edward Younger. New York: Oxford University Press, 1957.

Keckley, Elizabeth. *Behind the Scenes, Or Thirty Years a Slave, and Four Years in the White House.* New York: G. W. Carleton & Co., 1868.

Lincoln, Abraham. *The Collected Works of Abraham Lincoln.* Edited by Roy P. Basler. 9 vols. New Brunswick, N.J.: Rutgers University Press, 1953.

Mallory, Stephen R. "Last Days of the Confederate Government." *McClure's Magazine* 16, no. 3 (January 1901): 239–48.

McCulloch, Hugh. *Men and Measures of Half a Century: Sketches and Comments.* New York: Charles Scribner's Sons, 1888.

Miles, Nelson A. *Nelson A. Miles: A Documentary Biography of His Military Career, 1861–1903.* Edited by Brian C. Pohanka. Glendale, Calif.: Arthur H. Clark Co., 1985.

O'Conor, Charles. *My Own Cases: Lemmon's Slaves and Slavery Cases,* vol. 34. "The People of the State of New York, on the Relation of Louis Napoleon v. Jonathan Lemmon, A Citizen of the State of Virginia." Court of Appeals for the State of New York. Published by author.

Pierson, David. *Brothers in Gray: The Civil War Letters of the Pierson Family.* Edited by Thomas W. Cutrer and T. Michael Parrish. Baton Rouge: Louisiana State University Press, 1997.

Reagan, John H. *Memoirs: With Special References to Secession and the Civil War.* New York: Neale Publishing Co., 1906.

Shea, George. *Jefferson Davis: A Statement Concerning the Imputed Special Causes of His Long Imprisonment by the Government of the United States, and of His Tardy Release by Due Process of Law.* London: Edward Stanford, 1877.

Sherman, William Tecumseh. *Memoirs of General W. T. Sherman.* 2 vols. New York: D. Appleton & Co., 1875.

———. *Sherman's Civil War: Selected Correspondence of William T. Sherman, 1860–1865.* Edited by Brooks D. Simpson and Jean V. Berlin. Chapel Hill: University of North Carolina Press, 1999.

Stephens, Alexander H. "Alexander H. Stephens' Prison Life." *Confederate Veteran* 1, no. 6 (June 1893): 169–71.

———. *Recollections of Alexander H. Stephens.* Edited by Myrta Lockett Avary. Baton Rouge: Louisiana State University Press, 1998.

Stevens, Thaddeus. *The Selected Papers of Thaddeus Stevens.* Edited by Beverly Wilson Palmer. 2 vols. Pittsburgh: University of Pennsylvania Press, 1998.

Strong, George Templeton. *The Diary of George Templeton Strong: Post-War Years, 1865–1875.* Edited by Allan Nevins and Milton Halsey Thomas. New York: Macmillan, 1952.

Sublett, Emmie. *Ladies of Richmond: Confederate Capital.* Edited by Katharine Jones. Indianapolis: Bobbs-Merrill, 1962.

Sumner, Charles. *The Selected Letters of Charles Sumner.* Edited by Beverly Wilson Palmer. 2 vols. Boston: Northeastern University Press, 1990.

Taylor, Richard. *Destruction and Reconstruction: Personal Experiences of the Late War.* New York: D. Appleton & Co., 1870.

Webster, Daniel. *The Works of Daniel Webster.* 6 vols. Boston: Little, Brown, 1853.

Welles, Gideon. *The Civil War Diary of Gideon Welles, Lincoln's Secretary of the Navy.* Edited by William E. Gienapp and Erica L. Gienapp. Urbana: University of Illinois Press, 2014.

——. *The Diary of Gideon Welles.* Edited by Edgar T. Welles. 3 vols. Boston: Houghton Mifflin, 1911.

Wheeler, Joseph. "An Effort to Rescue Jefferson Davis." *Century Magazine* 56, no. 1 (May 1898): 85–90.

Wilson, James H. *Under the Old Flag: Recollections of Military Operations in the War for the Union, the Spanish War, the Boxer Rebellion, Etc.* New York: D. Appleton and Co., 1912.

Secondary Sources

Books and Pamphlets

A Voice from Rebel Prisons: Giving an Account of Some of the Horrors of the Stockades at Andersonville, Milan, and Other Prisons by a Returned Prisoner of War. Boston: Press of George C. Rand & Avery, 1865.

Ayers, Edward L. *The Thin Light of Freedom: The Civil War and Emancipation in the Heart of America.* New York: Norton, 2017.

Bigelow, John. "American Lawyer: Some Recollections of the Late C. O'Conor." N.d. Charles O'Conor file. New York Public Library.

Blair, William A. *Why Didn't the North Hang Some Rebels? The Postwar Debate over Punishment for Treason.* Milwaukee: Marquette University Press, 2004.

——. *With Malice toward Some: Treason and Loyalty in the Civil War Era.* Chapel Hill: University of North Carolina Press, 2014.

Blue, Frederick J. *Salmon P. Chase: A Life in Politics.* Kent, Ohio: Kent State University Press, 1987.

Bowers, Claude G. *The Tragic Era: The Revolution after Lincoln.* New York: Houghton Mifflin, 1929.

Brands, H. W. *The Man Who Saved the Union: Ulysses Grant in War and Peace.* New York: Doubleday, 2012.

Burgess, John W. *Reconstruction and the Constitution, 1866–1876.* New York: Charles Scribner's Sons, 1905.

Burke, Edmund. "Speech of Edmund Burke, Esq., on Moving His Resolutions for Conciliation with the Colonies." March 22, 1775. In *Longman's English Classics,* edited by George Rice Carpenter. New York: Longmans Green & Co., 1896.

Burlingame, Michael. *Abraham Lincoln: A Life.* 2 vols. Baltimore: Johns Hopkins University Press, 2008.

Charles O'Conor Memorials. New York: New York Law Institute, 1884.

The Chicago Copperhead Convention: The Treasonable and Revolutionary Utterances of the Men Who Composed It. Washington, D.C.: Congressional Union Committee, 1864.

Conroy, James B. *Our Once Common Country: Abraham Lincoln and the Hampton Roads Peace Conference of 1865.* Guilford, Conn.: Lyons Press, 2014.

Cooper, William J., Jr. *Jefferson Davis, American.* New York: Knopf, 2000.

Coulter, E. Merton. *A History of the South.* Vol. 8: *The South during Reconstruction, 1865–1877.* Baton Rouge: Louisiana State University Press, 1947.

Craven, John J. *The Prison Life of Jefferson Davis.* New York: Carleton Publisher, 1866.

Crofts, Daniel W. *Old Southampton: Politics and Society in a Virginia County, 1834–1869.* Charlottesville: University of Virginia Press, 1992.

Cummings, Homer, and Carl McFarland. *Federal Justice: Chapters in the History of Justice and the Federal Executive.* New York: Macmillan, 1937.

Davis, William C. *Jefferson Davis: The Man and His Hour.* New York: HarperCollins, 1991.

Dunning, William Archibald. *The American Nation: A History.* Vol. 22: *Reconstruction—Political and Economic, 1865–1877.* New York: Harper & Brothers, 1907.

Dyer, Brainerd. *The Public Career of William M. Evarts.* Berkeley: University of California Press, 1933.

Eckert, Edward K. *"Fiction Distorting Fact": The Prison Life, Annotated by Jefferson Davis.* Macon, Ga.: Mercer University Press, 1987.

Fellman, Michael. *The Making of Robert E. Lee.* New York: Random House, 2000.

Fleming, Walter Lynwood. *The Confederacy and Reconstruction.* Pt. 2: *The Sequel of Appomattox: A Chronicle of the Reunion of the States.* New Haven: Yale University Press, 1919.

Foner, Eric. *Reconstruction: America's Unfinished Revolution, 1863–1877.* New York: Perennial Classics, 2002.

Forgie, George B. *Patricide in the House Divided: A Psychological Interpretation of Lincoln and His Age.* New York: Norton, 1979.

Freeman, Douglas Southall. *A Calendar of Confederate Papers.* Richmond: Confederate Museum, 1908.

Freidel, Frank. *Francis Lieber: Nineteenth-Century Liberal.* Baton Rouge: Louisiana State University Press, 1947.

Gallagher, Gary W. "Another Look at the Generalship of R. E. Lee." In *R. E. Lee: The Soldier,* edited by Gary W. Gallagher, 275–89. Lincoln: University of Nebraska Press, 1996.

Goodwin, Doris Kearns. *Team of Rivals: The Political Genius of Abraham Lincoln.* New York: Simon & Schuster, 2005.

Hall, Kermit L., ed. *The Oxford Companion to the Supreme Court of the United States.* New York: Oxford University Press, 1992.

Harrison, Fairfax, ed. *Aris Sonis Focisque: Being a Memoir of an American Family, the Harrisons of Skimino and Particularly of Jesse Burton Harrison and Burton Norvell Harrison.* 1910. Reprint, Charleston, S.C.: BiblioLife, 2013.

Hess, Earl J. *Braxton Bragg: The Most Hated Man of the Confederacy.* Chapel Hill: University of North Carolina Press, 2016.

Hodes, Martha. *Mourning Lincoln.* New Haven: Yale University Press, 2015.

Hoffer, Peter Charles. *The Treason Trials of Aaron Burr.* Lawrence: University Press of Kansas, 2008.

Kermit L. Hall, ed. *The Oxford Companion to the Supreme Court of the United States.* New York: Oxford University Press, 1992.

Leonard, Elizabeth D. *Lincoln's Forgotten Ally: Judge Advocate General Joseph Holt of Kentucky.* Chapel Hill: University of North Carolina Press, 2011.

Lieber, Francis. *Lieber on Guerrilla Parties, Considered with Reference to the Law and Usages of War.* New York: D. Van Nostrand, 1862.

Malone, Dumas. *Jefferson and His Time.* Vol. 5: *Jefferson the President, Second Term, 1805–1809.* Boston: Little, Brown, 1974.

Marvel, William. *Lincoln's Autocrat: The Life of Edwin Stanton.* Chapel Hill: University of North Carolina Press, 2015.

McPherson, James M. *Embattled Rebel: Jefferson Davis as Commander in Chief.* New York: Penguin Press, 2014.

——. *The War That Forged a Nation: Why the Civil War Still Matters.* New York: Oxford University Press, 2014.

Milton, George Fort. *The Age of Hate: Andrew Johnson and the Radicals.* New York: Coward-McCann, 1930.

Narrative of Privations and Sufferings of United States Officers and Soldiers while Prisoners of War in the Hands of the Rebel Authorities. Philadelphia: Printed for the U.S. Sanitary Commission, King & Baird, Printers, 1864.

Neely, Mark E., Jr. *The Fate of Liberty: Abraham Lincoln and Civil Liberties.* New York: Oxford University Press, 1991.

Newmyer, R. Kent. *John Marshall and the Heroic Age of the Supreme Court.* Baton Rouge: Louisiana State University Press, 2001.

Nicolay, John G., and John Hay. *Abraham Lincoln: A History.* 10 vols. New York: Century Co., 1890.

Nicoletti, Cynthia. *Secession on Trial: The Treason Prosecution of Jefferson Davis.* New York: Cambridge University Press, 2017.

Niven, John. *Salmon P. Chase: A Biography.* New York: Oxford University Press, 1995.

O'Conor, Charles. *Negro Slavery Not Unjust: Speech of Charles O'Conor, Esq., at the Union Meeting at the Academy of Music, New York City, December 19th, 1859.* New York: Van Evrie, Horton & Co. 1859.

Oglesby, Thaddeus K. *The Shackling of Jefferson Davis, Read before the Atlanta Camp of Confederate Veterans, at the Capital, Atlanta, March 20, 1899.* Pamphlet. MS 382, Woodson Research Center, Fondren Library, Rice University.

Parrish, T. Michael. *Richard Taylor: Soldier Prince of Dixie.* Chapel Hill: University of North Carolina Press, 1992.

Procter, Ben H. *Not without Honor: The Life of John H. Reagan.* Austin: University of Texas Press, 1962.

Report of the Commission on the Andersonville Monument. Boston: Wright & Potter Printing Co., 1902.

Richards, Leonard L. *Who Freed the Slave? The Fight over the Thirteenth Amendment.* Chicago: University of Chicago Press, 2015.

Ripley, C. Peter, ed. *The Black Abolitionist Papers.* 5 vols. Chapel Hill: University of North Carolina Press, 1992.

Robertson, Davis. *Burr's Trial.* Vol. 2. Philadelphia: Hopkins & Earle, 1808.

Robinson, William M., Jr. *Justice in Grey: A History of the Judicial System of the Confederate States of America.* Cambridge: Harvard University Press, 1941.

Roland, Charles P. *Reflections on Lee: A Historian's Assessment,* Mechanicsburg, Pa.: Stackpole Books 1995.

Smith, Adam I. P. *The Stormy Present: Conservatism and the Problem of Slavery in Northern Politics, 1846–1865.* Chapel Hill: University of North Carolina Press, 2017.

Smith, Gerrit. *No Treason in Civil War: Speech of Gerrit Smith, at Cooper Institute, New-York, June 8, 1865.* New York: American News Co., 1865. Reprinted in *Sabin Americana, 1500–1926.* Farmington Hills, Mich.: Gale, 2012.

Speed, James. *James Speed: A Personality.* Louisville, Ky.: Press of John P. Morton & Co., 1914.

Stewart, David O. *Impeached: The Trial of President Andrew Johnson and the Fight for Lincoln's Legacy.* New York: Simon & Schuster, 2009.

Trefousse, Hans L. *Andrew Johnson: A Biography.* New York: Norton, 1989.

———. *The Radical Republicans: Lincoln's Vanguard for Racial Justice.* New York: Knopf, 1969.

Van Deusen, Glyndon G. *Horace Greeley: Nineteenth-Century Crusader.* Philadelphia: University of Pennsylvania Press, 1953.

White, Jonathan W. *Abraham Lincoln and Treason in the Civil War: The Trials of John Merryman.* Baton Rouge: Louisiana State University Press, 2011.

Wilson, James H. *The Life of Charles A. Dana.* New York: Harper & Brothers, 1907.

Winik, Jay. *April 1865: The Month That Saved America.* New York: HarperCollins, 2001.

Witt, John Fabian. *Lincoln's Code: The Laws of War in American History.* New York: Free Press, 2012.

Articles

Bloch, Susan Low. "The Early Role of the Attorney General in Our Constitutional Scheme: In the Beginning There Was Pragmatism." *Duke Law Journal,* no. 3 (1989): 561–653.

Chandler, Lucius H. "Speech of Hon. Lucius H. Chandler of Virginia, in the House of Representatives of the United States, in Defence of His Claim to a Seat in the Body for the Thirty-Eighth Congress." *Congressional Globe,* May 21, 1864.

Daly, Charles P. "Charles O'Conor: His Professional Life and Character." *Magazine of American History* 13, no. 6 (June 1885).

Davis, Jefferson. "Lord Wolseley's Mistakes." *North American Review* 149, no. 395 (October 1889): 472–82.

Dougherty, J. Hampden. "William M. Evarts, Lawyer and Statesman." *American Lawyer: A Monthly Journal Serving the Interests of the Legal Profession in America* (New York) (January 1902).

George, Joseph, Jr. "The Conspiracy Trial's 'Suppressed Testimony': An Attempt to Implicate Jefferson Davis in Lincoln's Assassination." *Lincoln Herald* 111, no. 2 (Summer 2009): 94–127.

Hanchett, William. "Reconstruction and the Rehabilitation of Jefferson Davis: Charles G. Halpine's Prison Life." *Journal of American History* 56 (1969): 280–89.

Hill, Frederick Trevor. "Decisive Battles of the Law: The Hayes-Tilden Contest—A Political Arbitration." *Harper's Monthly Magazine* (March 1907).

Jones, James P. "'Your Left Arm': James H. Wilson's Letters to Adam Badeau." *Civil War History* 12, no. 3 (September 1966): 230–45.

Lathrop, George P. "The Bailing of Jefferson Davis." *Century Magazine* (February 1887): 636–44.

Nichols, Roy Franklin. "United States vs. Jefferson Davis, 1865–1869." *American Historical Review* 31, no. 2 (January 1926): 266–84.

Nicoletti, Cynthia. "The American Civil War as a Trial by Battle." *Law and History Review* 28, no. 1 (February 2010): 71–110.

———. "Did Secession Really Die at Appomattox? The Strange Case of *U.S. v. Jefferson Davis.*" *University of Toledo Law Review* 41 (Spring 2010): 587–635.

Phillips, Christopher. "Lincoln's Grasp of War: Hard War and the Politics of Neutrality and Slavery in the Western Border States, 1861–1862." *Journal of the Civil War Era* 3, no. 2 (June 2013): 184–210.

"The United States Constitution and the Secessionists." *Westminster Review* (London) 29 (April 1866): 422–51.

Waugh, Joan. "'I Only Knew What Was in My Mind': Ulysses S. Grant and the Meaning of Appomattox." *Journal of the Civil War Era* 2, no. 3 (September 2012): 307–36.

White, Jonathan W. "The Trial of Jefferson Davis and the Americanization of Treason Law." In *Constitutionalism in the Approach and Aftermath of the Civil War,* edited by Paul D. Moreno and Johnathan O'Neill, 113–32. New York: Fordham University Press, 2013.

Nineteenth-Century Newspapers and Periodicals

Albany Evening Journal
Alexandria (Va.) Gazette
Atlantic Monthly
Augusta (Ga.) Chronicle
Augusta (Ga.) Daily Constitutionalist
Baltimore Sun
Boston Daily Advertiser
Boston Journal
Boston Post
Camden (N.J.) Democrat
Charleston (S.C.) Courier
Charleston (S.C.) Mercury
Chicago Legal News: : A Journal of Legal Intelligence
Chicago Tribune
Cincinnati Daily Gazette
Cincinnati Enquirer
Cleveland Leader
Cleveland Plain Dealer
Confederate Veteran (Nashville)
Critic-Record (Washington, D.C.)
Daily Advocate (Baton Rouge, La.)
Daily Age (Philadelphia)
Daily Albany (N.Y.) Argus
Daily Constitutional Union (Washington, D.C.)
Daily Constitutionalist (Augusta, Ga.)
Daily Eastern Argus (Portland, Me.)
Daily Globe (Washington, D.C.)
Daily Inter Ocean (Chicago)
Daily National Intelligencer (Washington, D.C.)
Daily National Republican (Washington, D.C.)
Elkhart (Ind.) Weekly Review

Evening Star (Washington, D.C.)
Frank Leslie's Illustrated Newspaper (New York)
Hartford (Conn.) Daily Courant
Illustrated New Age (Philadelphia)
Jamestown (N.Y.) Journal
Liberator (Boston)
Lowell (Mass.) Daily Citizen and News
Macon (Ga.) Telegraph
Massachusetts Spy (Worcester, Mass.)
The Nation
National Intelligencer (Washington, D.C.)
New-Hampshire Sentinel (Keene, N.H.)
New London (Conn.) Democrat
New Orleans Tribune
New York Bar Magazine
New-York Commercial Advertiser
New York Evening Post
New York Herald
New York Herald-Tribune
New York News
New York Reformer
New York Times
New York Tribune
New York World
Norwich (Conn.) Aurora
People's Advocate (Alexandria, Va.)
Petersburg (Va.) News
Philadelphia Inquirer
Portland (Me.) Advertiser
Portsmouth (N.H.) Journal of Literature and Politics
Richmond Examiner
Richmond Whig
Salem (Mass.) Register
Springfield (Mass.) Republican
St. Albans (Vt.) Messenger
Trenton (N.J.) Daily State Gazette
Weekly Eagle (Brattleboro, Vt.)
Winchester Virginian
Wooster Republican

Government Publications and Documents

Ashton, J. Hubley, ed. *Official Opinions of the Attorneys General of the United States.* Washington, D.C.: W. H. & O. H. Morrison, 1870.

Assassination of Lincoln: Report. Committee on the Assassination of Lincoln of the House of Representatives, 39th Cong., 1st Sess., Report No. 104. Washington, D.C., July 1866.

Cases of Contested Elections in Congress from 1834 to 1865, Inclusive. House of Representatives, Misc. Doc. No. 57, 38th Cong., 2d Sess. Washington, D.C.: Government Printing Office, 1865.

Congressional Globe. 46 vols. Washington, D.C.: Government Printing Office, 1834–73.

Documents of the Sanitary Commission. Vol. 2, nos. 61–95. New York: Wm. C. Bryant & Co., Printers, 1863.

Gales, Joseph, ed. *Debates and Proceedings in the Congress of the United States; with an Appendix, Containing Important States Papers and Public Documents, and All the Laws of a Public Nature; with a Copious Index.* 2 vols. Washington, D.C.: Gales & Seaton, 1834.

House of Representatives. Report No. 59, 38th Cong., 1st Sess., April 25, 1864.

Impeachment Investigation: Testimony Taken before the Judiciary Committee of the House of Representatives in the Investigation of the Charges against Andrew Johnson. 39th Cong., 2d Sess., and 40th Cong., 1st Sess. Washington, D.C.: Government Printing Office, 1867.

Johnson, Andrew. "Proclamation 179—Granting Full Pardon and Amnesty for the Offense of Treason against the United States during the Late Civil War," December 25, 1868. Online by Gerhard Peters and John T. Woolley, *The American Presidency Project.* http://www.presidency.ucsb.edu/ws/?pid=72360.

Journal of the Proceedings of the Senate of the United States in Executive Session. 37th Cong., 2d Sess., December 1861.

———. 38th Cong., 1st Sess., June 1864.

Kendrick, Benjamin B., ed. *The Journal of the Joint Committee of Fifteen on Reconstruction: 39th Congress, 1865–1867.* New York: Columbia University, 1914.

"Loyalty of Clerks and Other Persons Employed by Government, January 28, 1862." *Reports of Committees of the House of Representatives Made during the Second Session of the Thirty-Seventh Congress, 1861–1862.* Washington, D.C.: Government Printing Office, 1862.

"Opinion on the Constitutional Power of the Military to Try and Execute the Assassins of the President." James Speed, Attorney General. Washington, D.C.: Government Printing Office, 1865.

Pardon of William H. Wright by Andrew Johnson. May 6, 1868. In possession of the author.

Peters, Richard, ed. *The Public Statutes at Large of the United States of America.* Boston: Charles C. Little and James Brown, 1848.

Report of the Joint Committee on Reconstruction. Washington, D.C.: Government Printing Office, 1866.

Trial of Andrew Johnson, President of the United States, before the Senate of the United States, on Impeachment by the House of Representatives for High Crimes and Misdemeanors. 3 vols. Washington, D.C.: Government Printing Office, 1868.

Trial of Henry Wirz. Executive Documents of the House of Representatives. 40th Cong., 2d Sess., Ex. Doc. No. 23. Washington, D.C., 1867.

United States Census Records, 1860.

War of the Rebellion: A Compilation of the Official Records [*OR*] *of the Union and Confederate Armies.* 128 vols. Washington, D.C.: Government Printing Office, 1880–1901.

Winthrop, William, ed. *A Digest of Opinions of the Judge Advocate General of the Army.* Washington, D.C.: Government Printing Office, 1880.

Constitution, Statutes, Case Law, and Treatises

Black's Law Dictionary. 5th ed. St. Paul: West Publishing Co., 1978.

Cramer v. United States, 325 U.S. 1; 65 S.Ct. 918; 89 L.Ed. 1441 (1945).

Ex Parte Milligan, 71 U.S. 2, 18 L.Ed. 281, 4 Wall. 2 (1866).

Texas v. White, 74 U.S. 700 (1869).

United States Constitution.

United States Statutes at Large. Vol. 12. Boston: Little, Brown & Co., 1865.

INDEX

Page numbers in italic indicate illustrations